ESSAY ESSENTIALS

Sarah Norton
Centennial College

Brian Green
Niagara College

HARCOURT
BRACE
CANADA

Harcourt Brace & Company, Canada
Toronto   Montreal   Orlando   Fort Worth   San Diego   Philadelphia
London   Sydney   Tokyo

Canadian Cataloguing in Publication Data

Norton, Sarah, date
  Essay essentials

ISBN 0-03-922776-6

1. English language—Rhetoric. 2. Essay.
3. English language—Grammar—1950–
I. Green, Brian. II. Title.

PE1471.N67 1991   808'.042   C90-095525-2

Editorial Director: Heather McWhinney
Developmental Editor: Anne Venables Eigner
Director of Publishing Services: Stephen Lau
Production Manager: Sue-Ann Becker
Copy Editor: Maryan Malone
Interior Design: Bob Garbutt
Cover Design: Dave Peters
Typesetting and Assembly: Publications Development Company
Printing and Binding: Webcom Limited

♻ **This book was printed in Canada on recycled paper.**

4 5   95 94

OTABIND
Bound to stay open

Publisher's Note

This book has been specially bound using the
patented Otabind process. You can open this
book at any page, gently run your finger down
the spine, and the pages will lie flat.

Preface

Essay Essentials is designed for Canadian college students taking introductory courses in essay writing. Its numerous exercises are designed to teach and reinforce writing skills, and its examples and practical assignments emphasize the development of the techniques that lead to the effective communication of ideas.

The teaching of essay writing skills has evolved over the past few years into two distinct approaches: "bottom-up" and "top-down." *Essay Essentials* will be a useful text for either approach. We have provided instruction and reinforcing exercises applicable to the freewriting and brainstorming used in the bottom-up approach as well as to the more traditional heuristic method of the top-down approach, familiar to users of *The Bare Essentials*. We have found that different approaches (or even a combination of approaches) to generating ideas suit different students. Whatever approach is chosen, the goals are the same: well-organized thoughts, fully developed presentation of a subject, and clear and correct expression in essay form. Our aim in *Essay Essentials* is to assist students to achieve those goals through whichever process the instructor determines is most effective.

We have retained those features of *The Bare Essentials* that teachers and students have found most helpful and have directed them towards those elements of the writing process that are essential to students' academic and career success.

The units are presented as discrete sections, from focusing on a subject, through planning the paper and structuring the paragraphs, to revising, proofreading, and formating. This order is strongly recommended but is not essential; the instructor may introduce the units in a different sequence.

Many examples have been included, from both published works and students' assignments. Exercises that draw students' attention to the manner in which those examples have been developed and crafted are plentiful. The writing assignments that complement the exercises are designed to help students to apply the individual skills of good writing to the production of sound essays. The latter chapters present those elements of spelling, sentence structure, grammar, and punctuation without which the most carefully planned and organized essay must fail.

Writing with a word processor and adapting to public speaking the skills acquired in essay writing are treated in appendices.

For the convenience of students working through Units Six through Ten on their own, selected answers to the exercises are given in Appendix D. An asterisk appears alongside the number of each exercise for which an answer is provided.

We wish to express our appreciation to those colleagues who provided the ideas, inspiration, and, in some cases, the content of this text. Special thanks go to Marty Chan, a University of Alberta student, who wrote the sample research paper. We would like to thank our reviewers, Nina Butska, Maureen Dey, Brian Flack, Joan Pilz, and David Southmayd, for their detailed comments on our draft of *Essay Essentials*. Finally, we wish to acknowledge the significant contributions of D'arcy McHayle, Valerie Grabove, George Blazetich, Ian Lea, Tom Hartley, and Karen Jakob. Their advice, encouragement, and assistance have made this a finer and more useful book.

Sarah Norton
Centennial College
Scarborough, Ontario

Brian Green
Niagara College
Welland, Ontario

Publisher's Note to Instructors and Students

This textbook is a key component of your course. If you are the instructor of this course, you undoubtedly considered a number of texts carefully before choosing this as the one that will work best for your students and you. The authors and publishers of this book spent considerable time and money to ensure its high quality, and we appreciate your recognition of this effort and accomplishment.

If you are a student, we are confident that this text will help you to meet the objectives of your course. You will also find it helpful after the course is finished; its instruction on good writing will be important as you face the demands of your career. Hold on to *Essay Essentials* as a valuable addition to your personal library.

As well, please don't forget that photocopying copyright work means the authors lose royalties that are rightfully theirs. This loss will discourage them from writing another edition of this text or other books, because doing so will simply not be worth their time and effort. If this happens, we all lose—students, instructors, authors, and publishers.

And since we want to hear what you think about this book, please be sure to send us the stamped reply card at the end of the text. This will help us to continue publishing high-quality books for your courses.

Contents

UNIT FOUR   ## Revising the Essay

UNIT FIVE   ## The Research Paper

UNIT SIX   ## Sentence Structure

UNIT SEVEN   ## Grammar

UNIT EIGHT   ## Punctuation

What This Book Can Do for You

Let's face it: not many people enjoy writing essays. Can you imagine anyone including "essay writing" in a list of hobbies or favourite leisure time activities, or putting "career as an essayist" high on a list of vocational goals? So, you may be wondering, what does learning to write essays have to do with me and my future?

You may not be inclined to write for fun, but someday, in a manner of speaking, you will write for profit. The kinds of writing you will learn in this book are the kinds of writing you'll be expected to do in your job. If your résumé shows you've graduated from college or university, your prospective employer will assume that you are able to communicate in writing, frequently, correctly, and as a representative who will not mar the company's image. Are you ready for that? For some people, it's a frightening fact. What's even more alarming, judgements about your ability to perform your job will be based, to a large extent, on your skills as a communicator.

You won't need to be a Margaret Atwood or a Pierre Berton to succeed as an engineer, nurse, fashion consultant, or graphic artist. But in any job that requires communication beyond diagrams, charts, sketches, or mock-ups, you will be expected to be able to present your ideas in well-organized, readable prose that is clearly and correctly written. Whether your output is an interoffice memo, an accident report, a sales presentation, a patient history, or a legal brief, writing is the record of your activity—the evidence of the job you're doing and how well you're doing it. Ask any graduate who is currently working in your career field; ask any employer. College and university training personnel at all levels and in all disciplines are told again and again, "Teach them to communicate clearly." Over the past two decades, the most frequent lament of faculty at colleges and universities has been that entry level students lack basic communication skills, while those ready to graduate have not fully mastered them.

Before you can attempt the specialized kinds of communication that will be required of you in your career, you need to learn how to present your ideas clearly and correctly. In this book, you will learn to organize your thoughts, to develop your ideas in coherent paragraphs, and to express yourself clearly, concisely, and correctly. Adapting these essay-writing skills to the specific types and formats of written communication required on your job will be a fairly simple task. Learning to write well in the first place, however, is not easy for most people. It requires patience, concentration, and practice. The *ability* to write well is within the grasp of any college or university student; what's usually lacking is *motivation*. You can learn to write well if you're willing to work hard at it. We've designed this text so that you can master the theory of good writing and practise it confidently, producing effective essays in college and creditable communications in your career or profession.

Most composition texts claim that if you follow the authors' instructions carefully and do all the exercises faithfully, writing will become easy. This text makes no such claim. Nearly 200 years ago, Richard Brinsley Sheridan warned, "Easy writing's cursed hard reading." What will get easier as a result of this book is your readers' ability to read, understand, remember, and maybe enjoy what you've written. But that, you're smart enough to know, is everything any writer can hope for.

If you learn how to avoid frustrating or misleading your reader, how to keep your subject development on track, and how to include your significant information or arguments in a clearly organized, non-boring way, you'll probably be writing on the job for thirty to forty years, maybe even longer. Isn't it worth spending a term or two to learn how to communicate your ideas clearly and convincingly?

The Process of Writing

As noted in the Preface, this text offers you two approaches to the process of writing: top-down and bottom-up. The **top-down approach** assumes that you know what you want to say before you begin to write. You identify your subject and main points, establish your preview statement (the statement that orients your readers to the content of the paper), and plan your topic sentences (those sentences that identify the content of each paragraph).

The **bottom-up approach** is founded on the belief that, like most writers, you do not know what you want to say until you begin to write; you discover your meaning through the act of writing. With this approach, you rely on prewriting strategies such as brainstorming and freewriting to "get into" the process of writing.

You will probably need to use both approaches. In some circumstances, you will discover your subject through writing; at other times, use of strategies will help you to express clearly what you already know. You should experiment with both approaches so that you can comfortably use the one that is more appropriate for a particular writing task.

What Your Readers Expect

Whichever approach you use, your goal will be to make your finished essay easy for your readers to read and to understand. To achieve that goal, you must meet your readers' expectations.

Readers have five unconscious expectations when they begin to read a piece of extended prose. They expect:

1. To see paragraphs;
2. To have the first sentence of a paragraph orient them to the content of the paragraph by identifying its topic;
3. To see paragraph units that are coherent and unified, with each one exploring a single topic;
4. To have the paragraphs connect to each other according to some logical pattern that shows external as well as internal coherence;
5. To be introduced, very early, to the content of the whole, preferably through the writer's preview of the main points that are to be covered.

You should keep in mind, as you write, that your readers' overriding motive will be to obtain information quickly and easily, without unnecessary backtracking. A well-organized paper, with well-developed paragraphs, results in shorter reading time and in higher recall of the content. Your readers will rely on you to make efficient reading possible.

According to researchers, your readers will read with more ease and remember more of what they read if you include a preview statement to introduce them to the content and organization of the piece and if you begin each paragraph with a topic sentence, to identify the subject of that paragraph. If you do not organize and develop your paper and its paragraphs in a clearly identifiable way, your readers will impose their own organization on the paper. The result will be longer reading time, or difficulty in understanding and remembering the content, or, worse, the assumption that a paragraph or even the whole paper has a meaning

other than the one you intended. Writers can help readers to read efficiently if they follow the old adage: "Tell them what you're going to tell
them; tell them; then tell them what you've told them."

How to Begin

We have all listened to people who ramble on and on in conversation
and never seem to get to the point. Perhaps these speakers have no
point to make or are hoping one will turn up as they speak. For their
unfortunate listeners, the experience is both tiresome and frustrating.
Readers react similarly to poor writing. An essay—or any other form
of written communication—that has no point and that rambles on will
turn them off.

How can you avoid boring, confusing, or annoying your readers?

First, you need to have something to say and a reason for saying it. In
other words, you need to do some thinking before you begin to write.
Very few people can write an essay straight through from start to finish
without spending a considerable amount of time thinking and planning.
Some prewriting will help you to develop the structure more easily;
freewriting and brainstorming (Chapter 3 will explain these) are useful
to stimulate thinking.

Second, once you've determined what it is you want to say, you need to
arrange your main points in the most effective order possible. If you
organize your ideas carefully, you won't ramble. Writing an essay is like
building a house. If you have a clear plan or blueprint, you can construct
the house without the frustration of having to tear down misplaced
walls or convert windows to doors. You are less likely to need to double
back or even to start all over again from the beginning. A good plan
saves time.

As a general rule, the more time you spend on prewriting and planning, the less time you'll need to spend on writing and revising. Careful
up front planning will enable you to produce papers that your readers
will find clear and understandable.

The Parts of an Essay

An essay, like most other forms of oral and written communication, has
a beginning, a middle, and an end.

The beginning, or **introduction**, tells your readers the point, the purpose, and the scope of your paper. If your introduction is well crafted,
its preview statement will tell your readers what main points will be

discussed in the paragraphs that follow. Your introduction is to your readers what a highway sign is to travellers: it tells them where they're going and what main points of interest are to be found on the way.

The middle, or **body**, of an essay consists of several paragraphs that discuss in detail the points that are identified or previewed in the introduction. In a short essay, three, four, or more paragraphs will each focus on a separate main point.

Each paragraph should consist of two essential components: the **topic sentence**, which identifies the issue or subject to be examined in that paragraph; and the development, or **support**, of the topic sentence, which sets forth in additional sentences the detailed information the reader needs in order to understand the topic clearly. The topic sentence of each body paragraph connects to the preview statement, and the development of each paragraph supports and explains its topic sentence.

The end, or **conclusion**, of the essay is a brief final paragraph. After the main points of your paper have been introduced and developed, you summarize them to reinforce them for your readers. You then say good-bye with a memorable statement that will give your readers something to think about after they have finished reading your essay.

Bertrand Russell's short essay, "What I Have Lived For" (p. 6), is a good example of a well-structured essay. The introduction contains a clear preview statement. Each paragraph of the body consists of a clearly identifiable topic sentence and development sufficient to explain it. The conclusion is brief, pointed, and memorable.

What I Have Lived For

Bertrand Russell

Preview Statement

Introduction

Three passions, simple but overwhelmingly strong, have governed my life: the longing for love, the search for knowledge, and unbearable pity for the suffering of mankind. These passions, like great winds, have blown me hither and thither, in a wayward course, over a deep ocean of anguish, reaching to the very verge of despair.

Topic Sentence

I have sought love, first, because it brings ecstasy—ecstasy so great that I would often have sacrificed all the rest of life for a few hours of this joy. I have sought it, next, because it relieves loneliness—that terrible loneliness in which one shivering consciousness looks over the rim of the world into the cold unfathomable lifeless abyss. I have sought it, finally, because in the union of love I have seen, in a mystic miniature, the prefiguring vision of the heaven that saints and poets have imagined. This is what I sought, and though it might seem too good for human life, this is what—at last—I have found.

Topic Sentence

Body

Topic Sentence

With equal passion I have sought knowledge. I have wished to understand the hearts of men. I have wished to know why the stars shine. And I have tried to apprehend the Pythagorean power by which number holds sway above the flux. A little of this, but not much, I have achieved.

Love and knowledge, so far as they were possible, led upward toward the heavens. But always pity brought me back to earth. Echoes of cries of pain reverberate in my heart. Children in famine, victims tortured by oppressors, helpless old people a hated burden to their sons, and the whole world of loneliness, poverty, and pain make a mockery of what human life should be. I long to alleviate the evil, but I cannot, and I too suffer.

Conclusion

This has been my life. I have found it worth living, and would gladly live it again if the chance were offered me.

Planning the Essay

CHAPTER 1

Your Audience and You

Before you begin to write anything—an essay, a report, a letter to a friend, or even a shopping list—you must have not only something to write about (your subject) but also someone to write for (your audience). Writing is communication, and for communication to take place, you (the writer) must be able to make your ideas or message clear to your readers. If no one reads your piece, communication does not take place and your writing is just another exercise, a practice for the real thing.

Addressing Your Readers

It is vital that you keep your intended readers in mind at all times—when you plan, write, and revise your paper. Think of every piece of writing as if it were a letter. Letter writers always have their readers in mind; usually someone specific is addressed. As an essay writer, you can do the same thing. Think of your essay as a letter to specific people. Are your readers going to be interested in what you have to say? Is your information sufficiently new, different, thought-provoking, amusing, convincing, or instructive to make your readers stay with you to the end?

> Before you begin to plan an essay, write at the top of the page the name of a person who is your intended reader.

Naturally, your instructor is going to be reading your early (and your late) assignments, but, for your first draft, you should write at the top of the page the name of someone other than your instructor whom you might expect to be interested in your subject. Be creative; write the name of your supervisor, the Prime Minister, the editor of your local newspaper, a potential employer, a friend, an enemy, or even yourself. Keeping this reader in mind will help you plan, develop, and write your assignments in a tone and style appropriate to your message.

Spend a little time thinking about your subject in relation to your audience. Consider carefully these three questions when you are deciding what to include in your essay:

> 1. What do my readers know about my subject?
> 2. What is my readers' attitude towards my subject?
> 3. What are my readers' needs in regard to my subject?

Readers' Knowledge

The first question will help guide your choice of the amount and type of information you include. Are you writing for novices or for people with a fairly detailed knowledge of your subject? Do you have to cover the background and all the basics, or can you take it for granted that your readers are familiar with them? You don't want to bore your readers by telling them things they already know; but if you fail to provide information necessary to their understanding of your message, you'll turn them off or lose them entirely.

Readers' Attitudes

The second question helps you determine your approach to your subject. Will your readers be sympathetic to your point of view? If so, your aim will be to reinforce their agreement. You will want to state your opinion up front, to show you're on their side and to enlist their sympathy early. On the other hand, if they can be expected to resist your arguments, you might be wise to provide reasoning and support for your ideas before revealing your point of view. Gentle persuasion is usually more effective than confrontation—in writing and in life.

Readers' Needs

The third question helps you decide whether to persuade, or instruct, or compare, or classify. Which type of essay will best give your readers what they need to know about your subject? The answers to this question will determine whether you should be fairly general or quite specific in your comments. Is it your intention to add to or reinforce your readers' general knowledge, or is your information to be applied in specific situations?

Reflecting Yourself

Once you are clear about who your readers are, what they know, and what they need to know, you should spend a little time considering your own role in the communication process. Any time you speak or write, you present yourself in a particular way to the people who hear or read what you have to say. We all play a variety of roles. We choose a role, often unconsciously, that we hope will suit the expectations of a particular audience. These roles are not false or hypocritical; they are simply facets of our personality that we try to match to the needs of each communication encounter. Choosing and maintaining an appropriate role is essential in successful communication.

Each day, for example, you meet a variety of people. Some of them you know well—parents, siblings, friends, classmates, teachers, co-workers, supervisors. Others you know only casually—the cashier in a restaurant, a police officer in a radar trap, an enumerator for an upcoming election, a check-out person in a grocery store. With each of these people, whether the contact is casual or intense, you consciously or unconsciously adjust your language, in order to communicate well. If you speak to your spouse as you might to your dog, you'll be sleeping on the couch. If you speak to a salesperson as you would to a love interest, you'll get arrested.

Consider these three questions when you are deciding what role would be most appropriate in a particular communication situation:

1. What is my purpose in writing?
2. What is my attitude towards my subject?
3. What are my readers' expectations of me in this communication?

Your Purpose

The most common purposes of writing are to inform, to persuade, and to entertain. Your purpose will depend largely on the needs and expectations of your readers. It will influence your choice of supporting details to develop your points and will affect your tone. How you say something often has more impact on your audience than what you say.

Your Attitude

The second question requires you to clarify your attitude towards the subject of your paper. You've already considered what your readers' attitudes are likely to be; now it's important to determine whether your own attitude coincides or is in conflict. You might be positive or negative about a subject, depending on your purpose in writing and on your relationship with your readers. Your attitude towards your subject, like your purpose in writing, will influence your tone and the kinds of supporting evidence you will use to develop your points.

Your Role

The third question is designed to help you match your role to what your audience is likely to expect from you. What would your readers expect from someone in your position who is writing on your particular subject? Are you able and willing to meet these expectations? Taking the time to think through your relationship with your readers will help you make appropriate choices for your point of view, your support statements for your ideas, and your level of language.

Levels of Language

There are many **levels of language** in spoken English. They range from almost unintelligible mutters and groans, through colloquial slang and professional jargon, right up to the formal, correct English used in the law courts, in the Speech from the Throne, and on other formal occasions. A parallel range is possible in written English: from graffiti up to the formal report.

The key to finding the proper level for your message is to consider not only the subject but also the receiver. Sometimes compromises must be made, as when you send one message to a wide variety of receivers. In general, you aim at the highest level of receiver and trust that the others will understand. Thus, wedding invitations, even those to the bridegroom's buddies, are usually stylized and formal.

No one has to tell you what level of language to use when you communicate with your friends at lunch or after school; that level has been clearly established over many years. In other circumstances, however, it's not clear what level you should be using, and at such times a careful consideration of the needs and preferences of your receiver is necessary. If your sociology teacher wants you to write papers in a formal style, and you want to get good marks, you will have to write formally. Likewise, because employers, in general, favour formal letters of application over casual ones, if you want to get a job you will have to write your letter in a formal style. A more relaxed and personal style may be appropriate for a talk given to your class. Letters to friends and conversations with parents are still less formal, although they probably retain a degree of correctness not found in your conversations with your friends (or enemies).

There are no hard and fast divisions of language into levels; nevertheless, to help you choose the style most appropriate to the message and the receiver you are considering, we have outlined the basic characteristics of colloquial, general, and formal language.

	COLLOQUIAL	GENERAL	FORMAL
Vocabulary	casual, everyday; usually concrete; some slang, colloquial expressions, contractions	the language of educated persons; nonspecialized; balance of abstract and concrete; readily understood	often abstract; technical; specialized; no contractions or colloquialisms
Sentence and Paragraph Structure	sentences short, simple; some sentence fragments; paragraphs short	complete sentences of varying length; paragraphs vary, but often short	all sentences complete; sentences usually long, complex; paragraphs fully developed, often at length
Tone	conversational, casual; sounds like ordinary speech	varies to suit message and purpose of writer	impersonal, serious, often instructional
Typical Uses	personal letters, some fiction, some newspapers, much advertising	most of what we read: newspapers, magazines, novels, business correspondence	legal documents, some textbooks, academic writing, scientific reports

No level is "better" than another. Each has its place and function. Your message, your audience, and your purpose in writing are the factors that determine which level of usage is appropriate.

Read the following selections and consider each writer's purpose in writing, the audience for whom the message is intended, and how the writer's choice of language is appropriate to the readers, the subject, and the writer's purpose.

Colloquial

I love baseball the way some people love candy, but even I don't understand all the rules. I'd like to tell you about a rule that I do understand but, from what I've seen and heard at the ball park, not many other people have figured out. That's the balk rule.

The reason for the rule is so that a runner at first base can't be tricked unfairly by the pitcher. Let's say you've made it to first base. Your next goal is to get to second base. OK, I'm the pitcher and I've got two jobs. First, I've got to try to get the next batter out, and second, I've got to make sure you don't get to second base. Without the balk rule, I could wind up and make all the motions as if I were going to throw a pitch and then, at the last second, whip the ball over to the first baseman. Bingo! You're out because you've taken a lead away from the base toward second to get a head start. If I were allowed to do this, you'd never take a lead away from the base, would you? You'd stick right on the bag and wait until there was a safe hit before taking off for second. That would take a lot of the exciting plays out of the game. Plays like steals, and advancing to third on a single, and the hit-and-run would be out the window.

The only way to keep a balance between your being able to make it to second and my being able to get you out is to make sure I can't trick you like that. The balk rule says that I have to come to a complete stop before throwing the ball. After that pause, I have to throw to the plate or to first base, but I must move clearly one way or the other. In other words, I can't make a motion towards the plate, even with my knee or foot, and then throw to first. This protects you from being fooled by me and allows you to take a reasonable lead.

Who is the intended audience? These paragraphs are intended for general readers, but not people who are seeking a definitive and legal description of the baseball rule. The writer assumes some knowledge of and interest in the subject, but not much expertise.

What is the author's role? The author is seeking to inform readers, but not by coming across as a teacher or an expert. This sort of information is discussed among friends. One can imagine the writer and the audience sharing a relaxed and informal conversation about their favourite game.

How does the language work? The use of contractions and colloquialisms ("out of the window," "OK," "taking off") and especially the use of the first and second persons ("you," the baserunner, and "I," the pitcher) clearly make this an informal and friendly communication. Short sentences and many instances of conversational style ("a lot," "your being able to make it to second") add to the informal tone.

General

A good business letter is one that gets results. The best way to get results is to develop a letter that, in its appearance, style, and content, conveys information efficiently. To perform this function, a business letter should be concise, clear, and courteous.

The business letter must be concise. Little introduction or preliminary chat is necessary. Get to the point, make the point, and leave it. It is safe to assume that your letter is being read by a very busy person with all kinds of paper to deal with. Such a person does not want to spend very much time with a newsy letter about your ski trip or medical problem. Hone and refine your message until the words and sentences you have used are precise. This takes time for revision and rereading but is a necessary part of writing a good letter. A short business letter that makes its point quickly has much more impact on a reader than a long-winded, rambling exercise in creative writing. This does not mean that there is no place for style or even, on occasion, humour in the business letter. While it conveys a message in its contents, the letter also provides the reader with an impression of you, its author: the medium is part of the message.

The business letter must be clear. You should have a very firm idea of what you want to say, and you should let the reader know it. Use the structure of the letter—the paragraphs, topic sentences, introduction, and conclusion—to guide the reader point by point from your introduction, through your reasoning, to your conclusion. Paragraph often, to break up the page and to lend an air of organization to the letter. Use an accepted business-letter format: there are several, and they can be found in any book of business English. Reread what you have written from the point of view of someone who is seeing it for the first time, and be sure that all explanations are adequate, all information provided (including reference numbers, dates, and other identification). A clear message, clearly delivered, is the essence of business communication.

The business letter must be courteous. Sarcasm and insults are ineffective and can often work against you. If you are sure you are right, point that out as politely as possible, explain why you are right, and outline what the reader is expected to do about it. Always put yourself in the place of the person to whom you are writing. What sort of letter would you respond to? How effective would sarcasm and threats be in making you fulfill a request? Another form of courtesy is taking care in your writing and typing of the business letter. Grammatical and spelling errors (even if you call them typing errors) tell a reader that you don't think enough of him or her to be careful. Such mistakes can lower the reader's opinion of you faster than anything you say, no matter how idiotic. There are excuses for ignorance; there are no excuses for sloppiness.

The business letter is your custom-made representative. It speaks for you and is a permanent record of your message. It can pay big dividends on the time you invest in giving it a concise message, a clear structure, and a courteous tone.

Who is the intended audience? Readers of this essay will be seeking specific information about business-letter style. They will, therefore, have some knowledge about the subject and high-school-graduate levels of reading and writing ability.

What is the author's role? The author is providing information from an expert point of view but in a friendly way. The use of humour and casual language makes the instruction easy to take. A persuasive element in the essay makes it warmer and gentler than straightforward instruction would be.

How does the language work? There are no contractions or slang, as might be found in colloquial writing, but the vocabulary and writing style are easily understood by general readers. The use of the second person and direct address ("If you are sure you are right, point that out as politely as possible, . . .") adds to the personal nature of the language. Questions addressed to the readers in order to assist persuasion also make the tone more conversational than formal, without ever becoming colloquial. This message is designed to appeal to the widest possible audience.

Formal

Scorched Earth
David E. Loper

"The earth speaks of its internal movements through the silent voice of the magnetic needle." So wrote the Norwegian astronomer Christopher Hansteen in 1819, in eloquent summary of his conclusion that the slow wandering of magnetic north—the north of compass needles—is actually a reflection of movements deep below the surface. Hansteen

Reprinted with permission from *The Sciences*, September/October 1990: 23.

was not the first to make such a proposal. In 1635 the English cartographer Henry Gillibrand had published a chart showing that the direction of magnetic north, as measured at London, had changed by seven degrees in the preceding fifty-five years. Edmond Halley, of comet fame, presciently suggested in 1692 that such changes were caused by the slow rotation of a vast magnetized body deep within the earth. The annual change in the direction of magnetic north is now duly recorded on the legend of nearly every topographic map published by the U.S. Geological Survey.

But the voice of the magnetic needle was muffled until recently; through the nineteenth century and much of the twentieth a static view of the earth held sway. The planet's interior was seen as motionless and changeless except for a slow loss of heat and, by some accounts, the contraction of the cooling globe. Mountains had been uplifted by the contraction like wrinkles on a drying apple, but the continents as a whole, and the thousands of miles of rock below them, stayed put.

Twenty-five years ago that static image of the earth was replaced by the dynamic view of plate tectonics: the idea that the surface of the earth is made up of rigid plates, sixty miles thick on average, that are constantly shifting and jostling. Fittingly, the plate-tectonic revolution was triggered by new studies of the earth's magnetism. Magnetically polarized grains in cooling lava or compacting sedimentary rock record the direction of the magnetic field, just as a compass needle does. As the rock solidifies, the direction of the field freezes in. Layered deposits of volcanic or sedimentary rock thus yield vertical records of the magnetic field, which show that at intervals ranging from tens of thousands to millions of years the field reverses its direction, as if a giant bar magnet within the earth were sporadically flipping back and forth.

Who is the intended audience? The readers of this paragraph must be knowledgeable about and interested in the subject of geology. They must also be literate and well read. It is expected that this audience will be capable of studying and digesting abstract ideas without requiring the support of concrete examples.

What is the author's role? The author's purpose is to inform; the author's role is that of distant expert. The information is presented from the point of view of one who is extremely knowledgeable, and the tone and content assume that the readers are less well informed . . . students, perhaps.

How does the language work? The vocabulary is abstract and academic. The sentences are long and complex. There are no contractions, no colloquialisms, no references to first or second persons. Sentences are bookish in tone. The style distances the readers from the writer and ensures that their connection is purely in the realm of ideas; there is no attempt at personal or friendly contact.

EXERCISE 1

Read the excerpts below, and discuss the intended audience, the author's role, and the appropriateness of the language.

1. Have faith. Keep in mind those bizarre recipes where you mix unlikely stuff—a peanut butter–chicken stew, for instance—and end up with something great.

    In the case of this inspired comedy [*The Freshman*], the plot is a dignified bonkers combination of *The Graduate, The Sting, The Godfather* and *The Producers:* A naive young man comes to New York City to go to film school, gets suckered by a cheap crook, then gets introduced to a mobster you wouldn't believe.

    Actually, you might believe him since it's Brando, parodying his own *Godfather* role so closely that other characters keep starting to tell him, "Say, you look just like . . ." before henchmen shut them up. When someone asks Brando if he is making a promise, he pauses—anyone else forgotten what great comic timing he has?—and slowly replies in his raspy Don Corleone voice: "Every word I say, by definition, is a promise."

    (from *People Weekly*, July 30, 1990, 11)

Who is the intended audience? _____

_____

_____

_____

What is the author's role? _____

_____

_____

_____

_____

How does the language work? _____

_____

_____

_____

2. I have always disliked being a man. The whole idea of manhood in America is pitiful, in my opinion. This version of masculinity is a little

like having to wear an ill-fitting coat for one's entire life (by contrast, I imagine femininity to be an oppressive sense of nakedness). Even the expression "Be a man!" strikes me as insulting and abusive. It means: Be stupid, be unfeeling, obedient, soldierly and stop thinking. Man means "manly"—how can one think about men without considering the terrible ambition of manliness? And yet it is part of every man's life. It is a hideous and crippling lie; it not only insists on difference and connives at superiority, it is also by its very nature destructive—emotionally damaging and socially harmful.

(from Paul Theroux, "Being a Man")

Who is the intended audience? _____

_____

_____

_____

_____

What is the author's role? _____

_____

_____

_____

_____

How does the language work? _____

_____

_____

_____

_____

3. "Ignorance corrupts. Absolute ignorance corrupts absolutely." This paraphrase of a famous remark tells us something about the seeds of prejudice. Without ignorance, racism and discriminatory persecution would not be possible. Enlightened attitudes could not support the unfounded maltreatment of another human being. Nonetheless, ignorance is not a passive void waiting to be filled; it is an active rejection of civilizing insights. What causes this stubborn resistance to common sense? Some influences might be a deeply embedded traditional opinion, a deep-seated fear of change and growth, or a personal rigidity that cannot assimilate different or opposing views.

Who is the intended audience? _____

_____

_____

_____

What is the author's role? _____

_____

_____

_____

How does the language work? _____

_____

_____

_____

4.   A study of history reminds one that mankind has its ups and downs and during the ups has accomplished many brave and beautiful things, exerted stupendous endeavors, explored and conquered oceans and wildernesses, achieved marvels of beauty in the creative arts and marvels of science and social progress, loved liberty with a passion that throughout history has led men to fight and die for it over and over again, pursued knowledge, exercised reason, enjoyed laughter and pleasures, played games with zest, shown courage, heroism, altruism, honor and decency; experienced love, known comfort, contentment, and, occasionally, happiness. All these qualities have been part of human experience and if they have not had as important notice as the negatives nor exerted as wide and persistent an influence as the evils we do, they nevertheless deserve attention, for they currently are all but forgotten.

(from Barbara Tuchman, "Mankind's Better Moments")

Who is the intended audience? _____

_____

_____

_____

_____

What is the author's role? _____

_____

_____

_____

How does the language work? _____

_____

_____

_____

5.   More than any other time in history, mankind faces a crossroads. One path leads to despair and utter hopelessness. The other, to total extinction. Let us pray we have the wisdom to choose correctly. I speak, by the way, not with any sense of futility, but with a panicky conviction of the absolute meaninglessness of existence which could easily be misinterpreted as pessimism. It is not. It is merely a healthy concern for the predicament of modern man. (Modern man is here defined as any person born after Nietzsche's edict that "God is dead," but before the hit recording "I Wanna Hold Your Hand.") This "predicament" can be stated one of two ways, though certain linguistic philosophers prefer to reduce it to a mathematical equation where it can be easily solved and even carried around in the wallet.

    Put in its simplest form, the problem is: How is it possible to find meaning in a finite world given my waist and shirt size? This is a very difficult question when we realize that science has failed us. True, it has conquered many diseases, broken the genetic code, and even placed human beings on the moon, and yet when a man of eighty is left in a room with two eighteen-year-old cocktail waitresses nothing happens. Because the real problems never change. After all, can the human soul be glimpsed through a microscope? Maybe—but you'd definitely need one of those very good ones with two eyepieces. We know that the most advanced computer in the world does not have a brain as sophisticated as that of an ant. True, we could say that of many of our relatives, but we only have to put up with them at weddings or special occasions. Science is something we depend on all the time. . . . Science has taught us how to pasteurize cheese. And true, this can be fun in mixed company—but what of the H-bomb? Have you ever seen what happens when one of those things falls off a desk accidentally? And where is science when one ponders the eternal riddles? How did the cosmos originate? How long has it been around? Did matter begin with an explosion or by the word of God? And if by the latter, could He not have begun it just two weeks earlier to take advantage of some of the warmer weather? Exactly what do we mean when we say man is mortal? Obviously, it's not a compliment . . . .

(Reprinted with permission of Random House, Inc., from *Side Effects* by Woody Allen. Copyright 1980 by Woody Allen.)

*Who is the intended audience?*_____

_____

_____

_____

_____

*What is the author's role?*_____

_____

_____

_____

_____

*How does the language work?*_____

_____

_____

_____

_____

Role Playing

Now let's try an exercise in **role playing**—communicating effectively with an audience by adjusting your role (and your language) to suit your purpose, your message, and your audience.

Imagine, in each of the following situations, that you must deal with four different audiences face to face. Before you begin, analyze each audience in terms of knowledge, attitudes, and needs; then clarify your own purpose in communicating your message, your attitude towards your subject, and your audience's expectations of you.

EXERCISE 2

1. At 8:30 this morning, you got a phone call from your friend Jaron, who was calling from a police station. He had been arrested because,

according to the arresting officer, he had 37 unpaid parking tickets outstanding. He claims he's innocent; he's never had a parking ticket. He has called to ask you to come down and bail him out. If you do so, you will be late, possibly very late, for work. Jaron refuses to call his parents for help. Tell this story to

> your parents
> your boss
> a friend
> Jaron's parents.

2. You recently bought a pair of silk pants from Bottom Drawers Pants Company. They ripped in the crotch the first time you bent over. You were doing the lambada with a very attractive partner and were deeply embarrassed. Before you could recover your composure, the owner of the club asked you to leave immediately. Tell your story to

> Bottom Drawers
> a friend
> the owner of the club
> a tailor.

3. You recently saw a film in which a married man has an affair with an unmarried woman. He refuses to leave his wife and family; consequently, she decides to marry her old boyfriend in revenge. You enjoyed the film, but your date didn't. Describe the plot of the film, inventing any details you need, to

> a close friend of the same sex
> your eight-year-old sister
> a clergyman or priest
> a marriage counselor.

4. You are short of money—so short you can't even buy gas for your car. If you can't get gas money, you will be late for work and your boss is already annoyed because you've been late for work twice this week. Ask for money from

> your parents
> a friend
> someone who owes you money
> your boss.

5. Turn one of the sixteen role-playing situations above into a written assignment.

When you have a clear fix on your intended reader and on your own purpose and role in writing, it's time to turn to the first step in the actual writing of your essay: choosing a suitable subject for your paper.

CHAPTER 2

Selecting a Subject

Most of the time you devote to producing an essay should be spent on the planning stage. If you take the time to analyze your audience, to find a good subject, and to identify interesting main points to make about that subject, you will find that the mechanics of writing will fall into place much more easily than if you are going through the motions of writing an essay only because it's been assigned. After you have considered your readers' background, needs, and expectations, the next step is to choose a satisfactory subject to write about.

Even when you are assigned a topic for an essay, you need to examine it, focus it, and consider different ways of approaching it. Depending on your knowledge of the topic and the readers you are writing for, the range of specific subjects for any broad topic is almost endless. For example, given the broad topic "Microcomputers," here are some of the approaches you might choose from.

> How to buy a microcomputer
> The IBM PC and the Apple Mac: a comparison
> Graphics on the Amiga
> Computer programming on the Icon
> Why I love my laptop

Your first task, then, is to choose a satisfactory subject, one that satisfies the basic principles of the **4-S test:**

> A satisfactory subject is *significant, single, specific,* and *supportable.*

If it passes the 4-S test, your subject is the basis of a good essay.

Make Your Subject *Significant*

Your subject and your approach to that subject must be significant and meaningful both to you and to your readers. The subject you choose must be worthy of the time and attention you expect your readers to give to your paper. Can you imagine the subject "How to buy movie tickets" or "Why I hate pants with button flies," for example, as being significant for most readers?

EXERCISE 1

From the list below, choose those subjects that would be significant to a typical reader. Revise the others to make them significant, if possible. If not, suggest another, related subject that is significant.

1. Tips for traveling with small children
2. How to choose shoelaces
3. Using the Reference Library
4. How CDs have changed the world's listening habits
5. Page-turning techniques
6. The perfect vacation spot
7. How to find "r" on the computer keyboard
8. Television is a threat to Canadian independence
9. Colour television versus black-and-white
10. Why you should write on one side of the page only

Make Your Subject *Single*

Don't try to crowd too much into one paper. Naturally, different assignments in school and projects on the job will have varying requirements of length and scope, but be careful that your subject is not actually two or three related subjects masquerading as one. If you attempt to write about a multiple subject, your readers will get a superficial and possibly confusing overview instead of the interesting and satisfying detail they expect to find in a well-planned paper. A subject such as "The problem of league expansion in hockey and other sports" includes too much to be dealt with satisfactorily in one essay. You'd need to write a book to give your readers new and significant information on such a broad topic. In an essay, you and your readers will both benefit if you try something like "The problems of league expansion in the NHL" or "Why Halifax can't get an NHL franchise."

EXERCISE 2

From the list below, choose the subjects that are single and could be satisfactorily explored in a short essay. Revise the others to make them single.

1. Causes of inflation in Canada and South America
2. Pub night at different colleges
3. The instant replay in sports
4. How to change a tire and adjust the timing
5. Abortion and capital punishment
6. The importance of accuracy in newspaper and television reporting
7. Methods of preventing the spread of AIDS
8. Causes of injury in industry and professional sports
9. Nursing and engineering: rewarding careers
10. Vacationing on the islands of Corsica, Corfu, and Manitoulin

Make Your Subject *Specific*

Given a choice between a broad, general topic and a narrow, specific one, you should always choose the specific. Again, assignments and projects will vary in length and scope, but remember that your readers want to be both informed and interested in what you have to say. Most readers find concrete, specific details more interesting than broad generalizations.

It would be difficult to say anything very detailed about a huge subject like "The roles of women in history," for example. But, with some research, you could write an interesting paper on "The roles of women in medieval England" or "Famous women fliers." You can narrow a broad subject and make it more specific by applying one or more *limiting factors* to it. Try thinking of your subject in terms of a specific *kind,* or *time,* or *place,* or *number,* or *person* associated with it.

EXERCISE 3

In the list below, identify the subjects that are specific and could be explained satisfactorily in a short essay. Revise the others to make them specific by applying one or more of the limiting factors to each one.

1. Canadian politicians
2. Summer employment
3. Modern heroes
4. Enjoying winter weather
5. Drug abuse
6. The impact of the GST on low-income families
7. The problems of urban living
8. How to repair your home appliances
9. Planning your wedding
10. Female aggression

Make Your Subject *Supportable*

You must know something about your subject (preferably more than your readers know), or you must be able to find out about it. Remember, your readers want information that is new, interesting, and thought-provoking—not obvious observations familiar to everyone. You should be able to include *specific examples, facts, figures, quotations, anecdotes,* and other *supporting details.* (Think again about a reader whose name might be at the top of your page. What kind of supporting information will interest or persuade that person?) Supporting information can be gathered from your own experience, from the experience of other people, or from both. If you don't know enough about your topic to write anything but the obvious, be prepared to do some research.

EXERCISE 4

From the subjects given below, choose those that are clearly supportable in a short essay. Revise the others to make them supportable.

1. The principles of cold fusion
2. My career as a student
3. Movie review: *Jesus of Montreal*
4. Corporate mergers in the 1990s
5. The Chinese secret service
6. Religion in Canada
7. Space travel in the year 2100
8. Bass fishing techniques
9. Art through the ages
10. The hazards of working in a fast-food outlet

EXERCISE 5

Indicate with check marks (✓) whether each subject below passes the 4-S test by being *sig*nificant, *si*ngle, *sp*ecific, and *sup*portable. Revise each unsatisfactory subject (fewer than four check marks) to make it a satisfactory subject for a short essay.

The 4-S Test

SUBJECT	SIG	SI	SP	SUP	REVISION
1. The Canadian climate	—	—	—	—	_____
					_____
2. Boiled potatoes	—	—	—	—	_____
					_____
3. Whitewater rafting	—	—	—	—	_____
					_____
4. Insomnia and other stress-related disorders	—	—	—	—	_____
					_____
5. Blue: a nice colour	—	—	—	—	_____
					_____
6. Calgary in 200 years	—	—	—	—	_____
					_____
7. Dressing for an interview	—	—	—	—	_____
					_____
8. Canadian sports figures	—	—	—	—	_____
					_____
9. Architecture	—	—	—	—	_____
					_____
10. Life in the Andromeda galaxy	—	—	—	—	_____
					_____

Now that you've learned how to select an appropriate subject, it's time to move on to the next stage: identifying solid main points to support that subject.

CHAPTER 3

Managing the Main Points

While you were selecting subjects and testing them against the four principles presented in Chapter 2, you were thinking about some of the things you might say about each. **Main points** are the two or three or four most important things you have to say about your subject. Selecting them carefully is a vitally important part of the essay-writing process.

If you begin to write as soon as you have chosen a subject, and you march merrily down the page explaining everything that comes to mind, you will have to go back and revise your "thought flow" several times, writing draft after draft until your ideas take shape and are clear in your mind, let alone on the page. But if you take time, before you begin to write, to select strong main points and decide on the best order in which to present them, you will be able to get the essence of your essay down on paper in one or two drafts instead of three or more. A second or third draft will be necessary to refine the content and polish the writing, of course, but you will have a finished product in two or three drafts instead of needing five or six, or nine, or . . . .

Generating Main Points: The Bottom-up Approach

If you are feeling a little intimidated by your task and unsure about how to present your subject, some prewriting activities can be helpful. Writers use several methods to stimulate thinking and prepare for a productive first draft. Two techniques are especially effective: freewriting and brainstorming. Either will get your creative juices flowing; we recommend that you try both, to see which works best for you in particular situations. Understand that these techniques are used when you already have the necessary material in your head. Either you are writing from personal experience or you've done some research. (You'll learn about research in Unit Five.) Freewriting and brainstorming are designed to get your ideas on the page in any order, shape, or form. Don't worry about making a mess. You can clean up after.

Freewriting

Freewriting does what its name implies. It sets you free to write down your ideas by removing whatever may be inhibiting your thought flow: worries about grammar, spelling, punctuation, sentence structure, sequence, or word choice, for example. We are not suggesting that you abandon these important considerations forever. Just forget about them for a while, until you get some ideas down on the page. Here's how to go about freewriting:

1. Write your subject at the top of the page. Ideally, it will have passed the 4-S test, but if you're really stuck, you can begin with just a word or phrase.
2. Start writing. Don't worry about sentence structure. Ramble as much as you like. If you wander away from your subject, circle back and get on track. The important thing to remember is to keep writing. Don't pause for breath or thought or hand-cramp. If you are at a loss for words, repeat over and over the last phrase you've written, until something new comes to mind. (Don't worry, it will!)
3. Keep up this pace for a specified length of time. Start with two minutes and work up to four minutes, six minutes, or longer if necessary. You will be surprised how much paper you can cover in a limited time.
4. Put onto the page whatever comes into your mind. Forget about elegant phrasing, proper paragraphing, effective transitions, and the like. Don't stop. Don't pause to analyze your ideas or to evaluate them. This technique is designed to get thoughts into words as quickly as possible without self-consciousness. Don't edit what you're writing.
5. After your time is up, stop and stretch. Then take a look at the ideas and expressions you have discovered. Underline anything, even a single word, that is related to your subject. Much of your freewriting will be irrelevant nonsense that can be discarded. But what you have underlined will be useful in the next step, identifying the main points that you will focus on in explaining your subject.

6. Turn the fragments, words, and sentences that you have underlined into clear, understandable points. If you don't end up with at least a dozen points, continue freewriting for another few minutes and see what new points you can discover.

7. On a separate sheet of paper, list the points you have identified. Study the relationships among these points and cluster them under three or four main headings. These are your main points. Now you can move on to the next step, which is testing each main point to be sure it is satisfactory for your essay.

Here is an example of the freewriting technique. The subject was left open for students to choose. This student had recently bought a car and chose to write about how he selected his dream car.

Choosing My Car

I knew I wanted a sports car but I didn't know which one to get so I went out and compared a bunch of them so I could make the best buy. I compared the Corvette and the Porsche 944 and the Jaguar Vandenplatz. I liked the Corvette's speed because it was the fastest 0 to 100 in 6 seconds and has a really sexy body styling. The wheels they put on it are also really neat looking and add performance.

The Jag was really luxurious but I felt old when I drove it even though it has a good top end and moves pretty quick, not as quick as the other two. The interior is almost too nice and I felt I wouldn't be able to relax in the car and for sure I would never invite any of my friends to ride in it because they're such slobs. You should see my girlfriend's car it's a complete mess with candy wrappers and coffee cups all over the floor and dog hair from her German Shepherd thick all over the upholstery. Anyway, I would never let her in my car if I bought the Vandenplatz. It was sure the quietest of the three, but I kind of like the roar of a well tuned exhaust.

The Porsche was my favourite and it was the one I bought even though it cost more than the Corvette and didn't perform quite as well because it's a heavier car. It made it from 0 to 100 in 6.6 seconds and cornered better than the 'Vet but its braking is a shade slower. I've got the stats at home and can't remember all of them right now but I'll put them in the final essay. Neither of them were as quiet or luxurious as the Jag, but as I already said, I decided against the Jag for other reasons. Maybe when I'm old I'll get one of them for tooling along to the country club or something. Anyway, the Porsche isn't as sexy looking as the Corvette but everyone recognizes a Porsche and it really gets attention. Of the three, I'd guess the Corvette was most common. There are lots of Corvettes on the road.

I really like the Jag's looks, but most people think it's an old person's car.

Lucky for me I didn't have to worry about cost. Since my grandfather was buying it for me for graduating from college, I didn't really care,

> but since this is supposed to be a comparison, I'd say the Corvette was
> the better deal since it cost about $3000 less and gets better mileage
> and costs less to repair. But not having to worry about money I bought
> the one I wanted—the Porsche.

After completing this 10-minute freewriting exercise, the student underlined all the points he considered both significant and related to his
subject. He then clustered them into four main points:

1. Performance: 'Vet faster, better brakes
                     Porsche better handling
                     Jag quieter
2. Styling: 'Vet very sexy, great tires
                     Porsche I don't think is as nice, but better image
                     Porsche really gets attention
                     Jag has old image
3. Comfort: Jag is best
4. Cost: 'Vet costs less and is more economical

After thinking about these main points for a while, the student realized
that one of his selections, the Jaguar, weakened the comparison, because it had been eliminated almost from the beginning. Dropping
the Jaguar, he fleshed out the other two entries and developed a useful blueprint for a comparison paper. His last move before writing
the first draft was to eliminate the category "styling," because it
was highly subjective while the other criteria could be judged factu-
ally. After two preliminary drafts and the addition of the facts and
statistics that he had at home, the student submitted "Car Wars," the
essay on p. 148.

EXERCISE 1

Choose a subject, or work with an assigned subject. Generate some ideas
using the freewriting method.

Brainstorming

In *brainstorming*, you generate ideas by asking, about a specific subject,
all the questions you can think of: who? what? where? when? why? how?
You storm your brain for quick, spontaneous answers and for ideas
connected to those answers. The best brainstorming strategy is a direct
assault on a specific subject. Here's how to proceed.

1. Write your topic at the top of the page. Again, you'll save time if
   you've checked that your subject passes the 4-S test.

2. Ask all the questions you can think of about your subject, and record your answers in a list. Each point in the list might be only a word or a phrase. Work quickly. Don't slow yourself down by worrying about grammar or sentence structure or repetition. As in freewriting, working against the clock (allowing yourself two, four, six, or more minutes) can bring surprising results. Many of the points won't be usable in the final list; worry about that later.

3. Once you have generated a dozen or more answers to your questions, relax for a moment, then go down the list carefully. Underline the answers that seem most clearly related to your subject. Ignore any phrases that are unclear or off-topic. If you don't end up with at least three or four points that are meaningful to you, brainstorm again for a few minutes to generate more ideas.

4. Take your three or four most significant points and rephrase them in clear, comprehensible form on a clean sheet of paper. Now you're ready to move on to the next step: testing your points to ensure they are suitable for use in your essay.

The following example demonstrates how brainstorming can be used to overcome the most frustrating inertia. The subject was "The value of a college English course." As you might expect, the class groaned when the subject was assigned, but quick brainstorming produced some unique and interesting approaches to the topic. Through brainstorming, one student found he believed his career opportunities would improve if he learned how to communicate better. The time limit given for this exercise was four minutes.

The Value of a College English Course

- I have to take it
- I should like it but I don't
- People want me to take it
- I speak better
- People listen
- Speaking is important
- Speaking's easier than writing
- Writing is like speaking really
- Bosses will hire you if you can write
- You can get a job
- You can write a letter of application
- I have to write in my job
- I have to write to my boss
- I have to write to other departments
- I have to write to my customers
- I'm embarrassed I can't write well
- Nobody respects a poor speaker

- Nobody respects a poor writer
- Writing helps you think
- Writing helps you speak
- Think of the reports I have to do
- It's better to know how to do a good one
- I need to write to get promoted

This student's initial resistance gave way to some significant points. The phrases or sentences in his list were in no special order; in fact, he circled around and doubled back to the essential features of the relationship between writing and speaking and between good communication and job opportunities. After he underlined the points he felt were most important, he noticed that several points said almost the same thing. These he put together into one revised phrase. Here is his list of revised points.

College English is useful because

- it improves speaking skills and thinking skills
- you will get hired
- you will communicate better on the job
- you will get promoted.

Now it's your turn. Try your hand at the exercise below.

EXERCISE 2

Choose a subject, or work with an assigned subject. Brainstorm for five minutes, then underline your three or four best ideas.

Generating Main Points: The Top-down Approach

Another way to find suitable main points is to ask yourself some specific questions about the proposed subject of your essay. The top-down approach is more highly structured than the bottom-up approach, but top-down has the advantage of producing clearly identifiable main points with few or no off-topic responses.

The list of questions on p. 34 serves as a kind of filter. Apply each question to your subject until you find a question that produces answers that are solid main points. Applying each of these questions to your subject is especially helpful if you're stuck for ideas.

Notice that a particular question produces a particular kind of essay. When you come to Unit Three, you'll see how the various kinds of essays can be developed to satisfy the needs of your audience as well as your purpose in writing.

THE ANSWERS TO THESE QUESTIONS	WILL PRODUCE THESE KINDS OF ESSAY:
1. How is your subject *made* or *done?* 2. How does your subject *work?*	} *Process*
3. What are the main *kinds* of your subject? 4. What are the component *parts* of your subject? 5. What are the significant *features* or *characteristics* of your subject? 6. What are the main *functions* of your subject?	*Classification*
7. What are the *causes* of your subject? 8. What are the *effects* or *consequences* of your subject?	*Cause and Effect*
9. What are the *similarities* and/or *differences* between your subject and X?	*Comparison and Contrast*
10. What are the main *advantages/disadvantages* of your subject? 11. What are the reasons *in favour of/against* your subject?	*Persuasion*
12. What does your subject *look, feel, sound, smell,* and/or *taste* like?	*Description*
13. How did your subject *happen?*	*Narration*

By applying these questions to your subject, you will find at least one question to which you can give answers appropriate to your purpose. Your answers will be the main points of your essay. As an example, we've chosen the subject "Great rock bands." The subject passes the 4-S test: it is single, specific, supportable, and (we think) significant to our readers. Now let's apply the questions, to find our main points.

1. How is a great rock band made?

   Some ideas come to mind, but since great bands usually just "happen" rather than being deliberately put together, the answers to the question are going to be vague or, at best, not supportable with much detail.

2. How does a great rock band work?

   They all work differently, so we would have to answer the question separately for each band. No way.

3. What are the main kinds or types of great rock bands?

   This question presents possibilities. We could manage this one by distinguishing heavy metal bands, personality bands, dance bands, post-punk anarcho-machinist bands, and many more. We can put a star beside this question as the best possibility so far.

4. What are the main parts of a great rock band?

   This question produces answers (drums, keyboards, strings), but since great bands and terrible bands can have exactly the same instruments and personnel, it won't provide any useful information.

5. What are the significant features or characteristics of a great rock band?

   Bingo. We can begin to answer this question because, while bands are all different, we have some clear ideas about what characteristics make a *great* band: performance, determination, appeal, and adaptability, just to name a few. But let's try the rest of the questions, to make sure there isn't a better one.

6. What are the main functions of a great rock band?

   To entertain. The answer is so obvious that the question is useless.

7. What are the causes of a great rock band?

   This question doesn't produce any usable answers.

8. What are the effects or consequences of a great rock band?

   We could say something about a great band's effects on its fans, but specific answers to this question are hard to devise.

9. What are the similarities and/or differences between great rock bands and . . . what? lousy rock bands? great marching bands? great rock single performers?

   We can't think of a comparison that would be significant for our readers.

10. What are the advantages (or disadvantages) of a great rock band?

    Doesn't make sense.

11. What are the reasons in favour of (or against) great rock bands?

    Doesn't make sense.

12. What does a great rock band look, feel, and sound like?

    We could certainly describe how a particular great rock band looks and sounds, but every great rock band sounds different, and we can't describe them all.

13. How did a great rock band happen?

    We could tell how one particular band came about, but that wouldn't be very enlightening about great rock bands in general.

We found two questions that work for our subject. Now we can choose the question we think we have more to say about, and begin developing the answers that will become our main points.

We chose question 5 and found three answers that would serve as good main points: "The main characteristics of a great rock band are popular appeal, exciting stage performance, and ability to adapt." (To see how the essay worked out, turn to "Rock of Ages" on p. 124.)

Generating main points is not a difficult process, but it can be time-consuming. Don't rush; take the necessary time. This is a crucial stage in the writing process. To sharpen your skills, look at the sample subjects given here, the questions that might be applied to them, and the main points that could result. Study these samples until you're sure you understand how to find suitable main points for any subject. As you read these subjects and main points, imagine the essay that might result; you'll find the essay taking shape very easily in your mind.

SUBJECT	SELECTED QUESTION	MAIN POINTS
Hockey violence	What are the reasons in favour of violence in hockey?	• releases aggression • keeps players alert • attracts fans
Law enforcement officers	What are the main functions of law enforcement officers?	• preventing crime • apprehending criminals • enforcing the law • acting as role model
Dog ownership	What are the main disadvantages of dog ownership?	• damage to property • drain on nerves • drain on finances • damage to relationships
Job interviews	How do you make a negative impression in a job interview?	• be late • be inappropriately dressed • be ignorant about the company • complain about former employers
Essay topics	What are the characteristics of a satisfactory essay topic?	• single • significant • specific • supportable

EXERCISE 3

For each of the subjects listed below, apply the questions on p. 34. Select the question that produces the answers you like best, and list three or four of those answers as main points.

	SUBJECT	SELECTED QUESTION	MAIN POINTS
1.	Passing midterm tests		
2.	Teacher strikes		
3.	Blue jeans		
4.	Desk-top computers		
5.	Living away from home		
6.	Dating services		
7.	TV sitcoms		
8.	Quebec independence		
9.	Pie crust		
10.	Canadian Football League		

EXERCISE 4

Choose five subjects of your own that you think would be suitable for a short essay. Remember that satisfactory subjects are single, significant, supportable, and specific. For each of your five subjects, list at least three main points. Use the questions on p. 34 to help you identify main points.

SUBJECT	SELECTED QUESTION	MAIN POINTS
1.	_____	_____
	_____	_____
	_____	_____
	_____	_____
2.	_____	_____
	_____	_____
	_____	_____
	_____	_____
3.	_____	_____
	_____	_____
	_____	_____
	_____	_____
4.	_____	_____
	_____	_____
	_____	_____
	_____	_____
5.	_____	_____
	_____	_____
	_____	_____
	_____	_____

Testing Your Main Points

Now that you've practised identifying main points using freewriting, brainstorming, and the questioning approach, the next step is to examine the points you've come up with, to make sure each is going to work as a major component in your essay. Some may be too minor to bother with; some may overlap in meaning; some may even be unrelated to your subject. Here's how to test your main points to be sure they are satisfactory. Whether you've arrived at your main points through freewriting, brainstorming, or questioning, the test is the same:

> Main points must be
> *significant, distinct,* and *relevant.*

Are Your Main Points Significant?

Each main point should be worth writing and reading about. If you can't write at least one interesting and informative paragraph about a point, it probably is not significant enough to bother with. To waste your readers' time with trivial matters gains you only irritated readers. In the following example, one of the main points does not have the same "weight" or importance as the others. It should be eliminated or replaced.

Reasons for attending college
- to learn career skills
- to improve one's general knowledge of the world
- to enjoy pub nights
- to participate in student government

Are Your Main Points Distinct?

Each of the main points you choose must be different from all the others; there must be no overlap in meaning. Check to be sure you haven't given two different labels to what is really only one aspect of your subject. Eliminate or replace any main points that duplicate other points or that can easily be covered under another point. Here's an example of a list that contains a redundant main point.

Advantages of cycling
- improves fitness
- stimulates enjoyment of surroundings
- keeps one in shape
- doesn't damage the environment

Are Your Main Points Relevant?

The main points you choose must be clearly and directly related to your subject. They all must be aspects of that subject and must add to the development of your readers' information on the subject. In this example, the third main point listed is inappropriate because it does not relate to the stated topic. It must be eliminated.

The miseries of winter
- numbing cold
- layers of uncomfortable clothes
- Christmas presents
- dangerous driving conditions

EXERCISE 5

Circle the unsatisfactory main point in each group.

1. How to catch a cold
   - associate closely with infected friends
   - get wet and remain in damp clothing
   - take aspirin and drink plenty of liquids
   - make sure you are tired and run down

2. Levels of education
   - high school
   - primary school
   - preschool
   - college
   - secondary school

3. Why I drive a Ford
   - stylish body design
   - plenty of power
   - comparatively good value
   - substandard fit and finish
   - high acceleration and top speed

4. Causes of college failure
   - lack of preparation in high school
   - poor study habits
   - irregular attendance
   - card playing

5. Effects of cigarette smoking
   - smelly clothing
   - emphysema
   - heart disease
   - lung cancer

6. Major world religions
   - Roman Catholicism
   - Islam
   - Judaism
   - Christianity
   - Buddhism
   - Hinduism

7. How to choose a home
- determine your needs
- determine your budget
- select your favourite colour
- seek expert advice

8. Reasons in favour of waste recycling
- burning waste harms the environment
- we are running out of landfill sites
- it is wasteful
- recycling helps our economy

9. How to pour a beer
- open the bottle gently
- tip the glass to a 30-degree angle
- empty the bottle fast enough to produce the desired head
- drink with strong, steady pulls until the glass is empty

10. Comparison between the 1960s and the 1980s
- drug use
- musical tastes
- aspirations and ambitions of the young
- space travel
- personal style and fashion

Organizing Your Main Points

After you select the main points for your essay and check to make sure they are satisfactory, your final step in the planning process is to decide on the order of your main points for the best development of your topic. Some thought here can make a big difference in your readers' understanding of your instruction or explanation or argument. How you arrange your main points will determine, to a large extent, your readers' understanding of the relationship among the ideas you are presenting.

> There are four ways to order your main points: *chronological, climactic, logical,* and *random*.

Chronological Order

When you present your points in order of time from first to last, you are using **chronological order**. You will find it most appropriate in process essays, but it can be used in other essays as well. Here are two examples.

SUBJECT	MAIN POINTS
The process of getting dressed	• put on your underpants • pull on your socks (left first) • get into your shirt (button it if necessary) • pull on your pants • tuck your shirt into your pants • do up your pants and belt (if any) • put on your shoes and tie the laces (if necessary)
The evolution of a relationship	• attraction • meeting • discovery • intimacy • disillusionment

Climactic Order

Persuasion most often uses a climactic arrangement, but it is also common in papers based on comparisons and contrasts. In **climactic order**, you save your strongest or most convincing point for last (the climax of your argument). You lead off your essay with your second strongest point, and arrange your other points in between, as in this example.

SUBJECT	MAIN POINTS
Advantages of a college education	• development of skills • friendships and contacts with compatible people • higher income potential for life • discovery of one's own potential

Logical Order

Cause and effect essays, or any writing in which one point must be explained before the next point can be understood, use **logical order**. The points you are making will have a logical progression and you cannot take them out of order without confusing your readers. Consider the following sequence.

SUBJECT	MAIN POINTS
Main causes of juvenile delinquency	• lack of opportunity or motivation for work • lack of recreational facilities • boredom • quest for "kicks"

The logical links here are clear: because of unemployment, recreational facilities are needed. Because of both unemployment and inadequate recreational facilities, boredom and the quest for "kicks" become problems. Readers must grasp each point before the next can be explained and understood.

Random Order

When your points can be explained in any order without affecting your readers' understanding, you can use **random order**. A random arrangement of points is possible only if all your main points are of equal significance and are not linked together logically or chronologically. In this example, all three points have equal weight.

SUBJECT
The garbage disposal crisis

MAIN POINTS
- disposal sites are hard to find
- cartage costs are high
- new technologies are not yet fully developed

EXERCISE 6

Choose the type of order—chronological, climactic, logical, or random—you think is most appropriate for each subject. Arrange the main points in that order by numbering them.

SUBJECT	ORDER	MAIN POINTS
1. How to brush your teeth	_____	• use an up-and-down motion
	_____	• put about 2 cm of toothpaste on the brush
	_____	• brush continuously for at least 3 minutes
	_____	• rinse
2. Reasons for listening to the CBC	_____	• it offers informative programs
	_____	• your taxes are paying for it
	_____	• it provides a sense of Canadian unity
3. Causes of tomato plant failure	_____	• wet spring weather
	_____	• early frost
	_____	• lack of summer rain
	_____	• heavy rain at harvest

SUBJECT	ORDER	MAIN POINTS
4. How to get from Winnipeg to Regina	_____	• Portage la Prairie is the first major city
	_____	• go west out of Winnipeg on Portage Avenue
	_____	• cross the border into Saskatchewan
	_____	• Brandon, Manitoba is the next large centre
	_____	• about 200 km from the border you will enter Saskatchewan's capital, Regina
	_____	• Portage Avenue runs into Highway 1, which you follow all the way
5. Advantages of heating with wood	_____	• it gives a dry, comfortable heat
	_____	• it creates a pleasant atmosphere
	_____	• it costs less than other fuels
	_____	• it is a renewable resource
6. Methods of quitting smoking	_____	• laser therapy
	_____	• acupressure
	_____	• hypnosis
	_____	• cold turkey
	_____	• gradual withdrawal
7. How to train a dog	_____	• be consistent in use of commands
	_____	• be firm
	_____	• begin with easiest commands
	_____	• keep sessions short
8. Reasons for travelling abroad	_____	• meet new people
	_____	• practise and develop language skills
	_____	• see important cultural and historic sites
	_____	• practise self-reliance and "coping" skills
9. How to break into the Canadian film industry	_____	• go to acting school
	_____	• take bit parts and nonspeaking roles
	_____	• marry a producer
	_____	• get on the game shows
	_____	• work in live theatre
10. Causes of stress	_____	• change of employment
	_____	• financial problems
	_____	• death of a family member
	_____	• problems at school

In this chapter, you've learned how to identify main points, how to test them for suitability, and how to arrange them in the most appropriate order. You're ready now to go on to the next step—writing the preview statement—probably the most important sentence in your essay.

CHAPTER 4

Writing the Preview Statement

The key to clear organization of any essay is the preview statement—a sentence (or sentences) near the beginning of the paper that announces the subject and its scope. Your preview statement will be a tremendous help both to you and to your readers. It will help you plan your paper, and it will tell your readers exactly what they are going to read about.

> Specifically, a **preview statement** is one or more sentences that clearly and concisely indicate the subject of your essay, the main points you will discuss, and the order in which you will discuss them.

In fiction, telling readers in advance what they're going to find out would never do. But this "advance notice" works very well for practical, everyday kinds of writing. Essays, term papers, technical reports, research papers, office memoranda, and business letters are not suitable for suspense or surprises. Readers have expectations of these kinds of writing, and you're more likely to get and keep their interest if you indicate the subject and scope of your paper at the outset. Your preview statement acts like a table of contents, giving a clear indication of what is to follow. It maps the territory covered in your paper, to keep your readers (and you) on the right track.

The number of sentences in your preview statement depends on what your subject is, how best to phrase it, how many main points you have, and how they are expressed. The preview statement is usually found in the first paragraph of an essay.

To write a preview statement, you join your subject to your main points, after you have selected them and arranged them in the most appropriate order. A simple formula for constructing a preview statement is

S	**consists of**	**1, 2, 3 . . . n.**
(subject)		(main points)

Can you identify the subject and the main points in each of these examples of preview statements?

> Success in a broadcasting career depends on a combination of personal characteristics. Winners will be talented, motivated, and hard-working.
>
> Our trip to New York was expensive, exhausting—and exhilarating.
>
> The United States influences Canada's foreign policy, dominates our culture, and controls our economy. In fact, Canada is little more than an American satellite.
>
> Two cheers for democracy: one because it admits variety and two because it permits criticism. (E. M. Forster)
>
> The most prolific producers of unnecessary jargon are politicians, sports writers, advertising copy writers, and educators.

Now try your hand at analyzing the introductory paragraphs in the exercise below.

EXERCISE 1

Each of the five introductions below contains a preview statement. Underline the preview statement in each paragraph.

1. Suddenly a man steps into the road in front of me. He's wearing a uniform and he's waving his hand for me to pull over to the side. My heart pounds and my pores prickle with anxiety. I feel guilty but I don't know what I've done wrong—maybe speeding 10 km over the

limit, but no more. Anyone who has been caught in a radar trap knows this momentary feeling of panic, guilt, and resentment. We fear that the police officer will be brusque and blaming, but we are often surprised. There are as many kinds of police officers as there are people. Four kinds, however, dominate the profession: the confident veteran, the arrogant authoritarian, the cocky novice, and the friendly professional. As I roll down my window, I wonder which kind of police officer I've gotten.

2. After a hard day's work, do you relax with two or three stiff drinks? Do you enjoy a few beers while watching a game on TV? Do you believe mixed drinks make a party more fun? Do you cool off with gin fizzes on a hot afternoon? If you answered "Yes" to most of these questions, you are probably abusing alcohol. The line between excessive social drinking and a serious addictive habit is a blurry one. Most alcoholics don't know they are hooked until they try to stop drinking. What are the signs that a drinker is no longer drinking for pleasure only? If a person "needs" a drink, or drinks alone, or can fall asleep only after some drinks, and can find enjoyment only when drinking, that person is probably in trouble.

3. What does an interviewer look for in a new job applicant? Good credentials, good preparation, good grooming, and good communication are essential features for anyone who wants a job. No interviewer would seriously consider an applicant who comes to an interview without the required educational background and work experience, without information about the job and the company, without appropriate clothing, and without the ability to present ideas clearly in the interview.

4. Ours is a transient society. Most of us travel more miles in a year than our grandparents traveled in a lifetime. We move from one city to another, one province to another, and one country to another. In the course of moving, we inhabit many homes. The family home of the past might have been inhabited by several generations, consecutively or concurrently. Today's average Canadians will probably have ten or more addresses during their adult lives. Our restlessness is having numerous effects on the children in our migrating families. They have to leave familiar surroundings and friends, perhaps more than once, and they must adjust to a new environment, new habits, and, sometimes, a new language. They often have difficulty forming new relationships in a new setting. They are paying a heavy price for the mobility of modern impermanence.

5. Movie villains are a necessary evil in an adventure on the silver screen. Without them, movie heroes would have nobody to pit their strength and cunning against, nobody to save the female stars from, nobody to confront in a dramatic showdown, and nobody to defeat in the eternal battle between good and evil. This melodramatic summary of a typical cinematic contest invariably applies, in obvious or subtle form, to all Hollywood thrillers. Villains are even more important than heroes, perhaps because villains show the measure of heroes by the nature of the heroes' triumph over them.

Phrasing Your Statement of Subject

Your statement of subject should be as clear and concise as you can make it. This doesn't mean you can let it be boring, however. Beginning writers often fall into the trap of stating the obvious: "In this essay I am going to discuss . . ." or "The subject of this paper is . . . ." Your readers *know* it's your essay; you needn't hit them over the head by pointing out your authorship or the fact that the paper contains your ideas. Here are three examples of faulty subject statements and their revisions.

POOR	BETTER
In this essay, I am going to discuss violence in hockey.	Violence in hockey is misunderstood by the nonplaying public.
The problem of Canadian unity is the subject of this paper.	Canadian unity is neither possible nor desirable.
I am going to examine the three most common causes of student failure in college.	There are three important reasons for the large number of failures among first-year college students.

Phrasing the Main Points

When you combine your statement of subject with your main points to form your preview statement, be sure that all your main points are phrased in the same way, in grammatically parallel form. If point 1 is a single word, then points 2, 3, and so on must also be single words. If point 1 is a phrase, then all the points following it must be phrases. If point 1 is a clause or a sentence, then the succeeding points must also be in clause or sentence form.

The following sentence contains a main point that is not parallel with the others.

> There are many qualities that combine to make a good nurse, but the three most important are strength, intelligence, and she must be compassionate.

Rewritten to be grammatically parallel, this statement might read:

> There are many qualities that combine to make a good nurse, but the three most important are strength, intelligence, and compassion.

Or, the sentence could be rewritten this way:

> There are many qualities that combine to make a good nurse, but the three most important are that she or he be strong, intelligent, and compassionate.

Try the exercise below. You may have problems now with grammatical parallelism. We will be covering it in detail in Chapter 31.

EXERCISE 2

In each of the lists below, one point is not parallel with the others. Rephrase the incorrect item so that all are in grammatically parallel form.

1. I enjoy
   a. reading
   b. walking
   c. to cook
   d. talking
2. We have enjoyed vacations
   a. sunbathing at the beach
   b. relaxing at our cottage
   c. European travel
3. Our doctor is
   a. full of medical knowledge
   b. competent
   c. caring
4. I've noticed that my friends are increasingly
   a. concerned about smoking
   b. interested in fitness
   c. environmental awareness
5. To upgrade our educational system we need
   a. more effective teacher training
   b. better liaison between levels of education
   c. students must be motivated to learn

EXERCISE 3

Correct the following preview statements so that all the main points are expressed in the same grammatical form.

1. Important steps to improve your performance in a spor[t] [prac]tice on non-game days, warming up before the game, a[nd] hard during the game.

_____

_____

_____

2. Some effects of too much television viewing include increased passivity, interaction with others is reduced, and impaired imagination.

_____

_____

_____

3. A newspaper has three functions in our society: to inform the public about current affairs, to entertain with features and articles, and most importantly, persuasion about our political choices.

_____

_____

_____

4. All the box office hits of last year were violent action pictures, feeble comedies about sex, or repulsive horror melodramas.

_____

_____

_____

5. Common causes of failure in college are lack of responsibility, lack of discipline, and not knowing basic skills.

_____

_____

_____

6. Yuppies have three characteristics. They are highly materialistic, compulsive overachievers, and affluent in a highly conspicuous manner.

_____

_____

_____

7. We are victims of the fashion industry. We can buy only what the industry decides to make available; the products are shoddily made; the styles change too quickly.

_____

_____

_____

8. The Goods and Services Tax has several disadvantages for low-income Canadians. Most things cost more. Manufacturers are reluctant to lower their prices. The consumer pays twice for some services.

_____

_____

_____

9. Unlike American cities, Canada's large cities have low crime rates, streets that are unlittered, and graffiti-free public transit.

_____

_____

_____

10. If you want to be a good nurse, you have to love the job because the hours are long, you will work hard, and the pay you get is not that high.

_____

_____

_____

EXERCISE 4

Combine each of the following subjects with its main points to form a clear preview statement that is expressed in grammatical parallel form.

1. Factors in choosing a bicycle
   - sized to your body
   - meets your needs
   - priced to your resources

   Preview statement: _____

   _____

   _____

   _____

2. Advantages of fishing as a hobby
   - calm, relaxing activity
   - inexpensive to begin
   - can provide a delicious meal

   Preview statement: _____

   _____

   _____

   _____

   _____

3. Methods of quitting smoking
   - laser therapy
   - acupressure
   - hypnosis
   - programmed withdrawal

   Preview statement: _____

   _____

   _____

   _____

   _____

4. Comparison between Nike and Reebok aerobic shoes
   - comfort and fit
   - support and durability

   Preview statement: _____

   _____

   _____

   _____

   _____

5. Causes of stress
   - death of a family member
   - change of employment
   - financial problems

   Preview statement: _____

   _____

   _____

   _____

   _____

6. Steps in getting a job
   - research job advertisements
   - prepare letter of application
   - perform well in the interview

Preview statement: _____

_____

_____

_____

7. Ingredients of a successful party
   - friendly people
   - good music
   - tasty food
   - ample liquid refreshments

Preview statement: _____

_____

_____

_____

8. Evolution of a recession
   - unemployment causes general economic slowdown
   - consumer buying decreases, resulting in inflation
   - inflation causes fear and further decrease in consumer demand

Preview statement: _____

_____

_____

_____

9. Disadvantages of teenage parenthood
   - less time for fun
   - instant need for more money
   - reduced chances for a good job
   - less opportunity for higher education

Preview statement: _____

_____

_____

_____

_____

10. Effects of urban overcrowding
   • traffic jams
   • too much air pollution
   • high rate of homelessness
   • violence on the streets

    Preview statement: _____

_____

_____

_____

_____

You have now covered all the steps leading up to your own construction of a good preview statement. The earlier exercises have given you practice in the skills you need to phrase subjects and main points correctly and effectively. It's now time for you to write your own "live" example.

Exercise 5 will walk you through the process of developing a preview statement for a subject of your own choice. As you fill in the blanks in Exercise 5, you will be both reviewing the contents of the first four chapters and testing your mastery of the writing tasks they presented. You may want to refer to Exercise 5's step-by-step outline when you are starting your next paper or research report.

EXERCISE 5

1. Select a subject.

_____

_____

2. Test whether your subject is significant, single, specific, and supportable.

3. Identify three, four, or five main points in support of your subject.

_____

_____

_____

_____

_____

4. Test whether your main points are all significant, distinct, and clearly related to your subject.

5. Arrange your main points in the order that is most likely to guarantee your readers' understanding of your subject: chronological, climactic, logical, or random.

_____

_____

_____

_____

_____

6. Now rewrite your main points so that they are grammatically parallel: all single words, all phrases, or all clauses.

_____

_____

_____

_____

7. Combine your statement of subject with your main points, to produce your preview statement.

_____

_____

_____

_____

_____

CHAPTER 5

Drafting the Blueprint

Imagine for a moment that you are able to hire an architect to design your dream house. The architect produces some initial sketches, based on your wish list, but you decide you would like a wider courtyard, a southern exposure for the pool enclosure, and a larger skylight in the master bedroom. Finally, your architect creates an artist's rendering of how your house will look when it has been built to satisfy your needs and specifications. You approve the drawing and give the architect permission to proceed.

However, no builder can work from any representation of what the exterior of the building will look like when it is finished. Builders need a detailed blueprint that shows every structural component's proper place and exact measurements before they can set the first form of the foundation.

When you write, you are building words into sentences, sentences into paragraphs, and paragraphs into the written communication of your ideas. You need a blueprint when you start to structure your essay, and you should refer to it often when you write, revise, edit, and finally declare your "building" finished.

The model blueprint on the next page was drafted for building a short essay that has three main points. The blueprint can be adapted and expanded to other styles and lengths.

THE MODEL BLUEPRINT

Essay title _____

Introductory paragraph
Grabber _____

_____

Preview statement
(statement of subject _____
and main points)
_____

_____

Body paragraphs
1. Topic sentence _____

_____

Support of first _____
main point
_____

_____

2. Topic sentence _____

_____

Support of second _____
main point
_____

_____

3. Topic sentence _____

_____

Support of third _____
main point
_____

_____

Concluding paragraph
Summary or reinforce- _____
ment of main points
_____

_____

Clincher _____

_____

The following essay outline was developed using the model blueprint. Preparation of an outline would precede your writing of a first draft.

After the outline, we show the final version of "Flunking with Style," matched to the blueprint.

Essay title	Flunking with Style
Grabber	Challenge traditional view of failure in school
Preview statement (statement of subject and main points)	To fail your year in grand style, antagonize your teachers, disdain your studies, and cheat on your work.
1. Topic sentence	Antagonize your teachers
Support of first main point	• show boredom • slouch in desk • wear Walkman • talk to classmates • snort at teacher's points • respond "I dunno" to questions
2. Topic sentence	Disdain your studies
Support of second main point	• don't buy textbooks until midterm and don't make notes in them • never take notes in class • don't go to class—use clever excuses
3. Topic sentence	Cheat on your work
Support of third main point	• plagiarize research assignments • copy from a classmate's paper during exams • read notes written on your forearms • consult notes hidden in washroom • send in a ringer to write the exam for you
Summary or reinforcement of main points	If you follow these guidelines, you're guaranteed to flunk your year.
Clincher	The challenge is yours. Pick up the torch and fall with it!

Flunking with Style

Nell Waldman

Introductory paragraph

Grabber ————

Preview Statement

Body paragraphs

1. Topic Sentence

Support of first main point ————

2. Topic Sentence ————

Support of second main point ————

3. Topic Sentence ————

Support of third main point ————

People often remark that succeeding in school takes plenty of hard work. The remark implies that failure is a product of general idleness and zero motivation. This is an opinion I'd like to challenge. My long and checkered past in numerous educational institutions has taught me that to fail grandly, to fail extravagantly, to go down in truly blazing splendour, requires effort and imagination. To fail your year in the grand style, you must antagonize your teachers, disdain your studies, and cheat on your work. Keep the following guidelines in mind.

The first step, antagonizing your teachers, isn't difficult if you keep in mind what it is that teachers like: intelligent, interested, even enthusiastic faces in front row centre. Show that you're bored before the class begins by slouching in a desk at the back of the room. Wear your Walkman, and don't forget to turn up the volume when that teacher starts to talk. Carry on running conversations with your seatmates. Aim an occasional snort or snicker in the teacher's direction when she's putting a complex point on the board. Above all, never volunteer an answer and respond sullenly with an "I dunno" if the teacher has the nerve to ask you a question. Before long, you'll have that teacher bouncing chalk stubs off your head. Once you've earned the loathing of all your instructors, you'll be well on your way to a truly memorable failure.

The second step, disdaining your studies, is easy to master; they're probably B-O-R-I-N-G anyway. First, don't buy your books until close to midterm and keep them in their original condition; don't open, read, or note anything in them. Better yet, don't buy your texts at all. Second, never attempt to take notes in class. Third, stop going to class completely, but have lots of creative excuses for missed assignments: "My friend's aunt died;" "My gerbil's in a coma;" "My boyfriend was in another car wreck;" "My dog ate the lab report;" "I've got mono." You can bet your teachers will be really amused by these old stand-bys. By now, you are well on your way to disaster.

The third step, cheating, will deliver the *coup de grâce* to your academic career. Should an instructor be so sadistic as to assign a research paper, just copy something out of a book that the librarian will be happy to find for you. Your instructor will be astonished at the difference between the book's polished, professional prose and your usual halting scrawls; you're guaranteed a zero. During your exams, sit at the back and crane your neck to read your classmate's paper. Roll up your shirt-sleeves to reveal the answers you've tattooed all over your forearms. Ask to be excused three or four times during the test so you can consult the notes you've stashed in the hall or the washroom. Be bold! Dig out your old wood-burning kit and emblazon cheat notes on the desk. If you want to ensure not just failure but actual expulsion, send in a ringer—a look-alike to write the exam for you!

Reprinted with permission from Sarah Norton and Nell Waldman, eds., *Canadian Content*. Holt 1988.

Concluding paragraph —— If you follow these guidelines, you will be guaranteed to flunk your year. Actively courting failure with verve, with flair, and with a sense of drama

Summary or reinforcement of main point —— will not only ensure your status as an academic washout but will also immortalize you in the memories of teachers and classmates alike. The challenge is yours! Become a legend—pick up the torch and fall with it!

Clincher ——

Now it's your turn to develop your blueprinting skills.

EXERCISE 1

Read "Of Men and Machines" (p. 129) and "Lightweight Lit." (pp. 137–38). Identify in each essay the sentences that correspond to the major structural items in the model blueprint. You may not have studied some of the terms mentioned (if you're working through the units in order), but you should be able to make a good guess at identifying the grabber and the clincher.

Essay title   Of Men and Machines

Grabber   _____

_____

Preview statement   _____
(statement of subject)
and main points)   _____

_____

1. Topic sentence   _____

_____

   Support of first   _____
   main point   _____

_____

2. Topic sentence   _____

_____

   Support of second _____
   main point   _____

_____

3. Topic sentence _____

_____

Support of third _____
main point

_____

_____

_____

Summary or reinforce- _____
ment of main points

_____

_____

Clincher _____

_____

Essay title Lightweight Lit

Grabber _____

_____

Preview statement _____
(statement of subject
(and main points) _____

_____

1. Topic sentence _____

_____

Support of first _____
main point

_____

_____

2. Topic sentence _____

_____

Support of second
main point

_____

_____

_____

_____

3. Topic sentence

_____

Support of third
main point

_____

_____

_____

_____

Summary or reinforce-
ment of main points

_____

_____

_____

_____

Clincher

_____

_____

Writing the Paragraphs

CHAPTER 6

Understanding Form and Function

What Does a Paragraph Look Like?

Essays are divided into paragraphs. **Paragraphs** are sentence groups that are separated from each other in their physical presentation and in their thought content. They usually have an indentation at the beginning (on a typed page, the first word begins five spaces in from the left margin) and some white space at the end (the last line is left blank following the paragraph's last word). In between the indentation and the final period comes the paragraph: a group of sentences that explains a single idea or topic.

If you were to draw a blueprint for a single paragraph, it would look like this:

A sentence that introduces the **topic** (or main idea) of the paragraph goes here.

Three or more sentences that specifically support or explain the topic go in here.

A sentence that concludes your explanation of the topic goes here.

How Does a Paragraph Function?

Readers expect that a paragraph will present a unit of thought or a single, developed idea. The white space at the start of each paragraph defines your thought units and serves two other important functions. First, it provides visual cues that make your writing "reader-friendly." Imagine if the page you are now reading were one continuous block of printing. No headings, no indentations, no paragraphs. The page would look so intimidatingly difficult to read that few readers would even attempt it. Second, paragraphs divide your writing into linked but separate sections, helping both you and your readers to stay on track, always conscious of where you are in the development of the subject that is the focus of your essay. Without paragraphs, ideas would blur and blend one into another. Readers would find it difficult to identify them, let alone follow the organization and development of the writer's thoughts.

Paragraph indentations function in much the same way that commercial breaks function in TV situation comedy shows. Review a sitcom episode in your mind. The story will have a beginning, a middle, and an end, and these will be separated from each other by commercials. Since seven or eight minutes of each half-hour show are made up of commercials, writers have developed a format that divides any script neatly into segments. The opening scene presents the characters and reveals the story problem for the episode. After a commercial break, the story problem becomes complicated and more critical. Another commercial break interrupts, just before the crisis or climax of the show. The final commercial break precedes a brief ending that solves the problem, puts everything back together, and leaves you laughing so you'll tune in to the next week's show.

The paragraphs in an essay work much the same way. The white space at the beginning and end of the paragraphs sets them apart as separate "action" sequences. In a typical essay, an introductory paragraph is followed by paragraphs that add details and complexity to the ideas set out in the introduction. A concluding paragraph brings all the ideas together again and leaves the readers with the writer's complete thinking on the subject.

Your readers will be able to tell a great deal about your thinking by just quickly glancing at your page. A number of short paragraphs on your page will indicate a series of ideas, briefly (and perhaps superficially) explained. Newspapers traditionally use very short paragraphs, many of them only one sentence long, to attract readers. Long paragraphs—half a page or longer—suggest more complex ideas that require explanation and details; they signal serious thought.

As a general rule, you explore one major idea or main point in each paragraph. When you have finished exploring one topic and wish to move on to another, you signal this shift to your readers by beginning a new paragraph.

How Long Should a Paragraph Be?

The answer to this question depends on the *topic*, your readers' *knowledge* of the topic, and your *purpose* in writing. If your topic is complex, your readers' knowledge is limited, and your purpose is to persuade readers who do not share your point of view, then you'll probably need a fairly long paragraph to accomplish your goal. On the other hand, if you're writing about a fairly common idea that your readers can be expected to be familiar with, and your purpose is simply to share your understanding of that topic with your readers, you may be able to accomplish your task in a few sentences.

EXERCISE 1

Read the paragraphs below. After you've finished each one, answer the following questions:

- What is the topic of the paragraph, stated in a single word or short phrase?
- How much knowledge of the topic does the writer assume the readers have?
- What is the writer's purpose in this paragraph?

1. Violence as a way of achieving racial justice is both impractical and immoral. It is impractical because it is a descending spiral ending in destruction for all. The old law of an eye for an eye leaves everybody blind. It is immoral because it seeks to humiliate the opponent rather than win his understanding; it seeks to annihilate rather than to convert. Violence is immoral because it thrives on hatred rather than love. It destroys community and makes brotherhood impossible. It leaves society in monologue rather than dialogue. Violence ends by defeating itself. It creates bitterness in the survivors and brutality in the destroyers. A voice echoes through time saying to every potential Peter, "Put up your sword." History is cluttered with the wreckage of nations that failed to follow this command.

   (from Martin Luther King, Jr.,
   "Three Types of Resistance to Oppression")

2. Try to decide in advance from which side you want to dismount, and then *stick to your decision!* If you put off making up your mind until the

last possible minute or keep changing your plans, you may find yourself unable to decide at all and end up running around in a flurry of indecision. It is surprising how quickly any panic you feel can communicate itself to the elephant, who in turn may decide to go berserk. But that's nothing compared with how quickly *his* panic can communicate itself to you.

(from Richard L. Thomas, "How to Dismount from an Elephant")

3.   *Vinaya* means humility; it is the complete surrendering of the self on the part of the *shishya* [the disciple] to the *guru*. The ideal disciple feels love, adoration, reverence, and even fear toward his *guru,* and he accepts equally praise or scoldings. Talent, sincerity, and the willingness to practise faithfully are essential qualities of the serious student. The *guru,* as the giver in this relationship, seems to be all-powerful. Often, he may be unreasonable, harsh, or haughty, though the ideal *guru* is none of these. Ideally, he should respond to the efforts of the disciple and love him almost as his own child. In India, a Hindu child, from his earliest years, is taught to feel humble toward anyone older than he or superior in any way. From the simplest gesture of the *namaskar,* or greeting (putting the hands palm to palm in front of the forehead and bowing), or the *pranam* (a respectful greeting consisting of touching the greeted person's feet, then one's own eyes and forehead with the hands held palm to palm) to the practice of *vinaya* or humility tempered with a feeling of love and worship, the Hindu devotee's vanity and pretension are worn away.

(from Ravi Shankar, "Studying Music in India")

4.   Take William Lyon Mackenzie King, our prime minister through the war and, so it seemed, for all time until Pierre Trudeau came along and seemed to be prime minister for all time. King held power longer than any other Western politician in this century. How did such a pudgy, mundane little man do it? The truth is, he did it deliberately. He was shrewd and self-effacing, and he told his friends that he made every speech as boring as possible because then no one would ever remember what he said and hold it against him. Twenty-two years in power, droning on and on over the airwaves, and meanwhile, he was as crazy as a loon.

(from Barry Callaghan, "Canadian Wry")

5.   A word about balls. The *New Columbia Encyclopedia* says, "Despite the name, the ball used is not soft," which may be the understatement of the tome's 3,052 pages. There were three kinds of softballs, and each was about as soft as anthracite. The best was simply a big baseball, with seams that were pretty well flush with the horsehide cover. Then there was a solid rubber ball with fake seams. After a while, this ball did soften up, but on grounds it no longer hurt enough for competition, it was then retired for use only in practice. Then there was the "outseam"

ball. Perhaps it was not a sadist who invented it. Perhaps it was merely someone who sought durability in lean times. But the outseam was a quarter-inch ridge of leather so hard that, when you fielded a rifling, spinning grounder, the ball felt as though its real function was to rip the skin off your palms. The outseam ball was a character-builder.

(from Harry Bruce, "The Softball Was Always Hard")

CHAPTER 7

Crafting the Topic Sentence

The **topic sentence** in each paragraph is the sentence that clearly identifies your main idea in that paragraph—what the paragraph's about. The topic sentence focuses the paragraph, helps to unify it, and keeps both you and your readers on track. It ensures that both of you are starting from the same point. In some professional writing, the topic sentence is not the first sentence of the paragraph. Sometimes it is effective to wait and let the second sentence, or even the third, announce the topic of the paragraph. But professional writers, through years of practice, have earned the right to break the rules. Beginning writers should remember this: *most readers assume that the first sentence of a paragraph identifies the topic of that paragraph.* If it doesn't in your writing, you run the risk that your readers will proceed through your paragraph assuming the topic is something other than what you intended. This is not only a waste of the readers'—and your—time, it can be frustrating for both of you. To be absolutely clear to your readers, identify your topic up front.

A good topic sentence does three things:

> 1. It introduces the topic of the paragraph.
> 2. It makes a point about the topic.
> 3. It makes a statement that is neither too broad nor too narrow.

Readers appreciate writers who get to the point quickly, make the point clearly, and support or explain it adequately. They also appreciate writers who can make their points in an interesting way. Take the time to write topic sentences that are something more than straightforward, flat announcements of your main idea. Compare the following pairs of topic sentences.

WEAK	STRONG
This paragraph is about violence.	Violence as a way of achieving racial justice is both impractical and immoral.
I'm going to tell you how to dismount from an elephant.	Try to decide in advance from which side you want to dismount, and then *stick to your decision!*
My love of "trash" is the subject of this paper.	I'm ashamed to confess my secret vice—but since we're friends, I can tell you—I *love* "trash."

A good way of introducing the topic so that it is both interesting and effective is to make a point about it. You save your readers' time and eliminate the risk of confusion if you make clear at the outset your idea about or your attitude towards your topic. Consider these examples.

WEAK	STRONG
The third step is cheating.	The third step, cheating, will deliver the *coup de grâce* to your academic career.
You should know your audience.	Knowledge of your audience will enable you to devise an effective approach to your topic.
Let us consider the idea of manhood.	I have always disliked being a man.

Finally, the topic you choose must be "the right size"—neither so broad that you cannot support it adequately in a single paragraph, nor so narrow that it doesn't require support. The 4-S test that you used to determine whether a subject was suitable for a paper can also be applied to potential paragraph topics. If your topic is single, significant, specific, and supportable, it should form the basis for a solid paragraph. Take a look at these topic sentences.

WEAK	STRONG
Good teachers share certain characteristics.	A good teacher shows respect for her students.

WEAK	STRONG
I like ink.	Despite the almost universal preference for word processors, I still prefer to write with a pen.
Canadians are different from Americans.	What Canadians should be thankful for is what genuinely makes us different.
Censorship of books and movies is a necessary evil.	Censorship of movies is a necessary evil.
Today's teenagers have a hard time.	A teen's relationship with her mother is often a difficult one.

EXERCISE 1

Underline the topic sentence in each of the paragraphs below.

1. Besides being time-consuming, trying to find a part-time job can be humiliating. Some employers seem to feel that it is their right, and part of the hiring process, to point out all your faults and shortcomings during the interview. Here is a person you've just met telling you how useless you are! Until you learn to cope with rejection, being turned down for a job can be pretty humiliating, too. It's very humbling to be told that you're not smart enough to sell blue jeans or strong enough to ride a courier bike.

2. Such a seemingly minor irritant as sanitation can drive a wedge between generations of new Canadians. When I approached my grandfather about his spitting, a habit he picked up in China and continued to practise on the streets of Vancouver, he waited patiently for me to finish. I explained that it is unsanitary and unhealthy to spit on the street, and that to Canadians it is a disgusting habit. He smiled and quietly asked me in Mandarin, "What do these healthy Canadians do, then? Surely they don't swallow the stuff . . . *that* would be disgusting!"

3. No one seems able to explain the increasing death rate among loons. While some claim that acid rain has depleted the fish stock in the lakes, others maintain that mercury in the fish they eat is destroying their nervous systems. Evidence can be found to support both these views and several other theories as well. However, until we determine conclusively what is killing this wonderful bird, our efforts to save it will be haphazard and probably ineffective.

4. There is something magical about it. Baseball has a dimension far beyond mere athletic competition, a dimension that may encompass the mystical. *Field of Dreams*, the movie based on W. P. Kinsella's short story, "Shoeless Joe Jackson Comes to Iowa," comes closest to expressing this mysterious quality of the game. A corn farmer hears a

voice telling him to build a ball diamond that will attract the ghosts of long-dead players. He does, and it does. It isn't really surprising that thousands of people every year make a pilgrimage to the baseball diamond in Iowa that was carved out of a cornfield as the setting for the movie. The voice said, "If you build it, he will come." Baseball has that kind of magic.

5. The third consideration is perhaps the most important. Canada makes no economic sense. There may be excellent reasons for Canada's existence historically, socially, culturally, even geographically, but the lines of trade and commerce flow north–south. If a government's chief concern is the economy, that government will naturally draw us closer and closer to the United States, cinching in those belts of commerce that bind us to our southern partner. Only governments whose prime goals are cultural or social will loosen the longitudinal ties and seek east–west bonds.

6. The headlines in the supermarket tabloids are a revealing study of North American pop culture. For two years, "Elvis Lives!" headlines dominated the front pages. When readers got tired of seeing Elvis everywhere they turned, the headlines shifted to the always sure-selling aliens and UFOs. Some enterprising headline writers even combined the two: "Elvis was an Alien with a Mission" and "Aliens Take Off with Elvis' Frozen Body." Roseanne, Cher, and Madonna are ever popular subjects in the tabloids, along with deformity, depravity, and debauchery in forms previously unheard and even undreamt of. What the popularity of these checkout counter papers tells us, or may tell future anthropologists, about ourselves is frightening.

7. "Why do you want it?" This should be the first question a good computer salesperson asks a prospective customer. With the huge variety of computers now on the market, the determining factor in a purchase should be the job the machine will be expected to do. While colour monitors and graphics cards, stereo sound, and joysticks are great for video games, a user who is buying a word processor needn't spend money for any of them. Home users and small businesses often get carried away with the desire for gigantic memory capacity, lightning speed, and colour graphics capability, but these are advertising gimmicks rather than useful purchases for most small users. On the other hand, it can be a costly error for a buyer to underestimate long-term computer needs and buy a machine that must be upgraded or replaced in a year.

8. For millions of people around the world, the greatest annual sporting event is not the Stanley Cup or the Superbowl, but cycling's premier race, the Tour de France. Among the millionaire riders who compete in this grueling contest, none is more admired and respected than Canada's Steve Bauer. From a tiny village in Ontario's Niagara Peninsula, Bauer trained on the back roads and steep hills of the Niagara Escarpment. He first came to international attention when he took the silver

medal at the Olympics in 1984; he turned pro the same year, and quickly took his place among cycling's elite riders. When the greatness of many athletes is measured by their egos, and Canada's own international image is tarnished by drug use, it is refreshing to be represented in international competition by someone who so well reflects the qualities most valued by Canadians: modesty, determination, integrity, and grit. Steve Bauer is someone in whom we can all take pride.

9. If I were unable to go to France, my next vacation choice would be Greece. A visit to Greece combines the excitement of exploring some of the world's greatest historical treasures with the joy of unequalled recreation and relaxation opportunities. From the ruins of the first Olympic stadium in Olympia to the magnificent theatre in Epidaurus, from the sites of Greek mythology at Knossos and Mycenae to the wonders of Athens itself, impressive remnants of ancient Greece are everywhere. When tired of tramping through the magnificent temples and palaces of the past, one can take a break in the clear, warm waters of the Aegean Sea or lie on the white sand beaches of Corfu. Modern Greece is one of the world's most hospitable and enjoyable recreational destinations; ancient Greece is a bonus that makes the package almost irresistible.

10. Finally, then, there is the question of appearance and whether a beard mars or improves a man's looks. In my view, a bearded man is more interesting, more mature, and more attractive than his clean-shaven counterpart. It's impossible for most men to hide their feelings; emotion is written all over their bald faces. But bearded men project an air of depth, of mystery, simply because they aren't broadcasting their every feeling in the lines and frowns of their faces. Men whose chins make them appear weak, whose mouths betray indecision, whose babyish complexions make them look eternally seventeen, all can disguise their shortcomings while adding majesty and dignity with a full facial growth. There is something interesting and individual about a bearded man that his scraped and plucked friends lack.

EXERCISE 2

Study the topic sentences you underlined in Exercise 1, and determine whether each is satisfactory. Does it introduce the topic clearly? Does it make a point about the topic? Is it too broad or too narrow? Finally, rewrite the topic sentences of paragraphs 3 and 10 to make them more effective.

EXERCISE 3

Each of the following preview statements consists of a statement of subject and some main points. For each of these preview statements, develop the main points into effective topic sentences.

1. It is not easy for students to avoid bad eating habits, given the wide availability of junk food, the lack of time to prepare balanced meals, and the widespread ignorance about the importance of proper nutrition.

   - _____
     _____
     _____

   - _____
     _____
     _____

   - _____
     _____
     _____

2. Canadians emigrate to other countries for a variety of reasons, chief among them the search for a warmer climate, the search for better job opportunities, and the search for exotic experiences.

   - _____
     _____
     _____

   - _____
     _____
     _____

   - _____
     _____
     _____

3. Though both Canadians and Americans are part of a highly affluent society, Canadians seem to be more obsessed than their southern neighbours with personal savings, life insurance, and pension plans.

   - _____
     _____
     _____

- _____
  _____
  _____
- _____
  _____

4. Canada's Charter of Rights precludes discrimination on the grounds of sex, age, race, or religion.

- _____
  _____
  _____
- _____
  _____
  _____
- _____
  _____
  _____
- _____
  _____

5. Getting the job you want requires that you prepare a flawless résumé, research the firm you are interested in, respond intelligently in the interview, and follow up the interview appropriately.

- _____
  _____
  _____
- _____
  _____
  _____
- _____
  _____

- _____
  _____
  _____

6. Because maintaining a home involves considerable amounts of both time and money, one should consider very carefully the decision to buy a house.

- _____
  _____
  _____
- _____
  _____
  _____

7. The driver who caused your accident last weekend was probably one of four types: a road hog, a tailgater, a speed demon, or a Sunday driver.

- _____
  _____
  _____
- _____
  _____
  _____
- _____
  _____
  _____
- _____
  _____
  _____

8. The thought of moving to the country is attractive to many city dwellers because of the slower pace, the cleaner air, and the more closely knit communities.

- _____
  _____
  _____

* _____

_____

_____

* _____

_____

_____

9. Being unemployed, broke, and alone all contribute to depression.

* _____

_____

_____

* _____

_____

_____

* _____

_____

_____

10. Though their parents may have been interested in changing the world, today's college students seem primarily interested in finding a good job and making a good salary.

* _____

_____

_____

* _____

_____

_____

CHAPTER 8

Developing the Topic

After you've written your topic sentence, telling your readers what point or idea you're going to discuss in a paragraph, the next step is to develop that point or idea. An adequately developed paragraph will give enough supporting information to make the topic completely clear to your readers. Unless you are writing from a very detailed outline and have listed in front of you all the supporting material you need, a little thinking is in order at this point. Put yourself in your readers' place. What do your readers already know about your topic? Is their attitude towards your topic hostile or sympathetic? What do your readers need to know to understand your point clearly? If you ask yourself the seven questions listed below, you'll be able to decide what kind or kinds of development to use to support a particular topic sentence. The choice of development is up to you. Your topic and what your readers need to know about it will be the bases of your decision.

1. *Would telling a story be an effective way to get your idea across to your readers?* Everyone loves to read a story if it's well told and relevant to what's being discussed. Use of a personal anecdote to illustrate a point can be a very effective way of helping your readers not only understand your idea but also remember it. Below are two examples that illustrate the use of narration to develop a topic.

I first experienced culture shock when I travelled to Egypt. I was walking down the main street on the day of my arrival when it suddenly struck me that the crowds on the street were stepping aside to make way for me. It was 1980, and my height, blond hair, and blue eyes were so unusual to the Egyptians that I was an object of intense curiosity. The staring and pointing followed me everywhere. Finally, unable to cope any longer with being constantly on display, I took refuge in the Canadian Embassy and spent a couple of hours quietly leafing through back issues of *Maclean's* magazine.

I really enjoy literary discussions. I love it when people at trendy restaurants smack their lips in appreciation of the latest South American novelist, Egyptian poet, or Armenian essayist. By eavesdropping on these discussions, I can find out what's going on in the world of "great literature" so that when people ask me what I've read lately, I can pretend that I, too, am devoted to highbrow literature.

2. *Would a definition help your readers to understand?* A definition paragraph explains and clarifies the meaning of a word or idea that is central to your topic. Use the definition paragraph to explain a term that may be unfamiliar to your readers. (Write your own definition, please. Quoting from a dictionary is an overused and boring way to start a paragraph.) Below are definitions of terms that two writers wanted to be certain their readers understood.

Culture shock is the inability to understand or cope with experiences one has never encountered before. It commonly affects travellers who journey to lands whose climate, food, language, and customs are alien to the traveller. In addition to confusion and anxiety, culture shock may even produce physical symptoms: chills, fever, trembling, and faintness.

While the flood is a single bulb, strip lighting is a series of lamps set in a rectangular trough. It can be used for general illumination, but its primary functions are to blend the acting areas, illuminate shadows, and, with the use of colour, provide tone for settings and costumes. Strips can be hung as footlights, as border lights, or as special-purpose lights to illuminate backings for windows or doors.

You should include a definition, too, if you're using a familiar term in an unusual way. Here, Martin Luther King defines what he means by "the length of life."

Now let us notice first the length of life. I have said that this is the dimension of life in which the individual is concerned with developing his inner powers. It is that dimension of life in which the individual pursues personal ends and ambitions. This is perhaps the selfish dimension of life, and there is such a thing as moral and rational self-interest. If one is not concerned about himself he cannot be totally concerned about other selves.

3. *Would examples help to clarify the point?* Listing a number of examples is probably the most common method of developing an idea and

supporting a statement. Readers can become confused or suspicious when they read unsupported statements of "fact," opinion, or ideas. One of the best ways to support your opinion or ideas is by providing clear, relevant examples. Sometimes, as in the paragraph below, a single detailed example is enough to allow your readers to see clearly what you mean.

> Culture shock can affect anyone, even a person who never leaves home. My grandfather was perfectly content to be an accountant until he retired, and was confident that his company would need his services for the foreseeable future. Computers were "silly toys" and modern business practices just "jargon" and "a new fad." When he was laid off four years before his retirement, he went into shock. It wasn't just the layoff; it was the speed of change, the idea that he was stranded in a new and unfamiliar culture for which he was unprepared, and in which he had no useful role.

A number of examples may be necessary to illustrate a point, as in this next paragraph.

> All sports may be reduced to a few basic skills, which, if learned properly at the outset and drilled until they are instinctive, lead to success. Tennis is no exception; however, few people seem willing to spend the time needed to master the basics. Having been shown the proper grip and swing for a forehand, backhand, and serve, my students seem to feel they can qualify for Wimbledon. The basics are not learned that easily. Many tennis schools are now using a system first developed in Spain that is very successful in establishing the correct stroke in new players: for the first month of lessons, they aren't allowed to use a tennis ball. For that first month, correct positioning, proper swing, footwork, and technique are drilled without any of the distractions of keeping score, winning or losing, or chasing errant balls. That's how important the basics are to winning tennis.

4. *Would a quotation or paraphrase help to convince your readers?* Occasionally you will find that someone else—an expert in a particular field, a well-known author, or a respected public figure—has said what you want to say better than you could ever hope to say it. Relevant and authoritative quotations, as long as they are kept short and are not used too frequently, are useful in developing your topic. In the paragraph below, Martin Luther King uses a famous quotation to sum up and emphasize his point.

> As long as there is poverty in the world, I can never be rich, even if I have a billion dollars. As long as diseases are rampant and millions of people in this world cannot expect to live more than twenty-eight or thirty years, I can never be totally healthy even if I just got a good check-up at Mayo Clinic. I can never be what I ought to be until you are what you ought to be.

> This is the way our world is made. No individual or nation can stand out boasting of being independent. We are interdependent. So John Donne placed it in graphic terms when he affirmed, "No man is an island entire of itself. Every man is a piece of the continent, a part of the main." Then he goes on to say, "Any man's death diminishes me because I am involved in mankind, and therefore never send to know for whom the bell tolls; it tolls for thee." When we discover this, we master the second dimension of life.

A paraphrase is a summary, in your own words, of someone else's idea. Don't forget to indicate whose idea you are paraphrasing, the way King does here.

> Some years ago a learned rabbi, the late Joshua Liebman, wrote a book entitled *Peace of Mind*. He has a chapter in the book entitled "Love Thyself Properly." In this chapter he says in substance that it is impossible to love other selves adequately unless you love your own self properly. Many people have been plunged into the abyss of emotional fatalism because they did not love themselves properly. So every individual has a responsibility to be concerned about himself enough to discover what he is made for. After he discovers his calling he should set out to do it with all of the strength and power in his being . . . .

5. *Would a comparison help to illustrate or clarify your point?* A comparison shows similarities between things; it shows how two different things are alike in a particular way. If you have a difficult or abstract topic to explain, try comparing it to something tangible that is familiar to your readers, as this writer does.

> Being left on your own in a foreign land is a bit like being forced to play a card game when you're the only one who doesn't know the rules. As the stakes get higher and the other players' excitement and enjoyment increase, you get correspondingly more frustrated and miserable. Finally, in desperation, you want to throw your cards on the table, absorb your losses, and go home.

In this next paragraph, the writer uses an **analogy**—an extended comparison—between a date and a car to make the point both clear and interesting.

> The economy model date features cramped conditions and a lack of power. The econo-date thinks that his personality can make up for the fact that you never go anywhere except for walks, and never do anything that costs money. He tends to be shy, quiet, and about as much fun as an oil leak. It's not just that he doesn't have lots of money to spend; it's that he doesn't use any imagination or creativity to compensate for his lack of cash.

6. *Is a series of steps or stages involved?* Sometimes the most effective way to develop the main idea of your paragraph is by explaining how something is done, that is, by relating the process or series of steps involved. Make sure you break the process down into its component parts and detail the steps logically and precisely. Read how this writer explains the process of writing a good business letter.

> The business letter must be clear. You should have a very firm idea of what you want to say, and you should let the reader know it. Use the structure of the letter—paragraphs, topic sentences, introduction, and conclusion—to guide the reader point by point from your thesis, through your reasoning, to your conclusion. Paragraph often, to break up the page and to lend an air of organization to the letter. Use an accepted business-letter format: there are several, and they can be found in any book of business English. Reread what you have written from the point of view of someone who is seeing it for the first time, and be sure that all explanations are adequate, all information provided (including reference numbers, dates, and other identification). A clear message, clearly delivered, is the essence of business communication.

In writing a process paragraph, you need to pay particular attention to transitions, which are discussed in the next chapter, or you'll leave your readers gasping in the dust as you gallop through your explanation. The paragraph below illustrates a simple yet effective use of transitions.

> The second step, disdaining your studies, is easy to master. They're probably B-O-R-I-N-G anyway. First, don't buy your books until close to midterm and keep them in their original condition; don't open, read, or note anything in them. Better yet, don't buy your texts at all. Second, never attempt to take notes in class. Third, stop going to class completely, but have lots of creative excuses for missed assignments: "My friend's aunt died;" "My gerbil's in a coma;" "My boyfriend was in another car wreck;" "My dog ate the lab report;" "I've got mono." You can bet your teachers will be really amused by these old standbys. By now, you are well on your way to disaster.

7. *Would precise, detailed information or statistics make your ideas clearer or more credible?* Providing your reader with concrete, specific, descriptive details can be an effective way to develop your main idea. In some paragraphs, numerical facts or statistics are essential to make your argument convincing or to back up your opinion. (Just make sure that your facts are 100 percent correct!)

In the paragraph below, the writer uses specific details to support a comparison of two automobiles.

> Performance of the two cars was very close, especially when you consider the tiny difference at the speeds involved. However, I was able

to get the 'Vet from 0 to 100 kph in exactly six seconds, while the Porsche took more than half a second longer. In cornering, the Porsche was marginally superior, but the Corvette was the clear winner in braking. From 100 kph it came to a complete stop in 68 metres; the Porsche went almost two metres farther before stopping.

In this next paragraph, notice how Pierre Berton appeals to our senses in his description of the mixture he uses to season his famous baked beans:

When it [the seasoned liquid] tastes pungent and hot (remember that the pungency will be cut by the beans), stir in a large quantity of molasses. Most people don't use enough molasses, and yet this is the essence of all good baked bean dishes. For there comes a critical moment when the sweetness of the molasses is wedded to the sharpness of the vegetables and herbs, and it is this subtle flavour, baked indelibly into the beans and mingling with the pork fat, that brings a sparkle to the eyes.

(from Pierre Berton, "Baked Beans")

In writing your own paragraphs, you will often need to use more than one method of development to explain your point. The seven methods described in this chapter can be used in any combination you choose. Keep your readers' knowledge, attitude, and needs in mind as you consider what kinds of development to use in support of a point.

EXERCISE 1

To stretch your imagination and improve your mastery of the kinds of support you can choose from to develop a topic, write a short paragraph on each of the following topics, using only the methods of development specified.

1. Chinese food   example and narration
2. Headaches   specific detail and process
3. Physical fitness   comparison and quotation or paraphrase
4. Fast food   definition and specific detail
5. Making a video   narration and process

EXERCISE 2

The essay below has an introduction, a conclusion, and topic sentences, but it doesn't have any support for the main points. Using a variety of the kinds of paragraph development you've learned in this chapter, write four or five sentences to support each main point. Before you begin, decide on your readers: for whom is this essay intended?

Money Matters

"Money can't buy happiness," according to the old adage. Perhaps it can't, but certainly the lack of money can bring pain. I have no aspirations to be featured on "Lifestyles of the Rich and Famous," but I do want enough money to keep the wolf from my door. Money may not make me happy, but it will enable me to escape destitution, enjoy freedom from insecurity, and provide my family with the necessities of life.

Obviously, one needs enough money to keep off the streets and out of the soup kitchens. _____

_____

_____

_____

_____

_____

_____

_____

_____

_____

_____

_____

Peace of mind is very difficult to come by if you don't know where your next dollar is coming from. _____

_____

_____

_____

_____

_____

_____

_____

_____

_____

_____

_____

"Enough is as good as a feast," the proverb says, and I want "enough" so that I may provide for my family. _____

_____

_____

_____

_____

_____

_____

_____

_____

_____

_____

Relatively few people in Canada suffer the destitution, insecurity, and deprivation that lack of money brings. But only a blind man or a fool would believe that no one in our country suffers because there isn't enough cash for basic needs. A modest bank account may not buy one ounce of happiness, but it prevents a ton of misery, and preventing misery for all should be our individual and collective goal.

CHAPTER 9

Keeping Your Readers with You

As you write your paragraphs, keep in mind that you want to make it as easy as possible for your readers to follow you through your essay. *Unity*, *coherence*, and *tone* can make the difference between a paper that confuses or annoys your readers and one that enlightens and pleases them.

Unity

Unity means "oneness"; the contents of a paragraph must relate to a single main idea. All supporting sentences in the paragraph must clearly and directly relate to the topic sentence of that paragraph. A paragraph is said to be unified when it contains nothing that does not contribute to its main idea.

Achieving unity takes careful planning. You want to make the points you set out to make, not revise them or introduce other points that occur to you as you are writing. The time to set down whatever happens to come to mind is in the prewriting stage, not the paragraph development stage. Any material that does not clearly support the topic sentence should be deleted or moved to another paragraph in the essay—assuming, of course, that it is directly relevant there.

Take a look at the paragraph below. It contains several sentences that spoil the unity of the paragraph, because they do not clearly relate to the topic.

> I knew I wanted to return to school, but did I want to be a full-time or a part-time student? The major consideration was, not surprisingly, money. If I chose to go to college full time, then I would have to give up my full-time job. The resulting loss of income would reduce my buying power to zero. Even the tuition fees would be beyond my reach. Also, my choice of program would be a difficult decision, because I still wasn't sure which career path to follow. My other option was part-time education. If I kept my full-time job, I could at least pay for food, rent, and a modest amount of clothing. Also, I could afford the tuition fees. Going to school part-time costs less per year, because the expenditure is spread over a longer period of time than it is in the full-time program. Therefore, I chose to educate myself part time, through continuing education courses. While working, I could learn new skills in my spare time. My career choice would still be in doubt, but I would have a longer time in which to make up my mind. Money is scarce for a full-time, self-supporting student, but as a part-time student, I could have the best of both worlds: a steady income and a college education.

Draw a line through the sentences that do not logically and directly support the topic of the paragraph: the writer's decision whether to be a full-time or part-time student.

These are the sentences that you should have crossed out because they do not belong in this paragraph and are disruptive to its unity:

1. Also, my choice of program would be a difficult decision, because I still wasn't sure which career path to follow.

2. While working, I could learn new skills in my spare time.

3. My career choice would still be in doubt, but I would have a longer time in which to make up my mind.

EXERCISE 1

The paragraphs below have some irrelevant sentences. They do not support the topic sentence and thus they distract from the unity of the paragraph. Find and cross out the sentences that don't belong. (Hint: Read the entire paragraph before you cross out the unrelated material.)

1. A good pizza consists of a combination of succulent ingredients. First, you prepare the foundation, the crust, which may be thick or thin, depending on your preference. I like my crusts thick and chewy. The crust is spread with a layer of basil- and oregano-flavoured tomato sauce. Next, a rich smorgasbord of toppings—pepperoni, mushrooms, green peppers, bacon, anchovies—should be scattered over the tomato sauce. *Smorgasbord* is a Swedish word meaning a buffet meal; *pizza* is Italian in origin. Last of all, a double-thick blanket of bubbling mozzarella cheese should be spread over all. Pizza is simple to make—all you need is dough, tomato sauce, vegetables, sausage, herbs, and cheese—but the combination has an unbeatable taste.

2. Keeping a job is not easy in a tight market in which well-educated, unemployed job-seekers are plentiful. Here are a couple of hints you will find helpful in maintaining your "employed" status. First, you should not only apply your specialized knowledge on the job every day, but also continually update it by taking seminars and evening courses to enhance your skills. Doing your job effectively is difficult without falling prey to burnout. Second, good communication—with the public, your fellow workers, and your supervisor—is perhaps the most important factor in keeping you on the payroll. Upgrading your education and improving your communication skills are your best defences against the pink slip.

3. After the divorce, I found that most of my old friends' behaviour changed. Some of them behaved as they always had, treating my former wife and me with a mixture of friendly indifference and a stoic lack of curiosity. Others avoided us because they felt, I assume, that it would have been a betrayal of one of us to socialize with the other as if nothing had happened. My wife was surprised and hurt. Those who had been closer to me withdrew from her, and those who had been closer to her disappeared from my life. I can't imagine what they are saying about me now. One thing is sure, none of our old friends is quite the same with my wife or me as they were before our divorce.

4. Comedies are my favourite way to relax. Horror films terrify me, and adventures become tedious after the tenth chase; but comedies entertain and refresh me after a long shift at work. Woody Allen pictures, especially the early farces, help me to take my mind off the stress of the day. For example, *Bananas*, a satire about American politics in the '60s, is more relaxing for me than a double martini. It's also less fattening, and I've been trying to give up drinking. *Sleeper*, a futuristic spoof, has me laughing, on average, twice a minute. Perhaps my favourite, however, is *Annie Hall*. After viewing it, I am so weak with laughter that I can go to sleep within minutes. Now that all of Allen's comedies are available on video, I never need to feel tense and worn out for longer than it takes to insert a cassette.

5. I admit it: word processors have me completely baffled. There is a popular myth that a word processor is merely a complicated typewriter. No way. Typing is straightforward; you hit the keys and the words appear on the paper before you. Keying on a word processor is something quite different. For one thing, the processor uses code, and you, the novice, have to learn the code before you can key in even the first word. Learning the mystifying code—and every word processor is different—requires more time and patience than it would take to carve a research essay on a piece of marble using a dull chisel. It is time-consuming and annoying to have to translate English into another "language" before beginning to grapple with this electronic monster. My problem is I was never good at languages. I studied Latin for a year and never did understand the verb endings. Hungarian or Mandarin would be easier to master than the instructions in a Word Perfect manual. No word processor for me, thank you. I'll stick to English and my old typewriter.

EXERCISE 2

Choose one of the topic sentences below and develop it into a paragraph. Make sure that all your supporting sentences relate directly to the topic so your paragraph will be unified.

1. Co-operative education gives you a head start in the workplace.
2. Lotteries exploit the gullibility of those who want to get rich quickly.
3. Saturday nights are fun, but you pay for them Sunday morning.
4. Exams are a nightmare for those who don't prepare well.
5. An office romance is a dangerous self-indulgence.

Coherence

Coherence means "sticking together"; the sentences within each paragraph need to stick together, or cohere, as do the paragraphs within an essay. If your sentences and paragraphs are not coherent, your readers will have great difficulty trying to fit your bits of information together to make sense of the whole. Sorting out sentences as if they were pieces of a puzzle is not your readers' job. Your responsibility as a writer is to put the pieces together to form a complete and clear picture for your readers.

Coherence in achieved in two ways. First, you need to arrange the sentences in each paragraph according to an organizational principle. Remember the ways that you ordered the essay paragraphs in Chapter 3,

Managing the Main Points? You should arrange your ideas within paragraphs in the same ways: chronological, climactic, logical, or (infrequently) random order. (You may wish to turn to p. 41 to review these.)

Second, you achieve coherence by providing **transitions,** or connections between one idea and the next within a paragraph, and between one paragraph and the next within an essay. Why are transitions needed? Read the paragraph below and you'll see clearly that something is missing. The paragraph has adequate development, but no transitions.

> **We were bored one day. We didn't know what to do. It was Friday. We thought about going to the library. No one really wanted to do schoolwork. We went to the mall. For a short time we window-shopped. We discussed what to do. It was agreed that we would drive to the American side of the border. We would do our shopping. It was a short drive. We went to a discount mall. The bargains were great. We spent much more money than we intended to. We went home. We discovered that with the American exchange, prices are better at home. We should have gone to the library.**

Not very easy to read, is it? Readers are jerked abruptly from point to point until, battered and bruised, they finally reach the end. This kind of writing is unfair to readers. It makes them do too much of the work. The ideas may all be there, but the readers have to figure out for themselves how the ideas fit together. After a couple of paragraphs like the one above, even the most patient readers can become annoyed.

Now read the same paragraph, rewritten with transitions.

> **Last Friday we were so bored we didn't know what to do. We thought about going to the library, but no one really wanted to study, so we went to the mall and window-shopped for a while. After a long discussion about what to do next, we agreed to drive to the American side of the border for some serious shopping. A short drive later, we arrived at a discount mall where the bargains were so great we spent much more money than we had intended. Finally, we returned home where we discovered that, with the American exchange, prices were better at home after all. We should have gone to the library.**

Here the readers are gently guided from one point to the next. By the time they reach the conclusion, they know not only what ideas the writer had in mind but also how the ideas fit together to present a unit. The transitions make the readers' job easy and rewarding.

Transitions are necessary, and you can choose from an array of various transitional devices to improve the coherence of your writing. There are five techniques to master:

1. *Repeat a key word.* This technique focuses the readers' attention on an idea and creates a thread of meaning that runs through a paragraph (or a paper), tying the whole thing together.
2. *Use synonyms.* Frequent repetition of a key word can become monotonous after a while. You can keep the reader focused on the idea by using **synonyms,** various words that convey the same thought.
3. *Use pronoun references.* Another way of maintaining the focus but varying the wording is to use appropriate pronouns to refer back to a key noun. (This technique involves pronoun–antecedent agreement, a topic covered in Unit Seven.)
4. *Use parallel structure.* Phrasing your sentences in parallel form helps to maintain focus, reinforces the unity of your thoughts, and adds emphasis. Parallelism adds "punch" to your writing. (More punch is served in Chapter 31.)
5. *Use transitional phrases* to show the relationship between points in a paragraph as well as between paragraphs in an essay. Transitional phrases form a bond among the elements of a paragraph or a paper and allow smoother reading. They are like turn signals on a car: they tell the person following you where you're going.

The paragraph below is an excellent example of the use of transitional devices to achieve coherence. As you read, pay particular attention to the writer's use of repetition and parallelism.

> I want a wife who will take care of my physical needs. I want a wife who will keep my house clean. A wife who will pick up after my children, a wife who will pick up after me. I want a wife who will keep my clothes clean, ironed, mended, replaced when need be, and who will see to it that my personal things are kept in their proper place so that I can find what I need the minute I need it. I want a wife who cooks the meals, a wife who is a *good* cook. I want a wife who will plan the menus, do the necessary grocery shopping, prepare the meals, serve them pleasantly, and then do the cleaning up while I do my studying. I want a wife who will care for me when I am sick and sympathize with my pain and loss of time from school. I want a wife to go along when our family takes a vacation so that someone can continue to care for me and my children when I need a rest and change of scene.
>
> (from Judy Syfers, "I Want a Wife")

Here are some of the most common transitional phrases; you can use them to keep your readers on track.

TRANSITION FUNCTION	WORDS/PHRASES USED
1. *To show a time relationship between points*	• first, second, third • now, simultaneously, concurrently, at this point, while • before, to begin, previously • after, following this, then, later, next • finally, last, subsequently • during, meanwhile, presently, from time to time, sometimes
2. *To add an idea or example to the previous point*	• in addition, also, furthermore, besides, moreover, for the same reason • another, similarly, equally important, likewise • for example, for instance, in fact
3. *To show contrast between points*	• although, nevertheless, on the other hand, whereas • but, however, instead, nonetheless • in contrast, on the contrary, in spite of, despite
4. *To show a cause-and-effect relationship between points*	• since, because, thus, therefore, hence • as a result, consequently, accordingly
5. *To emphasize or repeat a significant point*	• in fact, indeed, certainly, undoubtedly • in other words, as I have said, that is to say
6. *To summarize or conclude*	• in brief, on the whole, in summary, in short • to conclude, in conclusion, last • therefore, as a result, finally

EXERCISE 3

Now it's your turn. Identify the transitional devices that create coherence in each of the sentence groups below.

1. The two girls spent the whole day tramping from car dealer to car dealer. Finally, they found a used Toyota they could live with, but the price was higher than they had hoped to pay.
2. Concern was etched in the face of the priest and mirrored in the eyes of the doctor. Janis felt her shoulders tighten and she fought to control her temper; their concern wouldn't help her now.
3. He knew that one good serve would end the match in his favour. As he walked slowly to the service line, he wondered if he had one good serve left in him.
4. Hamlet is an essentially noble man whose inaction brings about the tragedy that unfolds around him. The audience is then left with the problem of sorting out its own feelings about him.
5. The gypsy moth is invading our woodlands, killing trees that have resisted all other predators. Therefore, governments at both the local and provincial levels have begun a spray program.
6. As he scanned the menu, Philip knew his gourmet meal would have to wait. First, the merger had to be discussed.
7. There are many jokes about cats. Unfortunately, however, in most of them the cat is either very unhappy or dead.
8. There are those who think Quebec would thrive as a separate state. On the other hand, some feel that its economic viability depends on a close relationship with the rest of Canada.
9. The Volkswagen Beetle is probably the world's most loved car. It must be, since more people have owned Beetles than any other vehicle.
10. To feel secure, you must have a company pension. A company pension can only be obtained if you're willing to take on long-term employment.

EXERCISE 4

In each of the following sentences, supply transition words or phrases that will help the meaning become clearer and the sentence more coherent.

1. Small pets are important members of a family. _____ they provide companionship to those who live alone.
2. My first impression of him was that he was aloof and arrogant; _____ , I discovered I was wrong. He was painfully shy.

3. We had to reach the next town before dinnertime or the last motel rooms would be occupied. _____, we decided to break the speed limit.

4. At first I thought she didn't like me. _____ she confessed that she was playing "hard to get."

5. It's not hard to be a great basketball player. It helps, _____, if your parents are both seven feet tall.

6. Many best-sellers have become pathetic movies, now long forgotten. _____ many poor novels have been turned into movie classics, like *Gone With the Wind*, which last forever.

7. Many sports were discovered by accident. _____, one day at Rugby school in the 1830s, an English schoolboy, during a game of rugby, threw the ball overhand down the field. Football (as we call it in North America) was born.

8. Architecture in the twentieth century has become more streamlined, geometrical, and uniform. _____, it has become monotonous.

9. Batman and Robin were speeding off on a false lead. _____, the Joker was looting the coffers of the Gotham City bank.

10. The Fountain of Youth was rumoured to be in the swamps of Florida. _____ Ponce de Leon spent most of his remaining years looking for it there.

EXERCISE 5

Read the paragraphs below and underline in each the transitional devices that contribute to coherence.

1. Finally, developing the proper attitude is the true key to winning tennis. I define winning tennis as playing the game to the best of your ability, hitting the ball as well as you know you can, and enjoying the feeling of practised expertise. Winning tennis has nothing to do with beating an opponent. Naturally, if you play winning tennis by learning the basics, practising sufficiently, and concentrating, you'll win many matches, but that is the reward of playing well, not the reason for playing well. People who swear and throw their racquets when they lose are very useful; they are the most satisfying players to trounce. But I don't understand why they play a game that gives them such pain. Tennis players who enjoy the feel of a well-hit ball and the satisfaction of a long, skilfully played rally are winners, regardless of the score.

2. While education and relaxation are important, most of us read light novels to be entertained. "Entertainment" means different things to different people. Some enjoy being frightened half to death by the books of Stephen King or his colleagues; others get satisfaction from the sugary romance of Harlequin novels; many people find science

fiction absorbing and devour the works of Isaac Asimov or Jerry Pournel. Whatever subject or style grabs you, there are literally thousands of novels to suit your taste. I'm lucky because—with the exception of popular romance—I can find enjoyment in almost any type of reasonably well-written light novel.

3. Is there any reason for optimism? There is some evidence that Canadians are becoming more conscious of the environment, and consciousness can only lead to changes for the better. In 1989, one third of Canadians felt that the environment was the most important national issue. Only a year before that it was one in ten, and the year before that it was one in twenty. A majority of Canadians now favour tougher action against polluters, even if it means higher taxes, higher prices, and fewer jobs. However, this bit-by-bit heightening of concern is far from the concerted, all-out effort to save the planet that would result if we were threatened by an external force. How very much more difficult it is to mobilize resources and will when the enemy lies within!

Tone

As you write the paragraphs of your paper, try to be conscious of your tone. **Tone** is a word used to describe a writer's attitude towards the subject and the readers. The words you use, the examples, the quotations, and any other supporting materials you choose to help explain your main points—all these contribute to your tone. When you are trying to explain something, particularly something you feel strongly about, you may be tempted to be highly emotional in your discussion. If you allow yourself to "get emotional," chances are you won't be convincing. What will be communicated is the strength of your feelings, not the depth of your understanding or the validity of your opinion. To be clear and credible, you need to channel your enthusiasm (or your anger) into presenting your points in a calm, reasonable way.

Two suggestions may help you to find and maintain the right tone. First, never insult your readers, even unintentionally. Avoid phrases like "any idiot can see," "no sane person could believe," and "it is obvious that . . . ." Remember that what is "obvious" to you isn't necessarily obvious to someone who has a limited understanding of your subject or who disagrees with your opinion. Don't "talk down" to your readers, as though they were children or simpletons. Don't use sarcasm, and avoid profanity.

Second, don't apologize for your interpretation of your subject. Have confidence in yourself: you've thought long and hard about your subject, you've found good supporting material to help explain it, and you believe in its significance. Present your subject in a *positive* manner. If you hang back, using phrases like "I may be wrong, but . . ." or "I tend to feel that . . . ," your readers won't be inclined to give your points the consideration they deserve. Keep your readers in mind as you write, and your writing will be both clear and convincing.

EXERCISE 6

Rewrite the following paragraph, adding transitions where necessary and correcting any lapses in tone.

> If you like gardening, you're a wimp. It's such a dumb hobby, I don't even know where to begin listing the reasons I hate it. Flowers grow perfectly OK in the wild. Why force them into rows and beds? They claim it's relaxing. I know a guy who got a hernia from lifting manure and another who developed ulcers because his dahlias died. Inside the house, plants are a hazard. They attract insects, aggravate allergies, poison pets, and spread dirt. Gardening is a dangerous activity. Everyone I've met who likes it is a complete twit.

EXERCISE 7

Write a reply to this attack on gardening. Remember to keep your tone consistent, and don't forget transitions.

EXERCISE 8

Rewrite the following paragraph, adding transitions where necessary and correcting any lapses in tone.

> I'm no expert—in fact, I really don't know anything about it—but it seems to me that anyone who enjoys baseball is a masochist. I may be wrong (I usually am) but it's a very dull game, don't you think? About every third pitch the batter swings. The fielders do nothing. There are about fifteen hits in a three-hour game. The players actually do something for approximately seven-and-a-half minutes of an entire afternoon. Home runs are dull. One man trots around the bases. The others stand and watch. An awful lot of people seem to like baseball, so I guess there's something wrong with me. People who like baseball are probably boring people.

EXERCISE 9

Write a reply to this attack on baseball. Remember to keep your tone consistent, and use at least three different transitional devices in your paragraph.

CHAPTER 10

Writing Introductions and Conclusions

All of the concepts you've studied so far can be applied to any paragraph. However, two paragraphs, the first and the last in every essay, have special purposes and need extra care. All too often, the introduction and the conclusion of an essay are dull or clumsy and detract from its effectiveness. But they needn't be dull or clumsy: here's how to write good ones.

The Introductory Paragraph

The introduction is worth special attention because that's where your readers either sit up and take notice of your paper or sigh and pitch it into the wastebasket.

When we first discussed the concept of dividing a paper into paragraphs, we used the analogy of the TV sitcom, which is separated by commercials into distinct parts. The first section of the sitcom functions in ways the other parts don't. First, it attracts the viewers with a particularly funny moment, a fascinating situation, or an intriguing problem. Second, it sets the plot in motion or gets the action started. Your introductory paragraph has a similar role in your essay.

> There are two parts to an introductory paragraph: 1. a grabber; 2. a preview statement.

Grabbing and Holding Your Readers' Attention

Your readers must be attracted to your writing, or there's no point in putting pen to paper or fingers to keyboard. This doesn't permit you to use cheap tricks, however, like the classified ad that said:

SEX. There, now that I've got your attention, how would you like to own a 1981 Ford Comet?

The grabber must be appropriate both to the content of your essay and to your intended readers. If your audience is known for a solemn and serious approach to life and your topic is something of a serious nature (environmental ethics, for instance, or abortion), there is no point in leading off with a pun or joke, no matter how witty. Such an opening would be inappropriate and probably offensive to your readers.

Your grabber does not have to be a single sentence; in fact, good grabbers are often several sentences long. Your readers will be committing varying amounts of personal time and effort to reading your writing. You owe it to them to make your opening sentences clear, interesting, and creative.

An effective grabber should be followed by an equally effective preview statement, one that slides smoothly and easily into place. Your readers should be aware only of a unified presentation, not of the two parts you have blueprinted for your introductory paragraph.

Below are eight different kinds of grabbers you can choose from to get your readers' attention and lead up to your preview statement. In each of the illustrative paragraphs, note how the grabber and the preview statement are solidly linked to form a unified whole. To demonstrate that you can take many different approaches to a subject, depending on your purpose and your audience, we have used the same subject in all of the introductions: physical fitness, a subject that is much on the minds—and on the hips—of many Canadians.

1. *Begin with a well-phrased quotation.* You might choose a famous statement, a popular slogan, a widely known publicity gimmick, or a common saying by someone you know. Use a quotation when it sums up your point of view more succinctly and effectively than your own words could. As a rule, you should identify the source of the quotation.

"Who can be bothered?" "I'm much too busy." "I get all the exercise I need at the office." We've all heard excuses like these, excuses to avoid exercising regularly. Modern life with its distractions and conveniences tends to make us sedentary and lazy, but the human organism cannot tolerate inactivity and stress indefinitely. Eventually, it begins to break down. If you want to keep yourself in shape for the challenges of modern life, consider the benefits of working out a few times a week. Regular exercise can rejuvenate your body, refresh your mind, and improve your self-confidence.

2. *Use a provocative statement.* Sometimes a startling or surprising remark (not an insult or false exaggeration, please) is effective in getting readers' attention. A little known or striking fact will have the same effect.

After the age of thirty, the average North American puts on 25 to 40 pounds of fat. Presumably, the cause for this startling increase in avoirdupois is a combination of metabolic changes, decreased physical activity, and hundreds of pounds of junk food ingested since childhood. It's difficult to stop the spread of middle-aged corpulence, but experts tell us we *can* resist the rise in flab by reducing our caloric intake and increasing our physical activity. Regular exercise can rejuvenate the body, refresh the mind, and improve self-confidence.

3. *Ask a question or two.* Questions are often an effective way to encourage interest because your readers will find themselves thinking of answers. Some questions are rhetorical; that is, they will not have specific answers. Others might be answered in your essay.

Have you been feeling sluggish and exhausted lately? Has your blood pressure increased along with your waistline in the past few years? Are you stalled in front of the television set every night with potato chips and a beer? If so, you are probably suffering from a common middle-aged ailment called *flabitis*. This malady strikes most people over thirty: they put on unneeded pounds, have trouble concentrating, tire easily, and prefer watching sports to participating in them. Fortunately, there *is* a cure for flabitis: a three-times-weekly dose of exercise. With regular exercise, you can rejuvenate your body, refresh your mind, and improve your self-confidence.

4. *Point to the significance of your subject.* If its significance can catch your readers' interest, they will want to know more about it, especially if it is a subject that affects them directly.

More and more young people are dying of heart disease. Despite the statistics that say we, as a society, are living longer, thanks to advances in medicine and surgery, the figures can be misleading. It is a fact that people in their thirties and forties are dying from coronary problems that once threatened people in their fifties and sixties. What has caused this change? Certainly, the increase in stress, the fatigue of overwork, the rise in obesity, and the decline in physical activity are all contributing factors. To combat the risk of cardiovascular disease, we need physical activity. Regular exercise can forestall the ravages of heart disease and promote longevity.

5. *Start with a generalization related to your subject.* Generalizations can be useful to suggest the context and scope of your subject. They must, however, be narrowed down carefully to a focused preview statement.

Until the twentieth century, exercise was part of the normal workday. Our ancestors were farmers, pioneers, sailors, and so on. Few of our parents, however, made their living by ploughing the land or chopping down trees. In this century, the trend in work has been away from physical exertion towards automation. Today's generation uses technology to reduce physical activity even further: they pick up the phone, ride the elevator, and take the car to the corner store. Modern inactivity has negative consequences that only physical exercise can counter. To sustain good health, sharpen your mental edge, and have fun, you should take up aerobics or sports and use your body in the way it was intended—actively.

6. *State your intention to challenge a widely held opinion.* Perhaps your readers have also doubted the commonly held belief. Your preview statement can assert how false the opinion is, and the body of your essay can contain evidence to counter the validity of the view you are challenging.

Physical activity is for kids. Adults don't have time to hit a baseball or run around a field chasing after one, or to do aerobics and lift weights in a gym. They have to earn a living, raise families, and save money for retirement. They can leave exercise to their children. I firmly believed this until one morning when, late for work, I ran after a bus. My heart pounded; my lungs gasped; my head swam. It had been some years since my last stint of exercise, and I realized I wouldn't be around to do my job, support my family, or enjoy retirement unless I got into the habit of doing something physical to maintain my health. Regular exercise can rejuvenate your body, refresh your mind, and broaden your interests.

7. *Begin with a definition.* A definition is a good way to begin if you are introducing a key term that you suspect may be unfamiliar to your readers. If the subject of your essay depends on a personal meaning of a term that most people understand in a different way, a definition is essential.

> Myocardial infarction: the very term is frightening. It occurs when a person's muscles slacken from disuse, the veins clog up with sticky fats, and the heart has to work too hard to sustain even minor exertion like raking leaves or shoveling snow. The muscles of the heart become strained to exhaustion or balloon outward because the veins cannot pass blood quickly enough. In plain English, a myocardial infarction is a heart attack. If the victim is lucky enough to survive, physicians prescribe a regimen of less stress, low fat intake, and habitual exercise.

8. *Describe an interesting incident or tell an anecdote related to your subject.* Readers like stories; keep yours short and to the point by narrating only highlights. The incident or anecdote you select might be a story from the media, an event involving family or friends, or a personal experience.

> Last year, I got a free invitation to a fitness club in the mail. I responded, out of curiosity, but I needed to be convinced. After all, I was thirty-five, had grown a little paunch, and was a bit short of breath on the stairs; ten years had passed since I had last played sports. My first workout was a nightmare. My joints ached, my muscles throbbed, and my head spun. I was in worse shape than I thought. After a few weeks, those symptoms disappeared, and I began to enjoy myself. My paunch vanished and my muscles toned up. My capacity for concentration increased. Also, I met some new people who have become friends. Obviously, ten years is too long between workouts, because exercise rejuvenates your body, refreshes your mind, and improves your social life.

EXERCISE 1

Each of the following paragraphs is the introductory paragraph of an essay. Using the strategy indicated in parentheses, write an appropriate grabber for each paragraph.

1. (quotation) _____

_____

The words of my seventh-grade teacher are still very important to me. Mrs. Patronni has been one of the most important influences on my life so far. She not only taught me, she inspired me and set an example that I will always try to live up to.

2. (quotation) _____

_____

Every sport has its strange expressions, just as every sport has its devoted fans, its famous teams, and its legendary heroes. A sport that gets very little attention in Canada but is very popular in many parts of the world, especially Commonwealth countries, is cricket. Like the sports that millions of Canadians follow enthusiastically, cricket is an exciting and fascinating game once you become familiar with its rules and style. In fact, it compares very favourably to baseball in skill, pace, and strategy.

3. (provocative statement) _____

_____

The Canadian roads are overrun by drivers who are a danger to themselves, their passengers, and others on the road. Inept drivers demonstrate their inadequacies in so many ways that it would be impossible to list them all in one short paper. Nevertheless, bad drivers can be broadly categorized as traumatized turtles, careening cowboys, and daydreaming dodos.

4. (provocative statement) _____

_____

For many reasons, country and western music is Canada's national sound. It has universal appeal from coast to coast, it is more popular than any other single kind of music, and it expresses truly Canadian themes and values.

5. (question) _____

_____

Arranged marriages are a very important part of my culture. When my family moved to Canada, we left behind many of the traditions and customs that were as natural to us as breathing. However, my parents retained their right to choose a wife for me, even though they are aware that this custom is at odds with the Canadian way of life. While their decision was at first difficult to accept, I believe there are good reasons that an arranged marriage may be best for me. The decision will be made by mature people in a thoughtful manner, uninfluenced by the enthusiasms of youth; the decision will be made by people who have at heart the best interests of our family, the bride's family, and myself; and the decision will be made in accordance with a centuries-old tradition that has proven its success generation after generation.

6. (significance of subject) _____

_____

TV commercials that portray unrealistic and unattainable life-styles should be banned. While I do not support censorship, I feel there is sufficient evidence of the damage done by these advertisements to justify eliminating them, in the public interest. The objectionable commercials promote sexual stereotyping, set up unrealistic and dangerous expectations, and encourage irresponsible consumerism.

7. (generalization) _____

_____

My first roommate was the sort of person that nightmares are made of. It's been three years since she finally moved out of our apartment, but I still shudder when I recall our six months together. Denise was noisy, sloppy, and, worst of all, thoughtless.

8. (opinion you challenge) _____

_____

The evidence strongly suggests that overexposure to the sun can cause several forms of cancer at worst, and premature aging at best. We can't completely avoid the sun's rays, but there are several measures we can take to prevent the damage that normal outdoor activity might cause. To enjoy the summer without fear, use an effective sun block, cover sensitive skin completely, and limit your time in the sun.

9. (definition) _____

_____

The choice of corrective lenses is an individual matter, but many people go through a tough decision process when confronting the issue. In deciding whether contact lenses or eyeglasses are more suitable, one should examine such factors as comfort, convenience, and appearance.

10. (anecdote or incident) _____

_____

Black flies are just one of the pests that make life less than comfortable in Canada during the spring, but they tend to be the most irritating. No method of combating the pests is foolproof, but there are several methods that can be employed, either singly or together, to repel most of them. The campaign against the black fly begins with protective clothing, follows up with an effective repellant, and goes over the top with the secret weapon: garlic.

EXERCISE 2

Write an introductory paragraph for an essay on each of the following five topics. Put square brackets around your grabbers, and underline your preview statements.

1. Why I want to be a _____ (fill in your career choice)
2. Why I chose _____ (fill in your school)
3. How not to treat a friend
4. My favourite restaurant
5. The trouble with little brothers (or sisters)

The Concluding Paragraph

Like the introduction, the conclusion of your essay has a special form. Think back to your favourite television sitcom. The last section of the show wraps up the plot, explains any details that might still be unresolved, and leaves you with a satisfying sense that all is well, at least until next week. The last paragraph of your essay has two special, similar functions:

> 1. It *summarizes* or *reinforces* the main points of your paper.
> 2. It ends with an appropriate *clincher*.

Your summary statement should be as concise as you can make it, and must be phrased in such a way that it does not repeat word-for-word the portion of your preview statement that identifies the main points.

Your **clincher** is a memorable statement designed to leave your readers feeling satisfied with your essay and perhaps taking away with them something for further thought. Never end without a clincher. Don't just quit writing when your main points are covered or you'll leave your readers hanging, wondering what to make of it all.

Six strategies you can choose from in writing an appropriate clincher are described below. Each of the strategies is illustrated by a sample concluding paragraph. Try to identify the summary statement and the clincher in each conclusion.

1. *End with a relevant or thought-provoking quotation.* You can use this ending in two ways: repeat an earlier quotation but give it a new meaning, or give a new quote by an authority in the field, to place your subject in a larger context.

> Since I began lifting weights every second day, I have lowered my blood pressure, improved my productivity at work, and made some new friends at the fitness club. I may never be Arnold Schwarzenegger, but that isn't my goal. My muscles are pleasantly sore after a good workout,

but as Arnold says, "No pain, no gain." As long as the pain is so little and the gain is so great, I will continue to enjoy my regular workouts.

2. *Offer a solution to a problem discussed in your essay.* You can plan an organization for your essay that will allow you to resolve problems or neutralize negative consequences in your conclusion.

I've got the best intentions in the world. I know that exercise benefits me physically, mentally, and emotionally—but I still don't have the time. I didn't, that is, until last month when I was home from work for a week because I sprained my ankle while walking the dog. That never would have happened if I had been in shape. Since then, I have forced myself to manage my time to allow for a fitness program. Four hours of exercise a week is not a very big investment of time compared to four days in bed with a bandaged foot.

3. *End with one or more relevant or thought-provoking questions.* The advantage of clinching with a question is that readers tend to mull over a question automatically; a question stimulates thought. Before they know it, readers will begin to formulate answers to your question—and that activity automatically will make them remember your points. This technique carries one caution, however: be sure your question relates *directly* to your subject.

My life has improved considerably since I took up jogging three times a week: I'm enjoying better health, less brain-fog, and more confidence. And I'm inspired to continue jogging by the fact that coronary disease runs in my family. My father and grandfather both suffered heart attacks in their fifties. If they had done regular exercise, could they have reduced their chances of coronaries? Would they still be alive today?

4. *Point out the value or significance of your subject to your readers.* If you emphasize your subject matter at the end of your essay, you can stamp its importance on your readers' memory.

There aren't too many ways to stay in shape, be sharp, and feel strong; regular exercise is probably the best. Furthermore, there aren't too many ways to reduce the risk of arthritis, arterial decay, and heart dysfunction. Again, exercise provides an answer. In a country where the most common cause of mortality is coronary collapse, everyone needs to consider the value of consistent exercise. It's a small daily inconvenience with large and long-term rewards.

5. *Make a connection to a statement made in your introduction.* This strategy provides your readers with a sense of closure. They will recall your earlier remarks and feel satisfied that the loose ends have been tied.

Having exercised now for six months, I can run for the bus without losing my breath, sweating profusely, or feeling dizzy. My body is in better trim; my endurance and confidence on the job have grown. After a lapse of twenty years, I have even taken up the bicycle again and I go riding along local bike trails with friends. And now, when my children are playing baseball in the yard, I don't think, "Baseball is for kids." I'm first at the plate. Batter up!

6. *End with a suggestion for change or a prediction about the future.* Your suggestion for change will have a lasting influence if your readers have been persuaded by your arguments. Your predictions of events that *might* occur should not be misleading and exaggerated, or your readers will be sceptical of their validity. Make predictions that are possible and plausible.

If those of us who still prefer junk food, overwork, and television don't shape up, the incidence of coronary disease will continue to rise. Moderate exercise will benefit body, mind, and spirit. If we follow common sense and change our habits of self-pollution and self-destruction, all of us can lead long, active, and healthy lives.

EXERCISE 3

Each of the following is the concluding paragraph from an essay. For each paragraph, underline the summary statement and write an appropriate clincher.

1. Both games are enjoyable for spectators and create real enthusiasm among fans. High schools that chose soccer have seen no reduction in school spirit or fan support. For educational institutions to make the switch from football is really a "no-lose" proposition, because soccer provides dramatic advantages in reducing player injury, increasing player fitness, and shaving thousands of dollars from school expenses.

_____

_____

_____

_____

2. Far from fearing celibacy, young people should be enthusiastically supporting the idea. My energy is devoted to my schoolwork and two part-time jobs; my stress level is around zero; and I've got lots of money to spend on myself. These benefits and many more are easily attained by anyone strong enough to be an individual, to step off the dating–mating merry-go-round and choose, as I have done, the joys of a celibate life-style.

---

3. There's no mystery about achieving a baby-smooth face. By selecting the proper equipment, preparing your beard adequately, and following the procedures I've revealed, you, too, can have cheeks that beg to be touched. These carefully protected secrets have been used by generations of Hollywood makeup men and women on the faces of the stars; now they are yours.

---

4. Good friends are not easy to find. Anyone who says she has "dozens" doesn't know what a good friend is. I've been fortunate to have known four people who combine the qualities of patience, generosity, and intuition, people I'm proud and grateful to call my good friends.

---

5. Reviewers in the newspapers and on television were pretty well agreed about the two films, but moviegoers had quite a range of opinions. While *Dick Tracy* was the winner with the critics, *Batman* was more popular with the public. The remarkable similarities between the two films in scripting, style, and characterization make comparisons inevitable . . . and interesting. While my analysis favours "The Caped Crusader," there's lots of room for disagreement by the Tracy fans.

---

6. While the causes of dropout among first-year students are as individual as the students themselves, the effects are easier to categorize. Conflict with parents and others whose expectations have not been met comes first, followed by a loss of self-esteem. The determination to succeed despite this unfair setback is common, but statistics show that low-paying, dead-end jobs are the norm for the college dropout. The situation is much worse, of course, for those who don't complete high school.

_____

_____

_____

_____

7. I guess that you could say my evening out in Antigonish was less expensive, more fun, but less memorable than my evening out in Montreal. As time goes by, it's quite likely that memory will blur the events that occurred on those two evenings, and I'll probably end up telling my grandchildren wonderful tales about my Montreal adventure, while my quiet but delightful evening in Antigonish will fade. I hope this doesn't happen because I learned a great deal from both experiences.

_____

_____

_____

_____

8. Remember that some of the French wines we see in Canadian stores are "plonk" that the French won't drink. Dressed up in fancy labels and slapped with an impressively high price tag, they are designed to appeal to the snobbish but unsophisticated overseas buyer. At the same time, it is no longer a social blunder to present a good Canadian wine at your table. Choosing a good wine needn't be a mysterious ritual or a blind lottery. Just get good advice, don't be intimidated by packaging, price, or place of origin, and, when in doubt, let your taste guide you. Equipped with these three general rules, you should have no problem finding a wine to suit both your taste and your budget.

_____

_____

_____

_____

9. Great parties seldom just happen; they are the products of careful thought and planning. If a truly great party should occur spontaneously, then chance has brought the right ingredients together, just as chance can sometimes result in high marks on multiple-choice tests. The right people, brought together in the right place, for the right reason, will produce a memorable event every time.

---

10. Drinking and driving must be stopped. To stop it will require substantial commitment from all levels of government, both in terms of money and in terms of political will. The penalties for driving while under the influence of alcohol must be increased and more money for education and publicity must be spent. But, more than these measures, it will take the individual will of every Canadian to make the promise not to drive after drinking. Nothing will bring my sister back, but there are lots of other sisters out there—and brothers, and mothers and fathers—who can be saved.

EXERCISE 4

Write a short concluding paragraph for an essay on each of the following topics. Use the main points you developed for introductory paragraphs on these topics in Exercise 2.

1. Why I want to be a _____ (fill in your career choice)
2. Why I chose _____ (fill in your school)
3. How not to treat a friend
4. My favourite restaurant
5. The trouble with little brothers (or sisters)

Developing the Essay

CHAPTER 11

Process

College essays (and most business and technical reports) fall into three broad categories of writing:

1. Expository writing
2. Persuasive writing
3. Personal writing.

Expository writing includes essays of *process, classification, cause and effect,* and *comparison and contrast.* These categories are detailed here and in the next three chapters. Persuasive writing is covered in Chapter 15. Personal writing, which includes description and narration, is the topic of Chapters 16 and 17, the concluding chapters of this unit.

By carefully selecting an essay model and following the procedure for that model, you are focusing (as you always should) on your readers. The essay models clarify your thoughts and organize your writing, so that your readers are clearly informed of your purpose. After you have stated your subject and identified your main points, you should determine which of the essay models is best suited to your subject and what your readers need to know about the subject.

Each writing category is a pattern of organization. It represents a particular way of looking at your subject and is based on the interrelationship of your main points. Which organizational pattern or essay model you choose will depend in part on your subject and in part on what you want your readers to know or believe about your subject. How you put your ideas together is as important as the words you use in communicating with your readers.

What Is a Good Process Essay?

A **process essay** explains to your readers how to make or do something or how something works. It presents, in the order in which they must happen, the steps or stages necessary to perform a task or achieve a goal. A process essay subject may be very concrete, such as "How to fix a flat tire" or "Getting to the Resource Centre from the Registrar's Office"; or it may deal with something more abstract such as "Surviving the first week of college" or "How to get along with a difficult boss."

When you write a process essay, keep your language simple and clear. Your readers must be able to understand your instructions in order to follow them. The following instructions accompanied a simple box designed for preparing newspapers for recycling.

> **This paper recycler has been thoughtfully designed for ease of use and practical serviceability. Slide recycling binder material into recycling binder material placement slot in the upper frame opposite recycling binder material spool. Reel off sufficient recycling binder material to line the inside of the vertical housing unit and rest on the support struts. Place newspapers to be recycled lengthwise across support struts between vertical housing units, on top of recycling binder material. When newspaper stack reaches a height of 40 cm. reel off approximately 20 cm. of recycling binder material, remove end from recycling binder material placement slot, and tie securely. Cut off recycling binder material, remove newspaper bundle, and repeat.**

The instructions break the process down into simple steps organized in chronological order, but the writer has forgotten the most basic rule of good writing: *remember your readers*. Even the most determined environmentalist would be dismayed and discouraged by these directions. A successful process essay takes into account the readers' familiarity (or lack of it) with the process, their experience, and their level of vocabulary, and communicates the steps of the process in a way that holds their interest.

You should be knowledgeable about the process you are describing, but remember that your readers don't share your knowledge. One of the most difficult aspects of writing a process paper is making sure you have included all the necessary steps. Try to imagine yourself in your readers' place: a novice, reading the instructions for the first time.

Tips on Writing a Process Essay

1. List all the steps in the process in logical or chronological order. Include *everything* that your readers need to know. (See p. 41 and

p. 42 for definitions of chronological and logical order respectively.)

2. Write a preview statement that makes it clear what your readers are about to learn and what major steps are involved in the process.
   Example: To become a truly healthy person, you must follow a fitness program, develop good eating habits, and control stress.
3. In developing your points into paragraphs, be careful to use transitions within and between the paragraphs.
4. When editing and revising, put yourself in the position of a novice and test whether you can follow the instructions as they have been written, or have someone who really is a novice try to follow your directions.

EXERCISE 1

The following three essays show clearly how to direct readers through a step-by-step process. Read each one and answer the questions that follow.

How to Play Winning Tennis

As a tennis instructor for the past three summers, I've watched many people waste their money on hi-tech racquets, designer outfits, and professional lessons, and then loudly complain that in spite of all the expense, they still can't play the game. Unfortunately for them, a decent backhand is one thing that money can't buy. No matter what level of player you are, though, or what level you wish to be, there are four steps to accomplishing the goal of winning tennis. They can be summed up in four words: basics, practice, concentration, and attitude.

All sports may be reduced to a few basic skills, which, if learned properly at the outset and drilled until they are instinctive, lead to success. Tennis is no exception; however, few people seem willing to spend the time learning tennis basics properly. Having been shown the proper grip and swing for a forehand, backhand, and serve, my students seem to feel they can qualify for Wimbledon. The basics are not learned that easily. Many tennis schools are now using a system first developed in Spain that is very successful in establishing the correct stroke in new players: for the first month of lessons, they aren't allowed to use a tennis ball. For that first month, correct positioning, proper swing, footwork, and technique are drilled without any of the distractions of keeping score, winning or losing, or chasing errant balls. That's how important the basics are to winning tennis.

Having acquired the basics, a beginning player must now practise and practise and practise to remember and refine those important skills. It isn't very much fun sometimes to play against a ball machine that never swears or sweats, and doesn't care whether you hit a winning return. Drills and exercises won't do much for your social life while your friends are on the next court playing "pat-a-ball" with a couple of good looking novices. Those basic strokes that you must keep hitting correctly hundreds of times a day aren't as impressive as the sexy spins and tricky between-the-legs shots the club players are perfecting . . . but if you're going to play winning tennis, practice is vital. Your feet must move instinctively to get you to the ball properly positioned for an effective stroke; a smooth backhand must become automatic from everywhere on the court; a crisp forehand, hit with accuracy, must be as natural as breathing.

When you're finally ready for competition, everything seems calculated to make you forget all you've learned. It requires enormous concentration to shut out the distractions and continue to practise the basics that are essential to your game: watch the ball, keep your head down, turn ninety degrees from the path of the ball, keep your feet moving, and so on and so on. With an opponent opposite you, people watching, and your own self-esteem on the line, it's very difficult to keep your mind from wandering. Tennis is about fifty percent mental. Successful players are able to block out distractions and concentrate on making the racquet meet the ball with precision.

Finally, developing the proper attitude is the true key to winning tennis. I define winning tennis as playing the game to the best of your ability, hitting the ball as well as you know you can, and enjoying the feeling of practised expertise. Winning tennis has nothing to do with beating an opponent. Naturally, if you play winning tennis by learning the basics, practising sufficiently, and concentrating, you'll win many matches, but that is the reward of playing well, not the reason for playing well. People who swear and throw their racquet when they lose are very useful; they are the most satisfying players to trounce. But I don't understand why they play a game that gives them such pain. Tennis players who enjoy the feel of a well-hit ball and the satisfaction of a long, skilfully played rally are winners, regardless of the score.

1. Describe typical readers the author may have been thinking of. Consider their interests and goals.
2. What is the role of the author?
3. What are the main points the author covers in explaining the steps of improving performance in the game? Blueprint the main and supporting points that were employed while constructing this essay.
4. What functions does the introductory paragraph serve in this essay?
5. Discuss the final paragraph as an effective conclusion to the essay.

Baked Beans

Pierre Berton

Now we come to my famous (or infamous) formula for Klondike baked beans, the one that disturbed so many people because of its complexity. Well, winter is coming on and these beans will be needed, no matter how complex they seem to be. There is nothing quite like them. They are guaranteed to melt the frostiest heart, bring warmth to the palest cheeks, satisfy the most gnawing hunger, and rekindle the spark of hope in the coldest breast.

The Klondikers carried baked beans frozen solid in their packs and, when the trail grew weary and the stomach cried out for succour, they would chop pieces off with a knife and gnaw at them as they plunged onward. For beans carry a warmth locked within them, and when the human fire burns low, they act as hot coals to send the blood coursing through the veins.

My beans are more exotic than the 1898 variety, and they are not meant to be eaten frozen, but the principle is exactly the same.

I warn you that this is a lengthy task, so fortify yourself in any of the several ways known to cooks the world over. Step One is the simplest: simply take the quantity of navy beans that you require and soak them overnight in cold water.

The next morning, early, Step Two begins: simmer these soaked beans very lightly. Put them over a low heat and throw in a couple of crushed bay leaves, a handful of finely chopped parsley, some crushed garlic, oregano, thyme, chili powder, cloves, and salt. The idea here is to get the beans soft and to impregnate them with a basic flavour.

Let them simmer gently for an hour or two while you go over to the butcher's for some salt pork. Have him cut the pork—or good side bacon will do as well—into large cubes or chunks, the size of marshmallows. Get lots of pork; the makers of tinned beans skimp on the stuff, but we don't have to. There's nothing quite so good as pork or bacon cooked to a soft succulence in a frothing mass of beans and molasses.

You can tell if your beans are soft enough by picking a couple out of the pot and blowing on them. If the skins break, you're ready for Step Three. Turn off the heat and drain away the liquid, but for heaven's sake don't throw it away. It is nectar. What you don't use in the finished dish you can always save as soup stock.

Pour the drained beans in a big earthenware casserole and throw in the salt pork. I often serve beans at a party along with a good smoked ham; if you do this throw some of the ham fat in with the beans. Pour it right out of the pan, if you like.

Now we are into Step Three, and it is here that the boys are separated from the men, and the men from the women. Take a few cups of the liquid you poured from the beans and put it in a pot to simmer. Chop up some tomatoes and throw them in the pot with a few shots of chili sauce and a tin of tomato paste. Chop several onions, half of them very fine, so they'll disappear in the brew, and half in chunks, and throw them in. Green onion tops, chopped up, go well, too, if you can get them.

Now season this mixture, tasting carefully as you go, with dry mustard, freshly ground black pepper, Worcestershire sauce, crushed garlic, celery seed, a few squirts of tabasco, and some monosodium glutamate.

When it tastes pungent and hot (remember that the pungency will be cut by the beans) stir in a large quantity of molasses. Most people don't put in enough molasses, and yet this is the essence of all good baked bean dishes. For there comes a critical moment when the sweetness of the molasses is wedded to the sharpness of the vegetables and herbs, and it is this subtle flavour, baked indelibly into the beans and mingling with the pork fat, that brings a sparkle to the eyes.

Now pour this bubbling and fragrant syrup over the pot of pork and beans. Put a lid on the pot and bake the beans for several hours in a 250 degree oven. They should bake for at least six hours, but you can bake them much longer if you want. The longer they bake, the better they taste. This gives you time to work up an appetite, shovelling snow, chopping logs for the fire and so on.

About half-way through the baking, pull out the pot and taste the beans. *Taste*, I said! Don't eat them all up—they're nowhere near done. But at this point you ought to check the bouquet. Is it right? Are they too sweet or not sweet enough? Do they need more liquid? Don't let them get too dry.

Fix them up and put them back in for some more baking. One hour before they're ready you perform another important rite. Pour a cup of good sherry over them. Not cooking sherry—but the kind you drink yourself.

Do I see a small bird-like woman in the back row rise and denounce me for spreading debauchery and intoxication through the land? Control yourself, madam. I give you my bond that before this dish is done the alcoholic content of that fortified wine will have vanished, leaving only its delicate flavour behind, fused inseparably with a dish which supplies its own intoxication.

Now take some bacon strips and cover the entire top of the beans. Fifteen minutes before serving, take the lid off the pot so the bacon crispens into a thick crust.

By now you should be close to starvation, for the beans are meant to be devoured only when the tortured stomach pleads for sustenance. Call in your friends. Get some fresh bread with a hard crust. Tear open these loaves and rip out the soft insides. Now open the steaming pot, plunge a ladle through the bacon crust, spoon the bubbling brown beans, the soft globes of pork, and all the attendant juices, into the containers of bread.

Notice that the pork is sweet to the tooth, that the beans while still firm and round are infused with a delirious flavour, and that the simmering sauce is maddening to the palate.

Provide the company with mugs of steaming coffee. Now as you tear ravenously at the bread and feel the piping hot beans begin to woo your

taste buds, accept the homage of your friends, for you have earned it.
And, as your tired muscles lose their tensions, and the beans begin to
come out of your ears, and the day passes into history, give thanks to your
Maker for putting beans on this earth and giving men the wit to bake
them as they deserve.

1. Is this essay meant for a person who is in the kitchen about to cook
   dinner, or for other readers? How do you know?
2. What are the purposes of the first three paragraphs?
3. Comment on the tone of this essay. What attitude do you think the
   author wants us to have toward him? What has he done to make us
   feel this way about him?
4. Transitions between paragraphs are particularly noticeable in this
   essay. Underline transition words and comment on their effectiveness.

Lasting Impressions

Dating is a very important part of college life. In our quest to be educated
people, most of us must undergo some humiliation and embarrassment
as part of the maturing process. As a male who has gone through this
horrible ritual more times than he cares to remember, I have some
observations to offer to those women who are planning to gamble their
self-esteem for the chance of winning a partner. I'm twenty-four (next
month, the big "two-five") so my advice can be seen as coming from one
who is experienced. To make a lasting impression on that all-important
first date, it's important for a woman to be late, self-centred, and
unappreciative.

The best way to get the date off to a good start is to keep your new
prospect waiting for at least half an hour . . . longer if you can manage
it. This cooling-off period will make him appreciate you all the more when
you finally do put in an appearance. He will have had time to reflect on
how lucky he is to be going out with someone who is so careful about her
makeup that it takes forty-five minutes to apply it. His anticipation will
build and build to a fever pitch, so that by the time you present yourself,
he will be speechless with eagerness to impress you.

Once your prey has been properly softened up by his long wait, he is
ready to hear about your qualities and accomplishments. Now is not the
time to keep him in suspense, so get started right away and give lots of
detail. Tell him all about the many men who have sought your favour
over the past two or three years, the teachers who have given
testimony to your brilliance, the firms that have begged you to return
to their employ, the girlfriends who have turned their backs on you
because they were unable to compete. Your date will be enthralled
with your résumé of triumphs. After all, if you don't tell him how lucky
he is, how will he know?

By now your new man should be thoroughly infatuated with you, so
don't spoil the good impression you've created by showing any

appreciation for his efforts on the date. In fact, it is an excellent tactic to complain about as much as possible so that in future he will try to do better. Be sure to mention that his car is old-fashioned (or underpowered, or overpriced, or uncomfortable) and that other men you've dated drove much better vehicles. Criticize the meal if he has taken you to an expensive restaurant, and complain miserably about the band or the movie or the play or his friends, depending on what he has chosen for your entertainment. Your high standards will tell him all he needs to know about your style and expectations.

By following these simple steps you'll have no problem making that all-important first impression. You'll know, when he drops you at your door and takes off in a screech of tires, that he's trying in his own way to impress you, too. Being late, self-centred, and unappreciative are three important building blocks to creating a firm foundation for a relationship that will last minutes. Take it from one who knows.

1. This writer says that his purpose is to reveal how to make a lasting impression on a first date. What do you think his real purpose is in writing this essay?
2. What other main points might the author have used to add to his list of instructions?
3. List as many main points as you can for an essay on the same subject written from the female perspective. In other words, use the same technique to instruct a male how to make a lasting impression on a first date.
4. Select three good main points from your list in Question 3 and blueprint an essay on the subject.
5. Process essays often use irony (saying one thing but meaning something else). Think of as many subjects as you can that would make good ironic process essays. (Example: "How to lose friends")

For each of the exercises below, brainstorm your idea and use a question as your grabber. Devise a strong preview statement, then draft a clear blueprint for the rest of the essay.

EXERCISE 2

A friend from a distant town is staying with you and needs instructions on how to travel from your home to the building where this course is given, to meet you after class. In point form, describe how to get from your home to your classroom. On your next trip into class, test whether your instructions were complete.

EXERCISE 3

You have some expertise that is not shared by others; though others may be able to do it, no one does it as well as you. Your skill may be in serving customers, fly fishing, sleeping, eating spaghetti, or babysitting. Choose an activity at which you excel, and write a set of instructions for someone who wishes to become as expert as you are. For now, write your instructions in point form.

EXERCISE 4

Use the points written for Exercise 3 to develop an essay. Remember to consider your readers, to select and arrange your main points, and to develop the essay in paragraph units. Include an introduction and a conclusion.

EXERCISE 5

Write a process essay on one of these subjects, following all the guidelines to proper essay development.

How to keep friends
How to get fired
How to find a good part-time job
How to pack for a long vacation
How a hamburger is prepared in a fast-food restaurant
How a liar prospers
How to be popular
How to get a bargain
How to win an argument
How to unwind after a long day's work

CHAPTER 12

Classification

The **classification essay** is based on the natural human instinct for arranging things: we bring like things together into one category. For example, colleges put people who have similar degree goals and interests together in one curriculum program. Cars made in different parts of the world, by a multitude of manufacturers, may have many dissimilar features but they can still be categorized or classified as sports cars, luxury cars, or cars in a range of styles, sizes, and colours. A major category like *sports cars* can be subdivided into many smaller categories, and each of these subcategories could be analyzed and explained in another classification essay.

The procedure of **definition** also follows this pattern: we define a concept ("a good student") by dividing it into the characteristics that are shared by all members of that class ("a good student is one who is hard-working, interested, and creative.") Writing a classification essay requires either grouping similar things together to identify them as belonging to one class or examining an acknowledged class of things and breaking it down into constituent parts, or kinds, or characteristics. Here are four examples of essay topics that lend themselves to the classification model.

Saturday morning television
- cartoons
- sports shows
- interview programs

The ideal home
- affordable
- easy to maintain
- large enough for your family
- close to shopping and schools

Beer	• lager
	• ale
	• stout
	• bock
Insect	• head
	• thorax
	• abdomen

Tips on Writing a Classification Essay

1. The key to a good essay is choosing your main points carefully. Make sure that all points are of approximately equal weight and importance, that you have included *everything*, and that the points do not overlap.
2. Set out clearly in the introduction your reasons for choosing your main points. Are any aspects of the subject deliberately left out? If so, you must explain to your readers why you have limited your coverage.
3. Your preview statement must set out your subject and its main points, as in the following examples.

   Inanimate objects can be classified into three major categories— those that don't work, those that break down, and those that get lost.

   The perfect costume for school is comfortable, easy to get (and keep) clean, and, within limits, distinctive.

   Our softball team is made up of has-beens, might-have-beens, and never-weres.

EXERCISE 1

The following three essays demonstrate different types of classification. In the first essay, the subject is defined by a description of its characteristics; in the second and third essays, a large class of objects is subdivided. Read the essays and then answer the questions that follow each.

Rock of Ages

There are not many rock bands that can be defined as truly great. The history of rock is full of "one-hit wonders" and cult favourites, but very few groups have achieved both popular success and staying power. To be considered great, a rock band must have broad popular appeal, an exciting stage performance, and the ability to evolve with tastes and times.

Popularity is an important consideration in determining the greatness of a band, but because popular taste is so changeable, it can't be the only criterion. It takes great talent to produce lyrics and music, a style, and a personality that will keep a band in the public's favour for any length of time. Some bands manage to stay in business for years with a small, specialized following; others produce one platinum hit and are wildly popular for a few months before disappearing forever. But neither type of band qualifies for greatness.

Although popularity can be achieved with studio releases, a necessary ingredient in greatness is live performance. Studio bands can produce wonderful effects and a polished sound, but unless they can go on the road and demonstrate their abilities on stage, they will not be able to hold their audience beyond one or two albums. A stage performance need not be hi-tech or fantastically expensive to be successful; in fact, many groups who indulge in an excess of light shows and explosives to impress their fans are covering up for a lack of substance in the music. Great music well played, visually interesting performances, and appealing personalities are the characteristics of a great live performance.

Staying power is, in part, a product of popularity and performance, but versatility and adaptability are also needed if a band is going to have a long enough life span to qualify for greatness. Some bands that qualified under the other two categories fell apart over personality differences, money, drugs, or music style before they could become truly great. Others didn't have the talent to change their style or adapt their themes as musical tastes evolved. Truly great bands possess the musical ability and the collective strength to shape and set style, rather than labour to catch up with what's popular.

There have been a few great bands in the history of rock and some great individual performers. Naturally, personal tastes will differ, but no one can deny that popular appeal, spectacular live performance, and versatility and adaptability are the factors that made The Beatles, The Stones, Dire Straits, and others like them the great bands of rock.

1. Describe the audience this writer had in mind when writing the essay. Include age, education, interests, musical knowledge, and any other details you can.

2. What are the essential characteristics of "greatness," according to this writer?

   * _____

   * _____

   * _____

3. What other characteristics could have been used in writing an essay on this subject?

   * _____

   * _____

   * _____

4. Write a one-sentence explanation of the *function* or *purpose* of each of the five paragraphs in "Rock of Ages."

   • _____

   _____

   • _____

   _____

   • _____

   _____

   • _____

   _____

   • _____

   _____

5. "Rock of Ages" is about the factors that make a rock band "great." Think of three other topics for classification essays that include the word "great," such as "Great Canadian vacation spots" or "Great movies of the 1980s." Provide at least three kinds or parts or characteristics for each of your topics.

   Topic 1 _____

   a. _____

   b. _____

   c. _____

   Others _____

   _____

   Topic 2 _____

   a. _____

   b. _____

   c. _____

   Others _____

   _____

   Topic 3 _____

   a. _____

   b. _____

   c. _____

The Plot against People
Russell Baker

Washington, June 17—Inanimate objects are classified scientifically into three major categories—those that don't work, those that break down and those that get lost.

The goal of all inanimate objects is to resist man and ultimately to defeat him, and the three major classifications are based on the method each object uses to achieve its purpose. As a general rule, any object capable of breaking down at the moment when it is most needed will do so. The automobile is typical of the category.

With the cunning typical of its breed, the automobile never breaks down while entering a filling station with a large staff of idle mechanics. It waits until it reaches a downtown intersection in the middle of the rush hour, or until it is fully loaded with family and luggage on the Ohio turnpike.

Thus it creates maximum misery, inconvenience, frustration and irritability among its human cargo, thereby reducing its owner's life span.

Washing machines, garbage disposals, lawn mowers, light bulbs, automatic laundry dryers, water pipes, furnaces, electrical fuses, television tubes, hose nozzles, tape recorders, slide projectors—all are in league with the automobile to take their turn at breaking down whenever life threatens to flow smoothly for their human enemies.

Many inanimate objects, of course, find it extremely difficult to break down. Pliers, for example, and gloves and keys are almost totally incapable of breaking down. Therefore, they have had to evolve a different technique for resisting man.

They get lost. Science has still not solved the mystery of how they do it, and no man has ever caught one of them in the act of getting lost. The most plausible theory is that they have developed a secret method of locomotion, which they are able to conceal the instant a human eye falls upon them.

It is not uncommon for a pair of pliers to climb all the way from the cellar to the attic in its single-minded determination to raise its owner's blood pressure. Keys have been known to burrow three feet under mattresses. Women's purses, despite their great weight, frequently travel through six or seven rooms to find hiding space under a couch.

Scientists have been struck by the fact that things that break down virtually never get lost, while things that get lost hardly ever break down.

A furnace, for example, will invariably break down at the depth of the first winter cold wave, but it will never get lost. A woman's purse, which after all does have some inherent capacity for breaking down, hardly ever does; it almost invariably chooses to get lost.

Some persons believe this constitutes evidence that inanimate objects are not entirely hostile to man, and that a negotiated peace is possible. After all, they point out, a furnace could infuriate a man even more thoroughly by getting lost than by breaking down, just as a glove could upset him far more by breaking down than by getting lost.

Not everyone agrees, however, that this indicates a conciliatory attitude among inanimate objects. Many say it merely proves that furnaces, gloves and pliers are incredibly stupid.

The third class of objects—those that don't work—is the most curious of all. These include such objects as barometers, car clocks, cigarette lighters, flashlights and toy-train locomotives. It is inaccurate, of course, to say that they never work. They work once, usually for the first few hours after being brought home, and then quit. Thereafter, they never work again.

In fact, it is widely assumed that they are built for the purpose of not working. Some people have reached advanced ages without ever seeing some of these objects—barometers, for example—in working order.

Science is utterly baffled by the entire category. There are many theories about it. The most interesting holds that the things that don't work have attained the highest state possible for an inanimate object, the state to which things that break down and things that get lost can still only aspire.

They have truly defeated man by conditioning him never to expect anything of them, and in return they have given man the only peace he receives from inanimate society. He does not expect his barometer to work, his electric locomotive to run, his cigarette lighter to light or his flashlight to illuminate, and when they don't it does not raise his blood pressure.

He cannot attain that peace with furnaces, and keys, and cars and women's purses as long as he demands that they work for their keep.

1. Russell Baker is a journalist and humourist. What is the purpose of his classification essay? Who are his readers?
2. What is his role in this essay?
3. What are the three basic classifications in Baker's essay?

    - _____

    - _____

    - _____

4. Baker's preview statement includes three main points. In the paragraphs, however, he develops the main points in a *different order* from the order in the preview. Why has he chosen to do this? What effect does it have?
5. Baker's essay is broken into many short paragraphs. Why? What are the advantages? Disadvantages?
6. Tone is important in humourous satire. What is Baker's tone? How does it affect the relationship with his readers?
7. This essay was written before computers were in common use. Where might computers fit into Baker's classifications?

Of Men and Machines

There has got to be a better way! The North American system of mate selection by dating is so inefficient that I wonder why it works even as often as it does. If we selected cars using the same methods we employ to choose a mate, few of us would bother driving. Dates, like cars, have a few basic things in common: a body, an image, and (if you're lucky) insurance. Beyond the basics, however, each model is so individual that making a selection becomes a matter of guesswork. Nevertheless, for research purposes, we can classify cars and dates into these general types: the economy model, the standard North American model, and the exotic sports model.

The economy model date features cramped conditions and a lack of power. The econo-date thinks that his personality can make up for the fact that you never go anywhere except for walks, and never do anything that costs money. He tends to be shy, quiet, and about as much fun as an oil leak. It's not just that he doesn't have lots of money to spend, it's that he doesn't use any imagination or creativity to compensate for his lack of cash. The economy model's greatest ambition is someday to move up and compete with the standard North American model.

The standard North American date is big on comfort and appearance, but short on quality. He'll pay big money for an ordinary meal, then tip lavishly for poor service, thinking he's impressing you. He is loud, confident, and showy, and sure he is the best thing that could happen to you. Unfortunately, he can't carry on a conversation about anything but himself and, occasionally, sports. While he would never admit it, he secretly wants desperately to grow up to be an exotic sports type.

The exotic, high-powered sports date is rich, sophisticated, gorgeous, and nasty. If you should get a date with one of these creatures, you will be the envy of all your friends. Unfortunately, he has cultivated his vanity like a fine art, and your value to him is purely ornamental. Equality of the sexes is something he either doesn't understand or reserves for his equally wealthy and attractive friends. My mother always reminded me that "beauty is only skin deep;" the exotic sports date is proof that she was right.

If this sounds terribly pessimistic, I guess it is. If only we could select mates as intelligently and carefully as we choose cars! Of course, with my luck, I'd probably end up with something that has the power of an econo-model, the quality of the North American standard, and the repair bills of an exotic.

1. While planning "Of Men and Machines," the author had an audience in mind. Who were they?
2. Into what categories are dates classified in "Of Men and Machines"?

- _____

- _____

- _____

3. "Of Men and Machines" uses the technique of analogy. It makes a statement about types of men by comparing them to types of cars. Is this analogy accurate? Is it effective?
4. The conclusion makes a serious point. What is it? Does it work?

EXERCISE 2

This exercise is designed to improve your skill in identifying *unity* within a classification. In these preview statements, one of the points doesn't belong.

1. A good teacher doesn't bark at his students, give last-minute assignments, study for a test the night before, or grade unfairly.
2. The last movie I saw in the theatre was a boring mixture of unnecessary violence, annoying commercial interruptions, shallow characterizations, and nauseating sentimentality.
3. Newspapers are his main source of information. Every morning he reads *The Halifax Gazette, The Montreal Devoir, The Calgary Sun,* and *People Weekly.*
4. Toronto is noted for several important landmarks: the CN Tower, good civic government, the Royal York Hotel, and the SkyDome.
5. It's not easy to work for a perfectionist. She wants perfect results, double the work in half the time, unpaid overtime, and memos for almost everything.
6. Food is important for several reasons. It is a biological necessity, a pleasant focus for social activities, a sensual experience for gourmets, and a cause of environmental damage.
7. Baseball pitchers can be divided into four kinds: neurotic celebrities, stoic workhorses, speedy infielders, and anxious newcomers.
8. A media person has four important tasks to perform: to report news accurately, to collect a big salary, to prevent government control of information, and to entertain with social information.
9. There are several civic holidays during the spring and summer: Victoria Day, Canada Day, Labour Day, and Thanksgiving.
10. Tonight's entertainment consists of dinner at Maison Duchamp, a movie at the Bollinger cinemas, a midnight ferry-ride through the islands, and a miserable hangover in the morning.

EXERCISE 3

Humans have a strong instinct to classify everything. List at least ten classifications to which you belong.

EXERCISE 4

To help explain exactly what things are, we usually divide them up into their constituent parts. For each of the following terms, list several characteristics that would help to define it.

- a good teacher
- a successful résumé
- an ideal girlfriend/boyfriend
- a worthwhile course of study
- a good TV program

EXERCISE 5

Select one of the terms you used in Exercise 4 and expand your list of characteristics into an essay.

EXERCISE 6

Think of an example of a test question on a recent exam that required you to classify in order to explain, or make up a possible test question that would require a classification essay in response.

EXERCISE 7

Sports analogies are very common ("He can't get to first base," or "Just when she was making the right moves, she dropped the ball.") For each of the following subjects, give an analogy and an example that would help your readers' understanding in a classification essay.

SUBJECT	ANALOGY	EXAMPLE
Overwork	electronics	When the brain's circuits are overloaded, a fuse can blow, resulting in nervous breakdown.
Personal health	automechanics	_____ _____ _____
Marriage	travel	_____ _____ _____

SUBJECT	ANALOGY	EXAMPLE
Fashion	_____	_____
		_____
		_____

EXERCISE 8

Focus each of the following general subjects into a topic suited to a classification essay. For each, identify three types, categories, parts, or characteristics.

Restaurants Topic _____

• _____

• _____

• _____

Work Topic _____

• _____

• _____

• _____

Commercials Topic _____

• _____

• _____

• _____

Hobbies Topic _____

• _____

• _____

• _____

Soft drinks Topic _____

• _____

• _____

• _____

EXERCISE 9

Here is a blueprint for a classification essay on the characteristics necessary for career success. The preview statement and topic points are provided. Fill in appropriate topic sentences and support. When you are satisfied, turn your blueprint into a full essay.

Career Success

Grabber _____

_____

_____

Preview statement   To be successful in your career, you must prepare adequately in college, work hard on the job, and communicate well with employers, colleagues, and the public.

1. Topic sentence: _____
   (Preparation)

   _____

   Support: _____

   _____

   _____

2. Topic sentence: _____
   (Hard work)

   _____

   Support: _____

   _____

   _____

3. Topic sentence: _____
   (Communication)

   _____

   Support: _____

   _____

   _____

Summary _____

_____

_____

_____

Clincher _____

_____

EXERCISE 10

Write a classification essay on *one* of the following subjects.

The characteristics of
- an ideal job
- an ideal marriage
- a bad film
- a bad holiday
- a bad actor or actress
- a good athlete
- a good TV commercial
- a good book
- a good evening's entertainment
- an average Canadian

The main kinds of
- employees
- restaurants
- prime-time TV shows
- European sports cars
- housing accommodation
- sports fans
- pets
- college students
- insurance
- Americans

The component parts of
- a newspaper
- a five-course meal
- a sci-fi movie
- a citizenship review
- an ideal car
- a highway system
- a love affair
- a winning hockey team
- a golf swing
- a successful party

CHAPTER 13

Cause and Effect

- What are the causes of heart disease?
- What are the causes of acid rain?
- What are the effects of drug addiction?
- What are the consequences of bad posture?
- What are the results of a well-conceived business plan?

These are the kinds of subjects often discussed in **cause essays** and **effect essays.** On some occasions, cause and effect may be combined in one essay or report, but its length and complexity would put it out of the range of our introductory discussions here. Examples of such subjects might be "A discussion of hypertension" or "Share-splitting: a corporate strategy." For these topics, writers would likely include both the causes of the condition or activity and its probable effects. It is more usual, however, for essays to concentrate either on causes or on effects.

The most common problem found in student cause or effect essays is oversimplification. In the absence of solid facts, figures, or evidence, student writers have a tendency to generalize and to substitute unsupported opinions for reasons. This problem often originates from choosing a topic that is too big for the length of the paper. For example, one student decided to do an "effect" paper on Canada's immigration policy, a subject so big and so complicated that he could do nothing more than give vague and unsupported opinions. The result made him seem not only bigoted, but also ignorant and foolish. You can avoid this pitfall by choosing your subject carefully, focusing it into a limited topic, and supporting each main point with lots of evidence.

Tips on Writing a Cause or Effect Essay

1. Your preview statement should clearly indicate whether you are tackling cause or effect, and should present your main points in order. Consider these examples.

   > The chief causes of dissatisfaction among the workers in the office where I spent my placement are low wages, sexual harassment, and boredom.

   > The beneficial effects of my annual canoe trip include reduced stress and increased fitness.

2. Fully support your statements. You must provide proof of what you say, in the form of examples, facts, statistics, quotations, anecdotes, etc. (See pp. 80–85.)

EXERCISE 1

The following three essays demonstrate cause and effect writing. In the first essay, the writer employs facts to support statements of cause; in the second, effects are illustrated with examples; in the third, the writer uses facts, statistics, quotations, and examples as support in an effects essay. Read each essay and answer the questions that follow it.

"We Have Met the Enemy, and They Is . . . Us"

Our planet is being destroyed. If the cause of its destruction were some external force, such as aliens or a rogue comet, then we humans would band together and fight the threat with every resource at our disposal. We wouldn't count the cost in lives, effort, or money; we would throw every ounce of our strength and will into the effort. However, while the threat is just as real as if it came from space ships bombarding us with poison rays, we aren't doing much to save ourselves from destruction, because the evildoers are much closer to home. We see them daily in our mirrors. Motivated by greed and ignorance, we are wrecking our own environment with ruthless efficiency.

Greed—industrial, commercial, and personal—has motivated us to rape the earth's resources without giving thought to the consequences. A supplement appeared recently in a Canada-wide chain of newspapers. Printed on recycled paper, it outlined some of the environmental changes brought about by human greed. Since the industrial revolution, two-thirds of the world's rain forest has been cut or burned. The rain forest is (was?) the largest single source of the earth's oxygen supply. Around the world, we pave over, build on, or otherwise destroy one hectare of agricultural land every 14 seconds. In Canada, we fill our rivers with chemicals and sewage, kill our lakes and forests with industrial pollutants, poison the soil and the water table with toxic waste, all in the name of industrial growth and the jobs it creates. And we're one of the luckier nations. We are relatively rich in natural resources and, in the short term, can survive our attacks on the environment.

Often linked with greed, ignorance is the other prime motivator in our self-destruction. Ignorant and uncaring, we cling to our "freedom machines." Automobiles are the primary source of air pollution, and there are more than twice as many cars on Canadian roads today as there were twenty years ago. Canadians throw away some 275 000 tonnes of disposable (and nonbiodegradable) diapers every year. We munch our fast food in its environmentally harmful containers; demand that our paper products be bleached pure white despite the horrific pollution of our rivers that is caused by the bleaching process; recycle glass and plastics and papers reluctantly, if at all; and cheerfully accept—even demand—the plastic packaging, plastic bags, and plastic products our supermarkets peddle.

Is there any reason for optimism? There is some evidence that Canadians are becoming more conscious of the environment, and consciousness can only lead to changes for the better. In 1989, one third of Canadians felt that the environment was the most important national issue. Only a year before that it was one in ten, and the year before that it was one in twenty. A majority of Canadians now favour tougher action against polluters, even if it means higher taxes, higher prices, and fewer jobs. However, this bit-by-bit heightening of concern is far from the concerted, all-out effort to save the planet that would result if we were threatened by an external force. How very much more difficult it is to mobilize resources and will when the enemy lies within!

1. What is the main problem identified in "'We Have Met the Enemy . . . ,'" and what are its two causes?

   The causes of _____ are

   _____ and

   _____ .

2. Look at the concluding paragraph of the essay. How does it affect you as a reader? What is its purpose?
3. Describe the role that the author has assumed in developing this essay. Be as precise as you can.

Lightweight Lit.

I really enjoy literary discussions. I love it when people at trendy restaurants smack their lips in appreciation of the latest South American novelist, Egyptian poet, or Armenian essayist. By eavesdropping on these discussions, I can find out what's going on in the world of "great literature" so that when people ask me what I've read lately I can pretend that I, too, am devoted to highbrow literature. I'm ashamed to admit my secret vice . . . but, since we're friends, I can tell you . . . I *love* "trash." I'm embarrassed about it, and I know that my intellectual friends would ridicule me if they found out. Still, I have very good reasons for enjoying "light" literature so much. I find it educates, relaxes, and entertains in a way that more cerebral reading doesn't—at least, not for me.

The educational nature of popular or "junk" literature is often overlooked. From reading countless police novels, I know the workings of the Los Angeles and New York police departments inside out. I have a thorough grounding in the operations of the CIA, the KGB, MI6, and any number of less illustrious spy agencies. I'm eagerly awaiting the first novel about a hero from Canada's CSIS. Science fiction books have detailed for me the ways of life, war, travel, and even agriculture in outer space. My education even includes the laws of nature in alternate universes: I know about the society of Gor, the politics of Fionavar, and the nature of good and evil in a hundred other worlds.

Acquiring all this knowledge may sound tiring, but light novels are actually extremely relaxing. The way I read this kind of literature is slouched in my favourite chair with my feet up and a comforting drink close at hand, and, since I can't do anything else while I read, the overall effect is complete physical relaxation. Also, an absorbing novel will take me away from the concerns and stresses of everyday life, allowing me to escape to a world created by the writer. Since I can have no effect on this world, I can, with a completely clear conscience, let things unfold as they may and assume the relaxing role of observer.

While education and relaxation are important, most of us read light novels to be entertained. "Entertainment" means different things to different people. Some enjoy being frightened half to death by the books of Stephen King or his colleagues; others get satisfaction from the sugary romance of Harlequin novels; many people find science fiction absorbing and devour the works of Isaac Asimov or Jerry Pournel. Whatever subject or style grabs you, there are literally thousands of novels to suit your taste. I'm lucky because—with the exception of popular romance—I can find enjoyment in almost any type of reasonably well written light novel.

None of the novelists I read will ever win the Nobel prize for literature, and few of them will be studied in university literature courses. However, many writers have become wealthy from selling their fantasies to those millions of readers like me who seek entertainment, relaxation, and education from the novels they enjoy—even if they have to enjoy them in secret.

1. What is the main topic identified in "Lightweight Lit.," and what are its three effects?

The effects of _____ are

_____ ,

_____

2. What view is the author promoting to the audience? What role does the author perform in this essay?
3. Who are the readers? What do they expect from the essay? Will they be convinced of the causes for the author's literary preferences?
4. What purpose is served by the author's supposed embarrassment? How does this device affect you as a reader?
5. The author uses specific examples to demonstrate each point under the headings "Education," "Relaxation," and "Entertainment." List examples used to illustrate each point.

Indecent Exposure

Chuck Kraemer

I spotted my first one of the season on a warm day in mid-March, beside the Charles River near No. Harvard St., lying on his back with his shirt off, arms spread, palms up, chin high, letting the UV photons in the 3500–4000 angstrom range severely agitate the molecular structure of his keratin layer.

Actually, he was just sunbathing, but it was, biologically, a strange, masochistic bath indeed. Ultraviolet radiation was attacking his epidermis, sending its molecules into reactive states, producing dangerous reaction products. Deeper down, the dark pigment called melanin was being manufactured as a shield against the attack, but the process was slow, and if my sun worshipper was as unwary as most on this, his first exposure of the season, he probably killed off a few billion skin cells within fifteen minutes—long before his biological defenses could muster. It was truly a bloodbath—the blood being rushed through swollen vessels to the surface of the skin to begin repairing wounded tissue, producing the lobster-red color we call a sunburn.

The harmful effects of his worship were not as transient or superficial as this supplicant probably assumed, especially if he paid regular spring-through-September homage. The adverse vascular effects of a moderately severe burn may last for a year or more. Skin cancer is a distinct possibility. Twenty-three percent of all cancers in men and 13 percent in women are cancers of the skin, and of all those, 90 percent are sun-related. Most are cured, but often only by surgery.

Perhaps no less dire to the average narcissistic sunbather, the cosmetic toll can be very high. Prolonged exposure to the sun can cause

Reprinted with permission from *The Real Paper*, June 4, 1975.

long-lasting and permanent yellowing, wrinkling, spotting, freckling, and coarsening of the skin, such as that seen on the necks of sailors, farmers, and cowboys. It usually takes years, but it can start very early. Loss of skin elasticity has been found in solarphiles as young as 20 years—a condition interestingly omitted from the luscious body of the 20-year-old model in those Coppertone ads.

If only these war wounds were incurred for a just cause, maybe it would all make sense. But as far as I can see, sun worship is just plain demented—stranger than even its sister, star worship (astrology), which is bizarre enough but has no adverse physical effects, as far as I know. Getting a tan is, literally, self-abuse. As dermatologist John Knox of Baylor has said, "A suntan is a response to an injury." For anybody with an adequate diet, direct sunshine is medically useless at best, dangerous at worst.

Of course we justify our masochism on cosmetic grounds. Bronze is beautiful. Strident advertising by the suntan lotion companies, airlines, and Florida real estate outfits assures us of that, and fervently, by the peeling beachfuls, we believe. (One ad for a Bahamas vacation implores, "Get out of the kitchen and bake.")

But history shows that the tan body as a sign of health and status is only a rather long-running fad, rooted in ignorance and elitism. Before the nineteenth century a *pallid* complexion was considered fashionable and wholesome. The working classes toiled mostly outdoors, where they acquired the dark skins that marked them as socially inferior. The rich sensibly avoided the sun, preferring an iced tea in the shade, or a stroll in the filtered aura of an expensive parasol. Hence the poetic necks and bosoms "as white as alabaster," and upon them the consequently prominent blue veins—giving rise to the term "blue bloods."

Then came the Industrial Revolution, reversing the code of snobbery. Workers now spent their daylight hours in factories in coal-smoke-polluted cities, so sun became fashionable for those who could afford it. Sunshine was even seriously prescribed as a panacea for tuberculosis—a quaint overreaction to the plague of tuberculosis and rickets among the vitamin-D-deficient working classes.

Today, the summer tan is less a status symbol than an imagined necessity. (The status-conscious must now graduate to the *year-round* tan, which implies sufficient wealth to vacation in the South Seas.) There may not be a mass leisure class yet, but the masses manage to cram plenty of leisure into their summer outings at the Cape or Nantucket or Nahant, where they bask 10,000 per acre for hours on end, sizzling away like Cornish hens in a pit at the Kiwanis Memorial Day barbecue.

I have no sympathy for these folks, but I am obliged—this being a practical column—to advise them how to protect themselves from the sun, even as they so indecently expose themselves to it. Truth to tell, my secret desire is that if they're all going to abuse themselves this way they should fry to a crisp and get washed out to sea like bits of burned bacon, but I'll set prejudice aside for the moment and grudgingly offer the following three tips:

1. For the specific instructions on the absurdly complicated art of getting a tan without getting burned, see the May, June, or July issue of almost any women's magazine, where "Good Sense in the Sun" articles are a regular seasonal item. These are usually written by the in-house doc or a consulting dermatologist, and appear to be authoritative.

2. For the dullards among us who enjoy the outdoors and don't want to burn, but don't give a squint about skin color either, the solution is simple: stay in the shade.

3. The magazine pieces often go into greater detail on this, but, very briefly, the best sun lotions for preventing burns are those containing para-aminobenzoic acid, or PABA. Check the label—any product claiming to prevent sunburn must list the key ingredient.

See you at the beach. I'll be the one in long sleeves and work boots.

1. Kraemer has a firm point of view. What role does he use to support it?
2. Who is the audience for this essay? Will the readers see the *causes* that have encouraged Kraemer's view? Will they be convinced by the information that backs it up?
3. This is a persuasion essay as well as an essay of causes and effects. List the effects that will persuade the readers to stay out of the sun.

_____

_____

_____

4. Comment on the brief conclusion. Does it work?
5. Kraemer uses humour, despite his serious intent. What is the role of humour in this essay? How did it affect you as a reader?

EXERCISE 2

Develop each of the following preview statements by adding three good main points.

1. The main causes of divorce in adolescent marriages are _____

_____,

_____, and

_____.

2. The effects of secondary smoke inhalation by nonsmokers are serious; they include _____

_____,

_____, and

_____ .

3. Obesity, a common problem in North America, is the result of three major causes: _____

_____,

_____, and

_____ .

4. The positive effects of professional day care upon preschool children are _____

_____,

_____, and

_____ .

5. There are several causes for the present economic slump: _____

_____,

_____, and

_____ .

6. The major causes of air pollution are _____

_____,

_____, and

_____ .

7. The fitness craze was prompted by these causes: _____

_____,

_____, and

_____ .

8. Violence in professional hockey has several negative effects upon young hockey players: _____

_____,

_____, and

_____ .

9. There are several causes for the increase in numbers of full-time workers returning to college for part-time study: _____

_____,

_____ , and

_____ .

10. Three effects of superior Japanese technology in the North American marketplace are _____

_____,

_____ , and

_____ .

EXERCISE 3

Begin with the question "What are the causes of _____?" and fill in five topics that you know enough about to list at least three causes.

EXERCISE 4

Repeat Exercise 3, using the question "What are the effects of _____?"

EXERCISE 5

Choose one of the topics that you have developed in either Exercise 3 or Exercise 4 and work that topic into a full essay, taking care to select a subject about which you know enough to support your ideas.

EXERCISE 6

Write a cause essay or an effect essay on one of the following subjects. If you don't know enough to fully support your ideas, be prepared to do some research.

> *Causes*
> Yuppies are materialistic.
> Many people look forward to early retirement.
> Adolescence can be painful.
> My first job was a good (or bad) experience.
> My instructors think I am a good student.

Vandalism is a symptom of teenage frustration.
Too many criminal offenders are given probation.
Anorexia is a growing problem among young girls.
Homelessness has become widespread in large cities.
Runaways prefer the street to a dysfunctional home life.

Effects
Regular exercise is beneficial.
Technology is making us lazy.
A bad boss has a big influence on his employees.
Instant tellers have made banking more efficient.
Music can reduce tension.
Being an only child is a difficult way to grow up.
Poor driving skills are a hazard to everyone.
Alcohol is hard on the body.
Injuries resulting from overtraining are common among athletes.
Too many worries can age you prematurely.

CHAPTER 14

Comparison and Contrast

The difference between comparison and contrast is quite simple: if the similarities between two things (or ideas or concepts or points of view) are being emphasized, it's a **comparison essay;** if the differences are being emphasized, it's a **contrast essay.** Many people use the term "comparison" to cover both, and similarities *and* differences are usually discussed together in an essay.

You can choose from two approaches when you are organizing a comparison essay. In the first option, you discuss one item fully, then turn to the other item. This approach is sometimes called the **chunk** or **block method** of organizing. The alternative option is to compare your two items point by point. This approach is sometimes called the **slice** or **point-by-point method.** For example, suppose you decided to compare The Hulk and Macho Man. You might identify the following three points:

- physical appearance
- acting technique
- on-camera hysterics

Using the chunk method, you would first consider The Hulk in terms of these three points, then you would do the same for Macho Man. You would need to blueprint only four paragraphs for your essay:

1. Introduction
2. The Hulk's physical appearance, acting technique, and on-camera hysterics

3. Macho Man's physical appearance, acting, technique, and on-camera hysterics
4. Conclusion

The chunk method works best in short papers, where the points of comparison are easy to understand and remember. As comparisons get more complex, your readers will be able to see your points better if you present them side by side, using the slice method. You would then need to blueprint five paragraphs for your essay:

1. Introduction
2. Physical appearance of The Hulk and Macho Man
3. Acting technique of The Hulk and Macho Man
4. On-camera hysterics of The Hulk and Macho Man
5. Conclusion

The introductory paragraph in the comparison model usually tells readers what two things are to be assessed and what criteria will be used to assess them. The concluding paragraph may (or may not) reveal a preference for one over the other.

Tips on Writing a Comparison or Contrast Essay

1. Make sure that the two items you have chosen are appropriately paired; to make a satisfactory comparison or contrast, they must have something in common. Both might be baseball teams or both world leaders; but to compare the Montreal Expos to the Calgary Stampeders or to contrast Brian Mulroney to your Aunt Agatha would be futile and meaningless.
2. Your main points must apply equally to both items in your comparison. Reject main points that apply to one and have only limited application to the other. For example, in a comparison of typewriters and word processors, a category of screen colour would be pointless.
3. Your preview statement should clearly present the two items to be compared and the basis for their comparison. This is a tricky job and deserves some time. Consider these examples.

   The major points of comparison in automobiles are performance, comfort, and economy, so I applied these factors to the two cars in the running for my dollars: the Corvette and the Porsche.

   In comparing the top-of-the-line running shoes from Nike and Brooks, I looked at fit, cushioning, stability, and price.

EXERCISE 1

The following three essays demonstrate different approaches to writing comparisons or contrasts. After reading each essay, answer the questions that follow it.

The Canadian Climate

The student who comes to Canada from a tropical country is usually prepared for the cold of the Canadian winter, a sharp contrast to the hot northern summer. What the student may not be prepared for is the fact that Canadian personalities reflect the country's temperature range but are not quite so extreme. Canadian personalities fall into two categories: warm and cool. The two groups share the Canadian traits of restraint and willingness to compromise, but they are dissimilar in their attitudes both to their own country and to the foreign student's country of origin.

Warm Canadians are first of all warm about Canada, and will, at the first sound of a foreign accent, describe with rapture the magnificence of the country from the Maritimes to the West Coast, with loving descriptions of the prairies, the Rockies, and even the "unique climate of the far North." Canadian leisure activities are enthusiastically explained, with a special place reserved for hockey. "You must come out with us. So you've never skated? You'll learn. You'll have a great time." The Warm Canadian wants the newcomer to participate fully in the pleasures of life in Canada. When he turns his attention to the foreign student's homeland, he seeks enlightenment, asking questions about its geography, social and economic conditions, and other concerns not usually addressed in travel and tourism brochures. The Warm Canadian understands that the residents of these countries are not some tribe of wonderfully exotic flower children who sing and dance and have natural rhythm, but are individuals who, like people in Canada, face the problems of earning a living and raising a family.

Compared to the springlike optimism of the Warm Canadian, the Cool Canadian is like November. Conditions may not be unbearable for the moment, but they are bound to get much colder before there is any sign of a thaw. The Cool Canadian's first words on hearing the foreign student is from a warm country are, "How could you leave such a lovely climate to come to a place like this?" Not from him will one hear of Banff, or Niagara Falls, or anything except how cold and dark and dreary it gets in the winter. It sometimes seems that the Cool Canadian's description of his own country is designed to encourage foreign students to pack their bags and return home at once. As for the foreign student's country of origin, the Cool Canadian is not really interested, although he may declare, "I hear it's beautiful. I'd love to go there." Beyond that, however, he has no desire to receive information that may shake the foundations of his collection of myths, half-truths, and geographic inaccuracies. This type of Canadian, if he does travel to a tropical country, will ensure that he remains at all times within the safe confines of his hotel and that he returns to Canada with all his preconceived ideas intact.

The foreign student should not be upset by Cool Canadians; he should ignore their chilliness. Besides, like a heat wave in March, an unexpected thaw can occur and create extraordinary warmth. Likewise, a Warm Canadian may become a little frosty sometimes, but, like a cold spell in June, this condition won't last. When the weather changes, the foreign student is given a wonderful opportunity to display his own qualities of understanding, tolerance, and a fine "Canadian" acceptance of others as they are.

1. Which method of contrast has the author of "The Canadian Climate" chosen for his subject, chunk or slice? Is it the better method?
2. Why did the author choose this approach? Would the essay work as well if it were organized the other way? Blueprint the main points of comparison as they would look in the other style.
3. What are the main points of comparison in "Canadian Climate"?

_____

_____

_____

4. What other points of comparison or contrast between the two kinds of Canadians can you think of?

_____

_____

_____

5. What audience does this foreign student have in mind? What effect do you think the essay is likely to have on the readers?

Car Wars

Recently I was faced with a decision that sooner or later most of us confront: which car to buy. In Mr. Wright's economics class, we are taught to be careful consumers, so I spent many hours of research before I made my decision. The major points of comparison in automobiles, I discovered, are performance, comfort, and economy, so I applied these factors to the two cars in the running for my dollars: the Chevrolet Corvette and the Porsche 944 Turbo.

Performance of the two cars was very close, especially when you consider the tiny differences at the speeds involved. However, I was able to get the 'Vet from 0 to 100 kph in exactly six seconds, while the Porsche took more than half a second longer. In cornering, the Porsche was marginally superior, but the Corvette was the clear winner in braking. From 100 kph it came to a complete stop in 68 metres; the Porsche went almost two metres farther before stopping.

Comfort was my next concern, and here I gave a slight edge to the 944. Both have luxurious seats that provide support and comfort no matter what kind of twists and turns the car performs. The dash and instrumentation are a matter of personal preference, and I like the no-nonsense clarity of the European gauges better than the somewhat cluttered and flashy appearance of the Corvette interior. Fit and finish are superior in the Porsche, and the sound systems are pretty close, though I gave the nod to the 'Vet in this category after playing k. d. lang's "Absolute Torch and Twang" album at full volume on the built-in CD player in both cars.

Finally, keeping my economics class in mind, I examined the financial implications of each purchase. The list price is in the Corvette's favour by about $3000, and it gets almost one kilometre more for every litre than the German car. A quick check of typical repair bills and the cost of replacement parts sealed this category firmly in the Corvette's corner.

If I put all the factors on a balance sheet and made my decision based on the totals at the bottom of the page, I would purchase a Corvette without hesitation. However, there are many intangible factors that weigh heavily in a decision about cars. Mr. Wright would never understand (he drives a seven-year-old Hyundai), but as I got out my chequebook, I asked for the Porsche. The salesman seemed to understand.

1. Which method of organization has this writer used for his comparison? Is it the most appropriate one in this case?
2. Blueprint the essay as it would appear in the other method.
3. What other points might the writer have chosen in comparing two sports cars?
4. What audience does this writer have in mind for his essay? What is his purpose in writing?
5. What purposes does the last paragraph serve? What was your reaction to the writer's conclusion?

Perspectives

Michele Landsberg

As a teenager, I taught myself a trick of perspective. In moments of adolescent anxiety or gloom, I would ask myself, "One hundred years from now, will it matter whether I passed or failed a math test?" The sleight-of-mind worked. Peering down a tunnel of imaginary years seems to bathe most problems in a cool, calm light of distance.

Reprinted with permission from *Homemaker's*, October 1988: 190.

Physical distance has the same well-known and magical effect. Even the most disgruntled citizen is a patriot abroad. For the past three years, living in Manhattan, I had the pleasing luxury of two worlds—here-and-now New York, and the Canada I had temporarily left behind me and which came into brighter focus the longer I stayed away.

From my vantage point in crowded, filthy, dangerous, exciting New York, I could see for the first time that we Canadians have been selling ourselves short with clichés about our superior safety, order, cleanliness, and leafiness.

What we should be thankful for is what genuinely makes us different. We envy Americans their confidence and energy, but we forget that it sprouts from the same wealth, power, and headlong devotion to individualism that has made America dangerous in the world. They made heroes of lone cowboys and killers; we lionized red-coated Mounties and well-behaved team players.

Struggling with a smaller population, a harsher climate, and a blandly forgettable image, we Canadians formed a modest and realistic sense of our own importance. Instead of rattling swords, we set out to make colleagues of our sister countries in the Commonwealth. Today, our self-effacing generosity has made us loved and respected in the family of nations.

While Americans forged their cowboy myth into an ethic of unbridled capitalism, we tempered our respect for individual rights with a sensible impulse of mutual support. The vast majority of Canadians stubbornly insist that we continue to share, through our taxes, the cost of medical care, housing, arts and literature, and public amenities.

And though we do plenty of grousing about those burdens, they are indeed what makes us a humane and civilized country. Even as I savoured the rich stew of New York's cultural life, I nevertheless longed for the blessedly noncommercial voice of CBC radio, the security that comes from knowing that illness will not be financially ruinous, and that most of our politicians are not corrupted by ties to gigantic commercial interests.

We have another strength, too little noted. Thanksgiving is a good time to think about our threatened wealth of lakes, forests, and farmland, and to remind ourselves that it is we (though far from blameless ourselves) who are forcing the Americans to wake up to the environmental crisis.

Not much room for smugness, however. Americans may boast, but Canadians tend to belittle and begrudge. Traditionally, we've turned that belittling glance on both our neighbors and ourselves. But living "away" sharpened my perspective: I love both countries better now that I've gone and come back.

1. While the comparison is clear, the organization of this essay is much looser. What are the main points of comparison?
2. Choose either the chunk or the slice method of organization, and blueprint this essay to give it a clear structure. Which style do you prefer: the original, or the more tightly organized? Why?

3. What do you think is the intent of this essay? What reaction is Landsberg hoping to get from her audience?
4. Canadians are constantly comparing themselves to Americans. If you were to write an essay on this subject, what main points would you choose as the basis for your comparison?

EXERCISE 2

Briefly list (in point form) the characteristics of two people you know. Examine your lists and choose characteristics of each person that would make a basis for a comparison between the two. Then go back over the lists and choose characteristics that would make a basis for contrast.

EXERCISE 3

Contrast essays often turn persuasive, but they don't have to. When you are presenting a contrast, try not to be influenced by your own opinion. List the arguments on both sides of three of these controversial issues.

> gun control
> banning rodeos
> nuclear power
> euthanasia
> legalizing prostitution

EXERCISE 4

For one of the topics you worked on in Exercise 3, write an essay contrasting the views held by the two sides. Some research may be necessary, to find out exactly what the opposing arguments are and to explain those arguments to your reader.

EXERCISE 5

Write a comparison or contrast essay on one of the following subjects. Be sure to follow the guidelines for proper essay development, from selecting a subject, through managing your main points, to blueprinting your paper and writing your paragraphs.

> Cycling and driving
> Two beverages (two beers, two soft drinks, two wines, etc.)
> Gardening and marriage
> Two actors
> Two concerts
> Jogging and weight training (or rowing, or walking, etc.)

Two vacation destinations
Two bosses
Two business environments
Two careers

EXERCISE 6

Construct an essay of comparison or contrast, using one of the suggestions given below. Develop a preview statement that reflects the relationship of the two subjects. Before you begin writing, blueprint your thoughts, using either the chunk method or the slice method. Compare or contrast

Two provinces in Canada
Your spouse with the fantasy you had of a spouse before you were married
Two objects that have sentimental value for you
Two newspapers' coverage of a news event
Your life now with your life five (or ten or twenty) years ago
Full-time and part-time education
Living in an apartment and living in a house
A nurse's duties and a doctor's duties
Views of fidelity held by women and held by men
Two ways in which one of these pairs of products is advertised on television: beer and laundry soap; deodorants and diapers; candy bars and muffler repairs.

CHAPTER 15

Persuasion

In a **persuasion essay**, you go beyond simply trying to get your readers to understand your ideas and respect them. You attempt to bring your readers over to your point of view or to motivate them to take an action of some kind. For either task, thorough knowledge of your audience is necessary before you begin.

If you are trying to get your readers to agree with you, you must know (or be able to make an educated guess) what opinions they already hold, or to what degree they disagree with your views. If, for example, you want to convince your readers that urban living is more interesting than rural life, your approach will differ greatly, depending on the background, present location, and probable views of your readers. Do they love the city, hate it, or have no opinion?

If your readers are likely to disagree with your view or are known to oppose it, it is best to build your case with examples, illustrations, definitions, and the like *before* strongly stating your own opinion. Readers who are confronted early by a statement they disagree with are often less open to persuasion; instead, they are inclined to read the rest of the essay thinking of rebuttals and trying to pick holes in the arguments.

To win your readers' agreement with your point of view, you will need both an understanding of your readers and an ability to adapt your approach to them so that your essay will have the greatest possible impact. Persuading your readers to take action—to donate to a charity, lose weight, vote for the Green Party, or drink Canadian wines, for example—enlists the same knowledge and ability but may require a subtler technique. Readers who may be resistant to your views must be approached gently and convinced with facts before receiving your "pitch."

The following subjects lend themselves to development of a persuasion essay. Imagine a specific group of readers for each subject. Then decide whether you would use the direct approach (D) in your essay, because your readers are neutral or sympathetic to the argument, or the indirect approach (I), because your readers are going to be difficult to persuade.

SUBJECT	APPROACH (D or I)
Our secondary school system needs drastic reform.	_____
Buy a North American-built car.	_____
AIDS education should begin in primary school.	_____
Winter in Canada is the best time of year.	_____
The government should not restrict the distribution of pornography.	_____

You can use several techniques, in varied combinations, to persuade your readers. First, you may choose to use "facts and figures" to support your argument. Many readers are suspicious of **statistics** (usually, amounts expressed as percentages) because it's well known that they can be used to prove almost anything. If your statistics are accurate and presented fairly, however, they can be helpful in convincing your readers. When you read this chapter's sample essays, notice that the authors do not use numbers or statistics. They persuade with expression of ideas and presentation of facts. What numbers or statistics might each have included to help persuade readers? Would their inclusion have improved or cluttered the essays?

Second, you might use logic as a method of persuading, but be careful. Logical reasoning can be convincing if it is correctly presented, but it is also subject to all kinds of abuse and errors. The most common mistake is overgeneralization. "A is true; B is true; therefore C is true." Consider these examples:

> All dogs have tails; Digger is a dog; therefore Digger must have a tail.
>
> Everyone knows that hockey players are violent; Vince is a hockey player; therefore Vince must be the one who started the fight.

Which item in each set is overgeneralized?

Third, you can try to persuade your readers by citing an authority who supports your opinion. The trouble with this approach is that it's very likely that another authority, or a host of authorities, can be found to support the other side. It's also possible that the reputation and ability of your authority can be challenged, thereby weakening your "proof."

"I know it's true because I read it in *The Globe and Mail*," you say.

"But," say your opponents, *"The Globe and Mail* is a conservative newspaper and therefore an unreliable source on this issue."

"Is not," you cleverly reply.

"Is too," say your antagonists.

Your argument has been sidetracked. Instead of focusing on the issue and the validity of your case, your readers dispute the credibility of your "authority" and dismiss your argument. Choose your authorities carefully and provide ample proof that what they say can be believed.

The keys to good persuasion are to think carefully about what you are saying and to present honestly your reasons for believing it—*after* you have carefully analyzed your readers' level of knowledge, possible biases or prejudices, and degree of commitment to one side over the other. To persuade successfully, you need to be not only well organized and informative but also *tactful*, especially if your readers are likely to hold an opposing opinion.

Tips on Writing a Persuasion Essay

1. Thinking about your intended reader helps you to decide on a direct or an indirect approach for your persuasion.
2. In structuring your essay, remember that persuasion can come in several forms. Comparison/contrast or cause/effect essays can also be persuasive. Choose the organizational structure that will be most effective in persuading your readers.
3. Remember that there is another side to the argument. You can help your own cause by presenting the opposing viewpoint and refuting it.
4. For the direct approach, your preview statement should clearly present your opinion and the main points that support it.

   Example: Canada should switch immediately to full metric measurement because it is a more logical system and it is now the world standard.

   For the indirect approach, your preview statement should still state the main points you will be discussing. However, you should keep your opinion to yourself at the outset. In the course of your essay, you should win your reader over to your side.

Example: In choosing which candidates to vote for, we must consider their records, their platforms, and their characters.

EXERCISE 1

The following three essays illustrate persuasive techniques. The first is a straightforward argument; the second is quite gentle and philosophical by comparison; and the third attempts to persuade by presenting an example. Read the essays and answer the questions that follow each.

Let's Get Physical

As institutions where "education" is supposed to take place, colleges and universities are shirking their responsibility. By concentrating almost exclusively on intellectual development, they are only half educating their students. Physical development is important, too: it helps to make students healthier, happier, and even smarter. Physical education should be a significant part of every postsecondary school curriculum.

Let's acknowledge the obvious: training in physical fitness will produce healthier individuals. Cardiovascular development increases stamina for any task or activity and makes the recovery rate after exertion much shorter. It leads directly to a longer, more productive life and reduces time lost in sickness. In addition, a sound physical education includes attention to diet and promotes the elimination of harmful habits such as excessive caffeine, sugar, and nicotine intake, thereby significantly increasing the life span and productivity of the individual.

A healthier individual is a happier individual. With improved fitness comes an increased sense of well-being and enhanced self-esteem. Recreational and social activities multiply, and a more rounded and satisfying life-style commonly results from higher levels of fitness. Many people who participate in a college or university physical education program develop a lasting enthusiasm for specific games or fitness activities, such as swimming or jogging, that enhance their social, professional, and personal lives.

Healthier, happier, and—yes—smarter people are produced by good physical education. The brain, like the heart, the lungs, and the liver, is a physical organ that functions better when the entire organism is healthy. Oxygenated blood supplies the brain and removes wastes. A strong heart, healthy lungs, and unclogged veins and arteries have a direct impact on the brain's performance. Caffeine, nicotine, and other harmful substances impair the brain's ability to function, so their removal or reduction can enhance the organ's capability. A sense of confidence and well-being also helps to minimize the stresses and pressures that can have a negative effect on our ability to receive, process, and retain information.

We sometimes hear the argument (especially when budgets are tight) that educational institutions should concentrate on the development of the mind and leave development of the body up to the individual student. The division of the organism into separate compartments is not only poor zoology, it is harmful to the very process it attempts to promote: increased intellectual ability. For postsecondary institutions to ignore physical development in favour of intellectual development is to impair the health, happiness, and even the intelligence of the students whose interests they claim to serve.

1. Describe the readers whom the author of this essay has in mind. What are their attitudes, their goals, their levels of vocabulary?
2. Identify the essay's subject and main points. Draft a blueprint that the author might have used to construct the essay.
3. The author takes a very direct approach to persuasion. How might this essay have been structured if the author had wanted to be more subtle and to present the arguments before revealing a particular point of view? Draft a blueprint for such an essay.
4. The topic sentences in this essay refer to previous topic sentences each time they appear. What are the advantages of this technique?

Resisting the Revolution
David Suzuki

For years now, I have resisted the pressure to buy a personal computer. I am not mesmerized by technology, nor am I a technophobe (as proof, I have two VCRs and love my stereo system). I do admit to being intimidated by the hackers and the video parlour freaks. But having watched my secretary (I can't reveal her age lest she quit, but she is older than I and I'm almost 50) take to a word processor easily, the crunch has now come. I've rationalized my lack of interest in computers because I couldn't see a valid use for them but word processing is definitely something I now need. By the time this article is out, I am absolutely sure I'll find a portable word processor, with modem, indispensable.

One of history's remarkable lessons is the incredible seductiveness of technology. At first it's just convenient; but once we overcome initial reticence and conquer it, it becomes indispensable—it turns around and conquers us. I get annoyed as hell when my phone calls from Toronto to Vancouver don't go through right away—yet not long ago, I'd have to go through an operator and wait quite a while to make a transcontinental call. Indeed, we now take direct overseas dialing for granted. Yet in 1945, there was no transatlantic telephone cable at all; and until communications satellites went up in the '60s, there were fewer than 300 channels for all transatlantic calls. Does anyone out there remember when we had to book them days in advance?

Reprinted with permission of the author from *Science Dimensions*, vol. 17, no. 3: 30. Copyright 1985.

I was once waiting at the airport with a friend when his mother (originally an immigrant from Europe) arrived on the plane from New York. The jet had been full and the airport crowded, so it took almost an hour before her baggage arrived—and she spent the entire wait complaining bitterly about the inefficiency of the airlines. I found it amusing to think that it once took her two weeks to get from London to Montreal by boat; here she had just reached Vancouver in a 747 in six hours, yet felt enormously put out by an hour's inconvenience.

Once a technology is available, we rapidly forget what life was like before it, and simply take it as the norm. Today, we complain that amniocentesis takes up to four weeks for a diagnosis; yet twenty years ago, it wasn't possible to do any such analysis before birth. I get furious at the CBC office because our videotape machine is so "old." I can't rewind and view a tape at the same time, and it takes "so long" (meaning 15 seconds or so) to go back and forth from shot to shot. When our copier breaks down, I rant and rave without remembering all those smudged hands from ink and gels and stencils.

These technologies have transformed society beyond recognition from the one I knew as a child. My children grow up thinking of my childhood as an ancient way of life, long extinct. (Why, their dad is so old, there was no television when he was a kid!) And in spite of ourselves, we have been changed by technology in our values, in our expectations, and in the "needs" we feel.

In the summer of 1983, I spent time with the nomadic San people of the Kalahari Desert. One night, after they had slaughtered a cow we presented to them, they began to dance while we filmed the spectacle. As the camera zoomed in on a group of singers, we were astounded to find a huge, battery-driven cassette tape recorder blasting away. Where they got the machine, and how they got batteries for it, days away from the nearest settlement, is beyond me. But even they found value in its technology, thus ensuring that a chunk of their millennia-old culture will soon disappear.

We operate on simple faith that if we find any new technologies to have serious deleterious effects, we can always prohibit them. But when in history have we ever done that? Some suggest supersonic transport was scrapped because of its potential effect on the ozone layer. Nonsense! The Americans saw the enormous deficits it would pile up, and the Concorde is certainly proving them wise. Well, how about DDT? Yes, it was ultimately banned—in the industrialized countries—not so that we'd become less dependent on chemical technology, but only because there were alternative chemical pesticides. Technologies are too useful and convenient, and compel us ever onward. This leads us to depend on technological solutions to technological problems, thus assuring there will always be a price to be paid for the benefits.

And where does it all end? I am appalled at the effort that has gone into the development of embryo transplants for women. In a time when overpopulation, malnutrition, and parasitic disease cause global problems, medical science pursues non-life-threatening "problems" to satisfy desires. And once the new technology is in place, it is impossible to resist its use. Aside from the issue of whether it's a worthwhile use of medical expertise, the technology of embryo transplants has a deep impact on the very nature of biological lineage, by separating the "egg mother" from the "uterine mother" from the "social mother." Where that leads I have no idea, but it's not a trivial problem. I have watched, in horror, as parents pled for a liver to transplant into their mortally ill child—horrified at how far humans are prepared to go to fight nature, but also at the realization that were my child to develop a lethal liver condition, I would feel the same urge as those other distraught parents, now that the technology exists.

So, cognizant of and grateful for the utility of technology, I nevertheless feel that we ought to spend far more time weighing its benefits against its possible social costs. Does anyone out there agree or disagree?

1. This author does not use a precise preview statement. What, exactly, is this essay about? Write a preview statement for it.
2. Several incidents are used as examples. For each of these anecdotes, state the main point that it illustrates.
3. Comment on the tone of this essay. Describe the audience for whom you think it was intended.
4. We have seen that there are two main types of persuasion essay: one tries to convince readers to agree with the author, and the other tries to get readers to take an action. Into which of these categories does this essay fall? What is the author's purpose?

Canadians, Americans, and Football

Canadians are weird. They are impossible to understand. They claim to hate us Americans because we are domineering, arrogant, and stupid, but they want to be just like us. They ridicule our violence, but prefer our TV shows which depict it. They sneer at our politics, but know more about our political system than their own. They laugh at the way we manufacture our heroes, but worship them just the same.

Perhaps football best demonstrates this peculiarity in the Canadian psyche. Canadians are huge fans of football—*American* football. Even though they have a league that plays a distinctly Canadian brand of the game, Canadians stay away from their stadiums in multitudes, preferring to crowd around television sets to absorb the U.S. version of the game. Why? Because American football is a better game, right?

Let's suppose for a minute that the rules for the two games were reversed: Canadian football has four downs, a smaller field, and U.S. rules on kicking and scoring. American football gets the Canadian system. Here's how a Canadian would react.

"I always watch the American game. I have no interest at all in Canadian football because it's an inferior game. In the States, the three-down rule, the bigger field, and the emphasis on kicking really make football the exciting spectator sport it was meant to be.

"The four-down rule in Canadian football puts all the emphasis on a running game. Watching a 300-pound household appliance plough into the line time after time for three or four yards per carry is as exciting as watching paint dry. In the U.S. game, the ball is always in the air; there's always movement, excitement. Speed and finesse count for more than bulk in the American three-down game.

"The bigger field adds to the excitement. Broken field running is a lost art in Canada, where the small field ensures that big plays are rare. There's nothing more fun for the football fan than watching a man break free and dodge tacklers in the open field. With that little field all clogged up with massive blockers and more massive defenders, it can't happen with our Canadian game. The longer and wider field makes U.S. football spectacular.

"Finally, kicking in Canadian football is just a means of turning the ball over to the other side. I'm sure that eventually they'll do away with it altogether and just march the ball 50 yards down the field and let the other team take over from there. It's a routine, unexciting event the way it's done here with our fair-catch rule. But in the U.S., every kick is potentially a game-breaker. With no fair-catch, the Americans get to run back every kick, forcing both sides to play dramatic, dangerous football. For the fan, it's pure excitement. The Americans have kept the "foot" in "football"; in Canada, the game's beginning to look like Sumo wrestling."

I'm convinced that Canadians would react just the way I've outlined. Even when they have something clearly superior, like their football game, they covet the American model because . . . well, because it's American . . . and therefore *must* be better!

1. Describe the audience that the author had in mind. What are the characteristics of the essay's intended readers?
2. The essay begins by identifying several paradoxes in the Canadian attitude towards Americans. Why has the author begun the essay this way? Are there advantages to this beginning?
3. "Canadians, Americans, and Football" is an essay within an essay. The "umbrella" or "frame" essay is written by an American, and the "inside" essay is written by an imaginary Canadian. What is the subject of the "umbrella" essay? Identify the subject and the main points of the "inside" essay.
4. The author takes a very subtle approach to persuade the readers. Where does the author finally reveal clearly the point the essay is trying to make?
5. This essay could have taken the stance that everything Canadian is superior, as suggested in the opening paragraph. If that strategy had been followed, how would the essay have changed in its structure and support?

EXERCISE 2

Many people have firm convictions, yet few are willing to take action to uphold them. Everyone agrees, for example, that cancer should be cured, but not everyone donates to the Cancer Society. The same may be said for many other charitable causes. Choose a charitable cause in which you believe and list all the reasons why people should give money to support it. Then list all the excuses people would give for not donating.

EXERCISE 3

Write a few main points to support each of the following statements of subject. Make sure your points are persuasive.

Mandatory divorce should be enforced in cases of wifebeating.

There should be a uniform tax percentage for all citizens, regardless of their income.

Grading should be banned from higher education.

Music lyrics should be strictly monitored and censored.

The number of children in a family should be limited.

Prime-time television romances should reflect problems of real life.

Radio is a better news medium than television.

Nurses deserve higher salaries for the work they do.

The public school system should not stream its students.

Arsenio Hall is the King of Talk Shows.

EXERCISE 4

Choose a subject from the list below. Plan your preview statement, and blueprint your essay carefully. Make sure you have a strong point of view and valid reasons to support it. The statements are worded to allow a positive *or* a negative viewpoint. *Choose one side only.*

Women are (*or* are not) advancing in the workforce at an appropriate rate.

Life in the city is better (*or* worse) than life in the country.

Trial marriage is (*or* is not) a useful preparation for a legal union.

Erotic magazines are (*or* aren't) exploitive of the women who pose in them.

The attitudes of adult players have (*or* haven't) had a negative effect on junior sports players.

The greenhouse effect is (*or* is not) a serious threat to global survival.

All students should (*or* should not) be obliged to take mathematics courses in college, regardless of their program.

The government is (*or* isn't) avoiding its responsibilities to the native population.

Early childhood educators deserve (*or* don't deserve) better salaries.

Cheaters never (*or* always) prosper.

EXERCISE 5

Often, in an argument, we do not simply oppose or defend a certain point of view. Rather, we consider the degree to which a point of view can be upheld. For example, most North Americans agree that there should be a legal drinking age, but passionate debates are held to determine what that age should be. For the following subjects, a debate centres about *degree*. Choose three of the subjects, determine your own feelings, then list the reasons and evidence that you have for supporting your position.

The age at which people may buy alcohol

The age at which people are allowed to drive

The age at which people may marry

The amount of foreign ownership of Canadian business

Where smoking should (and should not) be allowed

EXERCISE 6

Expand your notes for one of the subjects in Exercise 3 into a persuasion essay. Remember to work through selecting a suitable subject, identifying, editing, and ordering your main points. Decide on an approach (direct or indirect) for your arguments, based on your analysis of your readers' opinions on the subject.

EXERCISE 7

Write a persuasion essay on a subject of your choice—one you feel strongly about. Aim your communication at a specific group of readers, and choose accordingly the approach you will take. If you don't feel strongly about anything, write about one of these subjects:

Tobacco products should be banned.

Seatbelt use should not be mandatory.

Quebec should (*or* should not) become an independent state.

Newfoundland should (*or* should not) become an independent state.

Homosexual couples should (*or* should not) be recognized as married.

Parenthood should (*or* should not) be strictly controlled and licensed, like driving.

Professional boxing should be banned.

Canadians are (*or* are not) just cold Americans.

Canada's heart lies in Saskatchewan (*or* _____).

Movies should be completely uncensored.

CHAPTER 16

Description

Description essays cover many writing applications, from the creative prose you might use to describe scenery, to the precise and concrete descriptions needed by law officers, medical staff, and emergency personnel to provide detailed reports. In all descriptive writing, the objective is to provide readers with a picture of what it was like to be there.

By learning to write good description, you will become better at all kinds of writing. Making your readers see what you have seen, even in your imagination, is the essence of communication.

Tips on Writing a Descriptive Essay

1. Engage all the senses, if possible: sight, sound, smell, touch, and taste.
2. Describe precisely, using words that create specific images. Don't say that something is "beautiful" or "impressive" or "wonderful," without telling your readers specifically how the object or event exhibited those qualities.
3. Select words with care. Never use a general word where a more specific, descriptive one could be used.

   Example: He walked towards the large figure sitting in the shadows.

   Examples, with nonspecific words replaced with descriptive ones:
   He strutted towards the large figure cowering in the shadows.
   He crept towards the large figure hulking in the shadows.
   He bounded towards the large figure poised in the shadows.
4. Choose a viewing point for your description. As the describer, you must take a position and describe what you see from that spot. Tell what is visible from left to right or from far to near, or "walk" your

readers around an object or along a defined pathway; but don't confuse them by changing your viewing point unnecessarily.

EXERCISE 1

Read the following description essays and answer the questions that follow each essay.

Diamonds Are Forever

Montreal's "Big O" and Toronto's "SkyDome" are wonderful places for loyal subjects to pay homage to baseball's royalty. We can watch the game in air-conditioned comfort, fearing neither rain nor cold, just as though we were at home viewing the proceedings on TV. While modern stadiums are fittingly lavish for highly paid major leaguers to perform their feats, baseball for most Canadians has a much different atmosphere. Many of us have in common the sights, sounds, smells, and "feel" of the dirt diamonds, grass outfields, wooden bleachers, and home-town crowds of small-time baseball.

Where I grew up, baseball meant the home-town "Star Cleaners" in their white uniforms with red trim. The infield of our diamond was hard red clay, raked over and loosened prior to game-time so that by the middle innings the players were covered in fine rust; latecomers could tell what inning it was by the degree of colour in the uniforms. A fastball would explode into the catcher's mitt in a satisfying cloud of dust, while a slide at second would sometimes be obscured from the bleacher crowd. In the early part of the season, the outfield grass was always bright green and as lush as a cemetery lawn. As the dry weather of August approached, however, brown patches would appear, until, by playoff time, the outfield was straw brown relieved by the odd green patch.

The newly mown outfield grass and, especially, the perfume of fried onions from the Lions Club snack bar behind the stands remain the most vivid scents of summer, and the *thwack!* of ball hitting leather the most exciting sound. The yelling of the home-town fans stirred excitement, and the hilarious jibes of the local wit in the back row of the bleachers brought comic relief, but the sounds on the field were what we were all there for. The smack of the bat on a well-hit ball, the umpire's guttural exclamations, the grunt of a player's effort, cries of encouragement from the players' benches: all these blended together in a happy symphony. But the slap of the ball into the leather of the first-baseman's glove, that breathless moment when so much is at stake, that's the sound that I crouched in the front row of the bleachers to hear.

Individual great plays still raise the hair on the back of my head when I recall them: "Moose" Christie catching a line drive in his bare, pitching hand; the reserve player/coach (his name now forgotten) who came off the bench in the sixteenth inning to hit a game-winning triple; my fifth-grade teacher, "Squirt" Dunsmore, striking out the side in the ninth inning; the entire, delirious game on a sunny Sunday when the "Star Cleaners" won the provincial championship. I love the Expos and adore the Blue Jays, and I live and die with them all season long. But somehow, their game is plastic, artificial, and remote beside the baseball being played on dirt diamonds by men and women who play for the love of it.

1. Sight, sound, and smell are the senses engaged in this essay. Identify specific words the author used to appeal to each of these senses.

   Sight: _____

   _____

   Sound: _____

   _____

   Smell: _____

   _____

2. What is the author's viewing point in this description?
3. This essay has elements of comparison/contrast. How do they add to the description?
4. In the introduction, the author begins with a brief description of other places before shifting to the real theme of the essay. Is this an effective way to start? Why?
5. Blueprint the essay, highlighting major and minor points.

Ode to a Café

Danielle Crittenden

There is a café in Toronto that I do not visit as much as I should since I moved from the neighbourhood. It is in an area known as The Beaches, where it has recently become impossible to buy a drink without a parasol in it. This was once a quiet district of clapboard cottages and empty stretches of sand, until the men with the pink neon and the white sportscars moved in. Now it looks something like a seaside village in drag. There are many cafés, and unless you are of a certain romantic temperament, it is unlikely you would wander into this particular one on your own. It is very small, about the size of a dry-cleaning outlet. On some days, depending upon the mood of the proprietress, only a few dishes are available.

Most prefer the café across the street, larger and more fashionable, decorated, like the rest, with black bentwood chairs and marble tables,

Reprinted with permission of the author from *The Idler*, May/June 1987.

and modern graphics on the walls. I have watched many people who go there, and it seems to be the choice of the Bohemian set. They sit by the windows wearing their berets and smoking French cigarettes, speaking of whatever is new.

Once, when my favourite café was closed, I had no choice but to eat lunch there. I listened to a couple near me discuss a significant development in art: a sculptor who coated small plywood houses with chewed bubblegum. The man was rapturous as he described the metaphysical repercussions this technique could have on the art world. The woman listened intensely, stirring her *espresso* absently many times before she finally sipped it. The waitress appeared to be an unemployed actress, because she put much theatre into taking the orders, rattling off the specials of the day like a succession of memorized lines, sighing dramatically if one took too long to decide, bringing and removing plates with great swoops and arabesques. The bill for a stale, paltry amount of food was large (including, I assume, the price of the show), and she was insistent that I pay it immediately and vacate, as she was going "off shift."

It made me realize that there are few really good cafés in this city, or any Canadian city. We are not a café society in the tradition of Europe; our eateries are efficient, productive places that use loud music to discourage lingering or prolonged discussion; staff are trained like chained bull terriers. In Paris one can rent a table for several hours for the price of a single cup of coffee, and sit there, watching the other customers in the greasy mirrors along the walls or the passers-by outside as they bustle home in the dying autumn light.

There is a photograph that I love, taken in Paris in 1950, of a couple embracing in front of an outdoor café. The two lovers and a nearby table are the only objects in focus—the rest of the world around them is blurred, a mad, monochromatic rush. To me it illustrates what a good café should be, an oasis amidst the swirling, arid winds of society. In North America, we want everything at a fast pace, and our cafés are indicative of this. They are sleek, impressive, and modern, but unwhimsical. The culture they serve is like a bland patty shaped by a production line and fried until flavourless. It sells, people eat it, but ultimately, it is fattening and unhealthy.

I had long given up on finding a European-style café in Toronto, until the day I went into the smaller place. It had a large window with "Café Natasha" painted on it in gaudy yellow, next door to a beauty salon and a gourmet candy shop. Inside were eight small tables covered in blue cloths, all taken, except for one seat at a table for four. The woman who appeared to be Natasha looked at me sympathetically, and waved her hand to the empty chair.

"Perhaps you would like that one?" she said in a dense accent, and as I opened my mouth to say "No," she was already announcing my arrival to the three diners. They looked up cheerily and waved me over, and I spent the evening with them in a conversation of some sort which was eventually lost in drink, as most good conversations are.

It took me many more trips to the café to learn about the woman who ran it. Occasionally, when she was not busy, she would sit with me by the window and smoke one of her skinny brown cigarettes and muse on the colour of the sky. On evenings when I stopped by for a glass of wine before closing, the lights would be dimmed, and the woman shimmied softly by herself to an old jazz tune.

Her age was somewhere between precocious and refined, forty, I think, but it doesn't matter. She belonged in another era: a Berlin coffee house in the 'thirties, perhaps, or a Paris dance hall during the 'twenties. She had deep red hair cut along the line of her chin, and black eyes which reflected the light, or absorbed it, depending on her mood. On a fine day she would be wearing an outrageous, colourful costume with a wide leather belt and lace-up shoes. On bad days she would dress bleakly, her hair would be rumpled, and she would smoke her dreadful cigarettes with particular ferocity. Most of the time I saw her she was between these two extremes, a lyrical creature arranging fresh flowers in a chipped, ceramic jug, or exclaiming about the seasons.

It was not her dress or the way she wore her hair that defined Natasha. Something about her reminded me of an exotic, uncatalogued species of bird, next to whom one felt flightless. When she moved, she danced, even to fetch a spoon. The music she played constantly in her café was the kind that evoked memories of other places, and other times. In the spring, it was always Vivaldi; in the hot summer, it would be the sultry pining of Billie Holiday; by autumn, red wine and Piaf; throughout winter, the blues of Bessie Smith.

Eventually, I learned that Natasha had left Yugoslavia with her husband many years ago to come to Canada. On the walls she had hung small mirrors and black and white photographs, and a few girlish sketches of people she had drawn at college in Dubrovnik. Natasha worked from eleven in the morning to eleven at night, cooking in the back and serving people out front. She offered simple food which she knew how to cook well: schnitzels and goulash, perogies and chicken soup, with thick, fresh bread. Half of the menu was available at any moment, as long as the dishwasher had not quit earlier that day, or the stove had not broken down, which happened rather frequently. At these times Natasha would be flying around the café like a startled, frantic sparrow, flapping her arms and calling out in her accented English.

Yet those who came did not do so for the food but to visit Natasha, and she developed a regular, eclectic clientèle who dropped by to drink and to talk. One pleasant gentleman would take a side table, order a carafe of wine, and sit for hours reading paperback novels. An older woman who lived alone dined every night at the café and often stayed until closing, watching the other customers benignly like an aged cat. One Eastern European fellow was there frequently, a bulky man who wore a dark jacket, steel-toed boots, and had a face like moulded concrete.

"Who is that?" I asked Natasha one day.

"Shhh," she said furtively. "KGB."

Sometimes she would stop in the middle of carrying out plates to the kitchen and gaze at her café with fond amusement. There might be an argument going on at one table, drunken outbursts of laughter from another, and two lovers in the corner watching each other as they ate.

You could easily spot the new customers. They would sit watching with uncertain grins on their faces. "You know," she would say with great pride, "this has become my private smoking and drinking club."

Mostly, though, there were conversations, hundreds of them, now scattered. We would sit with wine, and smoke and speak frivolously, which one does when one is drunk. Sometimes she would shut the café so we could dance late at night, or she would put up the closed sign so we could have privacy to drink in the afternoon. One forgot other things when around her, the world shrank until it could fit in her front window.

I left the city for several months, and when I returned, I found a flat in a different neighbourhood. When I saw her again recently, she scolded me for not coming by as often as I did when I lived near the café. I apologized, and we drank quietly, with the resigned understanding of friends who know that nothing can be done to change the circumstances. She is open less frequently now, and on some days, I have gone by and found the café dark, with a handwritten note taped to the door: "Sorry, dear friends, you are here but I am not."

I noticed that she has been sadder lately, the light catching only the shadows of her eyes. She speaks often about selling the café, opening one in Casablanca, or Havana, or Montparnasse. She knows they are all lost places, but then so are many dreams, and Natasha's café has become more of a state of mind than a place to eat. If she closes, there will be nowhere else. As we talked, I looked out the window at the café across the street. It was full.

Suddenly Natasha grasped my hand. "But my goodness, look how serious you and I have become!" she exclaimed, standing to fetch more wine. "Come, let's dance . . . ."

1. Crittenden uses contrast frequently to help her description. What points of difference does she give in comparing cafés in Europe with cafés in North America?
2. The description of Natasha is vivid on many levels; Crittenden describes her appearance, her manner, and her attitudes. How is Natasha's personality reflected in the atmosphere of her café?
3. What is the atmosphere of the café? Is the author's description effective? Does the description of the café's customers contribute to the overall picture?
4. Contrast Natasha's café with the café across the street. Why does Crittenden prefer Natasha's café?
5. What is Crittenden's purpose in this essay? Who are her intended readers?

EXERCISE 2

A list of general or nonspecific words is given below. Write at least three verbs that could replace each word listed, to provide readers with a clearer image of the activity.

look	(*Example:* stare)	_____	_____
talk	_____	_____	_____
cut	_____	_____	_____
fall	_____	_____	_____
laugh	_____	_____	_____

EXERCISE 3

For each of the verbs you provided in Exercise 2, write an effective sentence. Vary the subject content as much as possible.

EXERCISE 4

For one of the persons listed below, brainstorm until you have at least ten characteristics. Put the characteristics in order and then develop them into a good paragraph. Have a specific person in mind, not simply an abstract "character."

a class clown
a fitness instructor
your girlfriend/boyfriend, past or present
a best man at a wedding
a teacher

a grandparent
your favourite comedian
your present boss
a street runaway
a transit employee

EXERCISE 5

Choose a scenic photograph or painting that appeals to you, and write a paragraph describing in detail exactly what you see. A friend will be listening to your description over a telephone, in another city.

EXERCISE 6

To the paragraph you wrote in Exercise 5, add a paragraph that describes the sounds and smells that you might experience if you were in the scene depicted in the photograph or painting.

EXERCISE 7

Write an essay describing an interesting person you know. Remember that your objective in description is to make your subject come alive for your readers. Specific details (including mannerisms, possessions, and activities) will bring the character to life more than abstract descriptions of his or her personality, and a very detailed physical description will help to convey a clear impression.

EXERCISE 8

Write a descriptive essay about a place that is particularly memorable to you, not because a significant event occurred there, but because the place itself was interesting and unique. Try to isolate the place into a sharply defined "snapshot," rather than a "panorama." The locations listed below may remind you of a particular memory spot.

a stadium after a rock concert	a train (or bus) station
a cemetery	a junkyard
an all-night diner	a garage sale
a hospital waiting room	a highway at night
a classroom during an exam	a flea market

EXERCISE 9

We can learn a lot about people if we know what possessions they have and what activities they engage in. What might you infer about the character of a woman who writes with an engraved, gold-plated fountain pen? One who writes with a stubby pencil? Describe *one* person and convey that person's character in a paragraph that includes description of each of the following.

means of transportation	ring(s)
writing implement	lunch
favourite drink	wristwatch
favourite TV show	wallet or purse
shoes	leisure activities

CHAPTER 17

Narration

When you write a **narration essay**, you become a storyteller. Your purpose in telling a story may be to illustrate a point, persuade, or entertain, but all good storytelling follows a basic pattern. The introduction presents a thesis, an overall theme for the story. The story then unfolds, usually in chronological order, with sufficient detail and description that your readers can experience the events along with you. The conclusion brings the story to a satisfying end and reinforces the thesis.

Tips on Writing a Narration Essay

1. Blueprint your ideas, then fill in descriptive details. Blueprinting will help you to arrange your events in chronological order and to group the events appropriately. Begin each paragraph after a natural break in the narrative. Use transition terms to help the coherence of your narrative.
2. Make sure that your opening paragraph introduces the scene and major characters fully enough that your readers are not confused. In your closing paragraph, draw the strings together to leave your readers with a feeling of satisfactory closure.
3. Dialogue is a common device in narration, but use it sparingly. Traditionally, each exchange of dialogue is given a separate paragraph.
4. Don't use so much description that events are drawn out beyond their natural length; you may make your readers impatient.
5. Don't try to include too many events in a short narrative.

EXERCISE 1

Read the two narration essays that follow, and answer the questions after each essay.

The Incomplete Angler

While visiting a kind and well-meaning friend in Sarnia, I revealed myself to be an avid, if not very expert, sports fisherman. My friend confessed that he found fishing slightly less enthralling than watching algae grow in his swimming pool, but he had a pal who was a fishing fanatic. A phone call later, I was to be the special guest of "Ol' Jack" on an all-day fishing expedition to the Thames River the very next day. It has taken me four years to recover sufficiently from this adventure to tell you about it.

On the fateful day, Ol' Jack picked me up at 5:30 A.M. in his monstrous blue four-wheel-drive truck. Attached to the trailer hitch on the bed was a fourteen-foot aluminum tub with an outboard motor of adequate horsepower to push the Queen Mary. In the back of the truck about twenty fishing rods lay tangled together in a heap, together with assorted tackle boxes, coolers, paddles, and hip waders. Surmounting this mess of miscellaneous gear was a green fishing net that could comfortably have held Moby Dick. I was beginning to get a picture of the kind of fisherman Ol' Jack was.

I credit a tough constitution and my battered fishing hat for my survival during our trip to the river. Even with the protection of the hat, by the time we pulled up at the dock I was nursing a scalp wound and two goose-eggs on my skull from being tossed around the cab. Jack launched the boat, hurled the mound of fishing paraphernalia into the back, and we were off; no one was going to beat us to the "good spots." As we tore up the river, leaving a four-foot wake on either side, Jack pulled out a vodka bottle filled with an evil-looking red liquid. After taking a long swig, he handed me the bottle. "Bloody Mary," he said. "Just the thing to start the day." Gingerly, I sniffed the contents and took a tiny taste. Jack laughed as I recoiled and spat the stuff over the side. "Didn't have any tomato juice," he howled, "so I just dropped a little ketchup in the vodka!"

For the rest of the day, we thrashed up and down the river, dragging various strange devices behind us in a futile attempt to attract a fish. While Jack stood tall in the cockpit, handling throttle, wheel, fishing rod, and bottle, I huddled miserably in the stern, hoping I would not be recognized by any of the canoeists or fishermen we were swamping in our wake and sending scurrying for shore with our erratic trolling. Jack waved jauntily at the shaken fists and obscene gestures directed our way and tipped his baseball hat to those who favoured us with shouted curses.

Noon found me trying to decide whether sunburn, hunger, and exhaust fumes from the leaky outboard motor would end my misery before the inevitable collision and death by drowning or lynch-mob. I favoured whichever end would be quicker. By mid-afternoon Jack had decided we weren't using the right lures, so we swept up to several anchored boats to find out what was working. These manoeuvres added seasickness to my list of woes. When anyone admitted to having caught a fish, Jack offered to buy the successful lure on the spot. However, even with these measures, he failed to entice any fish into attaching themselves to our lines. By supper-time, even Jack was ready to admit defeat and head for the dock. I was beyond caring.

Back in Sarnia, Jack dropped me at my friend's house and roared off with the promise to pick me up the next morning at 4:30. I staggered into the house and, when the trembling stopped, told the story of the day's fun on the river. Later, as I was helped up the stairs for a hot bath and long night's sleep, I begged my friend to call Jack with the news that I had come down with bubonic plague and would be unable to join him in the morning. I haven't killed, caught, or eaten a fish since.

1. The narrative in this essay begins with the first sentence. There is not a general introduction, but the thesis is clearly implied in the first paragraph. State the thesis of the essay in a short sentence.

   _____

   _____

2. You learned in studying description essay writing that a person's possessions and actions can tell us a great deal about his or her character. List some of Ol' Jack's more significant possessions and actions and the characteristics they reveal about Ol' Jack.

   POSSESSION/ACTION   CHARACTERISTIC

   _____   _____

   _____   _____

   _____   _____

   _____   _____

   _____   _____

   _____   _____

3. This story is entertaining, but is there any moral that can be learned from the narrative? What did the author learn from his experience?
4. Who are the author's intended readers?
5. The author shows himself as the victim of this humorous escapade. What is his role? What is his purpose?

Mangiamania

Erika Ritter

It happened when I called up a friend to find out about her first date with a new man the night before.

"So how was it?"

"Terrific. We went to that new restaurant, the Italian place."

"Sounds romantic."

"No. Northern Italian, actually. The cuisine of Rome is spicier. This place has white sauces to die for and—"

"Wait a sec. What about your date?"

"Oh, he started with the *zuppa del giorno*, then moved on to—"

"No, what I'm asking is: How did the evening go?"

"Not bad. Sixty bucks for two, including wine and tip."

Click.

As I hung up the receiver, I suddenly recalled how my friend had met this new man. Over a tray of green peppercorns in a gourmet food shop. Somehow, it seemed significant.

And what also seemed significant, now that I thought about it, was the means by which three of my other friends had recently met *their* new guys. One in a cooking course titled "French Without Fear." Another while browsing through a copy of *Gourmet* magazine in a bookstore. And the third, reaching for the same package of *linguine verde* on the grocery shelf.

Click. Click. Click.

Yes, something was definitely happening here. I decided that a walk downtown would help me sort it all out.

Food, I realized, as I passed the fourth store window in a row proclaiming a sale on wine thermometers and lettuce driers, had completely taken over. The kind of enthusiasm people used to pour into collecting stamps and breeding chinchillas was now being squandered on *crème anglaise* and red lettuce.

And that wasn't all. As I stopped for a moment outside a love shop, where the red satin lips dangling in the window had a "Going Out of Business" sign pinned to them, the full horror of the situation dawned on me. The sensual thrill of erotica had been all but eclipsed by the new mangiamania.

Well, damn it all, I thought. The old libidinous order can't be allowed to just pass away. Not while there's breath in this oh-so-willing body. I squared my shoulders and, turning my back forever on lettuce driers, marched bravely into the love shop.

L'Amour français was the promising title of the video cassette I selected and carried home with me in the deepening dusk.

Ah, what a treat. Curled up in bed with a lushly smutty movie, devouring lustful images more eagerly than champagne truffles from Fauchon . . . .

The film opened with a pouty young French man picking up a pouty young French girl on a wharf in Marseilles. Exactly *how* he picked her up, however, I failed to notice, because for some reason my interest was caught by all the fish strewn on the pier. I could just imagine them pan-fried with a soupçon of butter, and some freshly crushed garlic.

By the time I pulled myself back to the story line, the pouty French couple (I didn't catch their names, I was too busy watching them nibble flaky croissants from a *pâtisserie*) were back at his place, feverishly removing their clothes.

At that point, things got pretty hot and heavy—at least, I imagine they did. Unfortunately, my attention had been totally captivated by a still-life painting over their bed, featuring a neatly peeled Seville orange, some Anjou pears, a pomegranate (out of season), and a loaf of crusty bread, sprinkled with—

Click.

Trembling and furious with myself, I snapped off the set. What on earth was happening to me?

Frantic now, I rummaged in my dresser drawer for a novel I'd picked up in the drugstore a day or two before. Ah, here it was. *First Blissful Encounter.* Now, surely a chapter or two of that was all I needed to reaffirm that what I was looking for was the food of love, not vice versa.

Trying to feel confident, I opened the book on the first page. "It all began," I read, "with a kiss from my companion." Now that, I thought, was a very routine way for an evening to begin. And did they *both* have to start with the kiss? Couldn't her companion have ordered something different?

"At first," the book went on, "his caresses seemed bland." Yes, I could imagine the kind of bland caresses her companion would serve up, seasoned without inspiration. Fondly I cast my mind back to some truly outstanding kisses I had read about, kisses of the delectable sort available in the great European capitals, where the men not only make them spicy, but also totally fresh.

"At last, he took me in his arms, tenderly, delicately." Good grief, I scoffed, you call *that* a hug? A hug should always be robust and full-bodied, and heated to such a temperature that it can completely melt any resistance that—

Oh my God. I slammed shut the covers of the book, the cold sweat pouring down my neck. Could it be that mangiamania had claimed another victim?

Striving to be calm, I padded out to the kitchen to see what I could find in the fridge. I don't know why, but I always think better with something to eat. A wedge of perfectly aged Gorgonzola, accompanied by fragrant muscat grapes, and perhaps a chilled glass of that incomparable Bordeaux that everyone is . . .

1. Humour works well in narrative. What events push forward the comic action?
2. Ritter uses "click" as a piece of comic punctuation. What purpose does it serve? Why is it effective?

3. "Mangiamania" is composed of short paragraphs. There are several reasons for this choice. What are they?
4. By the end of her narrative, Ritter is using vivid language usually associated with food to describe erotica. List six examples.
5. In the conclusion, Ritter succumbs to "mangiamania." Is this an effective ending to her narrative?

EXERCISE 2

You hear narration every day, when your friends, family, classmates, and teachers tell you about incidents that happened to them. Most of these are insignificant incidents that seemed important at the time but are soon forgotten. What makes a narrative memorable? What kinds of stories stick in your mind long after you have heard them? Why?

EXERCISE 3

Narration relies on the same principle as description: a detailed account that appeals to the senses. However, good narration adds the answer to the question, "What did it feel like to be a participant?" Imagine yourself as the central figure in a major event. Write a paragraph that will convey to your readers some of the emotion of the event. You might start with "As I walked from the on-deck circle towards the plate . . ." or "The director motioned for action, and I moved forward into the arms of Richard Gere . . . ."

EXERCISE 4

Using the same incident that you created in Exercise 3, write the narration as it might have been seen and felt by a minor participant, perhaps the batboy in the first example, or a lighting technician in the second.

EXERCISE 5

In good narration, the story told is often used as an example to illustrate a theme or point of view. Briefly blueprint a story you might tell from personal experience to demonstrate one of the following themes.

loneliness	overcoming great odds
friendship	loss
panic	jealousy
peer pressure	a close call
victory	obsession

EXERCISE 6

Using the blueprint from Exercise 5, write a narrative essay. Remember that good stories are carefully planned and structured; poor ones are often the products of writers who begin at the top of the page and stumble downward until the story comes to an end.

EXERCISE 7

Embarrassing incidents often make good narratives, both because most are entertaining and because listeners and readers can often learn a lesson from the embarrassing mistakes of others. Briefly rough out, in point form, a narrative of the most embarrassing thing that has ever happened to you. This may make a good essay when you are assigned a narrative to write. It might also be good therapy!

EXERCISE 8

Narrate the plot of a movie that you enjoyed and remember clearly. Give important details, beyond the simple facts of the story. Try to make the experience of reading your essay as vivid and interesting as viewing the movie itself.

EXERCISE 9

Your life is full of experiences that you share with many others: your first day at school, your first day at work, your wedding day, a memorable vacation, and so on. However, no two of these narrative experiences are the same; each person has a unique version. Below is a list of "first" or "last" or "only" experiences. Only *you* can narrate how yours happened. Plan and develop *one* of these events into a full essay. Remember to focus on a limited length of time and give most attention to highlights.

a speeding ticket	a surprise birthday party
my first car purchase	my first time skiing (or another sport)
my first love affair	moving day
the last day on a job	betrayal by a friend
the birth of a child	my first speech

Revising the Essay

CHAPTER 18

Reworking the Early Draft

Revision is the process of "re-seeing" your essay, or checking it to make sure you have said what you want to say in a way that will enable your readers to understand your message clearly and to receive it favourably. These two goals, *clear understanding* and *favourable reception,* are at the heart of good communication. Your work during the revision stage is to ensure that both goals are met. You can accomplish this aim only if you revise from your readers' perspective. By playing the role of the intended reader of your essay, you can avoid misunderstandings before they happen.

Your grammar, spelling, punctuation, and neatness have an impact not only on your readers' understanding but also on your readers' impression of you. Mistakes and messiness can lead to unclear meanings, and they will certainly lower your readers' opinion of you and your work. In a letter of application, an appeal for funds, a business proposal—to name just a few examples—irritants such as spelling errors, sentence fragments, or even misused apostrophes can be disastrous.

The aim of revising is to improve your writing's organization, accuracy, and style.

Begin your revision by asking yourself these questions:

1. Are there any gaps or logical inconsistencies?
2. Have I kept my audience in mind?
3. Have I done what I said I would do in my preview statement?

Your blueprint is the best place to begin checking for completeness and consistency. Keep your blueprint close at hand and change it, if necessary, as you revise your essay. Nothing is sacred. If your essay can be improved by shifting parts of it around at this stage, go for it!

Your preview statement is the guiding principle of your essay. It is your contract with your readers. There should be nothing in the preview statement that is not expanded on and developed in the body of the essay. Be sure that all the terms of your contract have been fulfilled.

The next step in the revision process is a check to make sure you have included all the major elements of an essay. Turn to Chapter 5, "Drafting the Blueprint," and match your essay against the model blueprint on page 58. Does your essay contain everything that's noted there?

Now review your draft in terms of the questions below. If you have omitted any of these considerations, you will need to include them in your revision.

Audience

Have you a clear idea of who your readers are?

- How much do they know?
- What is their attitude towards your subject?
- What are their needs in relation to the subject?

Your role

- What is your purpose in this essay?
- What is your attitude towards the subject?

Language and tone

- Is your level of language appropriate both to your subject and to your audience?
- Is your tone courteous, reasonable, and consistent?

Subject

Have you refined your subject?

- Is it significant? Does it avoid the trivial or the tedious?
- Is it single? Does it avoid double or combined subjects?
- Is it specific? Is it focused and precise?
- Is it supportable? Were you able to provide enough varied evidence to make your meaning clear and convincing?

Main points

Have you refined your main points?

- Are they significant? Have you deleted any trivial points?
- Are they distinct? Do any points overlap in content?
- Are they relevant? Do all points relate directly to the subject?

Have you chosen the best order for your main points?

- If they are ordered chronologically, are they presented in order of time sequence?
- If they are presented in climactic order, have you presented the most important point last?
- If your points are logically linked, is there a clear logical progression or cause–effect connection between them?
- If your points are ordered randomly, are all of equal weight and is each logically independent of the others?

Are your main points expressed in grammatically parallel form?

Have you joined your statement of subject together with your main points to form a clear and comprehensive preview statement?

When you have considered these questions, you have completed the first step in the revision process: you have covered the "large issues" of content, structure, and organization.

CHAPTER 19

Polishing the Later Draft

In this stage of the revision process, you will examine your introduction, body, and conclusion. You will look closely at the construction of each paragraph and review its content for unity and coherence. Don't be overly concerned at this stage about spelling, punctuation, or grammatical errors. These will be considered in the final editing and proofreading stage, which is described in the next chapter.

You should allow at least a couple of days—a week would be better—between your first revision and your second. Enough time must elapse to allow you to approach your essay as if you were seeing it for the first time. Use this list of questions to help you revise and improve this next-to-last draft.

Introduction

Grabber

Is your grabber appropriate for your subject?

Is it appropriate for your intended audience? (Or will it turn them off or confuse them?)

Does it employ one of these techniques:
- Is it a memorable quotation?
- Is it a thought-provoking statement or question?
- Is it a statement stressing your subject's significance?
- Is it a general statement indicating the context and scope of your subject?

- Is it an opinion you are challenging?
- Is it a definition?
- Is it an anecdote or account of an interesting incident?

Preview statement

Is your preview statement clearly identifiable?

Does it consist of a clear statement of subject and main points?

Is it in the most appropriate position in your paragraph (usually, at the end)? If not, should it be moved?

Body paragraphs

Topic sentence

- Does each paragraph have an identifiable topic sentence?
- Does each topic sentence expand upon a main point from the preview statement?
- Is each topic sentence the first or second sentence of the paragraph? If not, should it be moved?

Supporting sentences

- Do all sentences in the paragraph clearly and directly relate to the topic sentence?
- Do the supporting sentences represent a variety of evidence?
  series of steps or stages   quotation or paraphrase
  definition   comparison or contrast
  examples   specific details

Unity

- Do all sentences in the paragraph relate clearly and directly to the topic sentence?
- Have you avoided repetition or redundancy?
- Is each sentence in the best position in relation to other sentences to ensure clear meaning?
- Does each sentence flow naturally into the next?

Transitions

Does each paragraph employ transitions as necessary?

- to show a time relationship (first, next, finally)
- to add an idea or example (furthermore, for example)
- to show contrast (however, on the other hand)
- to show cause and effect (therefore, as a result)
- to emphasize or repeat (in fact, in other words)
- to summarize or conclude (in brief, in conclusion)

Conclusion

Summary

Have you included a brief summary of your main points?

Have you restated your points in fresh language to avoid word-for-word repetition?

Is the summary statement in the best position—at the beginning of the concluding paragraph? If not, should it be moved?

Clincher

Does your conclusion contain a clincher?

Is the clincher appropriate to what has preceded it?

Is the clincher appropriate to the intended audience?

Have you used one of the following clincher techniques?

- a thought-provoking quotation
- a solution to a problem presented by the essay
- a thoughtful question
- a statement indicating the significance of your subject
- a statement echoing one made in the introduction
- a suggestion for change or a prediction

CHAPTER 20

Editing and Proofreading

At long last you've reached the final stages in the writing process: editing—correcting any errors in grammar, sentence structure, and mechanics (spelling and punctuation)—and proofreading—correcting any errors in typing or writing that appear in the final draft. It is especially important at this stage that you allow some time to elapse between your latest revision and this final step. Ideally, you should wait two or three days between your "last" draft and your final edit. Otherwise, you will read what you *think* you've written, the words that are still fresh in your mind, not what you've actually written, the words that appear on the page.

Here are the questions you should ask yourself when you are reading through your "final" draft.

Sentence structure

Are there any fragments?

Are there run-ons or comma splices?

Are there any misplaced or dangling modifiers?

Are all lists (whether words, phrases, or clauses) expressed in parallel form?

Grammar

Do all verbs agree with their subjects?

Do all pronouns agree with their antecedents?

Have any vague pronoun references been clarified?

Are there any confusing shifts in verb tense within a paragraph?

Are there any confusing shifts in number or person within a paragraph?

Words

Spelling

Are all words spelled correctly?

Have you used the appropriate spelling of words that sound or look alike?

Have you used capital letters where they are needed?

Have you used apostrophes correctly for possessives (and omitted them from plurals)?

Usage

Have you eliminated clichés, jargon, and slang?

Have you eliminated redundant (or unnecessary) words?

Have you corrected any "abusages"?

Punctuation

Within sentences
- Have you used commas where needed for clarity and unity?
- Have you deleted commas where they have no purpose?
- Have you used colons and semicolons where appropriate?
- Have you used parentheses and dashes where appropriate?

Beginnings and endings
- Does each sentence begin with a capital letter?
- Are introductory words (Similarly, Besides, However,) followed by commas?
- Do all questions have question marks?
- Are quotation marks correctly placed?

Tips for Effective Proofreading

1. Read each sentence of your essay carefully. You can choose to do this either line by line, using a ruler to cover the next sentence, or sentence by sentence, starting at the last sentence of the essay and working forward to the first. This technique will help you focus on each sentence as a discrete unit, and will help you identify run-ons or sentence fragments.

2. Read your essay aloud. Imagine that you are presenting it as a speech to your audience of intended readers. Make a check or other mark beside any paragraph or sentence that is inappropriate to your listeners.
3. If you've been keeping a list of your most frequent errors in this course, you can do a scan of your essay looking specifically for the errors you know you are most likely to commit.
4. Using the Editing Checklist on the inside back cover of this book, make a final check of all aspects of your writing.

Your "last" draft may need extensive revision after your editing and proofreading review. If this is the case, take the time to rewrite the paper so that the version you hand in is clean and easy to read. (If a word processor is available to you, proofreading will be easy and quick, and you will be assured of a clean copy with minimal effort.)
DON'T FORGET TO KEEP A COPY FOR YOUR FILES.
Your communication is judged by your readers on three counts: what you say, how you say it, and how you present it. Each is important in getting from your readers the response you want. Whether you're writing an application letter, a love letter, or an interoffice memo, you and your message will be evaluated and rated on the appearance and style as well as on the contents of your message.

The Research Paper

CHAPTER 21

Writing a Research Paper

When you write a short essay, you can often rely on what you already know about a subject to generate the main points and supporting detail your readers need to understand your message. When the subject of the essay is unfamiliar or complex, however, or when you want to make your argument more convincing, you will need to do some research.

Writing a research paper is not usually a more difficult task than writing an essay, but it *is* more time-consuming. Remember that it takes longer, and plan your time accordingly. The major difference between the two is that a research paper includes **source material**—information taken from other writers—to support a discussion. Think of the options you'd have if you were asked to give a speech on a subject. You could stand up there and talk all by yourself—the verbal equivalent of an essay—or you could gather together a panel of experts and act as the moderator of the panel by leading the discussion. A research paper is comparable to a panel discussion.

You can't just gather your panel of experts together and then excuse yourself and go home. The research paper isn't simply a collection of what other people have had to say on the topic. It is your responsibility to shape and control the discussion, make sure that what the experts add is both interesting and relevant, and make observations and comments on the validity or significance of their remarks. It's *your* paper, *your* subject, *your* main points; the quotations and ideas you include from your sources should give valid support for *your* topic sentences.

A research paper gives you the advantage of not having to face your readers alone, but it creates the problem of clearly separating your ideas from those you took from your sources. Readers can't hear the different "speakers" when ideas are put on paper; you have to clearly show who "said" what. To separate your sources from one another and from your own ideas, research papers require **documentation**—a system of acknowledging your sources. Your documentation will give your readers a guide to the sources of the information contained in your research paper—a play-by-play of who is "speaking."

You may prefer writing research papers instead of essays. You may find it easier to develop an argument when you can use source material, and more interesting to have the chance to discover and use new information than to discuss what you already know. As a bonus, the research skills you develop while doing research-paper assignments will be useful when you want to do research for your own interests or to solve an on-the-job problem.

Generally, research papers are longer than essays. Therefore, the time you are allowed to complete a research assignment is usually longer than the time you are given to complete an essay. This extra time can work to your advantage. In addition to being able to find material that makes what you say about your subject more interesting and credible, you have more time to polish your writing. A research paper allows you to demonstrate both your research skills and your writing skills. This winning combination is a "fast track" to good grades.

Tips on Writing a Research Paper

1. Manage your time carefully. You need to allow yourself time to complete both the research and the writing stages of the paper.
2. Divide the work into a number of smaller tasks, and work according to a schedule. Last-minute cramming may give you an "adrenalin rush," but it does not produce a well-written paper.
3. Clearly define your subject before beginning your research.
4. Find out where to locate appropriate information.
5. Incorporate your information into your paper as smoothly as you can.
6. Write your research paper as clearly and correctly as you would write any other essay. Without careful attention to your writing skills, your effort will be wasted, not rewarded.

CHAPTER 22

Researching Your Subject

Your first step in writing a research paper is the same as your first step in any writing task: select a suitable subject. Whether you choose your own subject or are assigned one for your paper, don't rush off to the library right away. Take a little time to think about your subject carefully. If it has been assigned and you're not sure what the instructor expects, clarify what is required of you.

Check your subject with the 4-S test: is it significant, single, specific, and supportable? If not, refine it by using the techniques discussed in Chapter 2.

Next, consider the best approach to take in presenting your subject. Does it lend itself to a comparison? Process? Cause or effect? Deciding up front what kind of paper you're going to write will save you hours of time, both in the library and at your writing desk.

When you're sure your subject is appropriate and you've decided, at least tentatively, on the approach you're going to take, you've already begun to focus on the kind of information you're going to look for in your research. For example, if the subject is "Word processing programs make writing easier," you don't need to discuss the history of computers, computer crime, or the best accounting programs. You can focus your research in areas that will be relevant to your specific subject.

Once you have an idea of the information you will need to help develop your subject, it's time to find the best information you can. There are many places to find information, but the library is the most obvious place to begin.

Using the Library

Does your library intimidate you because you don't know how to find quickly the information you need? Your library will be less overwhelming when you realize that all of its contents are organized and classified to simplify finding specific information. All you need to do is figure out the organizational system your library uses, and you'll have the key that unlocks the information gates.

Books

The books in libraries are catalogued by subject, title, and author. This system gives you three different ways to track down a specific book. The library may have its catalogue on cards in file drawers, on microfiche, or on computers. No matter how the information is stored, the catalogue headings will be the same.

You could begin your search by looking under a subject heading, such as "Computers." Or, if you know the title of the book you want, you can go directly to the title headings and look up the title—*Computer Wimp*, for example—and find where the book is located in the library by using the call number given. If you know that John Bear wrote a book on computers, but you aren't sure of the title, you can look under the author headings to find "Bear, John."

Books are arranged on library shelves in a sequence of call numbers. The call numbers that catalogue the subject of each book originate from the numbers assigned under the U.S. Library of Congress classification system. (Some small libraries still use the Dewey decimal system of classification, but most college and university libraries follow the Library of Congress system.)

When you arrive in a new library, look for a map showing where the various categories of books are located. When you have noted from the catalogue files the call numbers of the books you want, use the map to find the shelves where the books are stored.

Periodicals

Your library's collections of **periodicals**—journals, magazines, and reviews—may contain useful articles on the subject you are researching. In fact, articles may be more useful than books because they are more recent and up to date. To find the specific articles you need, use the periodical indexes; these list articles according to subject, author, and title.

There are many different indexes to journal and magazine articles. The most comprehensive index is the *Readers' Guide to Periodical Literature*, which lists most of the popular magazines. Other general indexes include the *Canadian Periodical Index* and the *New York Times Index*. Specialized areas have their own indexes, such as the *Social Sciences Index, Applied Science and Technology Index, Art Index, Business Periodicals Index, Canadian News Index, Education Index, Humanities Index,* and *Music Index*. Once you've found the listings for the articles you want, check to see whether the library subscribes to the magazines or journals that published the articles. A list of the periodicals held in the library is often posted in the section where the indexes are shelved.

Encyclopedias

Another useful source of *general* information on a topic is an encyclopedia. There are many different types of encyclopedias. Some of the general ones include *The Canadian Encyclopedia, Collier's Encyclopedia, Encyclopedia Americana,* and *Encyclopaedia Britannica*. Specialized encyclopedias include the *Encyclopedia of Music in Canada, Encyclopedia of World Art, International Encyclopedia of Social Sciences,* and *Encyclopedia of Computers and Data Processing*. An encyclopedia article on your topic may give you a good overview and a bibliography to guide you to further reading. Encyclopedias do *not* contain current, up-to-the-minute information, however.

Other Sources

Your library may have a vertical file that contains newspaper clippings, short articles, and brochures related to your topic. This material *is* current. The vertical file cabinet will have information listed according to general subject categories. A list of the categories is usually kept near the file.

Finally, don't overlook the possibility of finding information from the audio-visual materials held in the library—video tapes, films, records, or slide presentations. Check the catalogue for these items.

The library is not the only source of information you can use. Interviews with people who are familiar with your subject are good sources because they provide a personal view and they ensure that your paper will contain information not found in any other paper the instructor will read. Other forms of research, such as surveys and questionnaires that you design and distribute, can add interesting information as well. This type of research is time-consuming and requires knowledge of survey design and interpretation, but it has the advantage of being original, unique, and current.

Selecting the Best Information

After you have gathered all the information you think you will need for your paper, the next step is to assess the quality of your information. If you have done your research thoroughly, you will have discovered much more about the subject than will be usable in your paper. It's time to analyze the information and select your best and most relevant material.

To test your information for usefulness, you must ask three questions.

> 1. Is the information relevant to the topic?

Sometimes, when you are researching, you can get sidetracked by information that is interesting but not relevant. Don't let this information distract you from your topic; focus on the information that supports your subject directly.

> 2. Is the information up to date?

Whether you need current information depends on the subject itself. If you are researching a field of knowledge that is changing quickly, then you need the most recent information available. For example, if you are writing a paper on computers, material from the 1950s would be useful only to give a historical perspective; it would have no place in a discussion of current computer technology.

Your most up-to-date information will come from your own research—the surveys or interviews you conduct yourself. Your next most up-to-date source of information is periodicals. To check for currency, look at the date an article was published. Generally, the more recent the publication date, the more current the source of the information. The time between the writing of an article and its publication in a periodical is shorter than it is for books. Even recently published books may contain information that is out of date by the time the books are released.

> 3. Is the information from a reliable source?

Some sources of information affect the credibility of what is said. For example, most readers trust information taken from a city newspaper more than they trust the information in a tabloid such as *The National Enquirer*. When you need reliable information, use sources that represent the recognized experts in the field.

Taking Good Research Notes

As you do your research, remember that it is critical to identify the exact source of each piece of information or quotation. Good research notes will help you to keep track of the different ideas you find for your paper and the data that identify your sources. In addition to the information your source yields about your subject, you will need information about the source itself. For each published source that you will use in your paper, you will need to know

- the title and edition
- the author and/or editor
- the publisher, the place of publication, and the date of publication
- the volume number of the journal or magazine
- the page(s) from which the quotation (or your paraphrase or summary) was taken.

Some researchers keep every different piece of information on a separate index card; they include all of the information needed for the documentation. Other writers keep their notes on sheets of paper, clearly separating their own ideas from the ideas and words taken from sources. Using different colours of ink will help you to distinguish at a glance your words and ideas and those from a book or article. Technology has improved the way notes can be kept. Computers allow researchers to separate information through the creation of a data base, and photocopiers, usually available in libraries, allow researchers to copy relevant pages of sources for later use. *Whatever system you use, it is very important to separate clearly one source from another and to keep track of the documentation information.* A little time spent on this step will save you hours of frustrating backtracking later on.

Avoiding Plagiarism

If you don't take clear and complete research notes, you'll easily get one source confused with another. The result of this confusion could be inaccurate documentation in your final paper. You must **credit** your sources; that is, you need to identify them for your readers. (The next chapter will show you, in detail, how to document your sources of information.) If you don't give adequate credit to the source of your information, your readers can become confused and may assume that everything in the paper is based on your own ideas. Readers who are confused about your sources may challenge you to identify where your information originated. If your readers are led to believe that all the ideas are yours and then find out that the ideas came from somewhere else, they may feel as though you have tried to deceive them. Whether you have deliberately or naively left your sources unidentified, the result is called plagiarism.

Plagiarism is a very serious offence. When committed by college students, the penalty varies from school to school, but it is usually severe. **Plagiarism** *means taking someone else's words or ideas without giving credit to the author of those words or ideas. Even if you paraphrase the original words or ideas, it is still considered plagiarism unless you identify your source.*

Intentionally trying to pass off someone else's work as your own is a form of cheating. Doing it unintentionally is unacceptably sloppy. What makes your paper unique is your interpretation of your research in relation to your subject. Your readers want to know not only what information you've found but also what you think of it and how you interpret it. It's *your* paper, after all. Here's how you can avoid plagiarism.

---

1. Keep good research notes.

Keep track of the documentation information you'll need for every idea or passage you take from your sources. As you are researching, ideas or interpretations that are not covered in the source material may occur to you. Note these ideas as your own, so that you can use them in the paper as well.

---

2. Organize your paper carefully.

If your paper is merely a collection of ideas from sources, it won't convey a clear message to your readers. Develop a good blueprint before you begin to write, and make sure that your source material is *supporting* your main points, not substituting for them.

> 3. Acknowledge all of your sources.

If you know where you got a fact or piece of information, give the source—even if you think the information is common knowledge. It's safer to give the source than it is to assume that "everybody knows that." Statistics should always have references because, as you know, the significance of numbers tends to change, depending on who is using them or who gathered the data.

> 4. If in doubt, ask your instructor.

If you aren't sure what to document, take your research notes and your blueprint for your paper to your instructor and ask. It's better to ask before the essay is submitted than to try to explain a problem after the paper is graded. Asking also saves you time.

CHAPTER 23

Documenting Your Research

As we have seen, in a research paper or report you bring together information on a subject from several different sources. You interpret it, organize it, and work it into a coherent presentation, part of which is your own and part of which is taken from your sources. Whether you are **quoting** (using the author's exact words), **paraphrasing** (putting the author's words into your own words), or **summarizing** (condensing the author's main idea and putting it into your own words), you must acknowledge your sources to let your readers know exactly where you found your quotations and any borrowed ideas. Acknowledging your sources is called **documentation.**

When you give credit to your sources within your research paper, you need to follow a system of documentation. There are many different systems of documentation, but one of the most widely used is the Modern Language Association (MLA) system. Most instructors in English and the humanities will expect your papers to conform to the principles of format and documentation that are outlined in this chapter. If you are assigned a paper in the social sciences, you may be expected to use the *Publication Manual of the American Psychological Association* (3rd ed.) (APA style). For research essays in the biological sciences, your teacher may insist on the format in the *CBE* [Council of Biology Editors] *Style Manual: A Guide for Authors, Editors, and Publishers in the Biological Sciences* (CBE style).

If you learn the principles set forth in the following pages, which conform to the style recommended by the Modern Language Association (MLA style), you will be able to convert the format of your documentation to that of other systems with little difficulty. The manuals containing these other systems are available in college and university libraries and most bookstores.

Acknowledging Your Sources

Whenever you include information from a source in your writing, you need to identify (in parentheses) that source within your paper. You also need to list that source among your "Works Cited" or "Works Consulted" at the end of your paper. The way the information is given in both the parenthetical reference and in the Works Cited is determined by the MLA (or another) style, and the style—including the order of information, capitalization, and punctuation—must be followed exactly. Not all sources are the same, and there is a specific format for every type of source you might need to use for your paper. Examples of the most common types of citations are given in this chapter; for more information, consult Joseph Gibaldi and Walter S. Achtert, *MLA Handbook for Writers of Research Papers*. 3rd ed. New York: Modern Language Association, 1988.

Using References within Your Paper

Quotations, summaries, and paraphrases should be woven smoothly into your paper, not just strung together without commentary. Use your own introduction to a quotation to tie the source material to your discussion, and follow the quotation with an observation about its significance, as in this example:

```
Word processing programs make writing easier by allowing

mistakes to be corrected instantly: "When a writer isn't worried

about spoiling a page, it is possible to try ideas and see how

they look before deciding to keep the text" (Smith 3). Reducing

anxiety makes writing a more pleasant experience and also

improves the quality of the writing. Writers are free to

experiment with sentences and keep the best of what they produce.
```

Your quotations should be similarly introduced and discussed. Putting quotations in a context of your own will create coherence within your research papers.

If you are using a short quotation, put quotation marks around the words from the source and give the parenthetical reference after the quotation marks but before the final period, as in this example:

```
"Computers are essential to increasing productivity and

improving recordkeeping systems" (Wood 12).
```

If your quotation is longer than four typed lines, indent it ten spaces from the left margin. When you indent a quotation, quotation marks are not used, as here:

```
Wood observes that

    Computers are essential to increasing productivity and

    improving recordkeeping systems. When the initial cost of

    the system is measured against the benefits of improved

    efficiency, computers are not a luxury in the modern office.

    Computers are vital to the success of the organization. (12)
```

You don't always have to use a direct quotation from your source. You can summarize a paragraph or an entire book by using your own words to give the ideas. However, when you summarize, you must still identify the original source. Consider this example:

```
In Computer Crime, J. B. Shaw describes the problems computers

create for security. He explains that, despite the complex

system of passwords and codes, computers are still susceptible

to criminal activity.
```

You'll notice that the summary does not require a page reference. Page references are given only for direct quotations.

Citing Parenthetically within Your Paper

Every time you use information from a source that is not identified within your paragraph, you must identify it in parentheses immediately following the sentence or paragraph containing the information. (In the past, footnotes were used to identify the sources within a paper. Now, footnotes are used only to give additional explanation of a term or idea.) The parenthetical reference gives your readers only enough information to find the full listing of the source in your Works Cited or Works Consulted list.

Use parenthetical references to identify the sources of all quotations, paraphrases, summaries, facts, and ideas you have found in your research and used in your paper. Your references should be clear, accurate, and as brief as possible. Normally, the author's surname and the exact page number(s) are all you need.

As a general rule, you need to include a piece of source information only once; don't repeat information unnecessarily. For example, if you've already mentioned the author's name in your paragraph, you need give only the page reference in your parentheses.

An excerpt from a research paper is reproduced below. Notice how the writer uses quotations and summary to introduce the results of the research. The excerpt shows you the correct way to *leave out* a word or words from a passage you're quoting, using **ellipses** (. . .), and how to *add* a word or words to a quotation for readability, using square brackets [around the words you add].

Between 1980 and 1982, unemployment rates in Canada rose by almost 50 per cent. The people hardest hit by this phenomenal increase were the "chronically unemployed, [those who] experience frequent bouts of unemployment of relatively long durations" (Shaw 144). Six separate groups, distinguished from each other and from the working population by factors such as occupation, sex, age, geographic location, ethnic origin, and level of education make up the chronically unemployed in our society (Shaw 143-44).

Workers in primary industries such as fishing, logging, or construction suffer unemployment more often and for longer periods than people in managerial, clerical, or sales jobs:

In 1982 unemployment rates ranged from 3.7 percent for managers and administrators to 8-9 percent for sales and clerical workers and 12.6 percent for service workers. This compares to 19 percent for construction workers and 32 percent for workers in forestry and logging. ("Selected Indicators" 134)

In A Longitudinal Analysis of the Canadian Labour Market, Robertson reported that periods of unemployment for primary industry workers last, on average, more than twice as long as

```
the periods of unemployment experienced by managers or

professionals (10).

    Of all the chronically unemployed, women with dependent

children suffer the greatest financial burden. In 1982, there

were approximately 67,000 unemployed women living in households

in which no one had a job. Of these, "about 57 per cent

maintain[ed] the family . . . as single, separated, divorced, or

widowed family heads" (Shaw 150).
```

Study the way the writer of this excerpt has used parenthetical references to identify information sources. The introductory paragraph contains a short quotation and a summary. For both, a parenthetical reference identifies the author of the article from which the information was taken (because the author's name does not appear in the paragraph) and shows the page or pages on which it was found. For complete information about the article, readers would turn to the Works Cited list at the end of the paper. Under "Shaw," listed in alphabetical order, should be a standard entry for a periodical article. The entry would include the author's full name, the title of the article, the name of the journal, the publication date, and inclusive page numbers for the whole article:

```
    Shaw, R. Paul. "The Burden of Unemployment in Canada." Canadian

        Public Policy/Analyse de Politiques 11.2 (1985): 143-60.
```

In the second paragraph, the writer includes a long quotation. ("Long" usually means longer than four typed lines.) The parenthetical reference includes the shortened title of an **unsigned article**—no author is identified in the source—and the page on which the quotation was found. Complete information about the source would appear in the end-of-paper alphabetical list, under "Selected Indicators":

```
    "Selected Indicators of Unemployment by Occupation." The Labour

        Force. Dec. 1982: 130-34.
```

In the third paragraph, the writer's parenthetical reference gives only the page on which the information was found, because the author and title are included in the paragraph. Complete information about the source would appear in the alphabetical list of Works Cited or Works Consulted, under "Robertson":

```
    Robertson, M. J. A Longitudinal Analysis of the Canadian Labour

        Market. Ottawa: Canadian Employment and Immigration

        Commission, 1982.
```

Sample Parenthetical References

Here are some typical examples of parenthetical references. Titles of whole publications (books, magazines, pamphlets, and similar entities) are underlined (printed in *italics*); titles of parts of publications (single chapters, articles, essays, poems, and so on) are placed in quotation marks.

1. Simple page reference, with the author's name given in your paragraph:

   ```
   Leo Panitch says that Canadians are deeply entrenched in the
   American empire "as their hewers of wood, drawers of water and
   drillers for oil" (14).
   ```

2. Identification of author, with the author's name not given in your paragraph:

   ```
   ". . . only a perspective which . . . recognizes the rights of
   Palestinians to demand and secure for themselves an escape from
   homelessness on a substantial part of their own land and in
   their own state and with equal prerogatives and obligations can
   help to avoid the mutual tragedy that is engulfing both peoples"
   (Panitch 35).
   ```

3. Identification of one of several titles by the same author, with the author's name given in your paragraph:

   ```
   Pierre Berton suggests a unique approach to divorce: "The ritual
   . . . should be held in a church and it ought to be presided over,
   whenever possible, by the same minister who forged the original
   bonds of matrimony" ("A Modest Proposal" 73).
   ```

   Whenever you are quoting from more than one article by the same author, you must give the title as well as the page reference, to let your readers know from which article the quotation was taken.

4. Identification of author and of one of several titles by the same author:

   ```
   The entire ceremony is turned around in order to poke fun at both
   marriage and divorce; the little people on the divorce cake are
   "facing resolutely away from each other" (Berton, "A Modest
   Proposal" 74).
   ```

When you refer in your paper to several articles or books by the same writer, your parenthetical reference for each quotation or summary should identify the author and include the title as well as the page reference, so your readers know which work is your source.

5. Reference to one of several volumes:

   ```
   Only once in his two-volume work does Erickson suggest
   conspiracy (2: 184).
   ```

   The number before the colon identifies the volume and the number(s) after the colon identify the page(s) you are referring to.

6. References to a literary classic or to the Bible:

   ```
   In Shakespeare's play, the duke's threat to give "measure for
   measure" (5.1.414) echoes the familiar passage in the Bible
   (Matthew 7.1-2).
   ```

   Use Arabic numerals separated by periods for act, scene, and line from a play, or to identify a biblical chapter and verse.

The List of Works Cited or Works Consulted

The final page in your research paper will be a list of **Works Cited** (only those sources from which you have quoted in your paper) or of **Works Consulted** (all the sources you found useful in preparing your paper). The list, together with the parenthetical references within your paper, provides your readers with all of the necessary information about the sources you used in preparing your paper: who wrote them, who published them, where and when they were published. *By acknowledging and crediting your sources in these ways, you avoid plagiarism.*

Your final list of Works Cited or Works Consulted should be arranged alphabetically. Each item in this list gives your readers answers to the following questions:

For Books, Pamphlets, and Government Publications
Who wrote (or edited) it?
What is the full title?
What edition was used (if relevant)?
Where was it published?
Who was the publisher?
When was it published?

For Articles
Who wrote it?
What is the full title?
What is the name of the periodical it appeared in?
What is the volume number of the periodical (if applicable)?
When was it published?
On what page(s) does the article appear?

In a list of Works Consulted, you may also wish to include information obtained from a lecture, a film, a TV show, or another nonprint source. The information required in these entries varies considerably, depending on the type of source you are documenting. Examples are provided below.

Once you have sorted your sources into alphabetical order (if there is no author, use the first word of the title—excluding *A*, *An*, and *The* —to alphabetize an entry), you are ready to confirm that all necessary information has been gathered and is listed in the proper style. Centre your heading, Works Consulted or Works Cited, double space throughout the list and indent the second and subsequent lines of each entry. The following examples will guide you in listing different types of sources.

Books, Pamphlets, and Government Publications

1. Book by one author:

   Barnard, Sandie. Speaking Our Minds. Scarborough, Ontario:
   Prentice-Hall, 1990.

   Note that the publisher is usually identified by a short form of the company's full name: for example, Holt, Rinehart and Winston, Inc. is identified as Holt; University of Toronto Press becomes U of T Press; Prentice-Hall Canada, Ltd. becomes Prentice-Hall.

2. Book by more than one author:

   Matte, Jacqueline, and Phyllis A. Richard. Allons Bi-Bi.
   Toronto: Centennial, 1974.

   Pyle, William W., Kermit D. Laison, and Michael Zin. Fundamental
   Accounting Principles. Homewood, IL: Irwin, 1984.

3. Book edited by someone other than author:

   Hookey, Robert, ed. Contest: Essays by Canadian Students.
   Toronto: Holt, 1991.

   Norton, Sarah, and Nell Waldman, eds. Canadian Content.
   Toronto: Holt, 1988.

Wilkinson, Anne. The Collected Poems. Ed. A. J. M. Smith.
Toronto: Macmillan, 1968.

4. Work in several volumes:

Erickson, Edward W., and Leonard Waverman, eds. The Energy
Question: An International Failure of Policy. 2 vols.
Toronto: U of T Press, 1974.

5. Article, essay, chapter, story, or poem in a collection:

Trudeau, Pierre Elliot. "The Ascetic in a Canoe." Canadian
Content. Eds. Sarah Norton and Nell Waldman. Toronto: Holt,
1988. 271-74.

6. Encyclopedia reference:

"Prospecting." Encyclopedia Canadiana. 1970 ed.

Swinton, George. "Inuit Art." Canadian Encyclopedia. 1988 ed.

7. Book by corporate author (company, commission, agency):

Apple Computer, Inc. Apple Computer Annual Report 1984.
Cupertino, CA: Apple Computer, Inc., 1984.

Carnegie Council on Policy Studies in Higher Education. Giving
Youth a Better Chance: Options for Education, Work and
Service. San Francisco: Jossey, 1980.

8. Pamphlet:
Use the same form as for books.

Home Insurance Explained. Toronto: Insurance Bureau of Canada,
1988.

Irwin, Michael. What Do We Know About Allergies? New York:
Public Affairs Committee, 1972.

9. Government publication:
If the author of the document is not named, identify the government
first, then the agency, then the title, and so on.

Government of Canada. Ministry of Labour. Establishment and
Operation of Safety and Health Committees. Ottawa: Minister
of Supply and Services, 1984.

Province of Ontario. Ministry of Education. Language Across the
Curriculum. Toronto: Ministry of Education, 1978.

Articles

1. Magazine or journal article with new page numbers starting for each issue:

   > Booth, David. "Distributorless Ignition Systems." Canadian
   >
   > Automotive Technician April, 1990: 17-22.

   > Hibler, Michelle. "Strollers." Canadian Consumer 20.2 (1990):
   >
   > 16-21.

   Canadian Consumer is an example of a periodical that publishes a number of "issues" each year, making up an annual "volume." Identify the volume number (here, 20) right after the periodical title, add a period, then give the issue number (here, 2) immediately before the year (1990).

2. Magazine or journal article with page numbers continuing through all the issues of an annual volume:

   > Denker, Debra. "Along Afghanistan's War-Torn Frontier."
   >
   > National Geographic 167 (June 1985): 772-97.

   > Kemper, S. L., and O. Fennema. "Water Vapor Permeability of
   >
   > Edible Bilayer Films." Journal of Food Science 49
   >
   > (Nov.-Dec. 1984): 1478-81.

3. Newspaper article, signed or with byline:

   > Dobson, Wendy. "Lessons for Canada in how Europeans deal with
   >
   > inflation." Globe and Mail 14 May 1990: B2.

4. Newspaper article, unsigned:
   Alphabetize under first word of the title, excluding *A, An,* or *The.*

   > "Ontario francophones seek links in Quebec." Toronto Star 8 May
   >
   > 1990: A10.

5. Editorial in magazine or newspaper:

   > "Sacrificing people to fight inflation." Editorial. Toronto
   >
   > Star 8 May 1990: A18.

   > "Town named Soo." Editorial. Our Times 9.2 (April 1990): 4.

6. Review of book, film, concert, or theatrical performance:

   > Low, Simone. "Rhymes on Fire." Rev. of Fabulous Rhyming
   >
   > Dictionary by Gary Barwin. Journal of Wild Culture 1.4
   >
   > (Winter 1988/89): 24.

O'Toole, Lawrence. "Farther down the Yellow Brick Road." Rev. of
 <u>Return to Oz</u>, dir. Walter Murch. <u>Maclean's</u> 8 July 1985: 48.

Other Media

1. Computer software:

   Clarence, Paula. <u>The Business Writer</u>. Computer software. IPCF,
    1984. TRS-80, cartridge.

   Microsoft Corp. <u>BASIC</u>. 2nd ed. Computer software. IBM, 1982.
    IBM PC-DOS 2.10, disk.

2. Information from a computer service:

   Sondak, Arthur. "The Importance of Knowing Your Employee's
    Needs." Supervisory Management May 1980: 13-18. DIALOG file
    15, Item 80009142.

3. Interview:

   Alexander, Lincoln. Personal interview. 10 June 1990.

   van Vogt, A. E. Interview. <u>Dream Makers: The Uncommon People Who
    Write Science Fiction</u>. Ed. Charles Platt. New York:
    Berkley, 1980.

4. Radio or TV program:
   (Include the title of the program, network, local station, city, and
   date of broadcast.)

   <u>Alex Colville: The Splendour of Order</u>. Prod. Dan Curtis and Judi
    Stevenson. CBC. CBLT, Toronto. 7 July 1985.

   Interview with Stephen Lewis. Conducted by Peter Gzowski.
    <u>Morningside</u>. CBC. CBLT, Toronto. 8 May 1990.

   <u>Morningside</u>. CBC. CBLT, Toronto. 7 April 1988.

5. Recordings:

   Fowke, Edith. <u>Sally Go Round the Sun: Songs and Games of
    Canadian Children</u>. RCA, T-56666, n.d.

   Shorr, Joseph E. <u>Psycho-Imagination Therapy</u>. Audiotape.
    Citadel, 33818, 1963.

   Whitman, Walt. <u>Song of Myself</u>. Read by Orson Welles. BBC Radio
    Enterprises, 1953.

6. Film, filmstrip, or videocassette:
   Include title, director, distributor (if known), and year. You may include the writer, performers, and producer after the title. The size
   and length of a film are included after the date.

   > French Canadians. Filmstrip. Moreland-Latchford, Toronto, n.d.
   >
   > 73 fr., 35 mm.
   >
   > Handling Complaints and Grievances. Film. American Management
   >
   > Association, 1967. 16 mm, 17 min.
   >
   > Lasers. Videotape. Ontario Educational Communications
   >
   > Authority, 1980. 1/2 in., 30 min.
   >
   > The Last Frontier: Oceans. Sound filmstrip. New York Times,
   >
   > 1972. 15 min.
   >
   > Rashomon. Film. Dir. Akira Kurosawa. With Toshiro Mifune and
   >
   > Machiko Kyo. Daiei, 1950.

7. Lectures, speeches, addresses:

   > Hume, Michael. "Gender Distinctions in Canadian Sitcoms." EN
   >
   > 102-3 lecture. Centennial College. Scarborough, Ontario.
   >
   > 23 March 1988.
   >
   > Warberg, Carolyn. "Aggressive Play Behaviour in Young
   >
   > Children." Paper presented to the Early Childhood
   >
   > Educators, British Columbia. Vancouver, BC. 4 May 1990.

The preceding examples show you the formats you are most likely to
need in preparing a research paper. Other questions may arise as you
grapple with the task of documenting all your sources accurately. Check
these more unusual formats before you panic.

1. More than one book by an author:
   Substitute a line of three hyphens for the author's name in the second
   and any additional entries.

   > Colombo, John Robert. Canadian Literary Landmarks. Toronto:
   >
   > Hounslow, 1984.
   >
   > ---, ed. Colombo's Canadian Quotations. Edmonton: Hurtig,
   >
   > 1974.

2. Book with a subtitle:
   Put a colon after the title; then add the subtitle.

> The Energy Question: An International Failure of Policy. 2
>
> vols. Toronto: U of T Press, 1974.

3. New edition of an older book:
   Give the edition number and the date of the source you used.

> Wells, Walter. Communications in Business. 3rd ed. Boston:
>
> Kent, 1981.

4. Paperback edition of a previously published book:
   Put the date the book was originally published before the publication date of the edition you consulted.

> Laurence, Margaret. The Stone Angel. 1964. Toronto: McClelland,
>
> 1968.

5. More than three authors or editors:
   Give the name of the first author listed on the title page and add "et al."

> Baugh, Albert C., et al. A Literary History of England. New
>
> York: Appleton, 1948.

6. Publishing information not given:
   Use "N.p." for "no place"; "n.p." for "no publisher"; "n.d." for "no date"; "n. pag." for "no page numbers."

> Bank of Montreal. The Mortgage Control Handbook. N.p.: n.p.,
>
> n.d., n. pag.

7. Source not formally published

> Harris, Jim. "So You Think You Had a Bad Day." Dove (John Howard
>
> Society of Metropolitan Toronto) January 1990: n. pag.
>
> Waldman, Nell. "Curriculum, Composition, and Cultural
>
> Literacy." Review of a review. 27 September 1988.

The sample list of Works Consulted, on the next page, shows what your final page should look like.

Works Consulted if all works you looked at are included; Works Cited if only works quoted from are included.

Lecture, speech, or other spoken presentation.

Magazine article, unsigned; pages numbered continuously throughout an annual volume.

Newspaper article, signed; includes section as well as page number where necessary.

Magazine article, signed; each issue is renumbered starting at page 1.

Personal interview

Book with more than one author and in a second or later edition.

Pamphlet by corporate author such as a business company; publishing information (publisher's city, name, date) missing; no page numbers provided.

Works Consulted

Chodirker, Barry. "Speakers and their Audiences." Human
   Resources Renewal Teaching-Learning Series
   workshop. Scarborough College. Scarborough,
   Ontario, 11 March 1986.

"IBM-compatible Computers." Consumer Reports 51 (March
   1986): 166-9.

Lush, Patricia. "Dominion Case Creates Worries on
   Pension Funds," Globe and Mail 24 March 1986: B1.

McQueen, Rod. "Crisis, What Crisis?" Toronto Life April
   1986: 27-30.

Mirvish, Ed. Personal interview. 15 March 1986.

Norton, Sarah, and Brian Green. The Bare Essentials,
   Form A. 3rd ed. Toronto: Holt, 1990.

Sunbeam Corporation (Canada) Ltd. Solaray Ultrasonic
   Cool Mist Humidifier Model 456: Use and Care
   Instruction Manual. N.p.: n.p., n.d., n. pag.

CHAPTER 24

Formating a Research Paper

Although an old saying says "You can't judge a book by its cover," the way a book looks often influences your decision to read it or pass it by. Similarly, your research report should present a positive image. Its appearance should reflect all of the effort you put into its preparation. Otherwise, your reader may be turned off even before beginning to read.

Find out whether your instructor has any special requirements for the format of your research assignment. If so, follow them carefully. Otherwise, use the recommendations in this chapter, which includes an example of what a completed research paper looks like.

Paper

Type or computer-print your final draft on plain white letter-size (8 ½″ by 11″) or A4-size paper. Be sure to use a good ribbon on your typewriter or printer. If your instructor will accept a handwritten assignment, use blue or black ink and write neatly on one side of the paper only. *Always keep a copy of your paper.* (Instructors have occasionally been known to lose things.)

Spacing and Margins

Double-space throughout your assignment, including the title, quotations, and list of sources. If your paper is handwritten, write on every other line.

Leave a 2.5-cm (1-inch) margin all around the page. Indent paragraphs five spaces from the left margin. Indent long quotations (more than four typed lines) ten spaces from the left margin.

Page Numbers

Beginning with page 1, number *all* pages of your paper, including the list of sources. Put the numbers in the upper right corner of the page, 1.25 cm ($\frac{1}{2}$ inch) from the top edge and 2.5 cm (1 inch) from the right edge. (You may want to include your surname just before the number.)

Heading and Title

You do not need a separate title page for short papers. Beginning at the left margin, 2.5 cm (1 inch) from the top of the page, type on separate lines your name, your instructor's name, your course number, and the date. Then double-space and centre your title. Leave a double space between the title and the first line of your paper.

Presenting Source Titles

If you are not working on a word processor that allows you to use italics for titles, present the titles of complete works (books, magazines, tapes, programs, pamphlets, and so on) with underlining (for example, <u>The Best Short Stories of the Modern Age</u>). Put titles of parts of whole works (a chapter in a book, an article in a periodical, an essay in a collection, an interview on a television program) in quotation marks (for example, "The Lottery" in <u>The Best Short Stories of the Modern Age</u>).

Projecting an Image

Your research paper should demonstrate your understanding of the subject, your research and writing skills, and your ability to follow specific requirements of documentation and format. Meeting the submission requirements is as important as any other aspect of the preparation of your paper. It may be the last stage of your writing task, but it is the first impression that your readers will have of your work.

The model shown here is a "live" paper, properly formatted; its author is Marty Chan, a University of Alberta student.

Study first the blueprint Marty drafted before writing his research paper. Notice how he included in his outline some notes on the sources he wanted to quote or paraphrase in each section. This technique saves hours of paper shuffling when you sit down to write.

Professor Pac-Man:

What Do Children Learn from Video Games?

Grabber: Debate about the pros and cons of video games is probably irrelevant. Children will continue to zap, blast, leap, and steer their way to video victory whether we approve or not.

Preview: A review of the pros and cons may help us guard against the negative effects and develop the positive educational values; we will consider escapism, interactivity, and reinforcement.

I. Escapism is the primary attraction.

   A. Critics suggest violent themes may promote real-life aggression. (Anderson and Ford)

   B. The appeal of fantasy can make the games a powerful teaching tool. (Greenfield; Meer; Loftus and Loftus)

II. Interaction is a second attraction.

   A. Video games demand active involvement of the player.

   B. Critics are concerned that video games are replacing social interaction. (Greenfield; Scheibe and Erwin)

   C. Video games can have positive, practical applications. (Loftus and Loftus)

III.   Reinforcement accounts for much of the games' appeal.

   A. Negative implications include "addiction." (Greenfield; Needham)

   B. Positive effects include motivating children to learn. (Loftus and Loftus; Malone)

Summary: Fantasy, interaction, and reinforcement give video games both positive and negative power over children. (Liss)

Clincher: Assessment of the effects of video games on children will eventually fall somewhere between the extremes.

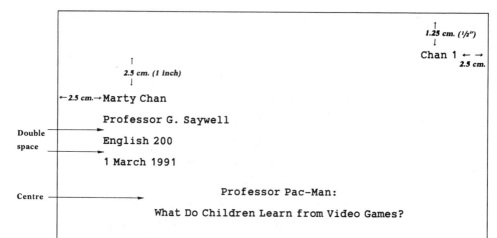

1.25 cm. (½″)

Chan 1 ← →
2.5 cm.

2.5 cm. (1 inch)

←*2.5 cm.*→Marty Chan

Professor G. Saywell

English 200

1 March 1991

Professor Pac-Man:
What Do Children Learn from Video Games?

Any debate about the pros and cons of video games is probably irrelevant; children will continue to zap, blast, leap, and steer their way to video victory regardless of our apprehension or approbation. Nevertheless, it is instructive to review the debate that pits those who fear the influence of the games against those who claim that playing them has value for young minds. Examining the evidence may enable us to guard against the negative social and psychological effects while recognizing and developing the positive educational values of The Mario Brothers and their ilk.

Video games owe their popularity to many factors. Escaping to a fantasy world where issues are straightforward and goals are clear is a major appeal. Another feature that draws players to the games is their interactivity; the passivity of the television viewer gives way to the excited participation of the role player in a personal adventure. Third, a clear and immediate reward for achievement in the games provides irresistible reinforcement and inducement to carry on through increasingly difficult skill levels.

Escapism is the primary attraction of video games. Whether controlling a dot-munching Pac-man or donning the trunks of a diminutive boxer named Little Mac, the players live for a time in a synthetic world. As long as they can compete with the machine, they will live happily in videoland--for good or ill.

Because the majority of popular video games draw on violent themes for their fantasies, critics suggest that there is a potentially dangerous carryover of aggression into real life. Craig A. Anderson and Catherine M. Ford concluded from experiments with college students that "aggressive video games [such as Zaxxon and Centipede] can have short-term negative effects on the game-player's emotional state. . . . The highly aggressive game [leads] to increased hostility and anxiety . . . " (398).

On the other hand, the producers of Sesame Street, the Children's Television Workshop, have proved that video games can present their action-oriented fantasy with positive, nonviolent themes (Greenfield 106). Regardless of the theme, UCLA psychology professor Seymour Feshbach asserts that fantasy is vital to child development (Meer 12). And, in an educational setting, learning can be enhanced by video games that use fantasy to "provide or provoke vivid images related to the material to be learned" (Loftus and Loftus 129). Children's literature from the Brothers Grimm to Dr. Seuss is rooted in fantasy. Should video games be censured for presenting the same themes electronically?

Chan 3

Another attraction of video games is interaction. Rather than passively watching the action, players participate in it. Typically, the player takes on the role of the main character in the video adventure and it is this character whom the player manipulates and controls with joystick, keypad, or power glove. The concentration required for success at most games and the absorbing nature of the interactive involvement lead to the undivided focus on the screen observed in many regular players.

The value of the interactivity of video games is a heated issue among critics. Because the player deals solely with the machine in most applications, worried parents fear that video games will replace social interaction. Combine this isolation with violent themes and the consequences could be dire:

> It may be that the most harmful aspect of the violent video games is that they are solitary in nature. A two-person aggressive game seems to provide a cathartic or releasing effect for aggression, while a solitary aggressive game (such as Space Invaders) may stimulate further aggression. (Greenfield 104)

Although crowds of teenagers gather in arcades, they rarely socialize with each other; the solitary nature of the games discourages human contact. The degree to which video interaction replaces social interaction among players was remarked in a study in which players were found to be talking to the machines as if they were human (Scheibe and Erwin 1979).

Video interaction can have positive applications, however. Besides increasing powers of concentration and honing motor skills, video games can be unequalled teachers. Video educational software can do something a teacher can't: provide prolonged individual attention to the student. Interactivity of this nature is described in a hypothetical video game described by Loftus and Loftus (133). The player learns Newton's law of motion by bombing ground targets from an airplane. Initially, the learning player drops the bomb when the plane is directly over the target, and the bomb overshoots the mark. After repeated tries, the player will eventually teach himself to release the bomb at the precise point when its forward motion will combine with gravity to carry it to the target. Without direct instruction, the player has learned to apply Newton's law of motion.

The effectiveness of the bomber game, described above, derives not only from the role playing of bombardier, nor only from the compelling interactivity of the game, but also from the instantaneous reward for a successful performance: an exploding target. Reinforcement is an integral part of the lure of video games. A rescued princess, an extra life, a defeated enemy: these are a few of the many forms of rewards provided. As long as the game encourages players by reinforcing a successful effort, they will continue to play.

Like video fantasy and interaction, continual reinforcement is not necessarily positive. Researchers have shown that it can foster addiction. Game designers produce increasingly complex games: "The existence of multiple levels [is] also responsible for the addictive properties of the games. . . . A video game player makes visible progress in the form of improved score and reaching the next level. Yet there is always another level to master" (Greenfield 122). The addiction produced by these never ending challenges can "spawn social problems such as gambling, vandalism, panhandling (for quarters), loan sharking, diversion of lunch money, and theft" (Needham 1983).

As any parent or teacher knows, reinforcement can be applied productively as well. For example, a spelling program rewards success by presenting a game of Asteroids on the screen (Loftus and Loftus 140). Once the students have finished playing the video game, the spelling program resumes. Knowledge that the game will reappear if they satisfy the program's spelling requirements motivates the players, providing them with a goal to work towards. In an experiment by Thomas Malone (1980), students learning about fractions were rewarded when their correct answers exploded balloons in a simulated darts game. A circus song trumpeted the players' success on popping three balloons. Visual and auditory rewards, instantaneously applied, encouraged success in learning fractions.

It is possible that the fantasy, interaction, and reinforcement that give video games their incredible power over children can have positive educational outcomes. At present, it must be admitted, the positive

Chan 6

is largely potential, while escapism and (often violent) entertainment are currently the chief attractions of the games. This may be changing, however, as companies like Nintendo, the giant in home video systems, begin exploring educational applications. Nintendo recently donated $3 million to the Massachusetts Institute of Technology's Media Laboratory to develop educational software (Liss 71). Their goal is to develop programs that exploit the powerful features of video games to make learning more effective and more fun.

What are our children learning from video games? At worst, they may be encouraged to violence, socially inhibited, and dangerously obsessed by their electronic fantasy worlds. At best, they may be stimulating their imaginations, learning their school lessons more effectively than ever before, and enjoying their video education. The dire predictions made about the destructive effects of rock 'n roll music, television, and even books have proven over time to be exaggerated. The wonderful educational potential predicted for new technologies has never fully materialized, either. Undoubtedly, the effects of video games on children will eventually fall somewhere between the extremes.

Works Consulted

Anderson, C. A., and C. M. Ford. "Affect of the Game
    Player: Short-term Effects of Highly and Mildly
    Aggressive Video Games." Personality and Social
    Psychology Bulletin 12.4 (1986): 390-402.

Greenfield, P. M. Mind and Media: The Effects of
    Television, Video Games, and Computers. Cambridge:
    Harvard University Press, 1984.

Liss, S. "Dr. Nintendo." Time 28 May 1990: 71.

Loftus, G. R., and E. F. Loftus. Mind At Play: The
    Psychology of Video Games. New York: Basic Books,
    1983.

Malone, T. W. What Makes Things Fun to Learn? A Study of
    Intrinsically Motivating Computer Games. Palo Alto:
    Xerox, 1980.

McDonald, M. C. "Video Games to Spot Problems."
    Psychology Today September 1983: 12.

Meer, J. "Mickey Mouse vs. Donkey Kong." Psychology
    Today September 1983: 12.

Needham, N. R. "The Impact of Video Games on American
    Youth." Education Digest 68.6 (1983): 40-42.

Rossel, R. D. "Addictive Video Games." Psychology Today
    May 1983: 87.

Scheibe, K. E., and M. Erwin. "The Computer as Altar."
    Journal of Social Psychology 108 (1979): 103-109.

Sentence Structure

CHAPTER 25

Cracking the Sentence Code

There is nothing really mysterious or difficult about sentences; you've been speaking them successfully since you were two. The difficulty arises when you go to write—not sentences, oddly enough, but paragraphs. Almost all college students, if asked to write ten sentences on ten different topics, could do so without an error. But, when those same students write paragraphs, sentence fragments and run-on sentences tend to creep in—errors that confuse or annoy readers.

The solution to fragment and run-on problems has two parts:

> Be sure every sentence you write
>
> 1. sounds right
> 2. has a subject and a verb.

Your ear is the best instrument with which to test your sentences. If you read your sentences aloud, you'll probably be able to tell by the sound whether they are complete, clear, and satisfactory. A complete sentence is one that makes sense by itself.

Read these sentences aloud:

Windsurfing is one of the world's newest sports.

Although windsurfing is still a young sport.

The second "sentence" doesn't sound right, does it? It does not make sense on its own and is in fact a sentence fragment.

Testing your sentences by reading them aloud won't work if you read your paragraphs straight through from beginning to end. The trick is to read from end to beginning. That is, read your last sentence aloud, and *listen* to it. If it sounds all right, then read aloud the next-to-last sentence, and so on, until you have worked your way back to the first sentence you wrote.

Now, what do you do with the ones that "sound funny"? Before you can fix them, you need to be able to "decode" each sentence to find out whether it has a subject and a verb. The subject and the verb are the bare essentials of the sentence; every sentence you write must have both. (The only exception is the **command,** in which the subject is understood rather than expressed. Consider this command: "Put your signature here." The subject *you* is understood.)

Finding Subjects and Verbs

A sentence is about *someone* or *something.* That someone or something is the **subject.** The word (or words) that tells what the subject *is* or *does* is the **verb.** The verb will express some sort of action, or condition, or occurrence.

Find the verb first. One way is by finding the word or group of words whose form can be changed to indicate a change in time. In the sentence

The prime minister has called an election.

has called (in the past) can be changed to *is calling* (present) or *will call* (future), so *has called* is the verb.

Once you have found the verb, find the subject by asking *who* or *what* the verb is referring to.

Look at these examples. We have underlined the subjects once and the verbs twice.

Jean helped me.
(Helped expresses an action and is the verb.
Who or what helped? Jean helped, so Jean is the subject.)

Finding verbs is relatively easy.
(Is expresses a condition and is the verb.
Who or what is [easy]? Finding, which is the subject.)

How you do it remains a mystery to me.
(Remains expresses a condition and is the verb.

Who or what <u>remains</u> [a mystery]? <u>How you do it</u>, which is the subject.
Notice that the subject can be more than one word.)

<u>Canada</u> <u><u>has been described</u></u> as "the land God gave to Cain."
(<u><u>Has been described</u></u> expresses an occurrence and is the verb.
Who or what <u><u>has been described</u></u>? <u>Canada</u>.)

Their rehabilitation <u>program</u> <u><u>seems</u></u> successful.
(<u><u>Seems</u></u> expresses a condition and is the verb.
Who or what <u><u>seems</u></u> [successful]? The <u>program</u>.)

Now try your hand at finding subjects and verbs. Throughout Units Six through Ten, for exercises marked with an asterisk (*), you can compare your answers with those given in Appendix D.

EXERCISE 1*

Find the subject and the verb in each of the following sentences. Underline the subject with one line and the verb with two. Check your answers on this exercise, and if you made even one mistake, carefully reread "Finding Subjects and Verbs." Be sure you understand this material thoroughly before you go on.

1. Algy met a bear.
2. A bear met Algy.
3. The bear was bulgy.
4. Sad to say, the bulge was Algy.
5. Grizzlies are famous for their unpredictability.
6. Meeting bears unexpectedly is clearly risky.
7. According to an old myth, bears never run downhill.
8. Take it from me. They do.
9. Females with cubs are known to be especially dangerous.
10. How to defend oneself presents a real problem.

Usually the subject comes before the verb in a sentence, but not always. Occasionally we find it after the verb:

Back to the refreshment stand for the fourth time <u><u>stumbled</u></u> the weary <u>father</u>.
(Who or what <u><u>stumbled</u></u>? The <u>father</u>.)

At the bottom of the page, in red ink, <u><u>was</u></u> my <u>grade</u>.
(Who or what <u><u>was</u></u>? My <u>grade</u>.)

In sentences beginning with *There* + some form of the verb *to be*, or with *Here* + some form of the verb *to be*, the subject is always found after the verb.

There <u>are</u> three good <u>reasons</u> for learning to write well.
(Who or what <u>are</u>? Reasons.)

There <u>will be</u> a <u>test</u> next week.
(Who or what <u>will be</u>? A test.)

Here <u>are</u> the <u>solutions</u> to last week's problem set.
(Who or what <u>are</u>? Solutions.)

In questions, the subject often follows the verb:

<u>Are</u> <u>you</u> sure about this?   <u>Is</u> <u>he</u> late again?
(Who or what <u>are</u>? You.)   (Who or what <u>is</u>? He.)

But notice that, in questions beginning with *who, whose, what,* or *which,* the subject and verb are in "normal" order:

<u>Who</u> <u>met</u> the bear?   What <u>happened</u> to Algy?
<u>Whose belly</u> <u>was</u> bulgy?   Which <u>grizzly</u> <u>ate</u> Algy?

To practise your skills, in each of the following exercises, underline the subject in each sentence with one line, the verb with two. Check your answers to each set before you go on.

EXERCISE 2*

1. Pierre Trudeau, like Jack Benny, is perennially middle-aged.
2. Here is an idea to consider.
3. Lucy Maud Montgomery was born in Ontario's Durham County before Confederation.
4. Who will eat the last pickle?
5. Eat slowly.
6. Physical activity builds strong bodies and healthy minds.
7. Keep your body fit.
8. Far behind the Liberals and New Democrats trailed the Conservatives, bringing up the rear.
9. Pride goes before a fall. (Biblical proverb)
10. Only in Canada is a so-called lack of national identity a distinctive national characteristic.

EXERCISE 3*

1. Toronto is a metropolitan centre with scores of distinct neighbourhoods.
2. The word "Toronto" is the Anglicization of the Indian term for "meeting place."
3. The Toronto Islands were originally a part of the mainland.

4. Are you a year-round island resident?
5. At a joint meeting of the councils, the city mayor opposed the Metro Council on behalf of island residents.
6. No evictions occurred last year.
7. The islanders' cohesiveness is the product of both genuine neighbourliness and common community concerns.
8. There is surprisingly little vandalism, the plague of other downtown areas.
9. For the average visitor to the Toronto Islands, the combination of private and public properties is acceptable and even enjoyable.
10. Minutes from the middle of the city nestles my sunny, serene island retreat.

More about Verbs

The verb in a sentence may be a single word, as in most of the exercises you've just done, or it may be a group of words. **Helping verbs** are often added to main verbs, so that an idea can be expressed precisely. The words *shall, should, may, might, can, could, must, ought, will, would, have, do,* and *be* are helping verbs.

> The complete verb in a sentence consists of the main verb + any helping verbs.

Here are a few of the forms of the verb *write*. Notice that in questions the subject may come between the helping verb and the main verb.

You <u>may write</u> now.
He certainly <u>can write</u>!
We <u>should write</u> home more often.
I <u>shall write</u> tomorrow.
He <u>could have written</u> yesterday.
She <u>is writing</u> her memoirs.
<u>Did</u> he <u>write</u> to you?

He <u>had written</u> his apology.
You <u>ought to write</u> to him.
We <u>will have written</u> by then.
I <u>will write</u> to the editor.
The proposal <u>has been written</u>.
Orders <u>should have been written</u>.
<u>Could</u> you <u>have written</u> it in French?

One verb form, in particular, always takes a helping verb. Here is the rule:

> A verb ending in *-ing* MUST have a helping verb (or verbs) before it.

Here are a few of the forms an *-ing* verb can take:

I am writing the report.   She must have been writing all night.
You will be writing a report.   You are writing illegibly.
He should have been writing it.   I was writing neatly.
Is she writing the paper for him? Have you been writing on the wall?

Beware of certain words that are often confused with helping verbs:

> Words such as *not, only, always, sometimes, never, ever,* and *just* are NOT part of the verb.

These words sometimes appear in the middle of a complete verb, but they are modifiers, not verbs. Do not underline them:

I have just won the lottery!
He is almost always chosen first.
Most people do not welcome unasked-for advice.

Test yourself with Exercises 4 and 5. Underline the subject once and the complete verb twice. Check your answers to each set before you go on to the next.

EXERCISE 4*

1. He has talked nonstop for three hours.
2. She should have been examining each package.
3. Could they return the goods tomorrow?
4. In the winter, the car starts more easily inside the garage than outside.
5. Where is the nearest gas station?
6. He is not going to drive.
7. Which horse does she prefer?
8. Parents will always perceive their offspring as small children.
9. The barometer has just fallen alarmingly.
10. Patiently and painstakingly, against all odds, struggled the little army.

EXERCISE 5*

1. In a couple of years, you will be a professional dancer.
2. By noon, he will have been sleeping for eighteen hours.
3. How are the club members identified?
4. The police will certainly stop all yellow cars on the road tonight.

5. How should the committee present this concept?
6. To some small degree at least, personal opinion is often presented as fact.
7. My boss does not understand me; neither does my husband.
8. Have you ever been to the Zanzibar tavern?
9. Little is known about his past, except that he visited here twice.
10. Isn't she going home now?

More about Subjects

Very often, groups of words called **prepositional phrases** come before the subject in a sentence, or between the subject and the verb. When you're looking for the subject in a sentence, prepositional phrases can trip you up unless you know this rule:

> The subject of a sentence is never in a prepositional phrase.

You have to be able to identify prepositional phrases, so that you will know where *not* to look for the subject. A prepositional phrase is a group of words that begins with a preposition and ends with the name of something or someone (a noun or a pronoun). Often a prepositional phrase will indicate the direction or location of something. Here are some prepositional phrases:

about the book	behind the desk	from the office
above the book	below the window	in the book
according to the book	beside the book	inside the office
after the meeting	between the desks	into the elevator
against the wall	by the book	in front of the door
along the hall	concerning the memo	like the book
among the books	despite the book	near the wall
among them	down the hall	on the desk
around the office	except the staff	onto the floor
before lunch	for the manager	of the typist
over a door	under the book	with a book
to the staff	until the meeting	without the book
through the window	up the hall	without them

When you're looking for the subject in a sentence, you can make the task easier by crossing out any prepositional phrases. For example,

The keyboard ~~of your computer~~ should be cleaned occasionally.

What <u>should be cleaned</u>? The <u>keyboard</u> (not the computer).

~~In case of an emergency~~, one ~~of the group~~ should go ~~to the nearest ranger station for help~~.

Who <u>should go</u>? <u>One</u> (not the group).

In the two exercises that follow, first cross out the prepositional phrase(s) in each sentence. Then underline the subject once and the verb twice. Check your answers to each set before going on.

EXERCISE 6*

1. According to the old proverb, a stitch in time saves nine.
2. I have had a stitch in my side, and I have often been in stitches.
3. Stitching, in my opinion, is best left to tailors and surgeons.
4. For today's prices, clothing manufacturers should be sewing triple seams in their clothing, all by hand.
5. From the beginning, each item of clothing should be separately designed.
6. After that, every pattern piece should be cut by hand.
7. Each piece of cloth should then be sewn with great care to the other appropriate pieces, by one person.
8. The same craftsperson should then pay attention to double seaming and to details of hand finishing.
9. Items of clothing produced in this way might justify today's high prices.
10. In this kind of manufacturing procedure, the individual maker of the item should receive a specified percentage of the wholesale price.

EXERCISE 7*

1. In the next twenty years, the average age of the Canadian population will increase significantly.
2. For those of us now in our forties, this trend is good news.
3. For those in their teens, however, the news is not so good. They will have to carry the burden of caring for the increasing numbers of elderly persons in society.
4. On the positive side, the leaders of tomorrow will have the experience and wisdom of a large segment of the population to draw on in their planning and decision making.

5. Throughout history, cultures around the world have traditionally associated age with wisdom.
6. Ironically, however, this assumption is not always supported by the evidence.
7. There are many examples from the past and in the present of young leaders with more wisdom and maturity than their aged counterparts.
8. Consider, for example, Alexander the Great. He had conquered the known world by the age of 19.
9. For a contemporary example, consider the success stories of youthful entrepreneurs like Bill Gates. Many young people, just out of college, have launched hi-tech ventures to compete with old, established companies.
10. Over the next two decades, with the maturing of the "baby boom," Canadians will encounter changes in life-style, in political focus, and in cultural attitudes towards the "young" and the "old."

EXERCISE 8

Write ten sentences of your own. Cross out all the prepositional phrases, and underline the subject once and the complete verb twice.

Multiple Subjects and Verbs

So far you have been working with sentences containing only one complete subject and one complete verb. Sentences can, however, have more than one subject and verb. Here is a sentence with a multiple subject:

Southlands and West Point Grey are suburbs of Vancouver.

This sentence has a multiple verb:

He elbowed and wriggled his way along the aisle of the bus.

And this sentence has a multiple subject and a multiple verb:

The psychiatrist and the police officer leaped from their chairs and seized the woman.

The elements of a multiple subject or verb are usually joined by *and* (but sometimes by *or*). Multiple subjects and verbs may contain more than two elements, as in the following sentences:

Clarity, brevity, and simplicity are the basic qualities of good writing.

I finished my paper, put the cat outside, took the phone off the hook, and crawled into bed.

EXERCISE 9 *

Underline the subjects once and the verbs twice. Be sure to underline all the elements in a multiple subject or verb.

1. The prime minister and the provincial premiers met at Meech Lake.
2. They debated and drafted amendments to the Constitution.
3. The anesthetist and the surgeon scrubbed for surgery and hurried to the operating room.
4. Blue spruce and hemlock are both northern imports to southern Ontario.
5. I tried and failed once, and then later tried again and succeeded.
6. My son or my daughter will drive me home.
7. The two dogs and the cat travelled a thousand miles in three months.
8. My retired father reads, travels, golfs, walks the dog, and loves all these activities.
9. Knock three times and ask for Joe.
10. Sight reading and improvising are necessary skills of the small-band musician.

EXERCISE 10

This exercise is a review. In these sentences, find and underline the subjects once and the verbs twice. Be sure to underline all the elements in a multiple subject or verb.

1. Consider the lilies of the field.
2. Melanie and Morris adjusted their chains, checked their earrings, and patted their spiked hair into place before stomping off to their job interviews.
3. I asked the necessary questions and recorded the householders' answers but was puzzled by one most unusual response.
4. In my house live my wife and I, our two teenagers, two dogs, one cat, and one ghost.
5. No other researcher got such a startling answer or finished a questionnaire so quickly.
6. On King Street, between St. Andrew's Church on the east and assorted small buildings on the west, lies Toronto's Roy Thomson Hall.

7. Ragweed, goldenrod, and twitch grass formed the essential elements in the bouquet for his English teacher.
8. He spun around the corner, whirled into a doorway, and careened up the stairs, with the police in hot pursuit.
9. Today's artists must mirror the real world rather than create an ideal one.
10. This theory of arts produces "slice-of-life" drama, encourages representational painting and visual art, engenders atonal music, and sells computers.

CHAPTER 26

Still More about Verbs

Every verb has four forms:

1. the **base form:** used by itself or with *can, may, might, shall, will, could, would, should, must;*
2. the **past tense** form: used by itself;
3. the **-ing form:** used with *am, is, are, was, were;* and
4. the **past participle** form: used with *have, has, had* or with *am, is, are, was, were.*

These forms are the principal parts of a verb. Here are some examples:

BASE	PAST TENSE	-ING FORM	PAST PARTICIPLE
walk	walked	walking	walked
learn	learned	learning	learned
seem	seemed	seeming	seemed
enjoy	enjoyed	enjoying	enjoyed

To use verbs correctly, you must know their principal parts. Knowing two facts will help you. First, your dictionary will give you the principal parts of certain verbs (irregular ones). Just look up the base form, and you'll find the past tense and the past participle beside it, usually in parentheses. If the past tense and past participle are *not* given, the verb is **regular.** So, the second thing you need to know is how to form the past tense and the past participle of regular verbs: by adding *-ed* to the base form. The examples listed above—*walk, learn, seem,* and *enjoy*—are regular verbs.

Many of the most common verbs are **irregular.** Their past tense and past participle are formed in a variety of ways. Following is a list of the principal parts of some of the most common irregular verbs. (We have not included the *-ing* form, because it never causes any difficulty. It is always made up of the base form + *ing*.)

The Principal Parts of Irregular Verbs

BASE (Use with *can, may, might, shall, will, could, would, should, must*.)	PAST TENSE	PAST PARTICIPLE (Use with *have, has, had* or with *am, is, are, was, were*.)
be (am, is, are)	was, were	been
bear	bore	borne
become	became	become
begin	began	begun
bid (offer to pay)	bid	bid
bite	bit	bitten
blow	blew	blown
break	broke	broken
bring	brought	brought
build	built	built
burst	burst	burst
buy	bought	bought
catch	caught	caught
choose	chose	chosen
come	came	come
cost	cost	cost
deal	dealt	dealt
dive	dived/dove	dived
do	did	done
draw	drew	drawn
drink	drank	drunk
drive	drove	driven
eat	ate	eaten
fall	fell	fallen
feel	felt	felt
fight	fought	fought
find	found	found
fling	flung	flung
fly	flew	flown

BASE	PAST TENSE	PAST PARTICIPLE
forget	forgot	forgotten/forgot
forgive	forgave	forgiven
freeze	froze	frozen
get	got	got/gotten
give	gave	given
go	went	gone (*not* went)
grow	grew	grown
hang (suspend)	hung	hung
hang (put to death)	hanged	hanged
have	had	had
hear	heard	heard
hide	hid	hidden
hit	hit	hit
hold	held	held
hurt	hurt	hurt
keep	kept	kept
know	knew	known
lay	laid	laid
lead	led	led
leave	left	left
lend	lent	lent
lie	lay	lain
lose	lost	lost
make	made	made
mean	meant	meant
meet	met	met
pay	paid	paid
put	put	put
ride	rode	ridden
ring	rang	rung
rise	rose	risen
run	ran	run
say	said	said
see	saw (*not* seen)	seen
sell	sold	sold
set	set	set
shake	shook	shaken
shine	shone	shone
sing	sang	sung
sit	sat	sat
sleep	slept	slept
slide	slid	slid
speak	spoke	spoken
speed	sped	sped

BASE	PAST TENSE	PAST PARTICIPLE
spend	spent	spent
stand	stood	stood
steal	stole	stolen
strike	struck	struck
swear	swore	sworn
swim	swam	swum
swing	swung	swung
take	took	taken
teach	taught	taught
tear	tore	torn
tell	told	told
think	thought	thought
throw	threw	thrown
wear	wore	worn
win	won	won
wind	wound	wound
write	wrote	written

In the following exercise, write on the blank line the correct form (either the past tense or the past participle) of the verb shown to the left of the sentence. Do not add or remove helping verbs.

EXERCISE 1*

1. come   Down from the high mountain that lay beyond the little town _____ the strangest creature they had ever seen.

2. spend   Appearing in the city square in the morning, he had apparently _____ the night crouched in a handy tree.

3. make   Odd-looking, but not frightening or ugly, he _____ even the early-morning dogs look his way.

4. be   He could have _____ a Hobbit, so much like Frodo did he look.

5. lose   Apparently he had _____ his way while picnicking with his friends in the foothills.

6. speak   The children from Miss Bundy's Nursery School
   find   _____ to him first and _____ him friendly and intelligent.

7. know   The townspeople all _____ the legend of a mountain

kingdom of little people.

8. have   Now they _____ evidence before their eyes for the

truth of the story.

9. choose   They could have _____ to ignore or do away with the

friendly little fellow.

10. tell   Instead, he stayed and _____ them more about the

lead   mountain kingdom and eventually _____ them

there to see it for themselves.

The sentences in Exercises 2 through 5 require both the past tense and the past participle of the verb shown at the left. Write the required form in each blank. Do not add or remove helping verbs.

EXERCISE 2*

1. win   Tom had _____ the long-distance run many times

before he _____ his first sprint.

2. wear   The white tuxedo had been _____ by Tom's brother,

but at yesterday's presentation Tom _____ it with

more pizzazz.

3. do   Tom _____ what he had never _____ before:

he made a speech.

4. forget   It was amazing: all his notes were _____ and he

even _____ to be nervous.

5. become Tom _____ quite good at speech-making on behalf

of the fitness cause; having _____ proficient, he was

asked to speak at many other meetings and banquets.

6. see   Having been _____ and mobbed on the street out-

side, Tom then _____ that he would have to avoid

recognition.

7. set   Having _____ a world record for the mile when he

was twenty, Tom _____ another one for the de-

cathlon when he was twenty-five.

8. fall   Tom had _____ and broken an ankle when he was twelve; he _____ again and broke his arm a year later.

9. meet   I was _____ at the door by this medical and athletic miracle; he surely _____ all my expectations.

10. keep   Now sixty, he had _____ himself in top condition over the years and still _____ up a daily exercise routine.

EXERCISE 3*

1. deal   Jane could not have _____ with the builders the way Jerry _____ with them.

2. drive   Because she is a woman, they would have _____ a much harder bargain than they _____ with Jerry.

3. fight   It was a crucial match; Rocky _____ as he never had _____ before.

4. grow   They could have _____ an excellent kitchen garden in the yard, but they _____ flowers instead.

5. bid   She would have _____ ten times more than he _____ last night at the auction.

6. begin   As they _____ to pick the cotton crop, they prayed that the weevils had not already _____ their harvest.

7. feel   She could have _____ cheated, but instead she _____ elated at being relieved of the responsibility.

8. cost   The effort to speak at his first AA meeting _____ Sean dearly, but his alcoholism had almost _____ him his life.

9. leave   Having _____ their place so early the last time, this time she _____ later, when everyone else did.

10. swing   The dancer was supposed to have _____ his partner
              into a stationary pose, but he _____ her into a pirou-
              ette instead.

EXERCISE 4*

1. teach   He had _____ the course for three consecutive
             years, but this year he _____ it so differently that it
             seemed like a new course.

2. hang   In Canada, convicted murderers were _____ until
             the 1950s; many still believe that murderers should be
             _____.

3. hold   According to her sentence, Sophia could have been
             _____ as a prisoner for thirty days; they _____
             her for only thirteen days.

4. drink   Sean would have _____ several bottles of wine at one
             party in the old days; at last night's party, he _____
             only soda water.

5. speed   He _____ out of the choppy, open water as quickly
             as he had _____ into it from the bay.

6. lay   Phyllis _____ the brake cables on the repair bench
             where the bicycle salesman had _____ them when
             the bike fell off the wall.

7. go   Having _____ home very late on Thursday, Robert
             _____ home at 4:00 P.M. on Friday.

8. freeze   They could have _____ four gallons of strawberries,
             but they gave away two gallons and _____ two.

9. dive   For safety's sake, he should have _____ from beyond
             the reef, but he _____ on the shallow west side instead.

10. break   He _____ his nose; he's lucky not to have _____
             his neck.

EXERCISE 5

1. bite   Though Trish wasn't _____ by the dog, the cat _____ her on the hand.

2. pay   The job _____ very poorly, but the experience has _____ off many times.

3. put   Having _____ the hat on his head, Duncan then _____ his head out into the rain.

4. sit   We _____ for as long as we could, but by the time we had _____ for an hour, we were sore.

5. fling   Susan _____ her paper to the floor; she might as well have _____ her books.

6. hold   Once they had _____ the fortress for a week, they knew they _____ the key to victory.

7. wear   Kevin _____ his best clothes to church, but having _____ them once, he gave them away.

8. hide   We would have _____ the children in the loft, but Bill _____ the money there last week.

9. wind   They _____ the clock daily until it was discovered that it had been _____ too tightly.

10. grow   In soil where nothing ever _____, the beanstalk had _____ fifty feet overnight!

CHAPTER 27

Solving Sentence-Fragment Problems

Any group of words that is punctuated as a sentence but that does not have a subject or a complete verb is a **sentence fragment**. Fragments are perfectly appropriate in conversation and in some kinds of writing, but normally they are unacceptable in college, technical, and business writing. You've already learned how to spot a sentence fragment: read the words aloud, and check to see whether the subject or the verb (or both) is missing. Let's look at a few examples:

Now, as always, is greatly influenced by her willful neighbour.
(Who or what <u>is influenced</u>? The sentence doesn't tell you. The subject is missing.)

Historians attempting to analyze Canada's role in WW II.
(Part of the verb is missing. Remember that a verb ending in *-ing* must have a helping verb in front of it.)

For motorcycle riders in every province but Manitoba.
(Subject and verb are both missing.)

Regarding the student we discussed last week.
(Subject and verb are both missing.)

Now, what do you do with the fragments you've found?

> To change a sentence fragment into a complete sentence, add whatever is missing: a subject, a verb, or both.

You may need to add a subject:

Now, as always, <u>Canada</u> is greatly influenced by her willful neighbour.

You may need to add part of a verb:

Historians <u>are attempting</u> to analyze Canada's role in WW II.

Sometimes it's better to change the form of the verb:

Historians <u>attempt</u> to analyze Canada's role in WW II.

You may need to add both a subject and a verb:

<u>Helmets</u> <u>are required</u> for motorcycle riders in every province but Manitoba.

And sometimes you need to add more than just a subject and a verb:

I <u>have written</u> to the registrar regarding the student we discussed last week.

Don't let the length of a fragment fool you. Students often think that if a string of words is long it must be a sentence. Not so. No matter how long the string of words is, if it doesn't have both a subject and a verb, it is not a sentence. Here is an example, taken from "The Men of Moosomin," by Sara Jeannette Duncan:

Here and there a ruddy little pond, like a pocket looking glass dropped on the prairie, with a score or so of wild ducks swimming in it, or a slight round hollow where a pond used to be, with the wild ducks flying high.

Do you know what's missing? Can you change the fragment into a sentence? Work through the exercises below to develop your sentence recognition skills.

In Exercises 1 through 3, read each "sentence" aloud. Put *S* before each complete sentence and *F* before each sentence fragment. Make each fragment into a complete sentence by adding whatever is missing: a subject, a verb, or both.

EXERCISE 1*

1. _____ Regarding myths and fairy tales.

2. _____ To decide on the basis of rumour, not facts.

3. _____ Sad to hear of the many occurrences of vandalism.

4. _____ Writing exams all evening, after working all day.

5. _____ The party members gathering in the campaign office.

6. _____ Anyone goes who so desires.

7. _____ Air attack cancelled because of cloud cover.

8. _____ Painting in a studio with bad lighting.

9. _____ Having worked outdoors all his life.

10. _____ Wanting to please them, she had coffee ready on their arrival.

EXERCISE 2*

1. _____ To exaggerate for the sake of personal image and for monetary gain.

2. _____ Hyperbole is an extravagant exaggeration used as a figure of speech.

3. _____ Exaggerating his own influence being of great importance to him.

4. _____ Knowing the truth.

5. _____ As usual, with some twisting of the truth.

6. _____ Speakers and listeners recognizing the tall tale for what it was.

7. _____ Let's hear it.

8. _____ Realizing their incredulity, she stopped speaking.

9. _____ The directions printed in the booklet included in the package.

10. _____ Does she really believe what she's saying?

EXERCISE 3*

1. _____ Unless he knows someone in the field.

2. _____ She is educated and intelligent but no social graces.

3. _____ The sweet smell of success is often mixed with less desirable aromas.

4. _____ Garth Drabinsky speaking on financial success.

5. _____ Because financial gain is, for most people, synonymous with success.

6. _____ The saying, "Nothing succeeds like success."

7. _____ For the moment, not looking at the money and power aspects of the question.

8. _____ To bring to actualization the best human instincts in oneself and others?

9. _____ The more personal aspects usually not considered when the topic comes up in ordinary conversation.

10. _____ In our culture, the tendency to equate financial worth with personal success.

Independent and Dependent Clauses

A group of words containing a subject and a verb is a clause. There are two kinds of clauses. An **independent clause** is one that makes complete sense on its own. It can stand alone, as a sentence. A **dependent clause**, as its name suggests, cannot stand alone as a sentence; it *depends* on another clause to make complete sense.

Dependent clauses are easy to recognize, because they begin with words such as these:

Dependent-Clause Cues

after	if	until
although	in order that	what, whatever
as, as if	provided that	when, whenever
as soon as	since	where, wherever, whereas
as long as	so that	whether
because	that	which, whichever
before	though	while
even if, even though	unless	who, whom, whose

Whenever a clause begins with one of these words or phrases, it is dependent.

> A dependent clause must be attached to an independent clause. If it stands alone, it is a sentence fragment.

Here is an independent clause:

I am a poor speller.

If we put one of the dependent-clause cues in front of it, it can no longer stand alone:

Because I am a poor speller

We can correct this kind of fragment by attaching it to an independent clause:

Because I am a poor speller, I have chained my dictionary to my wrist.

EXERCISE 4*

Put an *S* before each clause that is independent and therefore a sentence. Put an *F* before each clause that is dependent and therefore a sentence fragment. Underline the dependent-clause cue in each sentence fragment.

1. _____ What parents don't know.

2. _____ As she was led to believe.

3. _____ Where three roads meet.

4. _____ If he decides on that basis.

5. _____ So that the children could see the performance with no difficulty.

6. _____ Although she practised it constantly.

7. _____ Since the horse stepped on her.

8. _____ As soon as the troops arrived, the fighting stopped.

9. _____ Whichever route the cyclists choose.

10. _____ Before Phyllis bought her racer.

In Exercises 5 and 6, identify the sentence fragments by underlining the dependent-clause cue in each fragment you find.

EXERCISE 5*

Before the curtain went up on the lavishly decorated and beautifully lit set. The actor playing Frankie could be seen pacing up and down nervously. Although he was a veteran of many stage performances and several popular movies and was accustomed to appearing before large audiences. Which made it very strange that he would demonstrate the symptoms of stage fright so clearly. Looking closely, a careful observer might have noticed, however, that he wasn't studying his lines or rehearsing his role. In fact, unless one were right beside him and watching very closely. The real purpose of his pacing could easily be missed. Although he appeared to be alone. He was, in reality, exercising his pet cockroach.

EXERCISE 6*

Photographing wildlife can be a rewarding and entertaining experience. Provided that one is very careful and has the right photographic equipment. Whereas some photographers try to capture the essence of a bowl of fruit, and others aim for a spiritual quality in family portraits or wedding pictures. I prefer to capture on film an accurate reflection of true wildlife. So that I can achieve this goal, I follow some of my crazy friends around from party to party, recording their antics with my pocket camera. Since so many of my friends are, by any definition, wild. The reproduction of wildlife in my photo albums is quite remarkable. Whether it is Jayne trying to play baseball in an evening gown, or Tessa going to a ballet opening in her jeans. As long as I have friends like Terry, who carries a pair of scissors to cut off people's ties, or Phyllis, who insists that she is Princess Di. I will always have plenty of subject matter for wildlife photography.

Most sentence fragments are dependent clauses punctuated as sentences. Fortunately, this is the easiest kind of fragment to recognize and fix. All you need to do is join the dependent clause either to the sentence that comes before it or to the one that comes after it—whichever linkage makes better sense.

One final point: if you join your clause fragment to the independent clause that follows it, you must separate the two clauses with a comma (see Chapter 39, p. 333).

Read the following example to yourself; then read it aloud (remember, last sentence first).

> Montreal is a sequence of ghettos. Although I was born and brought up there. My experience of French was a pathetically limited and distorted one.

The second "sentence" sounds incomplete, and the dependent-clause cue at the beginning of it is the clue you need to identify it as a sentence fragment. You could join the fragment to the sentence before it, but then you would get "Montreal is a sequence of ghettos, although I was born and brought up there," which doesn't make sense. Clearly the fragment should be linked to the sentence that follows it, like this:

> Montreal is a sequence of ghettos. Although I was born and brought up there, my experience of French was a pathetically limited and distorted one.
>
> (from Mordecai Richler, "Quebec Oui, Ottawa Non!")

EXERCISE 7*

This paragraph contains both independent clauses and dependent clauses (fragments), all punctuated as if they were complete sentences. Letting meaning be your guide, join each fragment to the most appropriate independent clause. Remember to punctuate correctly. Then turn to the answer section to compare your sentences with the author's. (Adapted from Pierre Berton's introduction to Henri Rossier's *The New City: A Prejudiced View of Toronto*, 1961, cited in Alan Dawe's *Profile of A Nation*, Macmillan, 1969.)

The attitude to Toronto takes two forms. There is first the attitude of the non-Torontonians. Who live in places like St. John's, Maple Creek and Vancouver. Then there is the attitude of the Torontonians themselves.

The attitude of the outsider is compounded of envy, malice and pity. In about equal quantities. It is admitted that Torontonians make large sums of money. But not much else. Certainly they never have any fun. There is none of the leisurely gracious living that is to be found in Montreal, say. Or Halifax, or Okotoks, Alberta. When a young man sets out for Toronto. He is surrounded by a covey of friends, all commiserating with him and whispering to him. To look about for a job for them in the big city. It is generally acknowledged that the bereaved young man will return, but he rarely does. If he sees his friends again, he sees them in Toronto. Where they all have a good cry and talk over the grand old days. When they were poor in Pelvis or West Webfoot.

The attitude of the Torontonians is that they simply do not care. What people think of them. They live in Toronto and that is good enough for them. For years a host of magazine articles, newspaper editorials and commentators have baited Toronto. Toronto refuses to swallow the bait. One mayor tried to launch a campaign. To make the city popular but it fizzled out after a few days. Torontonians do not really care about being popular; in fact, about half the criticism about the city comes from its own people. Nobody baits Toronto quite as much as those who live there.

EXERCISE 8

Make each clause given below into a dependent clause by adding one of the dependent-clause cues. Then add an independent clause to make a complete sentence.

Example: He felt very nervous.
Although he felt very nervous (dependent-clause cue added).
Although he felt very nervous, *he gave a good speech* (independent clause added).

1. They are hopeful.

2. He ate the cold leftover pizza.

3. She won't know immediately.

4. I want to see the new house.

5. There are eleven now.

6. Nothing ever goes right.

7. He is usually more careful.

8. She washed it thoroughly.

9. According to those in the media, the parties' opinions vary greatly.

10. Everyone knows something about computers' probable impact on future employment.

EXERCISE 9

Using the following dependent-clause cues, write dependent clauses of your own. Then make each into a complete sentence by adding an independent clause. Watch your punctuation!

1. as long as

2. even though

3. until

4. in order that

5. whatever

6. though

7. whether

8. whom

9. which

10. after

EXERCISE 10

As a final test of your skill in correcting sentence fragments, try this exercise. Put *S* before each complete sentence and *F* before each sentence fragment. Make each fragment into a complete sentence.

1. _____ Although the class was long, boring, and frustrating for me because I hadn't read the assignment and couldn't understand the discussion.

2. _____ Pierre Berton's famous definition of a Canadian: "Someone who knows how to make love in a canoe."

3. _____ The point being that hard work, intelligence, and dedication are not always rewarded.

4. _____ Getting promoted is often a matter of knowing the right people and of being in the right place at the right time.

5. _____ Probably the fastest growing but least publicized of modern crimes being data theft, sometimes known as computer tapping.

6. _____ Help me figure this one out, would you please?

7. _____ As long as I've known you, an honest, patient, loyal friend.

8. _____ There are several things you should think about first.

9. _____ Goodman Ace's famous quip that television was called a "medium" because things on it were rarely well done.

10. _____ The problem resulting from our stumbling blindly into the future, ignorant of the harm technological advances can bring.

CHAPTER 28

Solving Run-On Problems

Just as a sentence can lack certain elements and thus be a fragment, so can it contain too many elements. A sentence with too much in it is a **run-on.** Run-ons most often occur when you write in a hurry or when you're disorganized and not thinking clearly. If you think about what you want to say, and proceed slowly and carefully, you shouldn't have any problems with them.

There are two varieties of run-on sentence: the comma splice and the true run-on.

The Comma Splice

As the name suggests, the **comma splice** occurs when two complete sentences (independent clauses) are joined together, with only a comma between them. Here's an example:

That dog's obedient, it's been well trained.

> The easiest way to fix a comma splice is to replace the comma with a semicolon.

That dog's obedient; it's been well trained.

To be sure you understand how to use semicolons correctly, read Chapter 40.

> Another way to fix a comma splice is to add an appropriate linking word between the two clauses.

Two types of linking words will work.

1. You can insert one of these words: *and, but, or, nor, for, so, yet.* These should be preceded by a comma.

   That dog's obedient, for it's been well trained.

2. You can insert one of the dependent-clause cues listed in Chapter 27, on p. 246.

   That dog's obedient because it's been well trained.

> The third way to fix a comma splice is to make the run-on sentence into two short sentences.

That dog's obedient. It's been well trained.

All three solutions to the comma splice problem require that you replace the comma with a word or punctuation mark strong enough to come between two independent clauses.

The sentences in the following exercises will give you practice in fixing the comma splice. Correct the sentences where necessary. Then check your answers. If you find that you're confused about when to use a semicolon and when to use a period, be sure to read p. 337 before going on.

EXERCISE 1*

1. The teacher's late, let's go!
2. Just let me do the talking, you'll get us a ticket if you open your mouth.
3. I keep buying lottery tickets, but I've only won once.
4. Hitting a golf ball may look easy, but it's not.
5. As long as you smile when you speak, you can say almost anything.
6. Montreal used to be called *Ville Ste. Marie,* I think, but before that it had an Indian name.
7. Students today need summer jobs, tuition and living costs are too much for most families.

8. Bryan will be going to college if he is accepted, his parents have lots of money.
9. My word processor makes writing much easier, though it doesn't seem to spell any better than I do.
10. I am seeking a hero after whom I can model my life, so far I've rejected Sly Stallone, Madonna, and Hulk Hogan.

EXERCISE 2*

1. The comma splice gets its name from the film splice, two pieces of film are taped, or spliced, together.
2. Old movies are sometimes choppy and disconnected, they have been spliced badly or too often.
3. Two sentences cannot be spliced together with a comma, you need to use a semicolon or a period or a linking word between them.
4. You should be particularly careful when using linking words like "however," "consequently," "therefore," and "moreover," these words need a semicolon before them and a comma after when they join two independent clauses.
5. This isn't a very difficult rule, in fact, it's one of the easiest rules to learn because it has no exceptions.
6. With one minute to go, the opposing team scored the winning goal, consequently no one on our team felt much like celebrating the end of the season.
7. The anti-smoking bylaw doesn't seem to have done much good, I often see people smoking in restaurants, stores, and even elevators.
8. One of the things I hope to learn at college is French, however I doubt if I'll ever learn to speak it fluently.
9. It's a pity that burning coal contributes to acid rain, we have an almost inexhaustible supply of coal in Canada.
10. Our country's culture, attitudes, and even politics are strongly influenced by television, that is why the CRTC insists on a high level of Canadian content in television broadcasting.

EXERCISE 3*

1. A Canadian who speaks three languages is called multilingual, one who speaks two languages is called bilingual, one who speaks only one language is called an English Canadian.
2. I'm sure the job couldn't have been as bad as he claims, maybe he just didn't try hard enough.
3. Meetings such as this are fine for small groups, large groups have to be handled in a different way.
4. I'll be glad to help you out, when you need me just call, I'll be here all day.

5. In Canada, winter is more than a season, it's a bad joke.
6. Perfection is probably impossible to achieve, but that doesn't mean you should stop trying.
7. It may seem foolish, especially after all the wrangling over our new constitution, but I still believe in a unified Canada, I believe in one nation extending from sea to sea. The Fathers of Confederation were right, a federation of provinces can work.
8. Career opportunities appear very good for students in a wide range of technical programs, however most employers are looking for people with experience as well as training.
9. People with high-technology skills are urgently required in several fields, plastics processing, mould-making, and tool- and die-making are three examples.
10. For college students in technology programs, then, the future looks bright, however a diploma does not necessarily guarantee job security.

The Run-On Sentence

In the true **run-on sentence,** too many ideas are crowded into one sentence. In general, a sentence should convey no more than two ideas. There is no hard and fast rule about how many clauses you may have in a sentence, but more than two independent clauses can result in a sentence that's hard to read and even harder to understand.

> There were still twelve people at the party, but after Janice went home we decided it was time to leave, so we collected our coats and said good-bye to the others, and, after a careful drive home at 50 km/h, we drank coffee and stayed up until 3:00 A.M. discussing the evening's events.

It's obvious that the storyteller who created this monster got carried away with enthusiasm for the tale and just scribbled everything down without much thought. Take your time and keep your readers in mind, and you probably won't make this sort of error. If you do find run-on sentences in your writing, however, follow this rule:

> Fix sentences that are too long by breaking them up into shorter sentences.

There were still twelve people at the party, but after Janice went home we decided it was time to leave. So we collected our coats and said good-bye to the others. After a careful drive home at 50 km/h, we drank coffee and stayed up until 3:00 A.M. discussing the evening's events.

EXERCISE 4*

Using the four types of corrections you've learned in this chapter, make these sentences easier to read. There is more than one right way of fixing them; just be sure your corrected sentences are easy to read and make sense. The answers we've provided are only suggestions.

1. Since you are interested in both careers, you should probably play hockey now and take up teaching in the future, usually the legs give out before the mind does.

2. In the past fifteen years, we have seen a remarkable increase in the health consciousness of the average North American, and the result has been a huge and growing industry that attempts to make fitness painless or even fun, from health clubs and aerobics classes to weight lifting and diet plans, we have an almost limitless choice of ways to spend our money on our bodies.

3. Joan is a complete hypocrite now that she is wealthy, insisting with every other breath that she hasn't changed a bit, she drives a Rolls, flaunts her furs, and wears diamonds in bunches.

4. The hockey season now extends well into the baseball season, which, in turn, encroaches on the football season, and football, being a fall and winter sport, extends halfway into the hockey schedule, and so it goes, with basketball overlapping the other three.

5. Following the high-speed chase and subsequent arrest of the car's driver, the police learned that the vehicle had been stolen and they

added a charge of theft to the reckless driving charge, and the young man spent the night in jail, there he came to realize the seriousness of his predicament, and he asked for permission to make a telephone call so he could get in touch with his parents' lawyer.

EXERCISE 5*

Correct the following sentences where necessary. Your answers may differ somewhat from ours.

Fourteen people live in Punkeydoodle's Corner, Ontario. A town famous for its funny name. Twenty-five kilometres west of Kitchener, Punkeydoodle's Corner was a stagecoach stop on the Huron Trail during the nineteenth century, when it was a bustling town of more than one hundred people, but as stagecoaches gave way to trains, which, in turn, gave way to automobiles, the little town dwindled and shrank until only three families were left to call it home.

Several different stories account for the origin of the town's name, the hero of one of these stories was a man called John Zurbrigg. Who was a Swiss settler and pumpkin farmer. According to the tale, Zurbrigg was a rather lazy man, preferring to "doodle" his time away rather than tend to his pumpkins. One of his neighbours, furious at Zurbrigg's idleness, is said to have labeled him "punkey doodle" during an argument, history does not record Zurbrigg's response.

Another story claims the town got its name from John Zurbuchen. The chubby, genial host of the old hotel in the town, who had been born in

Germany, then moved to Ontario in the 1860s with his family. Apparently, Zurbuchen never quite mastered English pronunciation, he loved to sing, though, and frequently entertained his beer-drinking customers with his version of "Yankee Doodle." Which he mispronounced "Punkey Doodle." Both of these stories seem a bit farfetched, if you ask me.

Its unusual name attracts hundreds of visitors to Punkeydoodle's Corner every year, however being a tourist attraction has one disadvantage, according to the townspeople. Every time they put up a sign to identify their village. The sign is stolen within a few weeks. Even when it is firmly embedded in concrete.

EXERCISE 6*

This paragraph contains several kinds of sentence error, all of which can be corrected by changing the punctuation of the passage. Make the necessary corrections; then compare your corrections with ours.

Until I moved to the country, I could never see the attraction of bird-watching as a pastime, my parents had enjoyed bird-watching as a hobby for years. Frequently boring me numb with their enthusiastic tales of warblers heard or kingfishers sighted. While I lived in the city I saw birds so infrequently that I was completely indifferent to my parents' enthusiasm, those birds I did see were always pigeons, sparrows, or starlings, anyway. Within a week of moving out of the city to take a new job. I began to take notice of my feathered neighbours, I was awakened three mornings in a row by squawking blue jays. Three days later a convention of crows descended on my property. Sending everyone indoors for two days. My bird-watching really became an obsession when I was dive-bombed repeatedly by an irate woodpecker. Which I had offended in some mysterious way. Now, protected by a surplus army helmet and armed with binoculars. I go on excursions with the most dedicated birders, however whereas they creep silently through the underbrush and meticulously record each sighting in a log book, I crash about, threatening and cursing any birds I encounter and now everyone regards me with pity or contempt and more than one former friend has suggested that I've gone "cuckoo."

EXERCISE 7

As a final test of your ability to identify and correct sentence errors, supply the appropriate sentence breaks to make this garble into a grammatically correct paragraph.

Gordon is convinced that he is a great musician all that he needs is to discover the instrument on which his genius can flower in the course of trying to make this discovery, he has tried the alto recorder, the B flat clarinet, the Spanish guitar, and the five-string banjo each of these instruments was taken up with enthusiasm and devotion, but each was cast aside within a few months as it revealed that it could not bring forth Gordon's hidden musical talents several suggestions were made at about this time in his musical career, the most memorable by his parents who had to endure the loud learning process on each instrument, but Gordon was certain of success and deaf to any hint that his lack of musicianship was due to anything but his bad luck in not being able to discover his proper medium his parents gave up his friends deserted him but still he persisted his refusal to quit was finally rewarded and now he may be heard recorded on several albums and live with his group at many music festivals after about twelve frustrating years of experimentation Gordon discovered the instrument that best expresses his talent: the kazoo.

CHAPTER 29

Solving Modifier Problems

The thieves were caught before much of the loot could be disposed of <u>by the police.</u>

<u>Stamping her feet and switching her tail to brush away flies</u>, Susan led the mare out of the barn.

<u>At the age of five</u>, the barber cut Jamie's hair, <u>which curled to his shoulders nearly</u> for the first time.

These sentences show what can happen to your writing if you aren't sure how to use modifiers. A **modifier** is a word or group of words that adds information about another word in a sentence. In the examples above, the underlined words are modifiers. Used correctly, modifiers describe or explain or limit another word, making its meaning more precise. Used carelessly, however, modifiers can cause confusion or, even worse, amusement. There's nothing more embarrassing than being laughed at when you didn't mean to be funny.

You need to be able to recognize and solve two kinds of modifier problems: misplaced modifiers and dangling modifiers.

Misplaced Modifiers

Modifiers must be as close as possible to the words they apply to. Usually, readers will assume that a modifier modifies whatever it's next to. It's important to remember this, because, as the following examples show, changing the position of a modifier can change the meaning of your sentence.

I told Mr. Jones only what I had done. (I didn't tell him anything else.)

I told only Mr. Jones what I had done. (I didn't tell anybody else.)

Only I told Mr. Jones what I had done. (Nobody else told Mr. Jones.)

I told Mr. Jones what only I had done. (No one else did it.)

> To make sure a modifier is in the right place, ask yourself, "What does it apply to?" and put it beside that word.

When a modifier is not close enough to the word it refers to, it is said to be misplaced. A **misplaced modifier** can be *a single word in the wrong place*:

The supervisor told me they needed someone who could type badly.

Is some company really hiring people to do poor work? Or does the company urgently need a typist? Obviously, the modifier *badly* belongs next to *needed*:

The supervisor told me they badly needed someone who could type.

> Be especially careful with these words: *almost, nearly, just, only, even, hardly, merely, scarcely.* Put them right before the words they modify.

Misplaced: I almost ate the whole thing.

Correctly placed: I ate almost the whole thing.

Misplaced: When he played goal in the NHL, Glenn Hall nearly threw up before every game.

Correctly placed: When he played goal in the NHL, Glenn Hall threw up before nearly every game.

A **misplaced modifier** can also be *a group of words in the wrong place:*

Scratching each other playfully, we watched the monkeys.

The modifier, *scratching each other playfully,* is too far away from the word it is supposed to modify, *monkeys.* In fact, it seems to modify *we,* making the sentence ridiculous. We need to rewrite the sentence:

We watched the monkeys scratching each other playfully.

Look at this one:

I worked for my father, who owns a sawmill during the summer.

During the summer applies to *worked* and should be closer to it:

During the summer, I worked for my father, who owns a sawmill.

Notice that a modifier need not always go right next to what it modifies; it should, however, be as close as possible to it.

Occasionally, as in the examples above, the modifier is obviously out of place. The writer's intention is clear, and the sentences are easy to correct. But sometimes modifiers are misplaced in such a way that the meaning is not clear, as in this example:

Lucy said on her way out she would give the memo to John.

Did Lucy *say* it on her way out? Or is she going to *deliver the memo* on her way out? To avoid confusion, we must move the modifier and, depending on which meaning we want, write either

On her way out, Lucy said she would give the memo to John.

or

Lucy said she would give the memo to John on her way out.

Now try your hand at relocating misplaced modifiers. Rewrite the sentences that contain misplaced modifiers, positioning the modifiers correctly. Check your answers to the first set before going on.

EXERCISE 1*

1. There is a library on the third floor that has a washroom.

2. He told us on the first day no one works hard.

3. It is usually only once in a lifetime that a golfer gets a hole-in-one.

4. My supervisor told me in January I would get a raise.

5. We almost applied for every job that was posted.

6. He played the guitar all the time I was there beautifully.

7. There just are enough pieces to go around.

8. They couldn't remember which house Sean was living in when they drove down his street.

9. Unless they're French or Italian, some people never go to movies.

10. By working night and day, he almost managed to pay for all the damage for which his brother had been charged.

EXERCISE 2*

1. One finds the best Chinese food in those restaurants where the Chinese eat usually.

2. He caught sight of a canary and several finches using his new binoculars.

3. Juan had played ball professionally before coming to the Blue Jays for several major American teams.

4. The football practices have been organized for players who are not with a team in the summertime as a keep-fit measure.

5. Vancouver is a wonderful city for anyone who likes rain and fog to live in.

6. Some games are less demanding in terms of time and equipment, such as tiddlywinks.

7. The Human Rights Code prohibits discrimination against anyone who is applying for a job on the basis of race, sex, or age.

8. I was able to loosen the clamp that held the broken cable in place with a screwdriver.

9. They waited breathlessly under the trees for the return of their dog, which had been sprayed by a skunk with an open can of tomato juice.

10. Tonight Sue Johansen will lead a panel discussion on relaxation, including how to tone and stretch muscles, how to relieve tension, and even how to sleep through sex.

Dangling Modifiers

A **dangling modifier** occurs when there is *no appropriate word in the sentence for the modifier to apply to.* Or, a modifier is said to be "dangling" when the sentence does not contain a *specific word* or *idea* to which the modifier could sensibly refer. With no appropriate word to modify, the modifier *seems* to apply to whatever it's next to, often with ridiculous results:

After four semesters of hard work, my parents rewarded me with a car.
(This sentence seems to say that the parents are going to school.)

Jogging along the sidewalk, a truck swerved and nearly hit me.

(The *truck* was jogging along the sidewalk?)

Dangling modifiers are trickier to fix than misplaced ones; you can't simply move danglers to another spot in the sentence. There are, however, two ways in which you can fix them. One way requires that you remember this rule:

> When a modifier comes at the beginning of a sentence, it modifies the subject of the sentence.

(The rule has exceptions called adverbial modifiers, but they won't give you any trouble. *Example:* Quickly she did as she was told.)

This rule means that you can avoid dangling modifiers by choosing the subjects of your sentences carefully. All you have to do is make sure the subject is an appropriate one for the modifier to apply to. Using this method, we can rewrite our two examples by changing the subjects:

> (After four semesters of hard work,) I got my reward. My parents bought me a car.
>
> (Jogging along the sidewalk,) I was nearly hit by a swerving truck.

Another way to correct a dangling modifier is by changing it into a dependent clause:

> After I had completed four semesters of hard work, my parents rewarded me with a car.
>
> As I was jogging along the sidewalk, a truck swerved and nearly hit me.

Sometimes a dangling modifier comes at the end of a sentence:

> McDonald's would be a good place to go, not having much money.

Can you correct this sentence? Try it; then look at the suggestions at the foot of the page.

Here is a summary of the steps to follow in solving modifier problems:

---

1. Ask "What does the modifier apply to?"
2. Be sure there is a word *in the sentence* for the modifier to apply to.
3. Put the modifier as close as possible to the word it applies to.

EXERCISE 3*

Most of these sentences contain dangling modifiers. Make corrections by changing the subject of the sentence to one the modifier can appropriately

---

Here are two suggestions:
1. Add a subject: Not having much money, I thought McDonald's would be a good place to go.
2. Change the dangler to a dependent clause: McDonald's would be a good place to go since I don't have much money.

apply to. There is no one, "right" way to correct each sentence; our answers are only suggestions.

1. Considering Michael's charm and good manners, his good looks are unimportant.

2. My supervisor gave me a lecture about punctuality after being late twice in one week.

3. After criticizing both my work and my attitude, I was fired.

4. Trying to bunt, the ball went over the fence at centre field for a home run.

5. When looking over their résumés, Carol and George have completely different backgrounds, but both could do the job.

6. Rated tops in his field, Stuart will run the first heats in the two-sprint relays and the last heat in the marathon relay.

7. Not realizing the implications of the weather reports, they set sail for the distant island.

8. Fifteen minutes after setting sail for the island, the storm struck.

9. After struggling desperately for almost two hours with high winds and torrential rains, it stopped as suddenly as it had begun.

10. Even in hot weather, the legs and feet should be warmed and stretched before doing any serious jogging.

EXERCISE 4

Correct the dangling modifiers in Exercise 3 by changing them into dependent clauses.

EXERCISE 5*

Correct the misplaced and dangling modifiers in any way you choose. Our answers are only suggestions.

1. As a college student constantly faced with new assignments, the pressure is sometimes intolerable.

2. Being horribly hung over, the only problem with a free bar is knowing when to quit.

3. Rotting slowly over the years, the villagers no longer drive cars or ride bicycles over the bridge.

4. The Canadian Brass receives enthusiastic acclaim for its witty presentation, its wide repertoire, and its clarity of tone from Vancouver to Halifax.

5. Carrying two shopping bags full of old clothes and several other bags, our hearts were wrung by the frail, unkempt, little woman.

6. I learned that the provincial premiers will meet in July in the *Vancouver Province*.

7. After looking at the gorgeous dress all week, they sold it before I got there on payday.

8. On the day I was demonstrating how to make a Caesar salad, I left the Parmesan cheese in my locker which was my favourite ingredient.

9. Barry will prepare a Japanese sukiyaki dinner for his guests cooked in a wok and served with steamed rice.

10. The person who has lived for a long time in most cases has lived a simple life.

EXERCISE 6

Correct the misplaced and dangling modifiers, using any solution you choose.

1. A worm-eating warbler was spotted by Hazel Miller while walking along the branch of a tree and singing.

2. When trying for your Red Cross bronze medal, your examiner will consider speed, endurance, and resuscitation techniques.

3. The University of Toronto's research in heart disease this month will be summarized in a special issue of the *Canadian Medical Journal*.

4. Trapped under a delicate crystal wine glass on the elegantly set table, his guests observed that most despised of uninvited dinner guests, a cockroach.

5. Not being reliable about arriving on time, I can't hire her to supervise others who *are* punctual.

6. The parks superintendent explained that reforestation was urgent in Ontario's northernmost provincial parks on Friday at the Toronto conference.

7. He maintains the tack, grooms the horses, and shovels manure just like his father.

8. At the age of five, his mother took Scott to the movie theatre that had been in the neighbourhood for many years for the first time.

9. We always pay our respects to our friends and relatives when they have passed on in a funeral parlour.

10. "This bus has a seating capacity of 56 passengers with a maximum height of 14 feet, 6 inches." (Sign on a double-decker bus in Charlottetown, P.E.I.)

CHAPTER 30

The Parallelism Principle

When writing about items in a series—such as main points in a preview statement, for example—you must be sure all the items are **parallel;** that is, they must be written in the same grammatical form.

> I like camping, fishing, and to hike.

The items in this list are not parallel. Two end in *ing*, but the third *(to hike)* is the infinitive form of the verb. To correct the sentence, you must make all the items in the list take the same grammatical form— either

> I like to camp, to fish, and to hike.
>   or
> I like camping, fishing, and hiking.

Correct faulty parallelism by giving the items in a series the same grammatical form.

One way to tell whether all the items in a list are parallel is to picture (or actually write) the items in list form, one below the other, aligning the similar elements. That way, you can make sure that all the elements are the same—that they are all words, or phrases, or clauses.

NOT PARALLEL	PARALLEL

Sharon is kind,
    considerate, and
  likes to help.
	Sharon is kind,
	    considerate, and
	  helpful.

I support myself by tending bar,
    piano, and
  shooting pool.
	I support myself by tending bar,
	    playing piano, and
	  shooting pool.

Her upbringing made her neat,
    polite, and
  an obnoxious
      person.
	Her upbringing made her neat,
	    polite, and
	  obnoxious.

Gordon tries to do what is right,
    different things, and
  make a profit.
	Gordon tries to do what is right,
	    what is different, and
	  what is profitable.

With his sharp mind,
by having the boss as his uncle, and
    few enemies,
he'll go far.
	With his sharp mind,
	  the boss as his uncle, and
	  few enemies,
	  he'll go far.
	
	or
	
	Having a sharp mind,
	  the boss as his uncle, and
	  few enemies,
	  he'll go far.

As you can see, achieving parallelism is partly a matter of developing an ear for the sound of a correct list. Practice, and the exercises in this chapter, will help. As you work through the exercises, try to spot faulty parallelism from the *sound* of the sentences, before you examine them closely to correct their mistakes. Check your answers to each set before going on.

EXERCISE 1*

1. I'm looking for a babysitter who is intelligent, patient, and who is basically a kind person.

2. Make sure your report is comprehensive, readable, and above all that it records everything accurately.

3. Those in community-service fields must be loving, patient, objective, and they must also be able to understand people's problems.

4. The location, staff, and the way it looked made that hospital a more pleasant place to stay than most.

5. We were told to study the report carefully and that we should make our recommendations in writing.

6. Their chances for a lasting relationship aren't good, considering their goals are extremely different, their temperamental differences, and their cultural differences.

7. Her small build, quick temper, and the fact that she has a criminal record will disqualify her from becoming a corrections officer.

8. Barry is everything a girl could want: handsome, intelligent, successful, and he's even kind to his mother.

9. The space-age kitchen, the pool and sauna, and a security system that was burglar-proof were what sold us on the apartment.

10. Mr. Redfern explained how the tape recorder worked, the microphone and camera, and how to use the video cassette recorder.

EXERCISE 2*

1. Body-building has made me what I am today: physically perfect, very prosperous financially, and practically friendless.

2. If there is no heaven, then hell can't exist either.

3. In my tiny home town, two significantly related crimes prevail: vandalism, and there is a lot of drug-trafficking.

4. I'd like to help, but I'm too tired, I'm too poor, and my time is already taken up with other things.

5. I wanted either a Mother's pizza or I wanted a Big Mac from McDonald's.

6. Garfield understands pretty clearly what he can get away with and what he can't.

7. My sister, who's trying to teach me to play tennis, says that my forehand and serve are all right, but to work on strengthening my backhand.

8. The two factors thought to be most important in a long-lasting marriage are how committed each partner is to the marriage and the willingness to compromise.

9. Barry claimed that, through constant repetition and being firm, he had trained his guppy to be obedient, quiet, and show loyalty.

10. The new budget must deal with several major problems, two of them being the devalued Canadian dollar and the fact that the inflation rate rose so high.

EXERCISE 3 *

Make the following lists parallel. In each case there's more than one way to do it, because you can make your items parallel with any item in the list. Therefore, your answers may differ from ours. Here's an example:

wrong:	stick handling	score a goal
right:	stick handling	goal scoring
or		
right:	handle the stick	score a goal

1. wrong: wine   women   singing
   right:

2. wrong: privately   in public
   right:

3. wrong: employers   those working for
                               the employer
   right:

4. wrong: lying about all   to do whatever I
               morning   please
   right:

5. wrong: individually   as a group
   right:

6. wrong: happy   healthy   wisdom
   right:

7. wrong: doing your best   don't give up
   right:

8. wrong: information   education   entertaining
   right:

9. wrong: insufficient time   too little money   not enough staff
   right:

10. wrong: French is the   English is the best   Profanity is best
               language of   language for   in German
               love   business
   right:

EXERCISE 4*

As a test of your mastery of parallelism, try these sentences.

1. Working with children is stimulating, challenging, and has its rewards.
2. Not being able to speak the language causes confusion, is frustrating, and it's embarrassing.
3. To prevent crime, attending to victims of accidents and crimes, and how to safely apprehend those suspected of crime are a police officer's responsibilities.
4. Being sound of mind and physically strong, the elderly man was able to live quite happily by himself.
5. Three of the issues the committee will have to deal with right away are camp maintenance, how to get staff for the camp, and promoting the camp.
6. His doctor advised him to eat less, exercise more, and no smoking at all.
7. For many people, attending AA meetings is first embarrassing, possibly even humiliating, then helpful, and finally it is a success.
8. A high level of motivation, experience in problem-solving, and not worrying about your decisions are necessary if you hope to run a successful business.
9. Influential factors in any nation's economic regression are bad management of natural resources, policies regarding national debt might be unwise, and the unions' inflationary demands.
10. Although the first applicant seemed scared and showed shyness, the second was a composed person and outgoing.

EXERCISE 5

Correct the faulty parallelism in this paragraph.

The dictionary can be both a useful resource and an educational entertainment. Everyone knows that its three chief functions are to check spelling, for finding out the meanings of words, and what the correct pronunciation is. Few people, however, use the dictionary for discovery and learning. There are several methods of using the dictionary as an aid to discovery. One is randomly looking at words, another is to read a page or two thoroughly, and still another is by skimming through words until you find an unfamiliar one. It is by this latter method that I discovered the word "steatopygous," a term I now try to use at least once a day. You can increase your vocabulary significantly by using the dictionary, and of course a large and varied vocabulary can be used to baffle your colleagues, employers will be impressed, and your English teacher will be surprised.

CHAPTER 31

Refining by Combining

To reinforce what you've learned so far about sentence structure, try your voice and your hand (preferably with a pencil in it) at sentence combining. You've freed your writing of fragments; you've cast out demon comma splices; you're riding herd on run-ons. You may find, however, that your sentences, although technically correct, are choppy or repetitious. And you may be bored with conveying the same idea in the same old way. Sentence combining will not only test your mastery of sentence structure but also enable you to polish and refine your writing.

What is sentence combining? Sometimes called sentence generating, sentence building, sentence revising, or embedding, **sentence combining** is a technique that enables you to avoid a choppy, monotonous style while at the same time producing correct sentences. You can combine sentences in three ways:

> 1. Link two or more short sentences into a longer one using connecting words such as *and, or, but.*
> 2. Merge two or more short sentences into a longer one using dependent-clause cues (see Chapter 27).
> 3. Combine clusters of related sentences into paragraphs.

Let's look at an example of two short, technically correct sentences that could be combined:

The paperboy collects on Fridays.
The paperboy delivers the *Winnipeg Free Press* on Saturdays.

There are several ways of combining these two statements into a single smooth sentence:

The paperboy delivers the *Winnipeg Free Press* on Saturdays and collects on Fridays.

The paperboy, who delivers the *Winnipeg Free Press* on Saturdays, collects on Fridays.

On Fridays, the paperboy collects for the *Winnipeg Free Press,* which he delivers on Saturdays.

The aim of sentence combining is to make good sentences, not long ones. Don't forget that clarity is essential and that brevity has force. By rearranging words, changing their form, deleting repetitious or unnecessary words or phrases, and adding clear connectives, you are able to combine a number of short statements into several acceptable sentences.
Here's an example:

1. Correct but stilted sentences conveying an idea:

Pierre Trudeau was an influence.
He influenced Canadian politics.
His influence was strong in the 1970s.

2. Correct and smooth sentences conveying the same idea:

Pierre Trudeau had a strong influence on Canadian politics in the 1970s.

Pierre Trudeau strongly influenced Canadian politics in the 1970s.

In the 1970s, Canadian politics was strongly influenced by Pierre Trudeau.

The skills that you learn by combining sentences identify you as a perceptive and sensitive writer. They are useful not only in writing and speaking, but also in reading, listening, and problem solving.
In the following exercises, make sure you rehearse your solutions *orally* before you write them. You may also want to refer to Chapters 39 and 40, on the comma and the semicolon.

EXERCISE 1*

Combine the following sentences, using the connecting words *and, but, or, nor, for, so, yet.*

1. The Beatles are a musical institution.
   Their music appeals to every generation.

2. Kate Bush does not give live performances.
   She does not tour with her music.

3. Janet Jackson has a famous brother.
   She had to work hard to create a unique sound.

4. Van Halen is a progressive rock group.
   They take offence at being labeled "heavy metal."

5. You can read about Elton John's suicide attempt in music magazines.
   You can listen to "Someone Saved My Life Tonight."

6. The Rolling Stones originated in the sixties.
   They are still performing now, in the nineties.

7. Madonna is considered a controversial artist.
   She has made several sexually explicit videos.

8. Phil Collins is a popular contemporary solo artist.
   His roots go back to Genesis.

9. Bryan Adams is to be commended for his work on "Tears Are Not Enough."
   Anne Murray, Cory Hart, and Salome Bey contributed to making the song a success.

10. The Nylons are renowned for singing *a cappella,* or without accompaniment.
    They occasionally feature background instruments.

EXERCISE 2*

Using dependent-clause cues (see Chapter 27), combine the following sentences into longer, more interesting units.

1. The Calgary Flames have been a mainstay in the NHL.
   The team moved from Atlanta.

2. Fred McGriff has a devastating swing.
   He is one of the most feared hitters in the American League.

3. Tim Wallach of the Montreal Expos won a "gold glove."
   It was in recognition of his outstanding defensive skills.

4. Bo Jackson is a talented athlete.
   He is playing baseball for the Kansas City Royals or football for the Los Angeles Raiders.

5. The Blue Jays always seem to win.
   The SkyDome roof is closed.

6. The Vancouver Canucks are now acknowledged as a team to be reckoned with.
   They struggled for years to improve.

7. The Montreal Expos draw impressive crowds to Olympic Stadium.
   They are winning.

8. The Montreal Canadiens have won many Stanley Cups.
   The Quebec Nordiques have yet to win even one.

9. Wayne Gretzky is an exceptional hockey player.
   Some sportswriters consider him a defensive liability.

10. George Bell is an important role model for his team.
    He is a bigger role model for children in the Dominican Republic.
    George Bell comes from the Dominican Republic.

EXERCISE 3*

Combine the following sentences, using the connecting words listed in Exercise 1 and the dependent-clause cues listed in Chapter 27 (p. 246).

1. Rudolf loses a girlfriend.
   He goes shopping for new clothes.

2. Failure breeds fatigue, according to Mortimer Adler.
   There is nothing more energizing than success.

3. Love one another.
   Make not a bond of love.

4. You must learn to love yourself.
   You can truly love someone else.

5. Marriage is for serious people.
   I have not considered it an option.

6. Divorce is an acknowledgment.
   There was not a true commitment in the first place.
   Some people still believe this.

7. Twenty percent of adults in America are illiterate.
   Fifty percent of the adults who *can* read say they never read books.
   This is an astonishing fact.

8. Canada is a relatively rich country.
   Most of us brush up against hunger and homelessness almost daily.
   We encounter men and, less often, women begging.
   They are on downtown streetcorners.

9. In his essay, "A Modest Proposal for a Divorce Ceremony," Pierre Berton proposed that Canada institute a formal divorce ceremony.
   The divorce ceremony would be like a formal wedding ceremony.
   All the symbolism would be reversed.

10. The bride, for example, would wear black.
    Immediately after the ceremony, the newly divorced couple would go into the vestry.
    They would scratch their names off the marriage register.

After you have combined a number of sentences, you can evaluate your work. Read your sentences out loud. How they *sound* is important. Test your work against these six characteristics of successful sentences:

1. Meaning   Have you conveyed the idea you intend?

2. Clarity   Is your sentence clear? Can it be understood on the first reading?

3. Coherence   Do the various parts of the sentence fit together logically and smoothly?

4. Emphasis   Are the most important ideas and phrases either at the end or at the beginning of the sentence?

5. Conciseness   Is the sentence wordy? Have you cut out all redundant or repetitious words?

6. Rhythm   Does the sentence flow smoothly? Are there any interruptions in the development of the key idea(s)? Do the interruptions help to emphasize important points, or do they merely distract the reader?

If your sentences pass all six tests of successful sentence style, you may be confident that they are both technically correct and pleasing to the ear. No reader could ask for more.

Grammar

CHAPTER 32

Subject–Verb Agreement

Errors in grammar are like flies in soup: they don't usually affect meaning any more than flies affect flavour. But, like flies, grammar errors are distracting and irritating. They must be eliminated if you want your readers to pay attention to what you say rather than how you say it.

One of the most common grammatical problems is failure to make the subject and verb in a sentence agree with each other. Here is the rule for subject–verb agreement:

> Singular subjects take singular verbs.
> Plural subjects take plural verbs.

Remember that *singular* words concern one person or thing . . .

The phone <u>rings</u>.   Geoff <u>watches</u> TV.

Plural words concern more than one person or thing:

The phones <u>ring</u>.   Geoff and Tess <u>watch</u> TV.

The rule for subject–verb agreement will cause you no problem at all, as long as you make sure that the word the verb agrees with is really the subject. To see how a problem can arise, look at this example:

One of the boys write graffiti.

The writer forgot that the subject of a sentence is never in a prepositional phrase. The verb needs to be changed to agree with *one:*

>One of the boys writes graffiti.

If you're careful about identifying the subject of your sentence, you'll
have no trouble with subject–verb agreement. To sharpen your subject-
finding ability, review Chapter 25, "Cracking the Sentence Code." Then
do the following exercises.

EXERCISE 1*

Rewrite each of the following sentences, using the alternate beginning
shown.

Example: She wants to learn about data processing.
>>They want to learn about data processing.

1. He sells used essays to other students.
   They
2. They often spend the weekend on their sailboat.
   He
3. The woman maintains that her boss has been ogling her.
   The women
4. Her flight has been delayed because of the storm.
   Their flights
5. That new computer affects the entire office procedure.
   Those
6. She likes to work with children, so she is looking for a job in a day-
   care centre.
   They
7. Everyone who shops at Pimrock's receives a free can of tuna.
   All those
8. That girl's father is looking for a rich husband for her.
   Those
9. The civil servant with an indexed pension stands to gain from future
   inflation.
   Civil servants
10. Each of her sons is successful in his own way.
    Both

EXERCISE 2*

Rewrite each sentence, switching the position of its two main elements.

Example: Chocolate milkshakes are my weakness.
>>My weakness is chocolate milkshakes.

1. Vince's first love in life is Atari games.
   Atari games
2. What Marcia spends most of her time on is movies.
   Movies
3. Hostess Twinkies are the only junk food Tim eats.

4. Frequent nights of debauchery were the cause of his downfall.

5. What the team needs now is a good pitcher and outfielder.

6. What keeps Superman strong is clean living and Lois Lane.

7. Frequently, absences from class and failed exams are the cause of failure.

8. Brown rice and tofu are what I least like to eat.

9. Something that I didn't understand was accounting procedures.

10. Your stunning good looks are the reason for your success in the aluminum-siding business.

So far, so good. You can find the subject, even when it's hiding on the far side of the verb or nearly buried under a load of prepositional phrases. You can match up singular subjects with singular verbs, and plural subjects with plural verbs. Now let's take a look at a few of the complications that make subject–verb agreement into such a disagreeable problem.

Six Special Cases

Some subjects are tricky: they look singular but are actually plural, or they look plural when they're really singular. There are six different kinds of these slippery subjects, all of them common, and all of them likely to trip up the unwary writer.

1. Multiple subjects joined by *or, either . . . or, neither . . . nor, not . . . but.* All the multiple subjects we've dealt with so far have been joined by *and* and have required plural verbs, so agreement hasn't been a problem. But watch out when the two or more elements of a multiple subject are joined by *or, either . . . or, neither . . . nor,* or *not . . . but.* In these cases, *the verb agrees in number with the nearest subject.* That is, if the subject closest to the verb is singular, the verb will be singular; if the subject closest to the verb is plural, the verb must be plural, too.

> Neither the prime minister nor the cabinet ministers are responsible.

> Neither the cabinet ministers nor the prime minister is responsible.

EXERCISE 3*

Circle the correct verb.

1. Neither the man nor his previous wives (know knows) who buried the treasure in the orchard.
2. Not high interest rates but high unemployment (is are) Canadians' first concern.
3. The college has decided that neither final marks nor a diploma (is are) to be issued to students owing library fines.
4. Either your job performance or your school assignments (is are) going to suffer if you continue your frantic life-style.
5. According to my guidebook entitled *Sightseeing in Transylvania*, not sharp stakes but garlic cloves (repel repels) the dreaded vampires.

2. Subjects that look multiple but really aren't. Don't be fooled by phrases beginning with such words as *with, like, as well as, together with, in addition to, including*. These phrases are NOT part of the subject of the sentence. Cross them out mentally; they do not affect the verb.

> My typing teacher, ~~as well as my counsellor,~~ has advised me to switch programs.

Obviously, two people were involved in the advising; nevertheless, the subject (teacher) is singular, and so the verb must be singular (has advised).

> All my courses, ~~including chemistry,~~ are easier this term.

If you mentally cross out the phrase "including chemistry," you can easily see that the verb (are) must be plural to agree with the plural subject (courses).

EXERCISE 4*

Circle the correct verb.

1. Prime Minister Mulroney, along with his cabinet ministers, (is are) held responsible for our economic woes by many Canadians.

2. Wayne Gretzky, like Bobby Orr and Gordie Howe, (has have) become a hockey legend.
3. My English teacher, in addition to my math and data processing instructors, (inflict inflicts) a considerable amount of pain on me.
4. The company Tim keeps, not to mention the places he frequents, (is are) highly suspect.
5. His parole officer, in addition to the police, (keep keeps) a close eye on him.

3. Words ending in *one, thing,* or *body.* When used as subjects, the following words are always singular, requiring the singular form of the verb:

everyone	everything	everybody
anyone	anything	anybody
someone	something	somebody
no one	nothing	nobody

The last part of the word is the tip-off here: every*one*, any*thing*, no*body*. If you focus on this last part, you'll remember to use a singular verb with these subjects. Usually, these words are troublesome only when modifiers crop up between them and their verbs. For example, no one would write "Everyone are here." The trouble starts when you sandwich a group of words between the subject and the verb. You might, if you weren't on your toes, write this: "Everyone involved in implementing the company's new policies and procedures are here." Obviously, the meaning is plural: several people are present. But the subject (everyone) is singular in form, so the verb must be *is.*

EXERCISE 5*

Circle the correct verb.

1. Everybody in the first and second years of this program (is are) affected by the cutbacks.
2. Anyone who has seen the Grateful Dead perform (love loves) them.
3. No one who had anything to do with these projects (was were) talking about them.
4. Everything I enjoy doing on weekends (is are) illegal, immoral, or fattening.
5. Nothing you can offer me, including your collection of Argonaut autographs, (is are) likely to induce me to change my mind.

4. *Each, either (of), neither (of).* Used as subjects, these take singular verbs.

Either <u>was</u> suitable for the job.

Each <u>wants</u> desperately to win.

<u>Neither</u> of the stores <u>is</u> open after six o'clock. (Remember, the subject is never in a prepositional phrase.)

EXERCISE 6*

Circle the correct verb.

1. Unless we hear from the coach, neither of those team members (is are) playing this evening.
2. Either of those courses (involve involves) field placement.
3. You will be pleased to hear that neither (has have) the measles.
4. Each of the women (want wants) to win the Ms. Oshawa bodybuilding competition.
5. Strict discipline is what each of those teachers (believe believes) in.

5. Collective nouns. **A collective noun** is a word naming a group. Some examples are *company, class, committee, team, crowd, group, family, audience, public,* and *majority.* When you are referring to the group acting as a *unit,* use a *singular* verb. When you are referring to the *members* of the group acting *individually,* use a *plural* verb.

The team is sure to win tomorrow's game. (Here *team* refers to the group acting as a whole.)

The team are getting into their uniforms now. (The separate members of the team are acting individually.)

EXERCISE 7*

Circle the correct verb.

1. The whole class (is are) attending the weekend seminar.
2. The Canadian public (prefer prefers) hockey to opera.
3. Right after breakfast, the family (leaves leave) for various schools and jobs.
4. After a performance by Teenage Head, the audience often (brawl brawls) among themselves for hours.
5. The committee (was were) unanimous in its selection of a spokesperson.

6. Units of money, time, mass, length, and distance. These require singular verbs.

Four dollars <u>is</u> too much to pay for a hamburger.

Three hours <u>is</u> a long time to wait, and <u>five kilometres</u> <u>is</u> too far to walk.

Seventy kilograms <u>is</u> the mass of an average man.

EXERCISE 8*

Circle the correct verb.

1. No wonder you are suspicious if seventy dollars (was were) what you paid for last night's pizza.
2. Tim told his girlfriend that nine years (seem seems) like a long time to wait.
3. Forty hours of classes (is are) too much in one week.
4. When you are anxiously awaiting the next gas station, thirty kilometres (is are) a long distance.
5. Seventy-five cents (seems seem) a fair price for a slightly tattered Kelly Gruber card.

In Exercises 9 and 10, correct the errors in subject–verb agreement. Check your answers to each exercise before going on.

EXERCISE 9*

1. My sense of the schools are that none of them are any good.

2. Neither of them remember who ran against Art Eggleton for mayor of Toronto.

3. Every one of the SUNshine Boys appeal to my sense of the sublime.

4. My whole family, with the exception of Fido, dislike anchovy pizza.

5. Popular belief notwithstanding, quicksand do not suck you under or pull you down.

6. It is the suction created by the victims that are responsible for the pulling effect.

7. Neither age nor illness prevents Uncle Alf from pinching the nurses.

8. Eight hundred dollars per term, all students agree, are too much to pay for their education.

9. The birth of quintuplets were too much for the mother to cope with.

10. Everything that we agreed to last night seem silly this morning.

EXERCISE 10*

Quebec City, along with Montreal, Toronto, and Vancouver, are among Canada's great gourmet centres. While Toronto is a relative latecomer to this list, neither Quebec City nor Montreal are strangers to those who seeks fine dining. Indeed, travel and food magazines have long affirmed that the inclusion of these two cities in a Quebec vacation are a "must." Montreal is perhaps more international in its offerings, but Quebec City provides exquisite proof that French Canadian cuisine and hospitality is second to none in the world. Amid the old-world charm of the lower city is to be found some of the quaintest and most enjoyable traditional restaurants; the newer sections of town boasts equally fine dining in more contemporary surroundings. The combination of the wonderful food and the city's fascinating charms are sure to make any visitor return frequently. Either the summer, when the city blooms and outdoor cafes abound, or the winter, when Carnaval turns the streets into hundreds of connecting parties, are wonderful times to visit one of Canada's oldest and most interesting cities.

EXERCISE 11*

Correct the following passage.

The interest in wrestlers and their managers, fans, and friends are fascinating proof that our society needs cheap thrills. The concept of good and evil fighting it out in epic battles are an enduring one. In simpler times, everyone who felt the need to witness such struggles were able to watch westerns on TV and see the Bad Guy (wearing the black hat) gunned down at high noon by the reluctant Good Guy (wearing the white hat). The complexity of our society, where good and evil is constantly redefined, mean that we seldom get a clear decision in the battles we see each day on the news, let alone witness the triumph of good over evil. Into this frustrating world comes Rowdy Roddy Piper, Hulk Hogan, The Junk Yard Dog, and King Kong Bundy. The variety of names, personalities, and "show biz" tricks are bewildering. Though the staging of the various moves and even the outcomes of the matches are obvious, the immense popularity of the matches, both on television and in the arenas, are undeniable. Like Rambo and Dirty Harry, the professional wrestler cuts through frustrating complexity and represents good or evil in its simplest, most dramatic form. To a great many people, wrestling—not to mention wrestlers—are irresistible.

EXERCISE 12

As a final check of your mastery of subject–verb agreement, correct the following sentences as necessary.

1. The rate of business bankruptcies are rising monthly.

2. All of us at the college feel that cheating and plagiarism is a serious offence.

3. Either French dressing or mayonnaise go well with that salad.

4. By the time we reached the Festival Theatre at Stratford, there was left only one seat in the balcony and two behind posts.

5. In Canada today, everyone who wants a good education can get it.

6. The variety of Richard's money-making activities are amazing: he plays cards, bets on horses, and sells socks.

7. One can't help noticing that the orchestra are playing better now that the conductor is sober.

8. At lunchtime our cafeteria, with its dreary salad bar, greasy chips, and soggy burgers, take away my appetite.

9. Canada's aboriginal people are thought to have come from Asia via the Bering Sea several thousand years before Europeans arrived in North America.

10. Neither subject–verb agreement nor run-on sentences presents any problem for me now.

CHAPTER 33

Pronoun–Antecedent Agreement

The title of this chapter may be formidable, but the idea is really very simple. **Pronouns** are words that substitute for or refer to the name of a person or thing. The word that a pronoun substitutes for or refers to is called the **antecedent.**

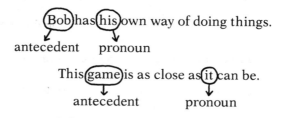

The basic rule to remember is this:

> A pronoun must agree with its antecedent.

You probably follow this rule most of the time, without even realizing that you know it. For example, you would never write

Bob has *its* own way of doing things.

or

This game is as close as *he* can be.

because you know that these pronouns don't agree with their antecedents.

There are three aspects of pronoun usage, however, that you need to be careful about. The first is how to use the relative pronouns—*which, that, who,* and *whom:*

> *Who* and *whom* are always used to refer to people.
> *That* and *which* refer to everything else.

The man *who* was hurt had to quit climbing.

The women *who* were present voted unanimously.

The moose *that* I met looked hostile.

Her car, *which* is imported, is smaller than cars *that* are built here.

The man *whom* the committee had decided to hire refused the job.

By the way, if you aren't sure whether to use *who* or *whom*, rewrite the sentence so you don't need either one: "The man the committee had decided to hire refused the job."

EXERCISE 1*

Correct the following sentences where necessary.

1. Yesterday's lecture was given by the English teacher that has a large

   wart on her nose.

2. Curling's most durable player is a man named Howard "Pappy"

   Wood, which competed in sixty-five consecutive annual bonspiels

   between 1908 and 1972.

3. Is this the car that was stolen by the man that escaped last night?

4. We are often attracted to people which are completely opposite

   to us.

5. When I entered the locker room, I knew the team who had lost had been there before me.

6. Liona Boyd is the musician that is scheduled to perform tonight.

7. The lasagna, which had been cooking all day, was hardly fit for the guests who were late.

8. Rudolf's grandmother always told him that people that couldn't fly as well as eagles should stay out of airplanes.

9. He remembered that sage advice the stormy night when the DC-9 in whom he was flying went into a sickening tailspin over Great Slave Lake.

10. The math problem that we worked out last night would have stymied anyone that hadn't attended class regularly.

The second tricky aspect of pronoun–antecedent agreement concerns words and phrases ending in *one*, *body*, and *thing:*

everyone	everybody	everything
anyone	anybody	anything
someone	somebody	something
no one	nobody	nothing
none		
each (one)		
every one		

In Chapter 32 you learned that when these words are used as subjects, they are singular and take singular verbs. So it makes sense that the pronouns that stand for or refer to them must be singular.

> Antecedents ending in *one*, *body*, and *thing* are singular and must be referred to by singular pronouns: *he, she, it, his, her, its.*

Everyone is expected to do *his* duty.

Each of the students must supply *his* or *her* own lunch.

Every mother deserves a break from *her* routine.

No one can truly say in *his* heart that *he* believes otherwise.

Another problem involves sentences that are grammatically correct but sound awkward:

If anyone is at the door, he'll have to knock louder.

Everyone arrives on time, but he leaves early.

It is wrong to write

If anyone is at the door, they'll have to knock louder.

Everyone arrives on time, but they leave early.

So, in order to make the sentences sound better, you need to rewrite them. Here is one way:

Anyone who is at the door will have to knock louder.

Everyone arrives on time but leaves early.

In speech it has become acceptable to use plural pronouns with *one*, *body*, and *thing* antecedents. Although these antecedents are singular and take singular verbs, often they are plural in meaning, and in conversation we find ourselves saying

Everyone clapped *their* hands with glee.

No one has to stay if *they* don't want to.

This usage is acceptable only in conversation; *it is not acceptable in written standard English.* Errors in pronoun–antecedent agreement are sometimes made because people are attempting to write **"gender-free" language**—that is, to write without indicating whether the person referred to is male or female.

"Everyone is expected to do *their* duty" is incorrect, as we have seen; however, it does avoid making "everyone" male, as one of the grammatically correct versions seems to do: "Everyone is expected to do *his* duty." It also avoids the awkwardness of "Everyone is expected to do *his or her* duty."

There are two better ways to solve this problem.

> 1. Revise the sentence to leave the pronoun out.

Duty is expected of everyone.

or

Everyone is expected to perform dutifully.

Such creative avoidance of gender-specific or incorrect constructions can be an interesting challenge. The results often sound a little artificial, however. The second method is easier to accomplish.

> 2. Revise the sentence to make the pronoun plural.

You are all expected to do your duty.

or

All are expected to do their duty.

Here are a couple of examples for you to study:

Problem: Each of the students has his or her assignment.
Revision 1: Each of the students has an assignment.
Revision 2: All of the students have their assignments.

Problem: Everyone will enjoy seeing his or her school friends again.
Revision 1: Everyone will enjoy seeing school friends again.
Revision 2: All graduates will enjoy seeing their school friends again.

EXERCISE 2*

Choose the correct word from the pair in parentheses. Check your answers before continuing.

1. Everyone in my crowd brings (his their) lunch to school.
2. Each of them would rather prepare it (herself themselves) than eat cafeteria food.
3. No one wants to be a failure in (her their) college career.
4. Unless we finish this job, no one will get (his their) pay cheque this week.
5. All of the people involved in the accident tried to extricate (his their) cars from the pile-up.

6. A child will often show fear or frustration in ways designed to get (his its their) parents' attention.
7. None of the films we saw could be considered offensive by (itself themselves), but the smutty jokes became tedious after a while.
8. Someone punched Tim in order to protect (her their) husband.
9. Accounting and finance were interesting in (its their) way even though (it they) took up a great deal of study time.
10. Everyone must look closely at (himself themselves) to determine whether (he they) is using all (his her their) potential.

Avoiding the third difficulty with pronoun–antecedent agreement depends on your common sense and your ability to think of your readers. If you try to look at your writing from your readers' point of view, it is unlikely that you will break this rule:

> A pronoun must *clearly* refer to the correct antecedent.

The mistake that occurs when you fail to follow this rule is called **vague reference**:

> Sam pointed to his brother and said that he had saved his life.

Who saved whom? Here's another:

> Jackie felt that Helen should have been more careful with her car when she lent it to her because she was a good friend of her husband.

Who owns the car? Who has the husband?

In these sentences you can only guess about the meaning, because you don't know who is being referred to by the pronouns. You can make these sentences less confusing by using proper names more often and changing the sentences around. Try it on our examples above.

Another type of vague reference occurs when a pronoun doesn't have an antecedent at all.

> He loves watching fast cars and would like to do it himself someday. (Do what?)

> Bicycling is her favourite pastime, but she still doesn't own one. (One what?)

How would you revise these sentences?

Be sure that pronouns have clear antecedents and that they agree with their antecedents in number. Both must be singular, or both must be plural. That, in short, is the rule of thumb for pronoun–antecedent agreement.

EXERCISE 3*

Correct the following sentences where necessary. There is more than one way to fix these; our answers are only suggestions.

1. Everyone who works in this car wash should pick up their cheque on Monday.

2. Women are treated as equals when she works in the fields.

3. A good manager must have an understanding of every employee and what makes them tick.

4. Do you know whether anyone in this neighbourhood wants to have their windows washed?

5. Men and women, whatever age they may be, are invited to take part in an experiment that will test their ability to enjoy themselves.

6. Virginia claims that every one of her male friends has a room of their own.

7. It is now time to listen to the voice of your conscience and what they have to say.

8. No one living in Canada today believes their country is thriving economically.

9. Anyone that has completed introductory sociology should know what a "peer group" is.

10. Everyone knows that Gordie Howe is the man that played 25 years in the NHL, but do they also know that he collected 500 stitches on his face?

EXERCISE 4*

Correct the following sentences where necessary. Some perfectly correct answers of yours may differ from the answers we've given. That's because the reference was so vague that the sentence could be understood in more than one way.

1. The gorilla was mean and thirsty because he had finished it all in the morning.

2. If your pet rat won't eat its food, feed it to the kitty.

3. Hockey is his favourite game, and he badly needs new ones.

4. Tim told Rocco his teeth were falling out.

5. Whenever Dennis and Bob played poker, he stacked the deck.

6. Every time Rudolf sat on the frog, he croaked.

7. You know that smoking is very bad for your health, but you won't throw them away.

8. Daphne backed her car into a garbage truck and dented it.

9. Lefty was suspicious of handgun control because he thought everyone should have one for late-night subway rides.

10. If Pierre and Joe begin to argue, he'll tell him that he's never had any use for him and that he ought to keep his crazy ideas to himself.

EXERCISE 5

Correct the following sentences.

1. Each of her suitors had their own faults, but Drusilla decided to choose the one that had the most money.

2. Embezzling is what he does best, but he hasn't been able to pull one off lately.

3. Everyone may pick up their exams after Tuesday.

4. Our instructor said that passing grades would be given to those that completed the field placement.

5. None of the people in Tuktoyaktuk feels safe without their mukluks.

6. Betty said to Liz that she had no idea how she felt when Alan broke up with her.

7. Everyone but me said that they would like to work for the company who gave me the job.

8. All of the girls are looked on as a sister here at Camp Kitsch-i-koo-mee.

9. Charles and Diana are a couple that don't have to worry where its next dollar is coming from.

10. Danny's boss always gave him directions, but sometimes he wasn't familiar enough with the procedure.

CHAPTER 34

Tense Agreement

Verbs are time markers. The different tenses are used to express differences in time:

I was fired two weeks ago; I hope I will find a new job soon.
    ↓   ↓   ↓
   past   present   future

Sometimes, as in the sentence above, it is necessary to use several different tenses in a single sentence to get the meaning across. But usually, whether you're writing a sentence, a paragraph, an essay, or a report, you will use *one tense throughout*. Normally you will choose either the past or the present tense. Here is the rule to follow:

Don't change tense unless meaning requires it.

Readers like and expect consistency. If you begin a sentence with "I worried and fretted and delayed," your readers will tune in to the past-tense verbs and expect any other verbs in the sentence to be in the past tense too. Therefore, if you finish the sentence with ". . . then I decide to give it a try," the readers will be abruptly jolted out of one time frame and into another. This sort of jolting is uncomfortable, and readers don't like it.

Shifting tenses is like shifting gears: it should be done smoothly and when necessary—never abruptly, out of carelessness, or on a whim. Avoid causing verbal whiplash: keep your tenses consistent.

> *Wrong:*   He kicked a stone from his path as he rambles up the winding driveway.
>
> *Right:*   He kicked a stone from his path as he rambled up the winding driveway.
>
> *Also right:*   He kicks a stone from his path as he rambles up the winding driveway.
>
> *Wrong:*   She hesitated but then began to climb the steps. Suddenly she hears a low groan.
>
> *Right:*   She hesitated but then began to climb the steps. Suddenly she heard a low groan.
>
> *Also right:*   She hesitates but then begins to climb the steps. Suddenly she hears a low groan.

In the exercises for this chapter, most of the sentences contain unnecessary tense shifts. Use the first verb in each sentence as your time marker, and change the tense(s) of the other verb(s) in the sentence to agree with it. If you get Exercise 1 entirely correct, skip ahead to Exercise 3.

EXERCISE 1*

1. Rolly goes home and kicked his cat.

2. Hank Aaron broke Babe Ruth's record of 714 home runs in a lifetime when he hits number 715 in 1974.

3. Children are quite perceptive and will know when you are lying to them.

4. We had just finished painting the floor when the dog runs through.

5. When Knowlton Nash walked into the room, the ladies go crazy.

6. You ought not to venture into that place until the police arrive.

7. Tim walked into the room, took one look at Lefty, and smashes him right through the wall.

8. First you will greet the guests; then you show them to their rooms.

9. The largest cheese ever produced took 43 hours to make and weighs a whopping 15 723 kilograms.

10. He watches television all evening until he finally went to sleep.

EXERCISE 2 *

1. Murphy's Law states that everything that can go wrong will.

2. I tried to warn him about her evil ways, and what thanks do I get?

3. The embarrassed girl didn't say anything. She just blushes and runs from the room.

4. Before Roger noticed the snowstorm, he's already up and dressed.

5. They agreed to our living here after we offer them a substantial bribe.

6. In the interests of good community relations and to prevent them from blowing up our house, I vote that we will pay what they asked for.

7. Drusilla looks like a sweet young thing; when she spoke, however, the toughest truck drivers blush.

8. Whenever I skip chemistry, it seemed old Mr. Bunsen was lurking in the hall to catch me.

9. The goons in hockey keep ruining the sport for those who want to play it the way it is intended to be played.

10. We attempted to change Rudolf's mind all day, but we didn't know he's already voted.

EXERCISE 3*

1. Are you going to see *The Blob?* It was a great movie!

2. *Prince of Space* and *The Blob* are the best movies I had ever seen.

3. The film begins with a clever sequence in which a girl met a boy and his dog.

4. Little do we realize what kind of dreadful creature our young lovers will encounter, or that it terrifies the whole town!

5. The Blob originates in a test tube as a tiny bit of green ooze that then grew to enormous proportions.

6. The slimy, pulsating mass gathers both speed and size as it moved towards our young lovers necking in a pick-up truck.

7. They repel the fearsome Blob with the defrost button and realized the monster couldn't stand heat, so they rush off to save the town.

8. The Blob is devouring patrons at a local bowling alley, and its increasing girth indicated that it enjoyed every morsel. What gruesome sights did this movie have in store for us next?

9. Much to our relief, our hero arrives and built a huge bonfire out of five-pins; the Blob withered and shrank away before our very eyes. The town was saved!

10. Is it any wonder that this movie was my favourite? I only wish I can see it with 3-D glasses.

EXERCISE 4*

Correct the faulty tense shifts in this passage. Use the italicized verb as your time marker.

As a boy, Jeffrey *had* a remarkable knack for making predictions. At age 7, he predicts to anyone who would listen that he would be a millionaire by the time he is old enough to vote. When he is 11, he predicts that he starred in a major motion picture by the time he could legally drive. At 14, he has prophesied that he would have been elected mayor before his 23rd birthday. Incredibly, his predictions came to pass, one after the other. At 16, he becomes the youngest person ever to play James Bond in a movie; this role leads to other pictures and a salary well into six figures. Careful investing makes him a millionaire within two years. With all that money behind him, there will be no stopping Jeffrey's campaign to have become, at 22, the youngest mayor in Moose Factory's history. However, his amazing early successes are not repeated, and Jeffrey becomes a has-been by the time he turns 25.

EXERCISE 5

Test your mastery of verb-tense agreement by correcting the following sentences.

1. We knew that he would fail math; he keeps skipping class.

2. Eric was quite the outdoor lover; he comes from Flin Flon, you know.

3. Tim likes to watch the dryer spin at the laundromat; he spent many happy hours there.

4. The teacher continues to talk, heedless of the uproar that was occurring in the classroom.

5. First they'll appeal to our finer instincts; then they whine and beg.

6. When the umpire asked for respect, we give it to him.

7. Toxemia is a dangerous illness during pregnancy and will be difficult to treat.

8. It was not until the Constitution Act of 1982 that Canada becomes fully responsible for its own destiny.

9. The city of Kitchener, Ontario was known as Berlin until World War II begins.

10. Jonathan Swift wrote a famous statement on corporal punishment: "Last week I saw a woman flayed, and you would hardly believe how much it alters her person for the worse." (from *A Tale of a Tub*)

CHAPTER 35

Person
Agreement

There are three categories of "person" that you can use when you write or speak:

> **first person:** I, we
> **second person:** you (singular and plural)
> **third person:** he, she, one, someone, they

Here is the rule for person agreement:

> Do not mix "persons" unless meaning requires it.

In other words, you must be consistent: if you begin a discussion in second person, you must use second person all the way through. Look at this sentence:

> If *you* wish to succeed, *one* must work hard.

This is the most common error—mixing second-person *you* with third-person *one*. Here's another example:

> *One* can live happily in Winnipeg if *you* have a very warm coat.

We can correct this error by using the second person throughout:

- *You* can live happily in Winnipeg if *you* have a very warm coat.

or by using the third person throughout:

- *One* can live happily in Winnipeg if *one* has a very warm coat.
  or
- *One* can live happily in Winnipeg if *he* has a very warm coat.

The bulleted sentences raise two points of style that you should be aware of:

1. Don't overuse *one*. Although the three versions are equally correct, they sound somewhat different from one another. The second sentence, which uses *one* twice, sounds the most formal—even a little stilted. The sentence in the second person sounds the most informal and natural—like something you would say. The third sentence is between the other two in formality and is the one you'd be most likely to use in writing for school or business.

2. Be aware of gender neutrality preferences—yours and your readers. As we noted in Chapter 33, the pronoun *he* is often used to represent both sexes. If this usage bothers you or seems inappropriate for your intended audience, you can substitute *he or she:*

> A person can live happily in Winnipeg if he or she has a very warm coat.

But if *he or she* occurs too frequently, the sentence becomes very awkward:

> A student can easily pass this course if he or she applies himself or herself to his or her studies.

You can fix sentences like these by switching the *whole sentence* to the plural:

> Students can easily pass this course if they apply themselves to their studies.

EXERCISE 1*

Choose the correct word from the parentheses for each of the following sentences. Check your answers before continuing.

1. If you want to make good egg rolls, I advise (them her you) to buy the ready-made wrappings.
2. If you win tonight's lottery, will (one he you) tell (one's his your) friends?
3. Even young children can learn to swim if (one they she) have a good instructor and apply (oneself themselves herself).
4. Every person working in this office should know that (they she) helped finish an important project.
5. When we toured the House of Commons, (you we he one) didn't see a single MP.

EXERCISE 2*

Correct the following sentences where necessary. Check your answers to each set before going on.

1. After the unfortunate brawl, Tim learned that if a person stomps on policemen, they can expect to end up in jail.

2. Everyone can expect to experience the horrors of nuclear war unless they raise their voices against nuclear proliferation.

3. If one leaves garbage at one's campsite, you may well have bears as midnight callers.

4. I knew she wasn't the girl for me when she asked me if Wayne Gretzky were the leader of Solidarity.

5. One will always think about the opportunities he's missed, even if you're happy with what you have.

6. Canadians who worry about street violence should keep in mind that, in comparison to New York, you are safe in downtown Kapuskasing after dark.

7. You should always wear garlic around the neck if one fears vampires.

8. Any woman who wears garlic won't have to worry about men harassing them, either.

9. Can one really know another person if you have never been to their home?

10. A sure way to lose one's friends is to eat all the Baskin-Robbins ice cream yourself.

EXERCISE 3*

Correct the errors in person agreement in the following passage. Use the second-person pronoun (you) wherever possible.

Anyone can enjoy classical music if you are willing to give it a chance and really listen. If we listen closely, you will find relaxation and enjoyment quite different from that which one might experience when listening to "pop," rock, country and western, or any of the other varieties of music. Of course, not all classical music appeals to everyone, but then, everyone doesn't find all rock music to your taste, either. Nevertheless, there are some classical selections we are sure to enjoy. Go to the public library and borrow one or two of the following records and put them on your turntable. If one then relaxes, puts one's feet up and really listens, you will be guaranteed an enjoyable experience. For your introduction to classical music, one might try Beethoven's Sixth Symphony *(Pastoral)*, Grieg's *Peer Gynt Suite*, and Tchaikovsky's *Romeo and Juliet*. These pieces appeal to almost everyone and are ideal selections with which to begin our exploration of a new musical world.

EXERCISE 4*

This exercise will test and reinforce your understanding of both tense and person agreement. Correct the following sentences where necessary.

1. If you're ready to learn how to operate a motorcycle, one should involve oneself in lessons, especially if you were interested in safety.

2. We often go to wrestling matches at the Gardens, and you're always sure of having a stimulating evening as one watches the Sheik make mincemeat of the Masked Marvel.

3. I don't know whether I can complete the program on time because it always seems either you had to wait for a terminal or the machines were down.

4. Until last week Marcia had us all believing her unlikely story; then we realize that she was lying.

5. You know that Cindy Nicholas holds the record for completing a double crossing of the English Channel, but were you aware that she has swum it a total of six times?

6. You know Orville was a troublemaker when you see his sneaky little face.

7. When one considered the issue carefully, you think better of the more expensive proposal. After all, quality workmanship was what we're looking for.

8. When summer arrives, our patio is where you will find one, relaxing and enjoying our leisure hours.

9. Many women think that the only way you can succeed in the business world is by wearing conservative three-piece suits similar to those men wore.

10. Actually, while you should dress appropriately, one needn't spend undue amounts of time and money trying to ape "the executive look."

Competence and ability always had more impact than appearance.

EXERCISE 5

Choose the right word from those in parentheses, keeping the person and number of the pronouns in agreement with the italicized word in the first sentence of each paragraph.

When *people* see a dreadful occurrences, such as a war, earthquake, or mass starvation on television, it does not always affect (you one them). It is one thing for people to see the ravages of war (yourself oneself themselves) and another thing to see a three-minute newsclip of the same battle, neatly edited by the CBC. Even the horrible effects of natural catastrophes that wipe out whole populations are somehow minimized or trivialized when (we people you) see them on TV. And while people may be shocked and horrified by the gaunt faces of starving children on the screen, (you one they) can easily escape into (our your their) familiar world of Egg McMuffins, Shake'n Bake, and Sara Lee Cheesecakes that is portrayed in commercial messages.

Thus, the impact of television on *us* is a mixed one. It is true that (you we they) are shown events, tragic and otherwise, which (you we they) could not possibly have seen before television. In this way (our their your) world is drawn together more closely. However, the risk in creating this immediacy, and perhaps the most tragic consequence of all, is that (we people you) may become desensitized and cease to feel or care about (your our their) fellow human beings.

Punctuation

CHAPTER 36

Question and Exclamation Marks

The Question Mark

Everyone knows that a question mark follows an interrogative, or asking, sentence, but we all sometimes forget to include it. Let this chapter serve as a reminder not to forget!

> The **question mark** is the end punctuation for all interrogative sentences.

The question mark gives your readers an important clue to the meaning of your sentence. "There's more?" is vastly different in meaning from "There's more!" and that difference is communicated to readers by the punctuation alone.

The only time you don't end a question with a question mark is when the question is part of a statement.

Are you going?   (question)

I asked if you are going.   (statement)

Do you know them?   (question)

I wonder whether you know them.   (statement)

EXERCISE 1*

Supply the correct end punctuation for these sentences. Then check your answers.

1. Did you ever think that the Canadian dollar would drop below the U.S. seventy-cents mark
2. Our trip to the States this summer is going to be very expensive, isn't it
3. The Blue Jays will never be a pennant contender unless they get some good relief pitchers
4. If you let me show you how to hold the ball properly, your bowling will improve
5. How can you just stand there while a man is being beaten
6. If we can't finish the project on time, I wonder if we will lose the contract
7. Finish your nice liver casserole, children, or you won't get any dessert
8. It's difficult to meet eligible bachelors in their 80s, isn't it
9. I don't know if you've ever thought about it, but we have no answer to the question of whether we could live happily in Iqaluit
10. Did you know that Harpo Marx was just as capable of talking as his brothers Groucho, Chico, Gummo, and Zeppo

The Exclamation Mark

The exclamation mark is a useful piece of punctuation for conveying your tone of voice to your readers. There is a distinct difference in tone between these two sentences:

There's a man behind you.

There's a man behind you!

In the first sentence, information is being supplied, perhaps about the line-up at a grocery-store check-out counter. The second sentence might be a shouted warning about a mugger.

> Use an **exclamation mark** as end punctuation in sentences requiring extreme emphasis or dramatic effect.

Please note that the exclamation mark will have "punch" or drama only if you use it sparingly. If you use an exclamation mark after every third sentence, how will your readers know when you really mean to indicate excitement? The overuse of the exclamation mark is a technique used in comic books. The writers of comics use the exclamation mark after every sentence to try to heighten the impact of their characters' words. Instead, they've robbed their exclamation marks of all meaning.

Practically any sentence may have an exclamation mark after it, but remember that the punctuation changes the meaning of the sentence. Read the following sentences with and without an exclamation mark, and picture the situation that would call for each reading.

He's gone   Don't touch that button

The room was empty   There she goes again

EXERCISE 2*

Supply the correct end punctuation for these sentences. In many cases, the punctuation you use will depend on how you want the sentence to be read. Notice the extent to which different punctuation can change the meaning of a sentence.

1. There's a vampire in my attic
2. Come here and say that. I dare you
3. I can't believe how badly the Maple Leafs play hockey
4. Oh no You've done it again
5. Congratulations You've finally graduated
6. Help There's no way I can pay this bill
7. Workers of the world unite (Karl Marx)
8. Can that guy ever run
9. Come and get me, copper
10. Oh no We're late for the last ferry to the mainland

EXERCISE 3*

Add the correct punctuation to these sentences. Choose a period, a question mark, or an exclamation mark.

1. We aren't sure if we're getting paid this week or not
2. Reginald wanted his broker to tell him whether pork bellies would be a good investment
3. Where in the world are you going with your hair dyed green and that safety pin in your nose
4. Arthur asked Catherine where she was going
5. Would you believe that the heaviest world champion boxer, Primo Carnera, weighed in at 123 kg in a 1933 fight

6. That's one king-size heavyweight
7. Do you mean to tell me that your lovely necklace is made of shellacked moose droppings
8. You must be kidding
9. Dr. and Mr. Widget arrived at the reception in their new Rolls Royce
10. Hooray This exercise is finished

EXERCISE 4*

Correct the punctuation in the following sentences.

1. The question was whether we would spend the night in Cornwall or push on for Montreal?
2. "Help," he screamed "The piranha has my finger"
3. Just think!! We have two glorious weeks free of English class!!!
4. Tim thought he looked lovely(?) in his new sharkskin suit!
5. If you think you're confused, just imagine how I must feel?
6. If I ever hear him tell that joke again, I'll box his ears!
7. Catherine asked Arthur if he would like to stay over?
8. Her Ph. D. didn't seem to impress her co-workers at the doughnut shop
9. Despite the fact that he was busy with his weightlifting, jogging, swimming, tumbling, etc., Jacques always had time for a little drinking?
10. We studied the poems of Irving Layton, who was born in Rumania, I think(?)

EXERCISE 5

Supply correct end punctuation for these sentences.

1. She would like to help with the preparations, but can she cook as well as her father
2. Who's been sleeping in my bed
3. Imagine our surprise when Mortimer appeared outside the window of our fourteenth-floor apartment
4. The students question whether this exam is fair
5. There has to be a better way, hasn't there
6. Are the Argos likely to win the Grey Cup Absolutely not
7. The angry parents descended on the board of education, waving "Save Our School" banners
8. After seeing your test results, I wonder if you read the textbook at all
9. When will you be finished with that job so that we can begin our vacation
10. Congratulations You've just mastered end punctuation marks

CHAPTER 37

Quotation Marks

Quotation marks (" ") are used to set off direct speech (dialogue), quoted material, and some titles. Quotation marks come in pairs; there has to be a set to show where the dialogue or quotation begins and a set to show where it ends. You must be absolutely sure that whatever you put between them is *exactly* the way it is stated in the source you are using. The only other thing you need to know about quotation marks is how to punctuate what comes between them.

Dialogue

When you quote direct speech, include normal sentence punctuation. If the speaker's name is included in your own sentence, set it off with commas. The comma or the end punctuation mark comes *inside* the final set of quotation marks.

> "Did you," Tim asked in a rage, "drink all of my Brador?"
> "No, there are a couple of swigs left," I said.

Be careful that you put quotation marks only around direct speech (someone's exact words). Don't use quotation marks with indirect speech:

Tim, in a rage, asked me if I had drunk all his Brador. (These are not Tim's exact words, nor is the sentence a question.)

A quotation *within* a quotation is punctuated by single quotation marks:

"If you really expect me to go out with you again," Lori told her date, "you'll stop calling me 'Babe.'"

Quoted Material

When you quote a *short* written passage (three lines of print or less), you can work it into your own sentence. Again, include normal sentence punctuation within the quotation marks.

"Marriage," wrote Dr. Johnson, "has many pains, but celibacy has no pleasures."

"The medium is the message," Marshall McLuhan points out in his book *Understanding Media*.

If your own introductory words form a complete sentence, use a colon:

Dr. Johnson made an interesting statement on wedded life: "Marriage has many pains, but celibacy has no pleasures."

Marshall McLuhan captured the imagination of a generation brought up on television: "The medium is the message."

All the lines of a *long* quoted passage (more than three lines of print) should be indented ten spaces from the left margin so that the quotation stands apart from your own text. An indented quotation is not enclosed in quotation marks. You will find an example of a long quotation in a research paper on p. 218.

Titles

If you are not using a word processor that prints out italics, titles of whole books or volumes should be *underlined;* titles of parts of those books or volumes should be placed in quotation marks. Thus, books, names of magazines, pamphlets, newspapers, plays, and films should be underlined. Titles of single articles, essays, stories, or poems should be placed in quotation marks.

"The Bear on the Delhi Road," by Earle Birney, in <u>Fifteen Canadian Poets</u>

"I Am Jane's Pancreas," in <u>Reader's Digest</u>

Note: In printed works—such as this text—titles of books are printed in *italics*, not underlined.

EXERCISE 1*

Place the quotation marks correctly and insert the necessary punctuation in these sentences.

1. Pardon me, boys, is this the Transylvania Station? asked the man in the black cape.
2. Every day Rudolf asked the same question When do you think E.T. will return?
3. The child asked when his mother would call.
4. This film exclaimed Granny is more explicit than *National Geographic!*
5. As *The Globe and Mail* put it The Canadian dollar went on a roller coaster ride yesterday.
6. It was the philosopher Ludwig Feuerbach who first said man is what he eats, and we here at Big Boy restaurants certainly agree with that.
7. Roger claimed that he was deathly afraid of airplanes.
8. Your every whim will be catered to promised the Sybaritic Spas brochure.
9. I wondered whether they would peel grapes for me and find slaves to perform lomi-lomi on my aching muscles.
10. If not I asked my friend why should we spend $800 for a weekend in Collingwood?

EXERCISE 2*

Place the quotation marks and punctuation correctly in these sentences. Check your answers before going on to the next exercise.

1. The Guinness Book of World Records claims that the oldest living thing is the California bristlecone pine tree which is almost 5,000 years old.
2. Did you see the strange look on his face asked Roderick.
3. Frank asked Rita if she would like to play bridge.
4. Of course she answered, usually willing to oblige.

5. Have you read my new essay, Dreaming Your Way to an Energized Future Dr. Piffle asked his numbed audience. It's in my next book entitled Upscale Networking in a Self-Actualized Cosmos.
6. The fellow to my left hissed I'd sooner be horsewhipped; where do they find these guys?
7. I forget whether it was John Paul Jones or George Chuvalo who said I have not yet begun to fight.
8. The vice-president had bad news for the staff Due to lack of funds and excessive vandalism at the parking gates, you're all terminated.
9. The book claims that someday we will get injections of our own white blood cells taken during our youth; these injections will ward off infections and aging.
10. Wow I said that's amazing!

EXERCISE 3

Now test your understanding of quotation marks and the punctuation that goes with them.

1. Look out he shouted. There's a dump truck behind you!
2. Cinderella had a few choice words for her fairy godmother How am I supposed to walk in glass slippers, anyway?
3. Would you rather the fairy asked go to the ball in your Nikes?
4. Many of the fans said they'd pay top dollar to see the Grateful Dead.
5. Joseph Conrad makes a chilling comparison in his novel *The Secret Agent*. The terrorist and the policeman are startlingly similar in character.
6. Pierre Trudeau once told Canadians that the state had no business in the nation's bedrooms.
7. Tim said That's sure a relief; I wouldn't want him to see what I've got growing on my windowsill.
8. You'll be glad to hear that we are planning to bring the whole family down from Moosonee for a month wrote Uncle Morty.
9. Good grief! said my wife. The last time they did that Aunt Madeline had to be bailed out of the Don Jail, and I ended up in a rest home she added nervously.
10. The instructor said she was pleased we all understood the mysteries of quotation marks so thoroughly.

CHAPTER 38

The Colon

The colon functions as an "introducer." When a statement is followed by a list or by one or more examples, the colon between the statement and what follows alerts the readers to what is coming.

> We have only two choices: for and against.
>
> There are three things I can't stand: brussels sprouts, cats, and John Candy's films.
>
> One person prevented her rise to wealth and fame: herself.

The statement that precedes the colon must be a complete sentence (independent clause). Therefore, a colon can never come after *is* or *are.* For example

> Two things I cannot stand are: cats and brussels sprouts.

This is incorrect because the statement before the colon is not a complete sentence.

The colon, then, follows a complete statement and introduces a list or example that defines or amplifies something in the statement. The information after the colon very often answers the question "what?" or "who?"

> There is a new danger to consider: (what?) inflation.
>
> He peered into the clear water to see his favourite friend: (who?) himself.

The colon is also used after a complete sentence introducing a quotation.

> Irving Layton is not fond of academic critics: "There hasn't been a writer of power and originality during the past century who

hasn't had to fight his way to acceptance against the educated pipsqueaks hibernating in universities." (Layton, in a letter to the *Montreal Star*)

The uses of the colon can be summed up as follows:

> The colon follows an independent clause and introduces one of three things: examples, a list, or a quotation.

EXERCISE 1*

Put a check next to the sentences that are correctly punctuated. Check your answers before going on.

1. _____ The three people having trouble with their nursing techniques course are: Tanya, Eddy, and Rufus.

2. _____ There are three people having trouble with their nursing techniques course, Tanya, Eddy, and Rufus.

3. _____ We lacked only one thing: money.

4. _____ The only thing we lacked was: money.

5. _____ Our friends are certain to remain loyal if we treat them with: courtesy, kindness, and honesty.

6. _____ There are three characteristics of a good paragraph: unity, coherence, and clarity.

7. _____ Two places I wouldn't want to visit are: Tuscaloosa and Moose Factory.

8. _____ I'll give you an example: Bruce Cockburn.

9. _____ Roderick's needs in life were: sex, drugs, and rock 'n roll.

10. _____ Two of Canada's highest awards in professional sports are the Stanley Cup and the Grey Cup.

EXERCISE 2*

Insert colons in the following sentences where necessary, and then check your answers. If you find you've made any mistakes, review the chapter, and be sure you understand why your answers were wrong.

1. We'll finish the repairs by tomorrow only if we work all night or call a plumber.

2. Unless you work consistently throughout the term and prepare thoroughly for your final exam, you will achieve only one result failure.

3. There are several troublesome implications of biological engineering, but one in particular is frightening to most people, the cloning of human beings.

4. Their credit consultant asked them an important question after their bankruptcy "Why don't you cut up your credit cards?"

5. Only one thing prevents me from pulverizing you the Masked Marvel, who is standing behind you.

6. Canada has attained international literary acclaim with novelists of the stature of Richler, Atwood, and Laurence.

7. The bulk of Canada's population is worn out and exhausted at the end of a long, hard winter, but most people console themselves with one thought, spring will arrive sometime in May or June.

8. There are a number of activities that will improve physical fitness; swimming, tennis, jogging, even brisk walking.

9. Melanie is trying very hard to accomplish two things a significant weight loss and success as a restaurant critic.

10. Several of the animals on the endangered species list are native to Canada the wood bison, the Northern kit fox, and the whooping crane.

EXERCISE 3*

Correct the incorrectly punctuated sentences in Exercise 1.

EXERCISE 4

As a test of your knowledge of colons, put a check before the sentences that are correctly punctuated.

1. _____ Several people missed yesterday's exciting meeting: Carol, Jack, George, and Bonita.

2. _____ There are several families that are considerably richer than the Rockefellers, the du Ponts, the Mellons, and the Gettys.

3. _____ Three qualities of a good computer programmer are: intelligence, accuracy, and patience.

4. _____ The TV is always asking me challenging questions "It's 11:05. Do you know where your children are?"

5. _____ He won a prize in spite of his ineptitude the slow-but-steady-progress award.

6. _____ He wants to talk to you: but he's afraid.

7. _____ You have all the qualities of a dog except one: loyalty.

8. _____ Three things that always make me mad are: "The Gong Show," Premier Vander Zalm, and beer commercials.

9. _____ In the paper are two career opportunities that Dudley may find intriguing undertaking and sky-diving.

10. _____ The desert is: hot in the day and cool at night.

EXERCISE 5

Now correct the incorrectly punctuated sentences in Exercise 4.

CHAPTER 39

The Comma

The comma is the most frequently used and the most frequently mis-used punctuation mark. The omission of a necessary comma can dis-tort the meaning of a sentence. Unnecessary commas can distract your readers and give your sentences a jerky quality. Perhaps nothing is so sure a sign of a competent writer as the correct use of commas, so it is very important that you master them. This chapter presents four rules that will give you a good indication of when you should use a comma. If the sentence you are writing is not covered by one of the four rules, remember this:

When in doubt, leave the comma out!

Four Comma Rules

In this section we present the four most helpful rules for using the comma.

---

1. Use commas to separate items in a series of three or more.

Required subjects are math, English, bookkeeping, and business law.
Walk up the hill, turn left, go two blocks, and you'll be there.

André went to the show, Joan went home in tears, Yasmin and Phil talked until dawn, and I went upstairs to bed.

The comma before the *and* at the end of the list is optional; use it or leave it out, but be consistent.

EXERCISE 1*

Insert commas where necessary in the following sentences.

1. Be sure to pick up gin tonic limes and ice.
2. Women and children are traditionally the first people into the life-boats.
3. Labatt Molson and O'Keefe are major breweries and patrons of sport and culture.
4. Americans and Canadians share a continent and a similar cultural heritage.
5. Tim stomped into the room threw himself into a chair drained a six-pack of Budweiser and crushed the cans against his forehead.

> 2. Use comma(s) to separate from the rest of the sentence any word or expression that is *not essential* to the sentence's meaning or that means the same as something else in the sentence.

Writing business letters isn't difficult, if you're careful.

The phrase "if you're careful" is not essential to the meaning of the sentence, so it's separated from the rest of the sentence by a comma.

Stephen Leacock, one of the world's great humorists, was a professor of economics at McGill.

The phrase "one of the world's great humorists" means the same as "Stephen Leacock." The two expressions refer to the same person, so the second is set off by commas. When a nonessential word or phrase occurs in the middle of a sentence, rather than at the beginning or the end, be sure to put commas *both* before and after it.

If it were up to me, Judy, I'd hire you right now.

The word "Judy," the name of the person spoken to, is unnecessary to the meaning of the sentence, so it's set off by commas.

EXERCISE 2*

Insert commas where necessary in the following sentences. Check your answers before going on.

1. The cheetah is of course the fastest animal on earth.
2. Everyone who sees the movie will be shocked.
3. Malcolm Lowry an alcoholic British expatriate wrote *Under the Volcano* perhaps the finest novel ever written in Canada.
4. Many children in this school it seems are coming in the morning without having had an adequate breakfast.
5. The lead singer in a bid for notoriety bit the head off a bat during the performance.

---

3. Place a comma between independent clauses when they are joined by these transition words:

and	nor	for
or	but	yet
so		

It was a good party, but last year's was better.

I'm not speaking to her, so you'll have to tell her.

I can't make it to class, yet I feel I should go.

Ross is a good student, for he studies hard.

Be sure that the sentence contains two independent clauses rather than a single subject and a multiple verb.

We ate very well in Quebec and gained 3 kilograms each. (Here We is the subject, and there are two verbs: ate and gained. No comma is needed between two verbs with a single subject.)

We ate very well in Quebec, and each of us gained 3 kilograms. (This sentence has two independent clauses—we ate and each gained—joined by an *and*. The comma is required here.)

EXERCISE 3*

Insert commas where necessary in the following sentences. Then check your answers.

1. I refuse to wear that turkey costume to the party nor will I go as a horse's rear end.

2. Yesterday he broke up with her but today he is begging for forgiveness.
3. We loved the book but hated the movie.
4. The boss told him to stop leering at the ladies or she would fire him.
5. Waving a red flag in front of a bull is supposed to enrage him yet experiments have shown that bulls are colour blind.

> 4. Put a comma after any word or group of words that comes before an independent clause.

Charley, you aren't paying attention. (The second rule applies here, too.)

Though tattered and torn, the book was worth a fortune.

Wherever you go, remember me.

If that's all there is, we'd better buy more.

Until he got his promotion, he was quite friendly.

EXERCISE 4*

Write out the four comma rules on a sheet of paper. Then insert commas where necessary in the following sentences. Check your answers when you're done.

1. Third insert your finger into the electrical socket.
2. Overwhelmed by the generous offer we spent the evening watching Paul's home movies.
3. If you work for an airline company policy states you are entitled to one free trip a year.
4. In addition your next of kin is entitled to reduced fares.
5. Unless you learn to use commas properly your writing will lack sophistication and polish.

One final note about the comma, before you try your hand at the review exercises: *never* place a *single* comma between a subject and its verb:

Right: Adam and Liz are going into business.

Never: Adam and Liz, are going into business.

However, two commas between a subject and its verb are all right *if* they are setting off nonessential material:

Adam and Liz, both recent graduates, are going into business.

Insert commas where necessary in the following exercises. Check your answers to each set and make sure you understand any mistakes, before you go on to the next exercise.

EXERCISE 5*

1. Caffeine which is present in coffee tea and cola stimulates the heart and raises blood pressure.
2. If a thing is worth doing it is worth doing badly. (G. K. Chesterton)
3. The agency interviewed tested investigated and rejected thirty applicants.
4. That man is guilty in my opinion and should be convicted of murder.
5. Roger checked his parachute carefully before take-off but he forgot to pull his rip cord after he jumped out of the plane.
6. Fortunately he landed in a tree and later that afternoon was found dangling helplessly.
7. Unfortunately he had some very nasty contusions and developed an entirely justifiable fear of flying.
8. However you choose to write your resignation is up to you.
9. Having left my wallet at home I am unable to buy lunch.
10. Having no money is embarrassing.

EXERCISE 6*

1. Fascinating challenging high-paying jobs are available to the people who transfer to our exciting Beirut branch office.
2. Oswald your lawyers agreed to work with you not against you didn't they?
3. Our guard dog a Doberman pinscher caught an intruder and maimed him for life.
4. Unfortunately my Uncle Ladislaw was the intruder and he intends to sue us for every penny we have.
5. The year 1945 marked the end of World War II and the beginning of assistance to war-torn nations.
6. All warm-blooded animals that give live birth and suckle their young are classified as mammals but no one knows how to classify the warm-blooded egg-laying chick-nursing platypus.
7. We are pleased with your résumé and we are offering you an interview this week.
8. We are pleased with your résumé and are offering you an interview this week.
9. Although Tim begged his girlfriend refused to wear a tattooed heart with his name in the middle.

10. Igor asked "May I show you to your quarters or would you prefer to spend the night in the dungeon?"

EXERCISE 7*

I sometimes wonder what our ancestors, were they able to observe us now would think of some of the activities we take for granted. I'm sure that breakdancing would seem peculiar to them as would surfing water-skiing and hang-gliding. However I suspect that our forebears would find even those strange activities understandable perhaps even enjoyable compared to jogging. The sight of otherwise perfectly reasonable people decked out in various types of colourful underwear doggedly puffing and sweating along every pathway road and trail would I am convinced put The Fear into Great Grandad and send him scurrying back whence he had come.

All kinds of people jog: there are short joggers tall joggers fat joggers thin joggers; serious joggers light-hearted joggers fashionable joggers and practical joggers; joggers with outfits of every hue from black to white and every shade in between. In fact there may be more people who jog than who don't!

I gave up on jogging some years ago with the excuse that although I adored distance running an old basketball injury prevented me from measuring up to my own expectations. This pitiful story together with a wistful sigh for lost youth usually gets me off the hook. While my friends claim to be fit and keen I take satisfaction in quoting Satchel Paige the famous baseball player who at age 60 pitched three scoreless innings in the major leagues. In his "Six Rules for a Long Life," Satch warns "On no account run." This is sound advice and I intend to live by this sensible and energy-efficient rule.

EXERCISE 8

To test your mastery of commas, provide the necessary commas for these sentences.

1. His face turned purple when he saw the exam results but he said nothing.
2. Clarity conciseness and courtesy are important in both personal and business communication.
3. The Blue Jays in case you haven't noticed have been playing better ball this season.
4. Unless you come with us now you won't be able to get to the island tonight.
5. Samuel de Champlain Jacques Cartier and Etienne Brûlé were among the first Europeans to explore what is now Canada.
6. In spite of its reputation the Spadina Hotel is I think a good place to have a drink.
7. Adam and Eve are supposed to have been the first people on earth but they apparently ran into some trouble with their supervisor.
8. Cedric why are you wearing those nose plugs?
9. Running jumping and shouting loudly the children ran across the yard and into the house.
10. Unless I am sadly mistaken you now have a firm grasp of the intricacies of comma use.

CHAPTER 40

The Semicolon

The colon and semicolon are often confused and used as if they were interchangeable. They serve very different functions, however, and their correct use can dramatically improve your readers' understanding of your writing. Here is one function of the semicolon:

> The semicolon can replace the period; in other words, it can appear between two independent clauses.

You should use the semicolon when the two clauses (sentences) you are joining are closely connected in meaning or when there is a cause-and-effect relationship between them.

> I'm too tired; I can't stay awake any longer.
>
> There's a good movie on tonight; it's a Canadian film called *Jesus of Montreal*.

A period could have been used instead of the semicolon in either of these sentences, but the close connection between the clauses prompted the writer to use a semicolon.

Certain connecting or transition words are sometimes put between independent clauses to show cause and effect or continuation of an idea. Words used in this way must be preceded by a semicolon and followed by a comma.

> Put a semicolon in front of these words and a comma after:
>
> | | | |
> |---|---|---|
> | ; i.e., | ; moreover, | ; furthermore, |
> | ; e.g., | ; besides, | ; in fact, |
> | ; consequently, | ; for example (e.g.), | ; thus, |
> | ; however, | ; nevertheless, | ; that is (i.e.), |
> | ; therefore, | ; otherwise, | |

We had hiked for two hours; consequently, we were glad for the rest.

There are only two of us; however, we're both pretty big.

The sun was very hot; therefore, we stopped at an ice-cream store.

Note, however, that when the words listed in the box are used as nonessential expressions rather than as connecting words, they are separated from the rest of the sentence by commas (rule 2 in Chapter 39).

Sometimes semicolons should be used in a list instead of commas:

> To make a *complex* list easier to read and understand, put semicolons between the items instead of commas.

Here's an example:

A few items are necessary: matches to start a fire; an axe or hatchet to cut wood; cooking utensils and eating implements; and, of course, the food itself.

EXERCISE 1*

Put a check next to the sentences that are correctly punctuated. Check your answers before continuing.

1. _____ We've eaten all the goodies, it's time to go home.

2. _____ Many doctors claim weather affects our health; in fact, barometric pressure has a direct effect on arthritis.

3. _____ Your instructor would like to pass you, however, there may be a small fee involved.

4. _____ Florence is going to Hollywood, she wants to appear on "Let's Make a Deal."

5. _____ We knew that the party was a huge success: Uncle Morty tap-danced across the top of the piano Aunt Madeline did her Big Bird imitation and Tim wrestled two of his cousins.

6. _____ Many people dislike hockey; because some of the players act like goons rather than athletes.

7. _____ Orville tried and tried; but he couldn't get the teacher's attention.

8. _____ He dangled one of his classmates from a window; that caught the teacher's eye immediately.

9. _____ First we'll have a cool drink then we'll see if we can find a way to start this car.

10. _____ Dudley left his clothes by the pool; so it's no wonder people in the lounge are looking at him strangely.

EXERCISE 2*

Correct the faulty punctuation in Exercise 1.

EXERCISE 3*

Correct the faulty punctuation.

1. Mrs. Reagan had a message for the unemployed: "There is no hunger in America, let them eat Kraft Dinner."
2. Most computer languages have been developed for a specific purpose, for example, COBOL is used in business whereas FORTRAN is used for mathematics, science, and engineering.
3. Some sociobiologists believe that human beings have evolved socially because female humanoids learned to barter sex for food and protection, however, this theory is controversial in academic circles.
4. Louis Riel led a Métis rebellion in Manitoba in 1885; but he was defeated, tried, and executed the same year, his death caused a deep rift between English and French Canada.
5. Go left at the next fork in the road, or you will end up at a nuclear-waste disposal site and come out all aglow.

EXERCISE 4*

Insert commas and semicolons where necessary in these sentences. Then check your answers carefully.

1. The entire town is in an uproar it seems Rudolf has been missing since yesterday.

2. Of course everyone knows Rudolf is a bit wacky he's been very strange since his close encounter of the fourth kind.
3. He claims that a hamburger-shaped chrome-coloured smoke-belching UFO pinned him under its wheels and its inhabitants kept him prisoner for several hours.
4. The creatures spoke to him through little slits however Rudolf says he got a good look at them.
5. According to him the aliens looked like a cross between Bonzo the Chimp and Sylvester Stallone.
6. The creatures told Rudolf many secrets one thing they told him was that they had searched the universe for a perfect specimen like him.
7. He considered this a friendly gesture and immediately felt more kindly toward the aliens.
8. In fact Rudolf later told us he is under the aliens' control perhaps this explains why he talks like Donald Duck.
9. But now everyone is beginning to worry there's an unexplained burned spot in Rudolf's yard and he's been gone since yesterday.
10. Do you think they've whisked him away for a tour of the galaxy?

EXERCISE 5*

Correct the punctuation in these sentences by changing commas to semicolons or colons where necessary.

1. I have grown fond of semicolons in recent years. The semicolon tells you that there is still some question about the preceding full sentence, something needs to be added.
2. It is almost always a greater pleasure to come across a semicolon than a period. The period tells you that that is that, if you didn't get all the meaning you wanted or expected, you got all the writer intended to parcel out and now you have to move along.
3. But with a semicolon there, you get a pleasant little feeling of expectancy, there is more to come, read on, it will get clearer.
4. Colons are a lot less attractive, for several reasons, firstly, they give you the feeling of being rather ordered around, or at least having your nose pointed in a direction you might not be inclined to take if left to yourself, and, secondly, you suspect you're in for one of those sentences that will be labelling the points to be made, firstly, secondly, and so forth, with the implication that you haven't enough sense to keep track of a sequence of notions without having them numbered.

Adapted from "Notes on Punctuation," in *The Medusa and the Snail,* by Lewis Thomas. New York: The Viking Press, 1979, 126–7.

5. Also, many writers use this system loosely and incompletely, starting out with number one and number two as though counting off on their fingers but then going on and on without the succession of labels you've been led to expect, leaving you floundering about searching for the ninthly or seventeenthly that ought to be there but isn't.

EXERCISE 6

Test your mastery of the semicolon by correcting the punctuation in these sentences.

1. Acid rain is a serious problem however until recently the U.S. has been unwilling to deal with it.
2. The lawn needs to be cut, get going on it right away.
3. The team lost seven games in a row consequently the coach was fired.
4. Lester Pearson won the Nobel Peace Prize in 1957, he was the only Canadian to do so.
5. Dragonflies have a fearsome appearance, nonetheless they are harmless insects.
6. I have a quick cure for insomnia, try to stay awake through a Sunday night episode of "The Nation's Business."
7. We've spent all our money, therefore we won't be dining out tonight.
8. The furniture looks like North York Provincial to me all the chairs are covered with plastic.
9. The abacus is an ancient computational device in skilful hands it can calculate sums as quickly as most modern gadgets.
10. The semicolon is an often misunderstood piece of punctuation now that you have mastered it your writing will be enhanced by its use.

CHAPTER 41

Dashes and Parentheses

When you are talking with someone, you use your voice and your delivery to punctuate: you pause for a short time (commas) or for a longer time (semicolons and periods); you shout (exclamation marks); or you query (question marks). When you write, your punctuation substitutes for your body language: it helps you make sure your writing will make sense to your readers.

One of the stylistic devices you can use to add variety and flexibility to your writing is the insertion into your sentences of words or phrases that add to but are *not essential* to the sentence's meaning. That is, the word or phrase could be omitted and the sentence would still be complete and would still make sense. It might, however, lack grace or interest.

You can use four punctuation marks to add non-essential material to your sentences: quotation marks, commas, dashes, and parentheses. You are already familiar with the first two. Here is your opportunity to master the last two: the **dash**—which looks like this—and **parentheses** (round brackets). (If you are typing, the dash is two hyphens with no space on either side.)

Dashes

Dashes are used to mark a break in thought or an abrupt shift in emphasis.

> 1. Use a dash to introduce a word, phrase, or clause that summarizes or restates what came just before.

I still love dried apricots and pickled beets—foods my mother gave me as treats when I was a child.

Perseverance, spirit, and skill—these three qualities ensure a good game.

Mulroney, Filmon, and Wells—all three share responsibility for the failure of the Meech Lake Accord.

> 2. Use a pair of dashes to enclose a series of items separated by commas.

Four of the managers—Laurence, Muhsin, Luis, and Neville—are new to the McDonald's franchise at the zoo.

Because they were afraid of the police, my so-called friends—Roman, Faye, and Mairi—all betrayed me.

The apartment he showed me would have been fine, had it not been for the tenants—moths, cockroaches, and silverfish—already making it their home.

> 3. Use a dash or a pair of dashes to mark off from the rest of the sentence a climactic or emphatic comment.

I expect—and I always will—that students at this level should be self-motivated.

Our neighbour—the accused murderer—is hanging out rabbit pelts to dry.

If you really want to go—even though you haven't been invited—I'll take you.

Note that dashes mark off material that is not grammatically part of the sentence. If you were to omit the words set off by dashes, the sentence would still make sense.

Dashes can be misused by appearing too frequently. Unless you are writing very informally—in a personal letter, for instance—save dashes for the very occasional phrase to which you want to draw emphatic attention.

EXERCISE 1*

Add dashes where they are appropriate.

1. The aboriginal tribes of England I've forgotten their name painted themselves blue.
2. My purpose in moving from Vancouver to Hope like that of hundreds of people before me was to find affordable housing.
3. We shall have to start without her again!
4. Skiing and skating if you like these sports, you'll love Quebec.
5. Tending to his garden, writing his memoirs, and dining with friends these were the pleasures Arnold looked forward to in retirement.
6. What is missing in his life is obvious rest and relaxation!
7. Zoe should do well in fact, I'm sure she will in the engineering program.
8. Rudolf was amazed positively thunderstruck when he learned Uncle Ladislaw had won a million dollars.
9. Historians, diarists, and chroniclers these are the recorders of our past.
10. Dashes allow you to insert with a kind of a shout the occasional exclamation into your sentences.

Parentheses

Like dashes, parentheses are used to enclose an interruption to a sentence. The difference between them is a matter of tone: dashes SHOUT—they serve to draw readers' attention to the material they enclose—but parentheses (which should be used sparingly) "whisper." Parentheses are similar to theatrical "asides"; they are subordinate to the main narrative or action but are not to be missed.

> 1. Use parentheses to enclose extra information that is not emphasized.

Yasmin's teaching schedule (she is in class seven hours a day) gives her little time to meet with students individually.

They brought me to their village and presented me to their chief (who was a woman) and to the tribal councilors.

Note the difference in tone your choice of punctuation makes. Compare the example above with this version:

They brought me to their village and presented me to their chief—who was a woman—and to the tribal councilors.

> 2. Use parentheses to enclose explanatory material that is not part of the main sentence.

"Lightweight Lit." (an essay presented earlier) was written by an English teacher who prefers to remain anonymous.

The Malagasy (people of Madagascar) like to eat a kapoaka of rice (enough to fill a condensed-milk can) three times a day.

> 3. Parentheses are used to enclose reference data in a research paper. (See Chapter 23.)

EXERCISE 2*

Add parentheses where they are appropriate.

1. Five of the students I was asked not to name them have volunteered to be peer tutors.
2. The apostrophe is explained in the unit on spelling pp. 347–87.
3. Jason complained that being a manager he became one in March was like being a cop.
4. I have enclosed a cheque for one hundred and fifty dollars $150.00.
5. More Canadian servicemen died in World War I 1914–1918 than in any war before or since.
6. Although Mozart lived a relatively short time he died when he was thirty-six, he composed hundreds of musical masterpieces.
7. As news of his "miracle cures" spread patients began to come to him from all over the province, the country doctor had to move his clinic to a more central location.
8. The new contract provided improved working conditions, a raise in salary 5 percent, and a new dental plan.
9. After years of producing undrinkable wine, Ontario now boasts a few very good wineries Inniskillin and Hillebrand are two that come to mind.
10. "One of the most important tools for making paper speak in your own voice is punctuation; it plays the role of body language; it helps readers hear you the way you want to be heard Baker, "How to Punctuate," 48–49.

EXERCISE 3*

Add dashes and parentheses where they are appropriate.

1. Lord Dunsany 1878–1957 wrote many fantastic tales.
2. A hoe, a rake, a spade, and a case of beer these are the essential tools for the weekend gardener.
3. Now that *Dick Tracy* has been so successful at the box office, I wonder if we will be treated heaven forbid to *Dick Tracy II, III, IV, V,* and even more?
4. Three of our best athletes Anne, Mei-ling, and Philomena have been declared ineligible.
5. At the last department meeting you should have been there! Ruth threw a lemon at Margaret.
6. Carefully arranged on a lacquer tray were deviled eggs, sushi, and kim chee all favourites of my wife and her lover.
7. These two famous satirical novels *Animal Farm* and *Gulliver's Travels* ought to be on every college student's reading list.
8. Do we *can* we graduate truly educated men and women after only three years of study?
9. The prisoner is supposed to have escaped if one can believe the witness by bending the bars of his cell.
10. The explanation is lengthy but easy to follow if you study the diagram see p. 77.

Spelling

CHAPTER 42

Three Suggestions for Quick Improvement

Of all the errors you might make in writing, spelling is the one that is noticed by everyone, not just English teachers. No piece of writing that is full of misspellings can be classified as good. Misspellings can cause misunderstanding, as when an English teacher promised his students a course with "a strong *vacational* emphasis." (Those students who weren't misled wondered what he was doing teaching English.)

Sometimes misspellings cause confusion. Take this sentence, for example:

Mouse is a desert with a base of wiped cream.

It takes a few seconds to "translate" the sentence into a definition of *mousse*, a dessert made with whipped cream.

Most often, though, misspellings are misleading, in that they spoil the image you want to present. You want, naturally, to be seen as intelligent, careful, and conscientious. But, if your writing is riddled with spelling errors, your readers will think you careless, uneducated, or even stupid. It is not true, by the way, that intelligence and the ability to spell go hand in hand. It *is* true, though, that people generally think they do. So, to prevent both confusion and embarrassment, it is essential that you spell correctly.

There are three things you can do to improve your spelling almost instantly:

---
1. Buy and use a good dictionary.

A good dictionary is an indispensable tool for any writer. You will need it *every time* you write. Most of your doubts about spelling can be answered if you take the time to check in your dictionary. The time you spend looking up words will not be wasted; your rewards will be the increased accuracy of your writing and the increased respect of your readers. Useful dictionaries are the *Gage Canadian Dictionary* (a Canadian reference, ideal for use at home or in the office), and the *Merriam-Webster Unabridged Dictionary*.

If you wonder how it's possible to look up a word that you can't spell, look at the dictionaries we've recommended. At the front of each is a "Guide to the Dictionary," and in the Guide is a chart showing the common spellings for all the sounds in the English language. If you know only how to pronounce a word, the chart will help you find its spelling. Another way to find a word you can't spell is to look up a **synonym**—a word that means the same thing. In the dictionary entry for the synonym, you'll probably find the word you're looking for.

Another useful tool, if you're writing your essay on a word processor, is a spell-check program. These aren't foolproof, though—as we'll see later—so don't count on your computer to solve *all* your spelling problems.

---
2. Ask a good speller.

Some people seem to have been born with the ability to spell. Such people are more reliable than a computer program. Often they are secretly proud of their talent and pleased to demonstrate it, so don't be afraid to ask. They probably aren't as good at something else as you are; you may have a talent they could use in exchange.

---
3. Learn three basic spelling rules.

English spelling is frustratingly irregular, and no rule holds true in *all* cases. But there are three simple rules that do hold for most words, and mastering these rules will help you avoid many common errors.

Before learning the three rules, you need to know the difference between **vowels** and **consonants**. The vowels are **a, e, i, o,** and **u** (and sometimes **y**). All the other letters are consonants.

Rule 1: Dropping the Final *e*

The first rule tells you when to drop the final, silent *e* when adding an ending to a word.

> *Drop* the final, silent *e* when adding an ending beginning with a vowel.
>
> *Keep* the final, silent *e* when adding an ending beginning with a consonant.

Keeping the rule in mind, look at these examples:

ENDINGS BEGINNING WITH A VOWEL	ENDINGS BEGINNING WITH A CONSONANT
-ing: amuse + ing = amusing	*-ment:* amuse + ment = amusement
-ed: live + ed = lived	*-ly:* live + ly = lively
-able: like + able = likable	*-ness:* like + ness = likeness
-ible: force + ible = forcible	*-ful:* force + ful = forceful
-er: use + er = user	*-less:* use + less = useless

In the three exercises that follow, combine each word with the ending to form a new word. When you have finished each set, check your answers.

EXERCISE 1*

1. desperate + ly =

2. crackle + ing =

3. generate + or =

4. atone + ment =

5. mate + ing =

6. rare + ly =

7. elevate + or =

8. emerge + ing =

9. positive + ly =

10. apologize + ing =

EXERCISE 2*

1. excite + ment =

2. interfere + ence =

3. desire + able =

4. continue + ance =

5. abridge + ing =

6. remove + able =

7. dissolute + ly =

8. acquire + ing =

9. shake + able =

10. aerate + ing =

EXERCISE 3*

Add *e* in the blank space wherever it's needed to complete the spelling of these words. If no *e* is needed, leave the space blank.

1. apologiz_____ing

2. encourag_____ment

3. nois_____y

4. issu_____able

5. fam_____ous

6. abridg_____ment

7. mov_____able

8. officiat_____ing

9. valu_____ation

10. realiz_____ing

Exceptions to Rule 1

Three common words do not follow the rule:

argue + ment = argument
nine + th = ninth
true + ly = truly

There is one more exception to rule 1: after soft *c* (as in *notice*) and soft *g* (as in *change*), keep the final, silent *e* when adding an ending beginning with *a* or *o*. Here are two examples:

notice + able = noticeable
outrage + ous = outrageous

Rule 2: Doubling the Final Consonant

The second rule tells you when to double the final consonant, when adding an ending to a word.

> When adding an ending beginning with a vowel (such as *-able*, *-ing*, *-ed*, or *-er*), double the final consonant of the root word if the word
> 1. ends with a *single* consonant preceded by a *single* vowel AND
> 2. is stressed on the last syllable.

Notice that a word must have *both* characteristics for the rule to apply. Let's look at a few examples:

begin + er	ends with a single consonant (*n*) preceded by a single vowel (*i*) and is stressed on the last syllable (*begín*), so the rule applies, and we double the final consonant:	beginner
control + ed	ends with a single consonant (*l*) preceded by a single vowel (*o*) and is stressed on the last syllable (*contról*), so the rule applies:	controlled
drop + ing	ends with a single consonant (*p*) preceded by a single vowel (*o*) and is stressed on the last syllable (there is only one: *dróp*), so the rule applies:	dropping

appear + ing	ends with a single consonant (*r*) preceded by *two* vowels (*ea*), so the rule does not apply, and we do not double the final consonant:	appearing
turn + ed	ends with *two* consonants (*rn*), so the rule does not apply:	turned
open + er	ends with a single consonant (*n*) preceded by a single vowel (*e*) but is *not* stressed on the last syllable (*ópen*), so the rule does not apply:	opener

(In words such as *equip*, *quit*, and *quiz*, the *u* should be considered part of the *q* and not a vowel. These words then follow the rule: *equipping*, *quitter*, and *quizzed*.)

Note: There is a group of words ending in *l*, *t*, or *s*, which, according to our rules, do not need a double consonant before the ending. (Examples are label, counsel, focus, and format.) You will sometimes see this consonant doubled (*labelled*, *counselled*, *focussed*, and *formatting*); this spelling is also correct. As a writer, you must use one spelling or the other consistently.

Following are four exercises that require you to combine each word with the ending to form a new word. Check your answers to each set before going on.

EXERCISE 4*

1. blot + ing =

2. span + ing =

3. submit + ed =

4. fail + ing =

5. blur + ed =

6. regret + able =

7. admit + ing =

8. bat + ing =

9. beg + ing =

10. entail + ed =

EXERCISE 5*

1. forget + ing =
2. confer + ed =
3. refer + ing =
4. strip + ed =
5. shoot + ing =
6. expel + ing =
7. grab + ed =
8. jar + ing =
9. knit + ing =
10. hinder + ed =

EXERCISE 6*

1. defer + ing =
2. remit + ance =
3. regret + ful =
4. cuddle + ed =
5. acquit + al =
6. concur + ed =
7. flag + ing =
8. pin + ing =
9. bar + ed =
10. refer + ed =

EXERCISE 7*

1. occur + ence =
2. persist + ence =
3. emerge + ence =
4. recur + ence =
5. persevere + ance =
6. consist + ency =

7. suffer + ance =

8. resist + ance =

9. concur + ence =

10. deter + ence =

When it comes to adding *-ence*, three words are especially trouble-some. *Prefer, refer,* and *confer* all appear to require a double final conso-nant. But they don't, because, when you add *-ence*, the stress shifts to the *first* syllable of the word. So you write:

prefér	preférring	preférred	*but*	préference
refér	reférring	reférred	*but*	réference
confér	conférring	conférred	*but*	cónference

Rule 3: Words Containing *ie* or *ei*

There are almost a thousand common English words containing *ie* or *ei*, so remembering the rule that governs them is worthwhile. It helps to keep in mind that *ie* occurs roughly twice as often as *ei*.

The old rhyme tells you most of what you need to know to spell these words:

> Write *i* before *e*, except after *c*
> Or when sounded like *ā*, as in *neighbour* and *weigh.*

If you remember this rhyme, you'll have no difficulty in spelling words like *belief, piece, ceiling, receive,* and *freight.*

Unfortunately, the rhyme covers only two of the cases in which we write *e* before *i*: after *c*, and when the syllable is pronounced with a long *ā* sound. An addition to the rule is necessary:

> If short *ĕ* or long *ī* is the sound that is right,
> Write *e* before *i*, as in *their* or in *height.*

This rule covers words such as *Fahrenheit, seismic, heir,* and *leisure* (pronounce it to rhyme with *pleasure*). *Either* and *neither* can be pro-nounced "eye-ther" and "nye-ther," so they too require *ei*.

There are, of course, exceptions. This silly sentence contains the most common ones:

The *friend* of a *weird species* of *sheik seized caffeine, codeine,* and *protein.*

These exercises will help you to pin down *ie* versus *ei.* Fill in the blanks with *ie* or *ei.* After you finish each set, check your answers.

EXERCISE 8*

1. br_____f
2. fr_____ndly
3. f_____lding
4. ach_____ve
5. rel_____ve
6. retr_____val
7. dec_____ve
8. l_____sure
9. rec_____pt
10. gr_____ve

EXERCISE 9*

1. p_____r
2. hyg_____ne
3. h_____rarchy
4. dec_____t
5. f_____rce
6. p_____ced
7. for_____gn
8. w_____ght
9. rec_____ve
10. spec_____s

EXERCISE 10*

1. Can we really trust _____ther of them, when we know th_____r
   bel_____fs to be so similar?

2. After all, anyone who thinks that we are dec_____ved by everything we perc_____ve must be a few grams short of a full kilo.

3. If we can't trust our own senses, what conc_____vable information
   is there that we can rec_____ve with confidence?

4. Frankly, it would be a great rel_____f if n_____ther of them ever
   appeared in my life again.

5. My n_____ghbour is so conc_____ted, she speaks to no one on
   our block. The children think she's w_____rd.

There are three or four more spelling rules we could explain here, but
we won't—for two reasons. First, there are many exceptions to the remaining "rules" for English spelling. And, second, you don't need to
memorize more rules *if you use your dictionary.* Now is the time to read
the "Guide to the Dictionary" in the front of your dictionary. Reading it
won't be very entertaining, but it will be well worth your while.

The Guide outlines the kinds of information given for each word in the
dictionary and explains the abbreviations and symbols that are used.
You will discover, for example, that you don't need to memorize long
lists of irregular plurals: your dictionary provides the irregular plurals
of the nouns you look up. It also gives the irregular forms of verbs,
adjectives, and adverbs. (If you've forgotten how *regular* plurals, verb
forms, adjectives, and adverbs are formed, the Guide will remind you.)
Your dictionary will also tell you how to add various endings to root
words and even where you can divide a word when you need to hyphen-
ate it at the end of a line. Take half an hour to read the Guide in your
dictionary; then do the following exercises.

EXERCISE 11*

Write the plural form of each word. Use your dictionary and check your
answers before going on to the next exercise.

1. hero

2. history

3. criterion

4. ghetto

5. personnel

6. crisis

7. data

8. phenomenon

9. nucleus

10. appendix

EXERCISE 12*

Combine each root word with the ending given. Again, use your dictionary and check your answers.

1. lonely + ness =

2. copy + ed =

3. crazy + ness =

4. easy + er =

5. pretty + est =

6. reply + s =

7. reply + ing =

8. thirty + eth =

9. unnecessary + ly =

10. traffic + ing =

EXERCISE 13*

Using hyphens, show where each word could be divided at the end of a line. (Some words can be divided in two or more places—for example, *ice-break-er.*)

1. employer

2. consists

3. success

4. management

5. process

6. shipping

7. accounting

8. through

9. distribution

10. business

CHAPTER 43

Sound-Alikes, Look-Alikes, and Spoilers

Using a dictionary, asking a good speller for help, and applying the three spelling rules will make an immediate improvement in your spelling. By following two additional suggestions you will further increase your spelling accuracy, but the skills involved will take longer to master. First, learn to tell apart words that are often confused because they sound or look alike. Second, learn to spell the words that most people find difficult—words we call Spelling Spoilers. Don't try to master all of these words at once. Instead, memorize a few each week, and review them frequently. In two or three months, you could be one of the people poor spellers turn to for help!

Sound-Alikes and Look-Alikes

Some of your spelling troubles are probably caused by your using words that either sound or look like the words you really want. A spellcheck cannot help you with these words because, if you're like most people, you don't misspell them. What makes the spelling "wrong" is the sense of the sentence in which you've used them. *Hear, our, meat, have* are, as isolated words, correctly spelled. But if you combine them into a "sentence"—*Meat me hear in have an our*—you end up with a tangle of misspellings no computer can unravel.

Careful pronunciation sometimes helps to correct this problem. For example, if you pronounce the words *accept* and *except* differently, you'll be less likely to confuse them in your writing. It is also useful to make up memory aids to help yourself remember the difference between words that sound alike but have very different meanings. We have included in this list a few pairs of words that do not look or sound alike, but that are commonly confused.

accept
except

Accept means "**t**ake." It is always a verb. **Ex**cept means "**ex**cluding."

Everyone *except* Brian *accepted* my explanation.

advice
advise

The difference in pronunciation makes the difference in meaning clear. *Advise* (rhymes with *wise*) is a verb. *Advice* (rhymes with *nice*) is a noun.

I *advise* you not to listen to free *advice*.

affect
effect

Affect as a verb means "influence." As a noun, it means "a strong feeling." *Effect* is a noun meaning "result." If you can substitute *result*, then *effect* is the word you need. (Occasionally *effect* can be a verb—meaning "bring about"—but you probably won't need to use it that way.)

Learning about the *effects* of caffeine *affected* my coffee-drinking habits.

Some disturbed people display appropriate *affect*.

a lot
allot

A lot (often misspelled *alot*) should be avoided. Use *many* or *much* instead. *Allot* means "distribute" or "assign."

He still has ~~a lot of~~ problems, but he's coping ~~a lot~~ better. [*many* / *much*]

The teacher will *allot* the assignments according to the students' interests.

amount
number

Amount is used with uncountable things; *number* is used with countable things.

You may have a large *number* of jelly beans in a jar, but a small *amount* of candy.

(Jelly beans are countable; candy is not.)

are
our

Are is a verb. *Our* shows ownership.

Marie-Claire Blais and Margaret Atwood *are* two of Canada's best-known writers.

Canada is *our* home and native land.

assure
ensure
insure

Assure means "state with confidence; pledge or promise."

She *assured* him she would keep his letters always.
Brian Mulroney *assured* the Inuit their concerns would be addressed in the near future.

Ensure means "make certain of something."

The extra twenty dollars will *ensure* your getting a good seat.
No number of promises can *ensure* that love will last.

Insure means "guarantee against financial loss." We *insure* lives and property.

Tom *insured* the book before he sent it airmail.
We have *insured* both our home and our car against fire and theft.

choose
chose

Pronunciation gives the clue here. *Choose* rhymes with *booze* and means "select." *Chose* rhymes with *rose* and means "selected."

Please *choose* a topic.
I *chose* film making.

cite
sight
site

To *cite* is to quote or mention. A lawyer *cites* precedents. Writers *cite* their sources in research papers. You might *cite* a comedian for her wit, or a politician for his honesty. A *site* is a place.

The Plains of Abraham is the *site* of a famous battle.
Tiananmen Square is the *site* of the massacre.
Pape and Mortimer is the *site* of our new communication arts centre.

A *sight* is something you see.

With her spiked hair and seven earrings, she was a *sight* to behold.

coarse
course

Coarse means "rough, unrefined." (Remember: the word *arse* is co*arse*.) For all other meanings, use *course*.

That sandpaper is too *coarse*.
You'll enjoy the photography *course*.
Of *course* you'll do well.

complement
compliment

A *complement* completes something. A *compliment* is a gift of praise.

A glass of wine would be the perfect *complement* to the meal.
Some people are embarrassed by *compliments*.

conscience
conscious

Your *conscience* is your sense of right and wrong. *Conscious* means "aware" or "awake"—able to feel and think.

> After Katy cheated on the test, her *conscience* bothered her.
> Katy was *conscious* of having done wrong.
> The injured man was *unconscious* for an hour.

consul
council
counsel

A *consul* is a government official stationed in another country. A *council* is an assembly or official group. Members of a council are *councilors*. *Counsel* can be used to mean both "advice" and "to advise."

> The Canadian *consul* in Mexico was very helpful.
> The Women's Advisory *Council* meets next month.
> Maria gave me good *counsel*.
> She *counseled* me to hire a lawyer.

continual
continuous

Continual refers to an action that goes on regularly, but with interruptions. *Continuous* refers to an action that goes on without interruption.

> The student *continually* tried to interrupt the lecturer, but his voice went on in a *continuous* drone.
> There is a *continuous* flow of traffic during rush hour.

credible
credulous
creditable

Credible refers to a story; *credulous* describes the person who believes an incredible story.

> Nell was fortunate that the police found her story *credible*.
> My brother is so *credulous*, we call him Gullible Gus.

Creditable means "worthy of reward or praise."

> After two semesters, Patti has finally begun to produce *creditable* work.

desert
dessert

A *désert* is a dry, barren place. As a verb, *desért* means "leave behind." *Dessért* is "double good," the kind of food you'd like two servings of, so give it two *s*'s.

> The tundra is Canada's only *desert* region.
> My neighbour *deserted* her husband and children.
> *Dessert* is my favourite part of the meal.

dining
dinning

You'll spell *dining* correctly if you remember the phrase "wining and dining." You'll probably never use *dinning*. It means "making a loud noise."

> The children are in the *dining* room.
> We are *dining* out tonight.
> The noise from the bar was *dinning* in our ears.

disburse
disperse

Disburse means "to pay out money;" that is what **burs**ars do. *Disperse* means "to break up"; crowds are sometimes *dispersed* by the police.

> The college's financial aid officer will *disburse* the students' loans at the end of this week.
> The students gathered in Tiananmen Square were *dispersed* by the army.

does
dose

Pronunciation provides the clue. *Does* rhymes with *buzz* and is a verb. *Dose* rhymes with *gross* and refers to a quantity of medicine.

> John *does* drive fast, *doesn't* he?
> My grandmother gave me a *dose* of cod liver oil.

farther
further

You'll have no trouble distinguishing between these two if you associate *farther* with *distance* and *further* with *time*.

> Dan wanted me to walk a little *farther* so we could discuss our relationship *further*.

faze
phase

Fazed usually has a *not* before it; to be *not fazed* means to be not disturbed, or concerned, or taken aback. *Phase* means "stage of development or process."

> Unfortunately, Theo was not the least bit *fazed* by his disastrous grade report.
> Since Cathy works full-time, she has decided to complete her degree in *phases*.

fewer
less

Fewer is used with countable things; *less*, with uncountable things.

> In May, there are *fewer* students in the college, so there is *less* work for the faculty to do.
> The *fewer* attempts you make, the *less* your chance of success.

With units of money or measurement, however, you use *less*:

> I have *less* than twenty dollars in my wallet.
> Walter's house is on a lot that is *less* than four metres wide.

forth
fourth

Forth means "**for**ward" or "onward." *Fourth* contains the number **four**, which gives it its meaning.

> Please stop pacing back and *forth*.
> The B.C. Lions lost their *fourth* game in a row.

hear
here

Hear is what you do with your **ears**. *Here* is used for all other meanings.

> Now *hear* this!
> Ray isn't *here*.
> *Here* is your assignment.

imply
infer

A speaker or writer *implies*; a listener or reader *infers*. To *imply* is to hint, or to say something indirectly. To *infer* is to draw a conclusion from what is stated or hinted at.

> I *inferred* from his sarcastic remarks that he was not very fond of Penny.
> In her introduction of Tom, Penny *implied* that she greatly admired him.

it's
its

It's is a shortened form of *it is*. The apostrophe takes the place of the *i* in *is*. If you can substitute *it is*, then *it's* is the form you need. If you can't substitute *it is*, then *its* is the correct word.

> *It's* really not difficult. (*It is* really not difficult.)
> The book has lost *its* cover. ("The book has lost *it is* cover" makes no sense, so you need *its*.)

It's is also commonly used as the shortened form of *it has*. In this case, the apostrophe takes the place of the *h* and the *a*.

> *It's* been a good year for us.

later
latter

Later refers to time and has the word **late** in it. *Latter* means "the second of two" and has two *t*'s. It is the opposite of *former*.

> It is *later* than you think.
> You take the former, and I'll take the *latter*.

loose
lose

Pronunciation is the key to these words. *Loose* rhymes with *goose* and means "not tight." *Lose* rhymes with *ooze* and means "misplace" or "be defeated."

> A *loose* electrical connection is dangerous.
> Some are born to win, some to *lose*.

miner
minor

A **miner** works in a **mine**. *Minor* means "lesser" or "not important." For example, a *minor* is a person of less than legal age.

> Liquor can be served to *miners*, but not if they are *minors*.
> For me, spelling is a *minor* problem.

moral
morale

Again, pronunciation provides the clue you need. *Móral* refers to the understanding of what is right and wrong. *Morále* refers to the spirit or mental condition of a person or group.

> People often have to make *moral* decisions.
> The low *morale* of the workers prompted the strike.

peace
piece

Peace is what we want on **ea**rth. *Piece* means "a part or portion of something," as in "a **pie**ce of **pie**."

> Everyone hopes for *peace* in the Middle East.
> A *piece* of the puzzle is missing.

personal
personnel

Personal means "private." *Personnel* refers to the group of people working for a particular employer or to the office responsible for maintaining employees' records.

> The letter was marked "*Personal* and Confidential."
> We are fortunate in having hired highly qualified *personnel*.
> Nellie works in the *Personnel* Office.

principal
principle

Principal means "main." A *principle* is a rule.

> A *principal* is the main administrator of a school.
> Oil is Alberta's *principal* industry.
> I make it a *principle* to submit my essays on time.

quiet
quite

If you pronounce these words carefully, you won't confuse them. *Quiet* has two syllables; *quite* has only one.

> The librarian asked us to be *quiet*.
> We had not *quite* finished our homework.

stationary
stationery

Stationary means "fixed in place." *Stationery* is writing paper.

> Did you want a portable or a *stationary* computer?
> Please order a new supply of *stationery*.

than
then

Than is used in comparisons. Pronounce it to rhyme with *can*. *Then* refers to time and rhymes with *when*.

> Peter is a better speller *than* I.
> He made his decision *then*.
> Ted withdrew from the competition; *then* he realized the consequences.

their
there
they're

Their indicates ownership. *There* points out something or indicates place. It includes the word *here*, which also indicates place. *They're* is a shortened form of *they are*. (The apostrophe replaces the *a* in *are*.)

It was *their* fault.
There are two weeks left in the term.
You should look over *there*.
They're late, as usual.

too **two** **to**	The *too* with an extra *o* in it means "more than enough" or "also." *Two* is the number after one. For all other meanings, use *to*.

He thinks he's been working *too* hard. She thinks so, *too*.
There are *two* sides *to* every argument.
The *two* women knew *too* much about each other *to* be friends.

weather **whether** **wether**	*Whether* means "which of the two" and is used in all cases when you aren't referring to the climatic conditions outside (*weather*). A *wether* is a castrated ram, so its uses are limited.

were **where** **we're**	If you pronounce these three carefully, you won't confuse them. *Were* rhymes with *fur* and is a verb. *Where* is pronounced "hwear," includes the word *here*, and indicates place. *We're* is a shortened form of *we are* and is pronounced "weer."

You *were* joking, *weren't* you?
Where did you want to meet?
We're on our way.

who's **whose**	*Who's* is a shortened form of *who is* or *who has*. If you can substitute *who is* or *who has* for the *who's* in your sentence, then you are using the right spelling. Otherwise, use *whose*.

Who's coming to dinner? (*Who is* coming to dinner?)
Who's been sleeping in my bed? (*Who has* been sleeping?)
Whose calculator is this? ("*Who is* calculator" makes no sense, so you need *whose*.)

woman **women**	Confusing these two is guaranteed to irritate your women readers. *Wo**man*** is the singular form; compare **man**. *Wo**men*** is the plural form; compare **men**.

A *woman's* place is wherever she chooses to be.
The *women's* movement promotes equality between *women* and men.

you're
your

You're is a shortened form of *you are*. If you can substitute *you are* for the *you're* in your sentence, then you're using the correct form. If you can't substitute *you are*, use *your*.

> *You're* welcome. (*You are* welcome.)
> Unfortunately, *your* hamburger got burned. ("*You are* hamburger" makes no sense, so *your* is the word you want.)

In the group of exercises that follows, choose the correct word in each pair. If you don't know an answer, go back and reread the explanation. Check your answers after each set.

EXERCISE 1*

1. Limiting (coarse course) selection so drastically will (affect effect) students' academic development and subsequent job opportunities.
2. (Are Our) you going to (accept except) the offer?
3. Eat your vegetables; (than then) you can have your (desert dessert).
4. If (your you're) overweight by fifty pounds, (loosing losing) the excess will be a long-term proposition.
5. It's (quiet quite) true that they did not get (hear here) until two in the morning.
6. Ironically, it is the saint, not the sinner, (who's whose) (conscience conscious) troubles him.
7. He (assured ensured insured) me he would keep the (amount number) of changes to a minimum.
8. (Its It's) hard to tell the dog from (its it's) owner.
9. To (choose chose) a (coarse course) of action contrary to your lawyer's (advice advise) would be foolish.
10. Constant (dining dinning) out (does dose) become boring after a while.

EXERCISE 2*

1. The (principal's principle's) high (principals principles) constrained him to request the offending teacher's resignation.
2. They (choose chose) the (forth fourth) house that the real estate agent showed them.
3. All day the rain poured down (continually continuously), and by evening our camp (cite sight site) was a (cite sight site) to behold.
4. (Your You're) being (conscience conscious) and in the classroom is a prerequisite, though not a guarantee, of learning.

5. I find it (incredible incredulous) that you would be so (credible credulous) as to believe any of our town (councilors counselors).
6. (Accept Except) for (miner minor) bruises, passengers wearing seat belts sustain fewer injuries in accidents than those who do not buckle up.
7. (Morales Morals) that have been judged as being (to too two) (loose lose) are reputed to have caused the downfalls of great empires.
8. The angry picketers were warned, "If you move one metre (farther further), the police will (disburse disperse) you."
9. Did you really intend to (imply infer) that your instructor (continually continuously) violates the no smoking policy in his classroom?
10. A (woman women) (who's whose) been out of the workforce for fifteen years (does dose) need some help in planning career choices.

EXERCISE 3*

1. Bartender, do you (hear here)? Over (hear here), we want beer.
2. (To Too Two) be (stationary stationery) for that long is to be dead.
3. (Loosing Losing) or winning is not important in the early stages of learning a sport; (its it's) the development of skills and attitudes that really matters.
4. Olerud, (your you're) being sent to the (miner minor) leagues!
5. He served her a (peace, piece) of rhubarb pie; (latter, later), she (complemented, complimented) him on his perfect crust.
6. The (weather whether) will have a major influence on (weather whether) we are able to land at Goose Bay.
7. He is handsome, clever, and talented, but his (coarse course) language entirely spoils the (affect effect) at his interviews.
8. The fact that I have (fewer less) friends than you do doesn't (faze phase) me.
9. (Woman Women) working in traditionally male areas of employment are the ones (who's whose) competence is most often questioned.
10. Rupert (choose chose) to (accept except) the (principal's principle's) apology.

EXERCISE 4*

(Their They're There) must be a better way to cope with house renovations. If I were to describe my (personal personnel) agony during the months it took for the construction workers and contractors to (acheive achieve) their final (affect effect), (you're your) heart would bleed. Plaster dust was the worst problem, because it gets into everything, making even (dinning dining) an uncomfortable experience. As the walls were torn (lose loose) and the house was gradually reduced to (it's its) skeleton, plaster dust found (its it's) way into every crack and corner. The noise and confusion (affected effected) my (moral morale), and I became inclined to use (course coarse) language, particularly with those who insisted on giving me (advice advise). (Later Latter), when my (conscience conscious) got the better of me, my feeble attempts at apology (were we're) not (accepted excepted). In the end, the renovations cost me my (peace piece) of mind, my (friends freinds), and more money (than then) I dreamed possible.

EXERCISE 5*

By the time we discovered that (there they're their) was (too to two) much cholesterol in fried foods, we (were we're where) already addicted. French fries and chicken wings, battered fish and doughnuts were an (excepted accepted) part of our diet. The (affect effect) that (dinning dining) on such foods has on us is evident in our (waste waist)lines and in the nation's heart disease statistics. The (desserts deserts) we tend to (chose choose) are the worst offenders, according to diet (councilors counselors), but (our are) main (course coarse) can be equally dangerous if (its it's) cholesterol count is high. Experts now (advice advise) us (too to two) be guided by the (principle principal) that "less is more." But this (advice advise) is more difficult to follow than one might expect in a society that has been conditioned to (believe beleive) "bigger is better." The (moral morale) seems to be that we must (chose choose) between foods that taste good and foods that do good.

Spelling Spoilers

Here is a list of words that are frequently misspelled. Have someone dictate the list to you. Circle the ones you misspell, and memorize them, a few at a time. Try to learn ten each week. Review your list often, until you have mastered every word. Making up memory aids for especially troublesome words will help you conquer them. Here are some examples to get you started:

accommodate: It means "make room for," and the word itself makes room for two c's and two m's.

business: Bus**in**ess is no **sin**.

environment: The word *env**iron**ment,* like the earth, has **iron** in it.

friend: He is a fri**end** to the **end**.

grammar: Poor gram**mar** will **mar** your writing.

absence
accommodate
achievement
acknowledge
across
adolescence
among
answer
argument
beginning
business
careful
category
clothes
committee
conscious
criticism
definitely
dependent
desperate
development
disappear
disappoint
discipline
dissatisfied
doesn't
eighth
embarrassed
environment
exercise
existence
explanation
extremely
familiar
February

finally
forty
friend
gauge
government
grammar
guarantee
guidance
height
hoping
hypocrisy
immediately
independent
laboratory
license (*or* licence)
likely
loneliness
lonely
maintenance
marriage
mentally
necessary
ninety
ninth
occasionally
omission
opinion
opportunity
paid
parallel
perform
planned
possess
prejudice
privilege

procedure
proceed
professor
psychology
recommend
relevant
repetition
restaurant
rhythm
ridiculous
safety
schedule
separate
shining
similar
somewhat
speech
studying
succeed
superintendent
surprise
technique
thorough
tragedy
truly
unnecessary
until
unusual
usually
vacuum
Wednesday
writing
written

EXERCISE 6

Make up sentences containing the words you misspelled when the list of
Spelling Spoilers was dictated. Underline the Spelling Spoiler(s) in each
sentence. (If you do this exercise once a week, you will master the list
very quickly.)

One final suggestion. You may find that, despite all your efforts,
there are a few words you just cannot spell correctly. The solution?

Either write them out on the inside cover of your dictionary or, even simpler, don't use them. Look in your dictionary or thesaurus to find synonyms (different words with the same or similar meanings), and use those instead. Two thesauruses are available in inexpensive paperback editions: *Roget's Thesaurus* and Soule's *Dictionary of English Synonyms*.

CHAPTER 44

Capital Letters

Capital letters should be used in a few specific places and nowhere else. Some people seem to have "capitalitis": they put capital letters on words randomly, regardless of whether the words are nouns, adjectives, or verbs. Like "exclamatosis," "capitalitis" is a disease communicated by comic books, which capitalize every word.

Not very many people have this problem; if you are in the majority who generally use capitals properly, skip this chapter and go on to the next one. If you are puzzled about capital letters, though, or have readers who are puzzled by your use of them, read on.

Capitalize the first letters of words that fit these descriptions:

1. the first word of a sentence:

    Put out the garbage.

2. the names of specific persons:

    Anne Murray   Mordecai Richler

    the names of specific places:

    Alberta   Elm St.
    Mars   Morocco
    Oz   Regina

    and the names of specific things:

St. Lawrence River
British North America Act
Hilltop Towers

3. the days of the week and the months of the year (but not the seasons):

Monday	July
Friday	summer
October	winter

4. the titles of specific people (but not the names of their positions), books, films, and courses (but not subject names, unless they're languages):

Governor General Ray Hnatyshyn	*but* the position of governor general
Pope John Paul II	*but* the position of pope
Mr. and Ms. O'Connor	
Essay Essentials	
Teenage Mutant Ninja Turtles	
Mathematics 101	*but* the subject of mathematics
English 101	*but* the English language

5. the names of specific companies, businesses, organizations, and departments:

Chateau Gai	Conservative Party
Arc Industries	Personnel Department
Winnipeg Rotary Club	

EXERCISE 1*

Correct the capitalization in these sentences.

1. why on Earth would you buy a toyota?
2. We need to get rid of some of our High-School habits when we start College.
3. have you read dr. Ernie l. Piffle's new book, *I'm OK — You're Fat: A Self-Help guide to fitness fascism*?
4. The loyalists were considered Patriots by inhabitants of upper Canada but Traitors by people in the united states.
5. I didn't do very well in my Fluid Power Course; maybe I'd better switch to Culinary Arts.
6. well, look who's here; it's mr. olympics.
7. Take a right at Yonge Street, a left at lawrence avenue, and a right at Avenue road.
8. My english teacher also teaches french to asian Immigrants.

9. Marcia's Father, being Conservative in his tastes, disapproved of Ronald's leather jacket and harley-davidson 750.
10. Neither was he amused when marcia ran off with Ron's Rock Group, the stoned angels.

EXERCISE 2*

1. Several Psychiatrists in california are developing Computer Programs to treat patients with mild forms of Depression or Neurosis.
2. They envision Computer Therapy Programs within the next fifteen years that will diagnose the Patient's problem (To be confirmed by a Psychiatrist) and select a Treatment Program.
3. The Computer would interact with the Patient and switch to various Subprograms to analyse his mental problems.
4. A tv camera could view the Patient to see if he exhibits signs of Stress, Nervousness, or Lying.
5. Thus, a computer with a sophisticated psychiatric program could appear to understand and empathize with a troubled patient.
6. Most psychiatrists are against such Unorthodox Treatment Methods, but proponents of Computer Therapy argue that it has many advantages.
7. These advantages include low cost and convenience: the Computer would function as a cheap Psychiatrist, available on Weekends and Holidays, Summer or Winter.
8. Other advantages are the long-term total Memory of the Computer and its appearance of honesty and objectivity.
9. Personally, I am surprised that anyone in the Medical Profession takes such a proposal seriously; treatment of complex Human Problems by machine seems perverse to me.
10. Taking my own personal depressions, fears, and phobias to a vdt would be likely to trigger a massive Anxiety Attack.

EXERCISE 3

Correct the capitalization in these sentences.

1. The way to a man's Heart is through his Stomach.
2. Dudley believes the World will end on december 31, 1999 a.d.
3. Dominion day is on july 1, but firecracker day is another name for queen Victoria's birthday in May.
4. The progressive conservative party seems to be a contradiction in terms.
5. May I introduce professor Eli Green?
6. Dr. Green teaches french, spanish, italian, and Modern Literature.

7. In the misfortunes of our Best Friends, we always find something which is not displeasing to us. (la Rochefoucauld)

8. If you want cheap curtains, come to crazy joe's next sunday for their big Sale.

9. This semester your Schedule will include Data Processing, Accounting, Math, philosophy, and english.

10. It's part of our Human Rights to be able to tell the Instructor what's bugging us on a daily basis.

CHAPTER 45

The
Apostrophe

Although it is easy to use correctly, the apostrophe is one of English's most misused punctuation marks. In fact, correct use of apostrophes is one of the best indicators of a careful writer. One large government corporation gives prospective employees a five-part grammar test, and three of the sections test the applicant's ability to use the apostrophe correctly. Clearly, this employer doesn't consider the apostrophe a frill.

In many sentences, an apostrophe is needed to enable your readers to understand what you're trying to say. Here's an example:

The teacher began class by calling the students names.

The teacher began class by calling the students' names.

There's a world of difference between those two sentences!

The apostrophe is used for two distinct purposes: to indicate contraction and to indicate possession.

Contraction

The rule about where to put apostrophes in contractions is one of the rare rules to which there are no exceptions. It *always* holds.

> When two words are shortened into one, and a letter (or letters) is left out, the apostrophe goes in the place of the missing letter(s).

they are → they're	you would → you'd
there is → there's	cannot → can't
we are → we're	is not → isn't
we will → we'll	who is, who has → who's
it is, it has → it's	will not → won't (Note the slight spelling variation here.)

EXERCISE 1*

Make these sets of words into contractions.

1. he will
2. you have
3. I am
4. do not
5. who has

6. would not
7. we are
8. who will
9. you will
10. did not

EXERCISE 2*

Place apostrophes correctly in these words.

1. cant
2. youre
3. theyre
4. shouldnt
5. wholl

6. dont
7. youll
8. were
9. theyve
10. itll

EXERCISE 3*

Correct these sentences by placing apostrophes where needed.

1. Yes, its a long way from Halifax to Vancouver, but weve been in training for three months.

2. Were taking the train to Antigonish and were biking to Halifax; then well begin the big trip west.
3. There isnt a dry eye in the theatre when Spielbergs film reaches its climax.
4. Those two havent made it through a meeting since the college adopted its No Smoking policy.
5. Wasnt it Mark Twain who said, "Its easy to stop smoking; Ive done it dozens of times"?

Possession

The apostrophe also shows ownership or possession. Here's the rule that applies in most circumstances:

> 1. Add *'s* to the word that indicates the *owner*.
> 2. If the resulting word ends in a double or triple *s*, erase the last one, leaving the apostrophe in place.

Examples:

person + 's = person's	clerk + 's = clerk's
people + 's = people's	Pamela + 's = Pamela's
women + 's = women's	Marx + 's = Marx's
sisters + 's = sisters's̸	mother-in-law + 's = mother-in-law's
teacher + 's = teacher's	teachers + 's = teachers's̸
Archimedes + 's = Archimedes's̸	goodness + 's = goodness's̸

When you're forming possessives, you must be careful to determine first whether the *owner* is singular or plural. For example:

the student's names (The names belong to a *student.*)

the students' names (The names belong to two or more *students.*)

If you remember that possession indicates belonging to, you can figure out where to put the apostrophe by "translating" your sentence like this:

Incorrect: The policeman asked Elmo for his drivers licence.
            1. Translation: the licence belongs to a *driver*
            2. Add *'s*:
Correct: The policeman asked Elmo for his driver's licence.
Incorrect: The college finally met the librarians demands.

1. Translation: the demands belong to—the
librarian? or the *librarians*? Here's where you
have to decide whether *one* or *more than one* is
involved.
2. Add *'s*:

Correct: The college finally met the librarian's demands.
(Only one librarian was involved.)

Also correct: The college finally met the librarians' demands.
(More than one librarian was involved.)

Possession does not have to be literal. The owner does not have to be a person or thing. Ideas or concepts can be "owners," too:

day's work = the work of, or belonging to, a day
arm's length = the length of, or belonging to, an arm
two cents' worth = the worth of, or belonging to, two cents

You should know that there are alternatives to the second part of the apostrophe rule for possessives given in the box above. Many writers prefer to keep the final *s* when forming possessives of one-syllable words ending in *s* and of some proper names. In these words, the *'s* represents a pronounced sound, and the *s* after the apostrophe is retained to reflect that sound. Here are some examples:

boss's temper   class's decision
Brutus's betrayal   Yeats's poem

Note that the following words, called **possessive pronouns**, are already possessive in form and do not take the *'s*:

my/mine   its
your/yours   our/ours
her/hers   their/theirs
his   whose

Four possessive pronouns are often confused with contractions that sound like them. The possessives are at the left in the following list, and the contractions are at the right. When you need to decide which word to use, you can separate the contraction into its two root words and try them out in the sentence. If the sentence makes sense, then the contraction is the word you need. If not, use the possessive. Better yet, you can memorize these words:

POSSESSIVES		CONTRACTIONS
their:	they own something	they're = they are
your:	you own something	you're = you are
whose:	"who" owns something	who's = who is, who has
its:	it owns something	it's = it is, it has

Examples: *They're* going to try *their* luck at cards.
You're losing *your* hair.
Who's been sleeping in *whose* bed?
It's obvious the car has a hole in *its* muffler.

EXERCISE 4*

Make the following words possessive.

1. their
2. Chris
3. her
4. gentlemen
5. strawberries
6. mystery
7. one
8. Burgess
9. chairmen
10. ladies

EXERCISE 5*

Make the bracketed words in the sentences possessive.

1. One (week) work under (he) supervision is enough.
2. By the (day) end, our (dogs) coats of fur were matted with burrs.
3. That (church) contributions to the Relief Fund were very generous, thanks to (it) (minister) hard work.
4. The (children) temperaments are not like (he); they're like (their) (mother).
5. (Today) television stars seem unable to resist (producers) temptations to make them into (tomorrows) film idols.

EXERCISE 6*

Correct these sentences by adding apostrophes where necessary.

1. A floppy discs quality is measured by its ability to store information without error.
2. Diplomatic ambassadors wives or husbands are often as important to a missions success as the ambassadors themselves.

3. Near Chicoutimi is one of the countrys most beautiful parks, where the skills of canoeists, fishermen, and wildlife photographers can all be put to the test on a summers day.
4. The Leafs forward and the Oilers defenceman were exchanged during the last days trading at the NHL meetings.
5. Janis career got its start when she sang fishermens songs in the yacht clubs dining lounge.

The following exercises will test and reinforce your understanding of both contraction and possession.

EXERCISE 7*

Choose the correct word from those in brackets. Check your answers before going on.

1. (Its It's) going to run (its it's) laps faster than yours, but I bet my (turtles turtle's) legs are shorter than your (turtles turtle's) legs.
2. (Its It's) strange what creatures people choose to race; (their there they're) going to have the national championship cricket race in Japan next week.
3. Where (your you're) going, (your you're) biggest problem will be maintaining (your you're) health.
4. (Joan's Joans') career goals involve the Humane (Society's Societies) plan to extend this (provinces province's) lost-animal services into their Manitoba and Saskatchewan facilities.
5. (Someones Someone's) got to take responsibility for the large numbers of domestic animals (whose who's) owners have abandoned them.
6. (Their There They're) isn't much chance that the (Jones's Jones' Joneses') animals will find (their there they're) way home, since (its it's) five hundred desolate miles from Moose Factory to Cochrane.
7. (Countries Country's Countries') that maintain (their there they're) neutrality find (their there they're) under pressure from super (power's powers powers') delegations.
8. The Ringling (Brothers Brother's Brothers') circus animals were well cared for compared to the animals of (todays today's todays') circuses.
9. My (fathers father's fathers') (uncles uncle's) hound could scent a (foxes fox's) ten-day-old trail even in dense (woods woods') teeming with other wildlife.

10. Contrary to some (people's peoples) opinions, postal (workers worker's workers') contracts are most often settled by both (sides side's sides') willingness to bend long before a (strikes strike's) necessary.

EXERCISE 8

Correct the following sentences where necessary.

1. Garlics effects should not be forgotten by those who's aim is to impress they're friends with close-up wit.

2. Noticing the customers' suspicious behaviour, David questioned her about her purses' contents.

3. Your playing well already, with only a years' practice.

4. Fort Garys history is revealed in the book's, document's, and historical artifacts' on display at the Art Galleries special show.

5. Admissions to the journalism program are down this term, but its not the director's fault; she toured the citys high schools to find interested students.

6. Your not going to improve your game beyond this point unless you concentrate on making the most of youre ability to intimidate the opposition.

7. Audiences shouldnt have to strain to hear what theyve paid good money for; its really annoying if the halls acoustics are poor.

8. The singers patience gave out when her two solo's were suddenly cut from the concert; shed been practising them for weeks.

9. Jerry Smith built a house that became known to our areas residents

as Smiths Folly, thanks to it's strange design and it's owners even stranger decorations.

10. Apostrophes don't seem very important until youve lost ten percent of your papers mark for leaving them out.

CHAPTER 46

The Hyphen

A **hyphen** (-) is required in three distinct writing situations: as part of the correct spelling of a word (e.g., mother-in-law, good-bye); to divide a word at the end of a line; and to separate or join two or more words or parts of words. There are five rules to follow.

> 1. Use a hyphen to divide a word at the end of a written or typed line.

Your dictionary shows where words can be divided. Most dictionaries mark the syllables of a word with a dot: syl · lables = syl-lables. Never divide a word of only one or two syllables; reserve the hyphen at the end of the line for words of three or more syllables: e.g., commu-nity. If the word is already hyphenated (e.g., self-reliance, ex-president), break it after the hyphen.

> 2. Use a hyphen to separate a prefix from the main word when two of the same vowels come together.

Examples: pre-empted, co-operate, re-elected, re-enter. When the two vowels are different, however, no hyphen is required: semiautomatic, realign, preamble.

> 3. Use a hyphen with compound numbers from twenty-one to ninety-nine, with fractions, and with dimensions.

Examples: forty-six, one-eighth, ninety-eight, six-by-eight.

> 4. Use a hyphen to join two or more words serving as an adjective *before* a noun.

Examples: The first-born child is often the best loved.

Word-of-mouth advertising is very effective.

A good writer has an up-to-date dictionary that is well thumbed.

> 5. Use a hyphen to avoid ambiguity.

Examples: The contractor re-covered the roof with asphalt shingles.

The contractor recovered his money.

The government's plan provided for nursing-home care. (care in a nursing home)

The government's plan provided for nursing home-care. (care at home by nurses)

The Prime Minister will address small business owners. (Do you really want to say he will talk only to short people?)

The Prime Minister will address small-business owners. (These people are owners of small businesses.)

EXERCISE 1*

Each of the following sentences requires one or more hyphens. Review the rules in the boxes above; then try your hand at correcting these sentences.

1. Nell decided to sublet her fifth floor apartment.
2. Anwar claims he is allergic to classical music but addicted to new wave music.
3. Chretien won most of the ethnic vote, which gave him a two thirds majority in a hard fought contest.
4. Hand knitted sweaters are usually more expensive than factory produced ones.
5. In 1950, at the age of forty seven, George Orwell died of tuberculosis.
6. For months after Nicolae Ceaucescu was overthrown, the world was shocked by revelations of the repression suffered by the Ruma nian people.

7. Would you relay this message to Mr. Chan: the masons would like to re lay the bricks this evening?

8. Our next door neighbour teaches in a high school but does not like to be known as a high school teacher.

9. A face to face meeting with an anti intellectual always gets my adrenalin going.

10. Because Angela was an attorney at law and had once been an all Canadian athlete, her forty five year old former coach was not surprised when she became Minister of Recreation.

The Finishing Touches

CHAPTER 47

Clichés, Jargon, and Slang

Clichés

A **cliché** is a group of words that was put together, quite creatively, long ago and that has been used and overused ever since. To write in clichés all the time is to write boringly or, even worse, to have your serious meaning found funny.

Spoken English is full of clichés. In the rush to express an idea, we often take the easy way, using ready-made expressions to put our thoughts into words. There is less excuse to *write* in clichés; writers have more time to think through carefully what it is they want to say. Taking the time to find appropriate words and interesting phrases demonstrates courtesy and concern for your readers.

> He was sick as a dog, but we got him to the hospital in the nick of time.

"Sick as a dog" and "nick of time" are clichés. They would have meaning for your readers, but they're tired, worn-out ways of expressing that meaning. It is difficult, if not impossible, to eliminate clichés from your writing, but you can be aware of them and try to use them infrequently. Don't write automatically. Spend some time thinking about what you want to say; then say it in your own words, not everyone else's.

EXERCISE 1

Rewrite these sentences, expressing the ideas in your own words.

1. As luck would have it, I was rewarded for not throwing in the sponge. Like a bolt from the blue, the announcement came; the announcer did not cut corners: "Ms. Fortune, you are the lucky winner of $2000, cold, hard cash."

2. When you are playing poker, it is good to keep your cool; otherwise, you can lose your shirt. If you hang in there, you can make your day.

3. By and large, the research team left no stone unturned. To cut a long story short, funds were eventually few and far between.

4. The customer is always right, say the managers. It doesn't matter that you are bone-tired, work till the wee small hours, or get falsely accused of giving someone the short end of the stick. To coin a phrase, you end up a sadder but wiser salesperson.

5. She worked like a beaver all day, sorting out her things. At the stroke of midnight, she hit the hay but tossed and turned all night long. Her better half, however, told her she had slept like a log.

6. Sick and tired of the gossip of her guests, Sally decided to catch 40 winks. Early in the game, she had lost the thread of the conversation and decided to give up the ghost.

7. It is clear as crystal that she has a heart as big as all outdoors. Good as gold, gentle as a lamb, and quick as greased lightning would

describe her general disposition. In the foreseeable future, she will in all likelihood take the manager's job—lock, stock, and barrel.

8. He liked the schedule in no way, shape, or form, so he gave advance warning of his intention to walk off the job. This drastic action, needless to say, was interpreted as a knee-jerk response. When all is said and done, the powers that be should see this serious crisis in terms of a moment of truth.

9. It was a dark and stormy night, raining cats and dogs. Jack stopped dead in his tracks, went pale as a ghost, and fainted dead away. When he came to, to his surprise, not only had his pockets been picked to the bone, but also his clothes had been ripped to shreds.

10. Ken was feeling like a million bucks. Little did he know that at that very moment, just around the corner, a group of desperate thieves was conspiring to take the wind out of his sails by leaving him high and dry without two cents to rub together.

Broadcasting is one of the chief refuges of the cliché. It's a rare newscast that doesn't include the expression "informed sources" or "claimed the life" or "skyrocketing inflation." Listening carefully for such overworked phrases on the radio and TV will make you more aware of them in your own writing and perhaps less likely to use them.

Jargon

Jargon, a special breed of cliché, is made up of technical words or phrases used in science, the trades, or the professions. Sometimes "shop talk" or "trade language" enters the everyday language we use outside our jobs. The sports world, for example, has a highly developed jargon: "the whole nine yards," "at the post," "on deck." Many of these expressions have found their way into everyday colloquial usage. The jargon of some professions is so highly technical and specialized it amounts almost to a private language: those in the profession are familiar with it and use it to communicate; those not in the profession are "outsiders" to whom the technical language is incomprehensible. Although jargon is useful, even necessary, in the context of the job, it is inappropriate in most writing—*it does not communicate.* Unless your reader shares your private language, your message will be lost.

As a writer, you need to be sensitive to the fact that your vocabulary—even the content of your language—is shaped and influenced by your experiences and the contexts within which you live and work.

Consider this example from *The Book of Jargon* by D. E. Miller:

> A group of people witness a car accident. What each person sees, and how he or she describes it, is determined to a large extent by the language each one normally uses. A doctor or nurse would see and describe contusions, lacerations, fractures, and hemorrhages. A lawyer would think in terms of civil liabilities and criminal negligence. A mechanic would see crushed fenders, bent axles, and damaged chassis. A psychologist would be concerned about stress reactions, trauma, and guilt. You or I might see and describe the pain and injury caused by a driver's error in judgment or lapse of skill.

The existence of jargon, then, is not the problem; the abuse of jargon is the problem. It limits your audience to those who have the same vocabulary you do. To the rest of the world, your writing will be difficult to understand or even meaningless. You can't expect to communicate with a general reader in sentences like this: "The professor replied with a logical uppercut that caught George right between the eyes and laid him out for the count." (Note that this sentence is an example of cliché as well as jargon.) This may be a colourful way to describe the winning of an argument, but it will be clearly understood only by readers who are boxing fans.

Be especially careful to avoid jargon that imitates a specialized vocabulary. Writers who are a little unsure of their subject matter or their audience sometimes try to impress their readers with jargon. Writing that has chains of abstract words and long, complicated sentences is sound without meaning, as the following sentence illustrates:

> Thus the meaningful verbalization of conceptual improvisation at the interpersonal interface is contraindicated by frustrations arising from idiosyncratic linguistic actualization, in terms of vocabulary, so that the verbalized formulations of the initiating consciousness actuate latent rejection mechanisms.

Who knows what this means? More important, who cares? Very few readers, dictionary in hand, would have the patience to go through this passage, trying vainly to translate such tortuous prose into plain English. The cure for this kind of jargon is consideration for your readers. If you really want to get your message across, write plainly and clearly in language your readers can be expected to understand.

EXERCISE 2

Write as many examples of jargon as you can identify for each of the following occupations.

1. auto technician: gapper, caliper, oscilloscope . . .

2. computer technologist: AT bus, real time, platforms . . .

3. salesperson: territory, distribution strategy, close . . .

4. sociologist: physical data categories, social stratification system . . .

5. your own career field:

Slang

Slang is nonstandard vocabulary that signifies an informal and close relationship among those who speak it to each other. There are innumerable examples of slang, from *A-OK* to *zowie*. Slang changes rapidly, and even dictionaries don't attempt to keep all the terms straight. Like jargon, slang serves to identify and reinforce membership in particular subgroups in society—students, the military, the police, criminals, or members of a trade or profession, for example. Unlike jargon, slang is highly colourful, nontechnical language, but it is often short-lived. On the street, you may be called "thick" ("stupid"), and outside of class, you may be known as a "grind" (hard-working student); for those in the military, "R and R" means "rest and relaxation," but to a mechanic it means "removed and replaced (or repaired)." Computer operators love slang: when a piece of computer equipment (especially software) ceases to function properly, it is said to "bomb" or "barf." A "bug" is a hitch, a fault, a problem. A "glitch" is the source of a malfunction: it is usually unexpected and can be anything from a loose wire to a power failure. "Wetware" is the human brain.

Slang can limit or even block your communication with your readers. It is the most quickly dated type of language: what is "in" today may well be laughed at in a few months. ("Right on, man. What a groovy scene. Far out!") The good news is that yesterday's slang may be today's **colloquialism** (highly informal, casual language) and tomorrow's standard English. It may surprise you to learn that the following words were once slang: fireworks, dwindle, clumsy, boardwalk, movies, blurb, stunt, fan, absurd, nice, awful, sneak, fake.

Because slang dates so quickly, and because it is understood by a limited group of people, you should avoid it in your writing. Unless you are quoting someone who has used slang, write Standard English. If you're in doubt as to the status of a word, check your dictionary. The notation *sl.* or *slang* appears after slang words or after a slang meaning of a word. (Some words, such as *neat* and *chick* and *hammered*, have both a general meaning and a slang meaning.) Taking the time to choose words and expressions appropriate to written English increases your chance of successful communication and demonstrates your concern for and courtesy to your readers.

CHAPTER 48

Wordiness

Wordiness is a problem that may develop if you try too hard to impress a reader with your use of words. Keep in mind that no reader wants to read "fill" or "padding." All writing should be as concise as it can be and still convey the message clearly. Even authors like Dickens and Michener, who have written huge quantities, chose their language carefully, trying not to waste their readers' time with unnecessary words.

Here's an example of what can happen when, in trying to impress, you lose sight of the need to communicate. Do you recognize any of your writing in this?

> In my own opinion, I feel very strongly indeed that the government of this Dominion of Canada is basically in need of an additional amount of meaningful input from its electors, the people of this country, at this point in time, frankly speaking. For too long a period of time, the leaders of this nation in Ottawa have, rightly or wrongly, gone heedlessly off on their own particular course of action without the benefit of consultation or dialogue with the people, who, it stands to reason, are most willing and able to provide, clearly and without doubt, a distinct and clear path to follow into the future world of tomorrow.

By eliminating wordiness, you could make this into a clear statement.

The following are some of the worst offenders we have collected from student writing. In some cases, many words are used when one or two would do; in others, the wording is **redundant** (says the same thing twice).

WORDY	ACCEPTABLE
"absolutely complete"	complete
"absolutely nothing"	nothing
"actual fact"	fact
"at that point in time"	then
"basic fundamentals"	fundamentals
"circled around"	circled
"collect together"	collect
"completely free"	free
"continue on"	continue
"could possibly" (also "may possibly" and "might possibly")	could (or may or might)
"dead bodies"	corpses
"disappear from view"	disappear
"entirely eliminated"	eliminated
"equally as good"	as good
"essential prerequisite"	prerequisite
"exactly identical"	identical
"few and far between"	rare
"final conclusion"	conclusion
"green in colour"	green
"having the same thing in common"	having in common
"I personally feel"	I feel
"in my opinion, I think"	in my opinion
"in this day and age"	now
"new innovation"	innovation
"personal friend"	friend
"proceed ahead"	proceed
"real, genuine leather"	genuine leather
"repeat again"	repeat
"repeat the same"	repeat
"seven A.M. in the morning"	seven A.M.
"small in size"	small
"such as, for example"	such as
"surround on all sides"	surround
"taking active steps"	taking steps
"true fact"	fact
"very (most, quite, rather) unique"	unique

> To avoid wordiness, eliminate clichés, repetition, redundancy, and unnecessary jargon.

EXERCISE 1*

Revise these sentences, making them more concise and understandable.

1. Even at that point in time, dead bodies were treated with respect, just as they are by civilized nations in this day and age.

2. My final conclusion concerning the real, genuine value of Bargain Barry's reduced price sale goods is exactly identical with yours.

3. Small in size as he was, and surrounded on all sides by strange children he didn't know, the quite uniquely courageous seven-year-old challenged the class bully to a fight.

4. The sergeant repeated again to the brand-new recruits, "You will be called at 5:30 A.M. in the morning, and you will have circled around the barracks on the double by 5:45. You will at that point in time be completely free until 6:00, when you will continue on to the barracks mess for breakfast."

5. The new recruits disappeared from view after the 7:00 A.M. breakfast, to discuss what they could do to get even with a sergeant who woke them up one full hour before the necessary time.

6. They personally thought that the sergeant would probably repeat the same obnoxious behaviour again each day, so they decided to proceed ahead with a new, innovative plan as an appropriate response.

7. The basic fundamentals of their plan included getting the sergeant very drunk one evening and putting him to bed at about 4:30 A.M.—

not in his own bunkhouse next to theirs, but in one that was next to the officers' quarters.

8. In my opinion, I must admit that I thought their plan was absolutely and completely foolproof, and that it was a great idea.

9. They had entirely eliminated the possibility that the sergeant would know where he was in the morning by bribing their friends in that bunkhouse to leave it empty and by arranging it like the sergeant's own personal barracks.

10. It is a real fact that, at 5:30 A.M., the sergeant, true to his own promise that nothing would prevent his wake-up call, staggered into the bunkhouse next to his and blasted with bugle and voice until he woke all the inhabitants. He never did a 5:30 A.M. morning reveille again.

CHAPTER 49

Abusages

Some words and terms that appear in writing are simply incorrect or used incorrectly. We've named these misspelled, misused, or made-up words **abusages**. The presence of abusages in writing makes the writer appear ignorant in the eyes of anyone who knows anything about the English language. The list of abusages that follows is a partial one but does include some of the worst offenders. You should add to it the abusages that your instructor hates most.

"alot"	There is no such word. Use *many* or *much*.
"anyways"	Also, "anywheres" and "a long ways." There is no *s* on these words.
"could of"	Also, "would of," "should of," and so on. The helping verb is *have:* "could have."
"didn't do nothing"	This, along with all other double negatives ("couldn't get nowhere," "wouldn't talk to nobody," and so on), is wrong. Write "didn't do anything" or "did nothing."
"irregardless"	There is no such word. Use *regardless.*
"irrevelant"	This is a misspelling. Spell the word *irrelevant.*
"media" used as singular word	The word *media* is plural. The singular is *medium.* Write "TV is a mass medium. Print and radio are also examples of mass media."
"off of"	Use *off* alone: "I fell off the wagon."
"prejudice" used as an adjective	It is wrong to write "She is prejudice against men." Use *prejudiced.*

"prejudism"	There is no such word. Use *prejudice:* "He should show no prejudice to either side."
"real" used as an adverb	"Real sad," "real swell," and "real nice" are wrong. Use *really* or *very.*
"reason is because"	Use "the reason is that": "The reason is that I don't use a deodorant."
"suppose to"	Also, "use to." Use "supposed to" and "used to."
"themself"	Also, "theirself," "ourselfs," "yourselfs," and "themselfs." The plural of *self* is *selves: themselves, ourselves,* and so on. Don't use "theirselves," though; there's no such word.
"youse"	There is no such word. "You" is used for both singular and plural. When waiting on tables, don't say "May I help youse?" to a group of English instructors, if you want a tip.

EXERCISE 1*

Correct the following sentences where necessary.

1. Nell should of gone with us to the beach; now she can't go nowheres.

2. Alot of us thought he might be prejudice, but actually he turned out to be a real nice man.

3. I'm suppose to see whether the reason for the delay is because it's raining.

4. They are suppose to get the ball themselfs, irregardless of where it is when they come off of the field.

5. Because I won't lend her my homework, she thinks I'm showing prejudism, but she is suppose to do her own homework anyways.

6. If youse don't do nothing about boarding the windows, you'll have pieces of glass everywheres in the house.

7. It's real sad to see signs of prejudism in young children, who must of been influenced by their parents.

8. It is irrevelant whether she fell off of or was pushed off of her bicycle; she is disqualified anyways.

9. They should of finished the race even though they were behind, since every entrant is suppose to finish unless disqualified or injured.

10. I didn't talk to nobody about seeing him cheat, since the judges don't consider a spectator's remarks to be revelant.

Polishing Your Pronouns

A whole category of abusages is created by misuse of pronouns.

> Him and I had a fight.
> Bob and her are the best spellers.
> It came down to a choice between she and me.

There are two groups of pronouns: those used for subjects and those used for objects. In Chapter 26, you reviewed how to find the subject of a sentence. When that subject is, or is referred to by, a pronoun, the pronoun should be one of these:

Subjective Pronouns

I	we
you	you
he, she	they

Whenever the pronoun is *not* the subject of the sentence, you should use one of these:

Objective Pronouns

me	us
you	you
him, her	them

He and *I* had a fight. (The pronouns are the subject of the sentence.)

Bob and *she* are the best spellers. (The pronoun is part of the multiple subject "Bob and she.")

It came down to a choice between *her* and *me*. (The pronouns are not the subject of the sentence.)

The girls in the blue uniforms are *they*. (The pronoun stands for the subject of the sentence, *girls*.)

He is more honest than *she*. (The verb *is* is understood at the end of the sentence, and *she* is the subject of that verb.)

EXERCISE 2*

Correct the pronouns in these sentences as necessary.

1. No one except you and I would go camping in this rain.

2. Him and I can't push this car any farther than you and her could.

3. Her and me did a really stupid thing.

4. He is a better cook than her, and she plays baseball better than him.

5. You and I can use the Caravan passports all week, and you and her can use them on the weekend when I'm not here.

6. As we walked along Bloor Street, we saw Marie and he going into Toby's restaurant.

7. The police stopped he and I at the door of our apartment building.

8. Everyone had to wait outside except them.

9. Us and them are not very good friends anymore.

10. No one is happier than me that youse got the job.

So far, you have identified and eliminated from your writing the main difficulties writers have with pronouns. In Chapter 33, you learned how to use relative pronouns; how to make pronouns agree with words ending in *-one*, *-thing*, and *-body*; how to rid your writing of sexism; and how to avoid vague and ambiguous pronoun references. In Chapter 35, you learned how to use pronouns (signalling "persons") consistently, not shifting from one pronoun to another unless meaning requires it. In Chapter 45, you learned that personal pronouns do not require an apostrophe in their possessive forms. With the help of this chapter, you have eliminated the worst of the abusages created by the misuse of pronouns.

To put the finishing touches on your mastery of pronouns, learn and remember three rules:

> 1. When the relative pronouns *who, which,* and *that* are the subjects of clauses, their antecedents determine the person and number of their verbs.

Examples: It is I who am trying to get through. (*I* is the antecedent of *who* and determines the person (first) and number (singular) of the verb, *am.*)

The dog that obeys is the dog for me! (*dog* is the antecedent of *that* and determines the person (third) and the number (singular) of the verb, *obeys.*)

Newfoundland, which has Canada's worst unemployment rate, entered Confederation in 1949. (*Newfoundland* is the antecedent of *which* and determines the person (third) and the number (singular) of the verb, *has.*)

> 2. After a preposition, a pronoun is always in its objective form.

Examples: Mario went shopping with Rita and me. (*me* is the object of the preposition *with.*)

One of us knew what was in the will. (*us* is the object of the preposition *of.*)

The police car chased after us. (*us* is the object of the preposition *after.*)

Our English teacher loves to ask questions of Rudolf and me. (*me* is the object of the preposition *of.*)

Hint: When you have two pronouns or a pronoun and a noun following a preposition, mentally cross out one of the pronouns or the noun. If you have only one pronoun to deal with, you are unlikely to make an error.

Examples: He and I (not *him* and *me*) have tickets for Blue Rodeo.
It will be up to him (not *he*) to raise the funds.

---

3. When using pronouns after *than/as well as/as*, if it is your intention to contrast the pronoun after *than* with the subject, use the subjective form of the pronoun; if it is your intention to contrast the pronoun after *than* with an object, use the objective form of the pronoun.

Examples: My brother is taller than I. (*I* is contrasted with *brother.*)
My sister is as tall as I. (*I* is contrasted with *sister.*)
Mairi likes Amin better than I. (*I* is contrasted with *Mairi.*)
Mairi likes Amin better than me. (*me* is contrasted with *Amin.*)
Gerald treats his dog better than I. (*I* is contrasted with *Gerald.*)
Gerald treats his dog better than me. (*me* is contrasted with *dog.*)

EXERCISE 3*

Try your hand at correcting the errors in pronoun usage in these sentences.

1. Leila was late because it was her who drove the boys home.

2. She is one of the accountants that made the error in my income tax.

3. She that laughs last, laughs best.

4. The hedge at the back of the garden is slightly shorter than me.

5. Geoff wasn't as hungry as me, so he gave his lunch to Brian and I to share.

6. Her and me wanted to see the circus, especially the horse who sings.

7. Us four girls have been friends since before youse were born.

8. I think it was her that had the nightmare.

9. The woman that won the lottery bought more tickets than you or me.

10. When asked to give the motto of the Dominion of Canada, either Jonah or him responded, "It's mainly because of the meat."

On-Screen Writing

The word processor is becoming common equipment in writing labs and is increasingly available to students both at school and at home. Different writers are comfortable with different tools; for some, the pen is really the most effective implement. If you write best with pen in hand, continue to use pen and paper for your writing until you have completed a first draft. At that point, however, you will find it worthwhile to transfer your thoughts to a screen for revising, editing, proofreading, and printing.

If you can use a word processor during all the steps in the writing process, the machine can improve your writing in many significant ways. However, a word processor demands two skills of you that the pen does not: reasonable keyboarding skill and a ready knowledge of the functions of the word processing program. Without these two skills, word processing can be a time-consuming and frustrating experience.

Some people like to use the word processor for freewriting or brainstorming. They key in words as fast as they can type, with no concern for spelling, organization, style, or structure. In this way, all the ideas they can think of are stored in the processor for recall on the screen. As they write draft after draft, revising and shaping, they can roll back to their original list to be sure no points have been omitted. Revisions are easy to enter, paragraphs can be relocated, and the latest draft is available for another reading.

By taking advantage of these capacities of a word processor, you can save time and effort and have an attractive final product. We suggest the following approach to creating essays on the word processor.

Organizing

1. Enter the subject of your paper in capital letters at the top of the page. If you've been assigned a specific subject, this is easy. If you are making up your own subject, or working with vague subject guidelines, enter a **working title**, one that serves to identify your paper but will probably be replaced later. Do you think you have enough to say on the subject? Should you do some research first, and begin work when you have notes in front of you? The guidelines in Chapter 2 for choosing a subject will lead you through this critical process.

2. Begin writing your main points, using a new line for each main point. Don't worry about writing complete sentences, or developing your ideas, or even spelling your words correctly. Get down as many points about your subject as you can think of.

3. Sit back and examine your main points very critically. Delete those that overlap with other points, those that don't relate directly to the subject, and those that are so weak you have nothing to say about them. Split up any entries that cover two or three points. Reduce your list to three or four solid main points. The more time and effort you spend here, the less you will need for the actual writing, and the better your finished paper will be.

4. Under each main point, write as much as you wish on how you will develop or expand that point. Don't worry about keeping the points in order, or about composing complete sentences, correcting your spelling, or following a particular organization. Get down all your ideas on the main points you've identified.

5. When you have written everything you can in rough form about each main point, use the block-move function on your word processor to arrange your points in the order you feel is most appropriate. See Chapter 3 for information on effective ordering of main points.

Save your file.

Writing

1. Print out the work you have produced so far.

2. Keep the printout close by, for reference, and write a paragraph for each of the main points. Remember to include a topic sentence, appropriate development of ideas, and a concluding sentence.

Save your file.

3. Read over your paragraphs. Is each one well developed? Is the order of the paragraphs appropriate? Taken together, do they deal adequately with your subject? This is the time to weave in more information, add or change main points, or rearrange the order of your statements.

4. Write your introduction and conclusion. Test each for effectiveness by reviewing the tips in Chapter 10. Writing your introduction and conclusion after you write the body of your essay is easier than doing the paragraphs in sequence. At that point, you know what you've said and how you've said it; you can introduce and conclude your subject better and in less time.

Save your file.

Revising

1. Some writers like to print out their work at this point, do their revising on paper, and then make changes on the screen. If you get a printout, you'll be able to see your whole essay (not just a screen at a time) and your reading will be easier. Alternatively, you can revise on-screen.

2. Read your essay slowly and critically. Use the Editing Checklist on the inside back cover as a guide.

3. Enlist your word processor's functions to help you eliminate errors. Use the "spellchecker" if your program has one (consider getting one if it doesn't), but remember that it is not foolproof; it can tell you that you have spelled *it's* or *accept* or *effect* correctly, but it doesn't know whether you have used them properly. The "find" function is useful to correct a repeated error. Tell the program to find each appearance of *it's*, for example, and read carefully to make sure you have used it correctly. Some programs have a "grammar checker," but these are, so far, very limited in what they can do.

4. Replace or rewrite any awkward words, phrases, or sentences. If something doesn't sound quite right to you, don't be satisfied until it does. Polish and revise until every sentence is as clear and well-expressed as you can possibly make it. The "thesaurus" function can be helpful, but don't use its most complex expressions in the hope of impressing your readers.

Printing

1. If you have not already done so, set your program to print "double space." This is a courtesy to your readers and will help you spot errors much more easily. (It's also required by most English teachers.)

2. Set your printer to the setting that will produce the darkest, clearest type. Don't make your readers strain their eyes to read faint print. Avoid the hard-to-read "draft" setting.

3. Print out your essay.

4. Reread it one more time to make sure you haven't missed an error. If you can, put the essay aside for a few days and then reread it again with a clear mind and a fresh point of view. One of the word processor's chief advantages is that if you should spot an error that must be corrected or an improvement that should be made, it's simple and painless to do so and then print out a new copy. Whiteout and messy pen insertions are considered relics of the past. Every paper you hand in can be clean, neat, and error-free.

From Essay to Speech

If you've worked your way with us from "What This Book Can Do for You" all the way through to the last page of "Abusages," you've finished the job you came to the book to do, right? Not quite. We've concentrated on essay writing in the pages you've completed, but two important topics that are related to essay writing have been saved for the appendices. We've told you in the previous appendix how to make maximum use of a computer or word processor for your writing; in this appendix we discuss preparing, writing, and delivering speeches.

If you're a typical college student, you may react by saying that you have no plans to become a political candidate or a presentations professional or a talk show host. All well and good; Phil, Joan, and Oprah will give audible sighs of relief. But you're also not headed for a hermit's life on a Hudson Bay island where the world and its people can't intrude. You're a member of a family, a community, a town or city or rural neighborhood; you'll be a trainer of some new workers on the job, or a liaison member of a rank-and-file–management task force, or a local environmental watchdog committee member, or a Little League coach, or a fund-raising activist, or a professional whose clear and persuasive language can lead others towards a better life. You *will* be a speaker, though no billboard announcements may ever display your name and the topic of your address. You *will* have the frightening, wonderful view of all faces turned to you, waiting expectantly to hear what you have to say. That will not be the moment to ask yourself, "*Now* what do I do?"

In the chapter on punctuation, we said that punctuation is a substitute for your body language; it conveys your tone, your exact meaning, and the purpose of your message. As a speaker, you deliver all the power of your words, sentences, and development of ideas that you have learned in essay writing, but you have the extra advantage of seeing, recognizing, and being able to respond to the reactions of your audience. Writing sends the ball into your readers' court; they're out there somewhere. Speaking zaps it right back to your court; your audience is right in front of you.

Our purposes here are to remind you of how prepared you are as a speaker if you're a good essay writer, and to guide you in fulfilling the unique demands of communication required in facing a live audience.

Speech writing attaches less importance to some aspects of essay writing; spelling, for instance, is less critical than pronunciation. But organizational principles are even more important than in essay writing. Unlike your readers, your listeners cannot return to a confusing section of your work or glance ahead to see how many more points you plan to make. You must make your audience aware of your organizational structure and use clear language that addresses them on their level.

When you practise the techniques of speech writing, you must concentrate on several aspects of writing which, in the struggle to achieve good style and correct grammar, sometimes receive too little emphasis in essays: analysis of your audience; careful attention to building and communicating your organization of ideas; drafting and revising; and using illustrations where appropriate to enhance your presentation.

Audience Analysis

When you planned your written essay assignments, you thought carefully about who your readers would be. This step is *absolutely vital* when you are composing a speech. You must give serious thought to your audience. Your analysis of the people who will be listening, even during a classroom presentation, will help you to determine the subject of your speech, your style of presentation, the depth and complexity of your content, your level of language, and your persuasive approach. No matter how little you think you know about your audience, you can make some judgements and guesses that will be valuable when you begin to write the speech.

What Chief Interest Will Be Bringing Them Together?

When you answer this question, you can begin to think of ways to appeal to your listeners. Are they all members of a club? If so, why have they joined; what does the club do; what can be assumed about them because they have joined this club and not another? If they are students in a public speaking class, then they go to the same school, share the same level of education, know many of the same people, and have many concerns in common. Brainstorm for all the descriptive qualities they might have. Use your audience profile to guide you in the direction of certain subjects, approaches, illustrations, and examples, and away from others. For example, if the group is a religious club, choose appropriate anecdotes and references. If your audience is a sales and marketing class, you can assume that examples from advertising and the business world will hit home.

What Physical, Social, Academic, or Geographic Characteristics Do They Share?

Can you determine, find out, or guess the average age, income, marital status, and education level of your listeners? Do they have children? Do they live in a definable geographic region? A subculture? If you are speaking to members of Elderhostel, an international association of retired people who wish to further their education, your approach and subject selection will not be the same as for a local Junior Achievement group. An audience of parents might be fascinated by a new preschool approach that improves academic performance by 50 percent, but most teenagers would be bored senseless.

What Do They Expect to Take Away with Them?

In simple terms, your audience will want to feel they made the right decision in coming to hear you because you gave them valuable information, you were interested in their needs, and you confirmed that their time was well spent.

Reflect for a moment on the questions you dealt with when you began your essay-writing exercises:

- What does your audience know about your subject?
- What are your audience's attitudes towards your subject?
- What are your audience's needs with respect to your subject?

Answers to these questions will help you begin the process of writing an effective speech, but you should be asking yourself many other questions about your audience. The more you know about them, the better prepared you will be. Good preparation is the key to good content and to controlling nervousness.

EXERCISE 1

A public address on each of the subjects listed below is to be delivered by someone who is an expert on that subject. Match each subject to its most appropriate audience by entering, on the fill-in lines, an identifying letter from the list of groups and organizations given. (Some subjects may be appropriate for more than one group.) Explain and justify your choices.

1. The Japanese art of flower arrangement _____

2. China's economy: opening doors to the West _____

3. Secrets of successful marriage _____

4. Make them want you: foolproof job interview techniques _____

5. Carving decoys for fun and profit _____

6. The Colt Peacemaker: the handgun that won the West _____

7. Making a career from your interest in sports _____

8. Where to get stuff cheap: a guide to intelligent shopping _____

9. The Targa story: everything there is to know about the Porsche 911 Targa _____

10. Florida's unspoiled vacation spots _____

    a. the college girls' basketball team
    b. a social group of retired doctors
    c. the local hunters' and anglers' club
    d. your English class
    e. the college marketing club
    f. the college Horticulture Department alumni association
    g. a boy scout troup
    h. The Entrepreneurs, a club of wealthy industrialists and influential business people
    i. the local Historical Society
    j. a social gathering of high-school teachers

EXERCISE 2

Imagine that you are *required* to give five speeches over the next three months to any five of the groups listed in Exercise 1. Select five subjects about which you are knowledgeable enough now, or in which you are interested sufficiently to acquire the knowledge, for your five addresses. Match your subjects with the appropriate audiences.

Content Structure

Everything you wrote down in black and white about the organizational structure of essays reappears in living color when you begin to prepare a speech. To get your audience's attention, you need a strong, interesting introduction that puts forth a compelling grabber and a clear, well-defined preview statement. To keep their attention, you need a well-organized body with clear divisions and smooth transitions. To send them away satisfied, you need an engaging conclusion that summarizes the points covered and/or calls for action. And, if you want any applause, you should end with a memorable clincher. Speech writing does have a few unique requirements, however.

First, your introduction for a speech tends to be longer than for an essay. A speech usually begins with a "preamble" or "warm-up" before the preview statement. Your warm-up can be—but doesn't need to be—amusing. A warm-up that is funny enough to draw laughter can be a great confidence builder; one that falls flat can have the opposite effect. Introduce yourself, perhaps with a personal anecdote, which always interests an audience. Good classroom teachers use this device—in moderation—when they feel their students' attention is beginning to wander.

Your preview statement is critical in speech writing; it reveals the scope of your speech. The main points you will cover and the order in which they will appear must be particularly clear so that your listeners can remember them and see how you are progressing towards your conclusion.

Second, the body of your speech will probably be longer than your average in-class essay assignment. You may have more points or more support for each point. In choosing a subject, make sure that you have (or can get) enough to say about it to speak for the length of time expected. As a guideline, broadcasters estimate that normal delivery time for half a page of double-spaced typing is 30 to 40 seconds. Your delivery during rehearsal will usually be about 20 percent slower than your delivery in front of your audience.

Third, transitions between points in your speech are very important, and should be made clear to your audience. They should always be able to follow along point by point and aware of where you are in the outline you gave them in your preview statement. The most effective technique to accomplish these goals is to use numeric transitions: first, second, third, finally. With clearly stated main points in your introduction, a well-structured body, and easy-to-follow transitions, your audience will be able to follow and remember your content.

Finally, your conclusion should be clear, firm, and dramatic—one that brings your audience's spontaneous applause. Don't finish with a lame "Thank you" to indicate you're through. If you can't think of a strong enough closing line, borrow from the great writers and speakers of the past and finish with a quotation: "Cystic fibrosis *can* be beaten, ladies and gentlemen; all it will take is money . . . and that's where you can help. In the words of Winston Churchill, 'Give us the tools and we'll finish the job!'"

Speaking Technique

Using the techniques of drafting and revision that you have learned in this book, write your speech as you would an essay (while keeping in mind the differences we've mentioned here). Once you have written your speech, read it through at a speed appropriate for delivery and make sure it's the length you want. Read it aloud and emphasize key words as you read; underline these words on your next read-through. Until you give the speech, continue to make yourself familiar with what you are going to say—familiar enough that the notes you take to the front of the room with you will be only point-form reminders to keep you on track. As you read the speech over and over, begin reducing it to a skeleton outline that represents every sentence. Then reduce it to a note for each paragraph, just enough to ensure you will cover all your main points. When your speech notes have been reduced to a single page of two- and three-word points, you're ready.

Important "Don'ts"

Don't take the full text of your speech with you to the front of the room. At your first hesitation or near loss of place, your head will bob down to the paper in front of you, and then, as if held there by some gigantic, invisible hand, you will stay bent, eyes down, and you will read your speech. An extremely competent reader can manage to do this and still maintain eye contact with an audience, continuing to hold their interest. However, for most of us, this is not possible. Short of keeling over in the middle of the speech, reading is the worst thing you can do.

Don't memorize your speech word for word. Become familiar with your content, remember key words and phrases, but don't sit down and memorize the thing from beginning to end. Amateur speakers who try to do this end up either rolling their eyes to the ceiling and spouting the words in a monotone as quickly as they can speak, or going blank at about the third paragraph and then repeating the last line they can remember, hoping to restart the memory engine.

Here is an example of the notes a speaker might use to deliver a speech based on the essay "We Have Met the Enemy and They Is . . . Us" (pp. 136–37).

I.   Our planet is being destroyed!
    A. external threat: aliens, rogue comet
    B. but, while threat is just as real, we aren't doing much
    C. evil doers close to home . . . in mirrors
    D. greed, ignorance
II. Greed: industrial, commercial, personal
    A. 2/3 of rain forest cut or burned
    B. one hectare every 14 seconds
    C. Canada—chemicals and sewage in rivers
        —industrial pollutants, toxic waste
        —lucky because rich in natural resources
III. Ignorance:
    A. "freedom machines" . . . twice as many as 20 years ago
    B. 275 thousand tonnes of diapers
    C. fast-food containers, bleached paper, recycling, plastics
IV. Optimism?
    A. more consciousness
    B. 1989: 1/3 said environment most important, up from 1/10 in 1988 and 1/20 in 1987
    C. majority want tougher action
V.   But this is far from concerted, all-out effort if threat were external . . . difficult to mobilize when *enemy lies within.*

EXERCISE 3

Write outline notes, like the ones you have just read, for the essay "Let's Get Physical" on pp. 156–57.

Visual Aids

In most speaking situations, you should try to use **visual aids**— overhead projections, chalkboard, large illustrations, or even 35mm slides that can illustrate your talk or list your main points. The use of such devices accomplishes two important goals: your audience's attention, comprehension, and enjoyment are increased; and your nervousness is reduced by diverting their attention away from you and directing it toward your visual aids.

For the effective use of visual aids, be prepared. Before the audience arrives, check the bulb in the overhead or slide projector, focus and aim it, and lower the screen. Check your slides to make sure they will appear right-side-up, and arrange for someone to turn off the lights at your signal. Be sure your overhead projections are arranged in front of you in the proper order.

Equally important, be sure your illustrations are visible. Holding up a small newspaper photo to an audience of 30 people will frustrate and annoy them. Use slides that are well-produced and clear; mount pictures on cardboard and arrange to have an easel or display stand. Make sure that any illustrations you wish to show are clearly visible to all . . . or don't use them.

EXERCISE 4

For each of the main points you included in your outline votes in Exercise 3, write a list of the visual aids you could use to make the address more effective and enjoyable for your audience.

Reducing Nervousness

For some people, giving a speech looms as a fright night. If you are afraid of speaking in public, you are not alone; a 1985 study to find out what North Americans fear most in life showed that people fear speaking in front of an audience more than death, injury, serious illness, or bankruptcy. However, situations in your career will inevitably make it necessary for you to give presentations. Many people find that once they get over their fear and actually give a speech, they enjoy the experience. Even professionals admit to some nervousness before every speech; some find that nervousness gets them "up" for an energetic performance. Only experience can make you a confident and relaxed speaker, but you can employ a few techniques to reduce and control your nervousness.

1. Preparation is the key to confident speaking. If you have spent sufficient time in writing, revising, and rehearsing your speech, you will have nothing to fear when the time comes to deliver it. On the other hand, if you are poorly prepared and not sure that you can remember what you have to say, then you have every reason to be terrified and you deserve the embarrassment of a poor performance.

2. Topic selection is an important element in confident speaking. Good speakers become **message oriented**; that is, they are eager to convey the information they have because they are interested in it and wish others to hear about it. Always choose a topic that you find

significant and interesting. If you aren't interested in your topic, how do you expect to make others interested in it? Most successful speakers talk about things they have experienced for themselves: travel, business success, hobbies, charitable causes, expertise in a particular field.

3. Proper breathing techniques aid enormously in controlling nervousness. When you are rehearsing your speech, practice breath control. Take deep, even breaths that allow you to pause where appropriate, without gulping for air in the middle of every sentence. Before you go to the podium, a few deep breaths and some conscious relaxation will help you get started. Proper breathing, meditation, and muscle control are dealt with in public speaking classes or stress management courses.

4. Use visual aids. Something as simple as a chalkboard on which you have printed the main points of your speech will both deflect attention away from you and provide you with a prop that you can refer to on occasion, instead of constantly facing the audience.

5. Remember that the people in your audience are on your side. They want you to succeed and are prepared to be interested in what you have to say; they don't know why you should be afraid of them. *Never* tell your audience that you are nervous. Chances are that you don't appear half as uncomfortable as you are, and to tell your listeners that you are nervous only makes them embarrassed and uneasy on your behalf; automatically, they will begin looking for signs of your fear instead of concentrating on your message.

Remember that a close relationship exists between effective writing and effective speaking. If you can write a well-organized, clear, and coherent essay, you can write an effective speech. Delivering a speech effectively requires mastery of the principles we've outlined here—and lots of practice.

List of Grammatical Terms

adjectives	words that modify (describe, restrict, relate to, make more precise) nouns and pronouns. They answer the questions *What kind? How many? Which?*—e.g., the *competent* student; *five* home runs; my *last* class.
adverbs	words that modify verbs, adjectives, and other adverbs. They answer the questions *When? How? Where? Why? How much?*—e.g., Elmo talks *fast* (*fast* modifies the verb *talks*); he is a *very* fast talker (*very* modifies the adjective *fast*); he talks *really* fast (*really* modifies the adverb *fast*). Adverbs often—but not always—end in *-ly*.
antecedent	the word that a pronoun refers to or stands for. Literally, it means "going before, preceding." The antecedent usually comes before the pronoun that refers to it. E.g., *Karen* believes *she* is possessed. (*Karen* is the antecedent to which the pronoun *she* refers.)
clause	a group of words that contains a subject and a verb. If the group of words can stand by itself and makes complete sense, it is called an **independent clause**

(or **principal clause** or **main clause**). If the group of words does not make complete sense on its own but is linked to another clause (depends on it for its meaning), it is called a **dependent** or **subordinate clause.** E.g., *The porch collapsed.* This group of words can stand by itself, so it is an independent clause.

But: *when Kalim removed the railing with his tractor.* This group of words has a subject, *Kalim,* and a verb, *removed,* but it does not make complete sense on its own. It depends for its meaning on *The porch collapsed;* therefore, it is a dependent clause.

colloquialism   word or group of words that we use in casual conversation or in informal writing.

> Steve *flunked* his accounting exam.
> *Did* you *get* what the teacher said about job placement?
> I can't believe that *guy* is serious about learning.

comma splice   the error that results when the writer joins two independent clauses with a comma. E.g., *The comma splice is an error, it is a kind of run-on sentence.*

dependent-clause cue   word or word phrase that introduces a dependent clause. E.g., *when, because, in order that, as soon as.*

modifier   word or group of words that adds information about another word (or phrase or clause) in a sentence. See **adjective, adverb, dependent clause.**

nouns   words that name persons, places, and things and have the grammatical capability of being possessive. There are **concrete** nouns that are **proper** (*Calgary, Beijing, Gaza, January, Sharon*); **common** (*woman, man, city, car, animal*); and **collective** (*group, audience, swarm, jury, committee*). There are also **abstract** nouns (*truth, softness, pride, confidence*). Unlike their concrete cousins, abstract nouns refer to concepts, ideas, characteristics—things we know or experience through our intellect rather than through our senses.

objects   the "receiving" part of a sentence. The **direct object** is a noun or noun substitute (pronoun, phrase, or clause) that is the target or receiver of the action expressed by the verb in a sentence. It answers the question *what?* or *whom?* of the verb. E.g., John threw the *ball.* (John threw *what?*)

He wondered *where the money went*. (He wondered *what?*)

Munira loves *Abdul*. (Munira loves *whom?*)

The **indirect object** is a noun or pronoun that is the indirect target or receiver of the action expressed by the verb in a sentence. It is *always* placed in front of the direct object. It answers the question *to whom?* or *to what?*

John threw me the ball. (John threw *to whom?*)

Lisa gave her composition a title. (Gave *to what?*)

The **object of a preposition** is a noun or noun substitute (pronoun, phrase, or clause) that follows a preposition. E.g., after the *storm* (*storm* is a noun, object of the preposition *after*); before *signing the lease* (*signing the lease* is a phrase, object of the preposition *before*; He thought about *what he wanted to do*. (*what he wanted to do* is a clause, object of the preposition *about*).

Notice that what follows a preposition is always its object; that is why the subject of a sentence or clause can never be found in a prepositional phrase.

participle   form of a verb that can be used as an adjective (the *completed* work, the *weeping* willows) or part of a verb phrase (am *succeeding*, have *rented*).

The present participle of a verb ends in *-ing*.

The past participle of a regular verb ends in *-d* or *-ed*. For a list of irregular verbs, see pp. 236–38 and a dictionary.

person   a category of pronouns and nouns. **First person** refers to the person who is speaking (*I, we*). **Second person** refers to the person being spoken to (*you*). **Third person** is the person or thing being spoken about (*he, she, it, they*, and any noun or pronoun that may substitute for these).

phrase   a group of meaning-related words that acts as a noun, verb, adjective, or adverb within a sentence. Phrases do not make complete sense on their own because they do not contain both a subject and verb.

Behind the garage is the best place. (phrase acting as noun)

I *must have been sleeping* when you called. (verb phrase)

Travelling in Spain, my friends saw some monuments *of the Spanish Civil War.* (phrases acting as adjectives)
In this weather, portaging is a chore. (phrase acting as adverb)

prefix	a meaningful letter or group of letters added to the beginning of a word (1) to change its meaning or (2) to change its word class.

1. *a* + moral = amoral
   contra + indication = contraindication
   an + hydrous = anhydrous
   a + sexual = asexual
   dis + establish = disestablish
2. *de* + nude (adjective) = denude (verb)
   in + dent (noun) = indent (verb)
   in + put (verb) = input (noun)
   a + maze (noun) = amaze (verb)

Some prefixes require a hyphen; as here:

anti-Meech Lake
all-Canadian
mid-February
de-emphasize
re-establish

preposition	a word that connects a noun or pronoun or phrase to some other word(s) in a sentence. The noun or pronoun is the *object* of the preposition. (That is why the **subject** of a sentence is never found in a prepositional phrase.)

I prepared the minutes *of the union meeting.* (*of* relates *meeting* to *minutes*)
One *of the parents* checks the children every half hour. (*of* relates parents to *One*)

prepositional phrase	a group of grammatically related words having the function of a noun, adjective, or adverb and beginning with a preposition. See the list on p. 230.
pronouns	words that are noun-like. They usually substitute for nouns, but sometimes they substitute for other pronouns.

He will market *anything that* brings in money.
Everyone must earn *her* badges.

There are several kinds of pronouns:

personal: I, we, you, he, she, they, me, us, him, her, them

possessive: theirs, ours, my, mine, its, his, hers, your, yours

demonstrative: this, these, that, those

relative: who, which, that, whom, whose

interrogative: who? whose? whom? which? what?

indefinite: all *"-one, -thing, -body"* pronouns such as *everyone, something, anybody; each, neither, either, few, none, several.*

subject   In a sentence, the person, thing, or concept that the sentence is about—the topic of the sentence. In a paper, what the essay is about—the topic of the paper.

suffix   a letter or group of letters that is added to the end of a word (1) to change its meaning, (2) to change its grammatical role, or (3) to change its word class.

1. king + *dom* = kingdom
   tooth + *less* = toothless
   few + *er* = fewer
   home + *less* = homeless
2. love (base form) + *s* = loves (third person singular, present tense)
   student + *'s* = student's (possessive singular)
   eat (base form) + *en* = eaten (past participle)
   teacher + *s* = teachers (plural)
3. your (adjective) + *s* = yours (pronoun)
   happy (adjective) + *ily* = happily (adverb)
   act (verb) + *ive* = active (adjective)
   activate (verb) + *ion* = activation (noun)

With the help of a dictionary, count how many prefixes and suffixes are in *antidisestablishmentarianism.*

tenses   Verbs indicate past, present, or future time. The different forms of the verb used to indicate time are called *tenses*. The verb ending (e.g., play*s*, play*ing*, play*ed*) and any helping verbs associated with the main verb (*will* play, *has* played, *had* played, *will have* played) show the tense of the verb.

There are simple tenses:

    present: ask asks
    past: asked
    future: will ask

and perfect tenses:

present: have (has) asked
past: had asked
future: will (shall) have asked

The simple and perfect tenses can also be **progressive**: am asking, having been asking, etc.

transitions	words or phrases that help readers to follow the text smoothly from one paragraph to another, or from one sentence to the next. See p. 94.
verbs	words that say something about a person, place, or thing and whose form may be changed to indicate tense. They may make a statement, ask a question, or give commands. They may express action (physical or mental), occurrence, or condition (mode of being).

> George *hit* an inside curve for a home run. (physical action)
> Laurence *believed* the Blue Jays would win. (mental action)
> Father's Day *falls* on the first Sunday of June. (occurrence)
> Helen eventually *became* interested in English. (condition)

Some verbs are called **linking verbs**: they help to make a statement by linking the subject to a word that describes or explains it.

> William Hubbard *was* Toronto's first black mayor. (*was* links *William Hubbard* to *mayor*)
> Mohammed *looks* tired. (*looks* links *Mohammed* and *tired*)

In addition to *am, is, are, was, were,* and *been*, some common linking verbs are *appear, become, feel, grow, look, taste, remain, seem, smell, sound*.

Another class of verbs is called **helping verbs**. They show the time of a verb as future or past (*will go, has gone*), or as a continuing action (*is* reading); and they show the passive voice (*was* completed).

voice	verbs may be **active** or **passive**, depending on whether the subject of the verb is *acting* (active voice) or *being acted upon* (passive voice).

> In 1988, Brian Mulroney *introduced* another set of tax reforms. (active)
> Another set of tax reforms *was introduced* in 1988. (passive)

Answers to Selected Exercises

UNIT SIX: Sentence Structure

Chapter 25: Cracking the Sentence Code

EXERCISE 1

1. Algy met a bear.
2. A bear met Algy.
3. The bear was bulgy.
4. Sad to say, the bulge was Algy.
5. Grizzlies are famous for their unpredictability.
6. Meeting bears unexpectedly is clearly risky.
7. According to an old myth, bears never run downhill.
8. (You) Take it from me. They do.
9. Females with cubs are known to be especially dangerous.
10. How to defend oneself presents a real problem.

EXERCISE 2

1. Pierre Trudeau, like Jack Benny, is perennially middle-aged.
2. Here is an idea to consider.
3. Lucy Maud Montgomery was born in Ontario's Durham County before Confederation.
4. Who will eat the last pickle?
5. (You) Eat slowly.

6. Physical activity <u>builds</u> strong bodies and healthy minds.
7. (You) <u>Keep</u> your body fit.
8. Far behind the Liberals and New Democrats <u>trailed</u> the <u>Conserva</u>-tives, bringing up the rear.
9. <u>Pride</u> <u>goes</u> before a fall. (Biblical proverb)
10. <u>Only</u> in Canada <u>is</u> a so-called <u>lack</u> of national identity a distinctive national characteristic.

EXERCISE 3

1. <u>Toronto</u> <u>is</u> a metropolitan centre with scores of distinct neighbour-hoods.
2. The <u>word</u> "Toronto" <u>is</u> the Anglicization of the Indian term for "meeting place."
3. The Toronto Islands <u>were</u> originally a part of the mainland.
4. <u>Are</u> <u>you</u> a year-round island resident?
5. At a joint meeting of the councils, the city <u>mayor</u> <u>opposed</u> the Metro Council on behalf of island residents.
6. No evictions <u>occurred</u> last year.
7. The <u>islanders'</u> <u>cohesiveness</u> <u>is</u> the product of both genuine neigh-bourliness and common community concerns.
8. There <u>is</u> surprisingly little <u>vandalism</u>, the plague of other downtown areas.
9. For the average visitor to the Toronto Islands, the <u>combination</u> of private and public properties <u>is</u> acceptable and even <u>enjoyable</u>.
10. Minutes from the middle of the city <u>nestles</u> my sunny, serene island <u>retreat</u>.

EXERCISE 4

1. He <u>has talked</u> nonstop for three hours.
2. She <u>should have been examining</u> each package.
3. <u>Could</u> <u>they</u> <u>return</u> the goods tomorrow?
4. In the winter, the <u>car</u> <u>starts</u> more easily inside the garage than outside.
5. Where <u>is</u> the nearest gas station?
6. He <u>is</u> not <u>going</u> to drive.
7. <u>Which</u> horse <u>does</u> she <u>prefer</u>?
8. Parents <u>will</u> always <u>perceive</u> their offspring as small children.
9. The <u>barometer</u> <u>has</u> just <u>fallen</u> alarmingly.
10. Patiently and painstakingly, against all odds, <u>struggled</u> the little army.

EXERCISE 5

1. In a couple of years, you will be a professional dancer.
2. By noon, he will have been sleeping for eighteen hours.
3. How are the club members identified?
4. The police will certainly stop all yellow cars on the road tonight.
5. How should the committee present this concept?
6. To some small degree at least, personal opinion is often presented as fact.
7. My boss does not understand me; neither does my husband (understand me).
8. Have you ever been to the Zanzibar tavern?
9. Little is known about his past, except that he visited here twice.
10. Isn't she going home now?

EXERCISE 6

1. According to the old proverb, a stitch in time saves nine.
2. I have had a stitch in my side, and I have often been in stitches.
3. Stitching, in my opinion, is best left to tailors and surgeons.
4. For today's prices, clothing manufacturers should be sewing triple seams in their clothing, all by hand.
5. From the beginning, each item of clothing should be separately designed.
6. After that, every pattern piece should be cut by hand.
7. Each piece of cloth should then be sewn with great care to the other appropriate pieces, by one person.
8. The same craftsperson should then pay attention to double seaming and to details of hand finishing.
9. Items of clothing produced in this way might justify today's high prices.
10. In this kind of manufacturing procedure, the individual maker of the item should receive a specified percentage of the wholesale price.

EXERCISE 7

1. In the next twenty years, the average age of the Canadian population will increase significantly.
2. For those of us now in our forties, this trend is good news.

3. ~~For those in their teens,~~ however, the news <u>is</u> not so good. They <u>will have to carry</u> the burden ~~of caring for the increasing numbers of elderly persons in society.~~

4. ~~On the positive side,~~ the leaders ~~of tomorrow~~ <u>will have</u> the experience and wisdom ~~of a large segment of the population~~ to draw on ~~in their planning and decision making.~~

5. ~~Throughout history,~~ cultures ~~around the world~~ <u>have</u> traditionally associated age ~~with wisdom.~~

6. Ironically, however, this <u>assumption</u> <u>is</u> not always <u>supported</u> ~~by the evidence.~~

7. There <u>are</u> many examples ~~from the past~~ and ~~in the present of young leaders with more wisdom and maturity~~ than their aged counterparts.

8. (You) <u>Consider,</u> ~~for example,~~ Alexander the Great. He <u>had conquered</u> the known world ~~by the age of 19.~~

9. ~~For a contemporary example,~~ (you) <u>consider</u> the success stories ~~of youthful entrepreneurs like Bill Gates.~~ Many young <u>people,</u> just ~~out of college,~~ <u>have launched</u> hi-tech ventures to compete ~~with old, established companies.~~

10. ~~Over the next two decades, with the maturing of the "baby boom,"~~ Canadians <u>will encounter</u> changes ~~in life-style, in political focus,~~ and ~~in cultural attitudes~~ towards the "young" and the "old."

EXERCISE 9

1. The <u>prime minister</u> and the provincial <u>premiers</u> <u>met</u> at Meech Lake.
2. They <u>debated</u> and <u>drafted</u> amendments to the Constitution.
3. The <u>anesthetist</u> and the <u>surgeon</u> <u>scrubbed</u> for surgery and <u>hurried</u> to the operating room.
4. Blue <u>spruce</u> and <u>hemlock</u> <u>are</u> both northern imports to southern Ontario.
5. I <u>tried</u> and <u>failed</u> once, and then later <u>tried</u> again and <u>succeeded</u>.
6. My <u>son</u> or my <u>daughter</u> <u>will drive</u> me home.
7. The two <u>dogs</u> and the <u>cat</u> <u>travelled</u> a thousand miles in three months.
8. My retired <u>father</u> <u>reads</u>, <u>travels</u>, <u>golfs</u>, <u>walks</u> the dog, and <u>loves</u> all these activities.
9. (You) <u>Knock</u> three times and <u>ask</u> for Joe.
10. <u>Sight reading</u> and <u>improvising</u> <u>are</u> necessary skills of the small-band musician.

Chapter 26: *Still More about Verbs*

EXERCISE 1

1. came
2. spent
3. made
4. been
5. lost

6. spoke, found
7. knew
8. had
9. chosen
10. told, led

EXERCISE 2

1. won, won
2. worn, wore
3. did, done
4. forgotten, forgot
5. became, become

6. seen, saw
7. set, set
8. fallen, fell
9. met, met
10. kept, kept

EXERCISE 3

1. dealt, dealt
2. driven, drove
3. fought, fought
4. grown, grew
5. bid, bid

6. began, begun
7. felt, felt
8. cost, cost
9. left, left
10. swung, swung

EXERCISE 4

1. taught, taught
2. hanged, hanged
3. held, held
4. drunk, drank
5. sped, sped

6. laid, laid
7. gone, went
8. frozen, froze
9. dived, dived (*or* dove)
10. broke, broken

Chapter 27: *Solving Sentence-Fragment Problems*

We have made the sentence fragments into complete sentences only for the first two sets and only to give you an idea of how the sentences might be formed. Many different sentences can be made out of the fragments given; just be sure each of your sentences has a subject and a verb.

EXERCISE 1

1. F He is the college's expert regarding myths and fairy tales.
2. F It is silly to decide on the basis of rumour, not facts.
3. F Coming home, he was sad to hear of the many occurrences of vandalism.
4. F Those students were writing exams all evening, after working all day.
5. F The party members gathering in the campaign office called for a recount of the ballots.
6. S
7. F The air attack was cancelled because of cloud cover.
8. F The young artists were painting in a studio with bad lighting.
9. F Having worked outdoors all his life, upon retirement he spent his time in his garden.
10. S

EXERCISE 2

1. F To exaggerate for the sake of personal image and for monetary gain is a sure way to lose credibility among your friends.
2. S
3. F Exaggerating his own influence is of great importance to him.
4. F Knowing the truth, we paid little attention to his stories.
5. F He told his story as usual, with some twisting of the truth.
6. F Speakers and listeners both recognized the tall tale for what it was.
7. S
8. S
9. F We followed the directions printed in the booklet included in the package.
10. S

EXERCISE 3

1. F
2. F
3. S
4. F
5. F
6. F
7. F
8. F
9. F
10. F

EXERCISE 4

1. F What
2. F As
3. F Where
4. F If
5. F So that

6. F Although
7. F Since
8. S
9. F Whichever
10. F Before

EXERCISE 5

<u>Before</u> the curtain went up on the lavishly decorated and beautifully lit set. The actor playing Frankie could be seen pacing up and down nervously. <u>Although</u> he was a veteran of many stage performances and several popular movies and was accustomed to appearing before large audiences. <u>Which</u> made it very strange that he would demonstrate the symptoms of stage fright so clearly. Looking closely, a careful observer might have noticed, however, that he wasn't studying his lines or rehearsing his role. In fact, <u>unless</u> one were right beside him and watching very closely. The real purpose of his pacing could easily be missed. <u>Although</u> he appeared to be alone. He was, in reality, exercising his pet cockroach.

EXERCISE 6

Photographing wildlife can be a rewarding and entertaining experience. <u>Provided that</u> one is very careful and has the right photographic equipment. <u>Whereas</u> some photographers try to capture the essence of a bowl of fruit, and others aim for a spiritual quality in family portraits or wedding pictures. I prefer to capture on film an accurate reflection of true wildlife. So that I can achieve this goal, I follow some of my crazy friends around from party to party, recording their antics with my pocket camera. <u>Since</u> so many of my friends are, by any definition, wild. The reproduction of wildlife in my photo albums is quite remarkable. <u>Whether</u> it is Jayne trying to play baseball in an evening gown, or Tessa going to a ballet opening in her jeans. <u>As long as</u> I have friends like Terry, who carries a pair of scissors to cut off people's ties, or Phyllis, who insists that she is Princess Di. I will always have plenty of subject matter for wildlife photography.

EXERCISE 7

The attitude to Toronto takes two forms. There is first the attitude of the non-Torontonians, who live in places like St. John's, Maple Creek and Vancouver. Then there is the attitude of the Torontonians themselves.

The attitude of the outsider is compounded of envy, malice and pity in about equal quantities. It is admitted that Torontonians make large sums of money, but not much else. Certainly they never have any fun. There is none of the leisurely gracious living that is to be found in Montreal, say, or Halifax, or Okotoks, Alberta. When a young man sets out for Toronto, he is surrounded by a covey of friends, all commiserating with him and whispering to him to look about for a job for them in the big city. It is generally acknowledged that the bereaved young man will return, but he rarely does. If he sees his friends again, he sees them in Toronto, where they all have a good cry and talk over the grand old days when they were poor in Pelvis or West Webfoot.

The attitude of the Torontonians is that they simply do not care what people think of them. They live in Toronto and that is good enough for them. For years a host of magazine articles, newspaper editorials and commentators have baited Toronto. Toronto refuses to swallow the bait. One mayor tried to launch a campaign to make the city popular, but it fizzled out after a few days. Torontonians do not really care about being popular; in fact, about half the criticism about the city comes from its own people. Nobody baits Toronto quite as much as those who live there.

Chapter 28: Solving Run-On Problems

EXERCISE 1

1. The teacher's late; let's go!
2. Just let me do the talking; you'll get us a ticket if you open your mouth.
3. correct
4. correct
5. correct
6. correct
7. Students today need summer jobs. Tuition and living costs are too much for most families.
8. Bryan will be going to college if he is accepted. His parents have lots of money.
9. correct
10. I am seeking a hero after whom I can model my life. So far I've rejected Sly Stallone, Madonna, and Hulk Hogan.

EXERCISE 2

1. The comma splice gets its name from the film splice; two pieces of film are taped, or spliced, together.
2. Old movies are sometimes choppy and disconnected because they have been spliced badly or too often.
3. Two sentences cannot be spliced together with a comma; you need to use a semicolon or a period or a linking word between them.
4. You should be particularly careful when using linking words like "however," "consequently," "therefore," and "moreover." These words need a semicolon before them and a comma after when they join two independent clauses.
5. This isn't a very difficult rule; in fact, it's one of the easiest rules to learn because it has no exceptions.
6. With one minute to go, the opposing team scored the winning goal; consequently, no one on our team felt much like celebrating the end of the season.
7. The anti-smoking bylaw doesn't seem to have done much good. I often see people smoking in restaurants, stores, and even elevators.
8. One of the things I hope to learn at college is French; however, I doubt if I'll ever learn to speak it fluently.
9. It's a pity that burning coal contributes to acid rain since we have an almost inexhaustible supply of coal in Canada.
10. Our country's culture, attitudes, and even politics are strongly influenced by television. That is why the CRTC insists on a high level of Canadian content in television broadcasting.

EXERCISE 3

1. A Canadian who speaks three languages is called multilingual; one who speaks two languages is called bilingual; and one who speaks only one language is called an English Canadian.
2. I'm sure the job couldn't have been as bad as he claims; maybe he just didn't try hard enough. *Or:* I'm sure the job couldn't have been as bad as he claims. Maybe he just didn't try hard enough.
3. Meetings such as this are fine for small groups, but large groups have to be handled in a different way.
4. I'll be glad to help you out. When you need me just call; I'll be here all day.
5. In Canada, winter is more than a season; it's a bad joke.
6. correct
7. It may seem foolish, especially after all the wrangling over our new constitution, but I still believe in a unified Canada. I believe in one

nation extending from sea to sea. The Fathers of Confederation were right: a federation of provinces can work.

8. Career opportunities appear very good for students in a wide range of technical programs; however, most employers are looking for people with experience as well as training.

9. People with high-technology skills are urgently required in several fields; plastics processing, mould-making, and tool- and die-making are three examples.

10. For college students in technology programs, then, the future looks bright; however, a diploma does not necessarily guarantee job security.

EXERCISE 4

1. Since you are interested in both careers, you should probably play hockey now and take up teaching in the future. Usually the legs give out before the mind does.

2. In the past fifteen years, we have seen a remarkable increase in the health consciousness of the average North American. The result has been a huge and growing industry that attempts to make fitness painless or even fun. From health clubs and aerobics classes to weight lifting and diet plans, we have an almost limitless choice of ways to spend our money on our bodies.

3. Joan is a complete hypocrite now that she is wealthy. Insisting with every other breath that she hasn't changed a bit, she drives a Rolls, flaunts her furs, and wears diamonds in bunches.

4. The hockey season now extends well into the baseball season, which, in turn, encroaches on the football season. Football, being a fall and winter sport, extends halfway into the hockey schedule. So it goes, with basketball overlapping the other three.

5. Following the high-speed chase and subsequent arrest of the car's driver, the police learned that the vehicle had been stolen. They added a charge of theft to the reckless driving charge, and the young man spent the night in jail. There he came to realize the seriousness of his predicament, and he asked for permission to make a telephone call so he could get in touch with his parents' lawyer.

EXERCISE 5

Fourteen people live in Punkeydoodle's Corner, Ontario, a town famous for its funny name. Twenty-five kilometres west of Kitchener, Punkeydoodle's Corner was a stagecoach stop on the Huron Trail during the nineteenth century, when it was a bustling town of more than one hundred people. But, as stagecoaches gave way to trains, which, in turn, gave way to automobiles, the little town dwindled and shrank until only three families were left to call it home.

Several different stories account for the origin of the town's name. The hero of one of these stories was a man called John Zurbrigg, who was a Swiss settler and pumpkin farmer. According to the tale, Zurbrigg was a rather lazy man, preferring to "doodle" his time away rather than tend to his pumpkins. One of his neighbours, furious at Zurbrigg's idleness, is said to have labeled him "punkey doodle" during an argument; history does not record Zurbrigg's response.

Another story claims the town got its name from John Zurbuchen, the chubby, genial host of the old hotel in the town, who had been born in Germany, then moved to Ontario in the 1860s with his family. Apparently, Zurbuchen never quite mastered English pronunciation. He loved to sing, though, and frequently entertained his beer-drinking customers with his version of "Yankee Doodle," which he mispronounced "Punkey Doodle." Both of these stories seem a bit farfetched, if you ask me.

Its unusual name attracts hundreds of visitors to Punkeydoodle's Corner every year; however, being a tourist attraction has one disadvantage, according to the townspeople. Every time they put up a sign to identify their village, the sign is stolen within a few weeks, even when it is firmly embedded in concrete.

EXERCISE 6

Until I moved to the country, I could never see the attraction of bird-watching as a pastime. My parents had enjoyed bird-watching as a hobby for years, frequently boring me numb with their enthusiastic tales of warblers heard or kingfishers sighted. While I lived in the city I saw birds so infrequently that I was completely indifferent to my parents' enthusiasm; those birds I did see were always pigeons, sparrows, or starlings, anyway. Within a week of moving out of the city to take a new job, I began to take notice of my feathered neighbours. I was awakened three mornings in a row by squawking blue jays. Three days later a convention of crows descended on my property, sending everyone indoors for two days. My bird-watching really became an obsession when I was dive-bombed repeatedly by an irate woodpecker, which I had offended in some mysterious way. Now, protected by a surplus army helmet and armed with binoculars, I go on excursions with the most dedicated birders; however, whereas they creep silently through the underbrush and meticulously record each sighting in a log book, I crash about, threatening and cursing any birds I encounter. Now everyone regards me with pity or contempt, and more than one former friend has suggested that I've gone "cuckoo."

Chapter 29: Solving Modifier Problems

EXERCISE 1

1. On the third floor there is a library that has a washroom.
2. He told us no one works hard on the first day.
3. correct
4. In January, my supervisor told me I would get a raise. (Or: My supervisor told me I would get a raise in January.)
5. We applied for almost every job that was posted.
6. He played the guitar beautifully all the time I was there.
7. There are just enough pieces to go around.
8. When they drove down his street, they couldn't remember which house Sean was living in.
9. Some people never go to movies unless they're French or Italian.
10. By working night and day, he managed to pay for almost all the damage for which his brother had been charged.

EXERCISE 2

1. One usually finds the best Chinese food in those restaurants where the Chinese eat.
2. Using his new binoculars, he caught sight of a canary and several finches.
3. Juan had played ball professionally for several major American teams before coming to the Blue Jays.
4. The football practices have been organized as a keep-fit measure for players who are not with a team in the summertime.
5. Vancouver is a wonderful city to live in for anyone who likes rain and fog.
6. Some games, such as tiddlywinks, are less demanding in terms of time and equipment.
7. The Human Rights Code prohibits discrimination on the basis of race, sex, or age against anyone who is applying for a job.
8. With a screwdriver, I was able to loosen the clamp that held the broken cable in place.
9. With an open can of tomato juice, they waited breathlessly under the trees for the return of their dog, which had been sprayed by a skunk.
10. Tonight Sue Johansen will lead a panel discussion on relaxation through sex, including how to tone and stretch muscles, how to relieve tension, and even how to sleep.

EXERCISE 3

1. Considering Michael's charm and good manners, I think his good looks are unimportant.
2. My supervisor gave me a lecture about punctuality after I was late twice in one week.
3. After criticizing both my work and my attitude, my boss fired me.
4. Trying to bunt, the batter hit the ball over the fence at centre field for a home run.
5. When looking over their résumés, you can see that Carol and George have completely different backgrounds but that both could do the job.
6. correct
7. correct
8. Fifteen minutes after setting sail for the island, they were struck by the storm.
9. After struggling desperately for almost two hours with high winds and torrential rains, they were relieved by the storm's stopping as suddenly as it had begun.
10. Even in hot weather, runners should warm and stretch their legs and feet before doing any serious jogging.

EXERCISE 5

1. As a college student constantly faced with new assignments, I find the pressure is sometimes intolerable.
2. Being horribly hung over, I realized that the only problem with a free bar is knowing when to quit.
3. The villagers no longer drive cars or ride bicycles over the bridge that has been rotting slowly over the years.
4. The Canadian Brass receives enthusiastic acclaim from Vancouver to Halifax for its witty presentation, its wide repertoire, and its clarity of tone.
5. Our hearts were wrung by the frail, unkempt little woman carrying two shopping bags full of old clothes and several other bags.
6. I learned in the *Vancouver Province* that the provincial premiers will meet in July.
7. When I finally got to the shop on payday, the gorgeous dress I had been looking at all week had been sold.
8. On the day I was demonstrating how to make a Caesar salad, I left the Parmesan cheese, my favourite ingredient, in my locker.
9. Barry will prepare his guests a Japanese sukiyaki dinner cooked in a wok and served with steamed rice.
10. In most cases, the person who has lived for a long time has lived a simple life.

Chapter 30: The Parallelism Principle

EXERCISE 1

1. I'm looking for a babysitter who is intelligent, patient, and kind.
2. Make sure your report is comprehensive, readable, and accurate.
3. Those in community-service fields must be loving, patient, objective, and understanding.
4. Its location, staff, and appearance made that hospital a more pleasant place to stay than most.
5. We were told to study the report carefully and to make our recommendations in writing.
6. Their chances for a lasting relationship aren't good, considering their differences in goals, temperament, and culture.
7. Her small build, quick temper, and criminal record will disqualify her from becoming a corrections officer.
8. Barry is everything a girl could want: handsome, intelligent, successful, and kind.
9. The space-age kitchen, the pool and sauna, and the burglar-proof security system were what sold us on the apartment.
10. Mr. Redfern explained how to use the tape recorder, the microphone and camera, and the video cassette recorder.

EXERCISE 2

1. Body-building has made me what I am today: physically perfect, financially prosperous, and practically friendless.
2. If there is no heaven, then there is no hell.
3. In my tiny home town, two significantly related crimes prevail: vandalism and drug-trafficking.
4. I'd like to help, but I'm too tired, too poor, and too busy.
5. I wanted either a Mother's pizza or a McDonald's Big Mac.
6. correct
7. My sister, who's trying to teach me to play tennis, says that my forehand and serve are all right, but that my backhand needs strengthening.
8. The two factors thought to be most important in a long-lasting marriage are the commitment of each partner to the marriage and the willingness of each partner to compromise.
9. Barry claimed that, through repetition and firmness, he had trained his guppy to be obedient, quiet, and loyal.
10. The new budget must deal with several major problems, two of them being the devalued Canadian dollar and the high rate of inflation.

EXERCISE 3

1. wine   women   song
2. privately   publicly
3. employers   employees
4. lying about all morning   doing whatever I please
5. as individuals   as a group
6. happy   healthy   wise
7. do your best   don't give up
8. information   education   entertainment
9. not enough time   not enough money   not enough staff
10. French is the language of love
    English is the language of business
    German is the language of profanity

EXERCISE 4

1. Working with children is stimulating, challenging, and rewarding.
2. Not being able to speak the language causes confusion, frustration, and embarrassment.
3. To prevent crime, attend to victims of accidents and crimes, and safely apprehend those suspected of crime are a police officer's responsibilities.
4. Being mentally sound and physically strong, the elderly man was able to live quite happily by himself.
5. Three of the issues the committee will have to deal with right away are camp maintenance, staffing, and promotion.
6. His doctor advised him to eat less, exercise more, and quit smoking.
7. For many people, attending AA meetings is first embarrassing, possibly even humiliating, then helpful, and finally successful.
8. A high level of motivation, problem-solving experience, and confidence in your decisions are necessary if you hope to run a successful business.
9. Influential factors in any nation's economic regression are bad management of natural resources, unwise policies regarding national debt, and inflationary demands of unions.
10. Although the first applicant seemed scared and shy, the second was composed and outgoing.

Chapter 31: Refining by Combining

EXERCISE 1

1. The Beatles are a musical institution, for (*or* and) their music appeals to every generation.

2. Kate Bush does not give live performances, nor does she tour with her music.
3. Janet Jackson has a famous brother, so (*or* and) she had to work hard to create a unique sound.
4. Van Halen is a progressive rock group, but they take offence at being labeled "heavy metal."
5. You can read about Elton John's suicide attempt in music magazines, or you can listen to "Someone Saved My Life Tonight."
6. The Rolling Stones originated in the sixties, and (*or* yet) they are still performing now, in the nineties.
7. Madonna is considered a controversial artist, for she has made several sexually explicit videos.
8. Phil Collins is a popular contemporary solo artist, but his roots go back to Genesis.
9. Bryan Adams is to be commended for his work on "Tears Are Not Enough," and Anne Murray, Cory Hart, and Salome Bey contributed to making the song a success.
10. The Nylons are renowned for singing *a cappella*, or, without accompaniment, but they occasionally feature background instruments.

EXERCISE 2

1. Since the team moved from Atlanta, the Calgary Flames have been a mainstay in the NHL.
2. Because Fred McGriff has a devastating swing, he is one of the most feared hitters in the American League.
3. Tim Wallach of the Montreal Expos won a "gold glove," which was in recognition of his outstanding defensive skills.
4. Bo Jackson is a talented athlete, whether he is playing baseball for the Kansas City Royals or football for the Los Angeles Raiders.
5. The Blue Jays always seem to win when (*or* whenever) the SkyDome roof is closed.
6. After struggling for years, the Vancouver Canucks are so improved that they are now acknowledged as a team to be reckoned with.
7. The Montreal Expos draw impressive crowds to Olympic Stadium as long as they are winning.
8. The Montreal Canadiens have won many Stanley Cups, but the Quebec Nordiques have yet to win even one.
9. Wayne Gretzky is an exceptional hockey player, even if some sportswriters consider him a defensive liability. *or*
   Although Wayne Gretzky is an exceptional hockey player, some sportswriters consider him a defensive liability.
10. Although George Bell, who comes from the Dominican Republic, is an important role model for his team, he is a bigger role model for children in the Dominican Republic.

EXERCISE 3

1. Whenever Rudolf loses a girlfriend, he goes shopping for new clothes.
2. According to Mortimer Adler, failure breeds fatigue, and there is nothing more energizing than success.
3. Love one another, but make not a bond of love. (Kahlil Gibran)
4. You must learn to love yourself before you can truly love someone else.
5. Marriage is for serious people, so I have not considered it an option. *or* Because marriage is for serious people, I have not considered it an option.
6. Some people still believe that divorce is an acknowledgment that there was not a true commitment in the first place.
7. It is an astonishing fact that twenty percent of adults in America are illiterate, and fifty percent of the adults who *can* read say they never read books.
8. Although Canada is a relatively rich country, most of us brush up against hunger and homelessness almost daily, when we encounter men and, less often, women begging on downtown streetcorners.
9. In his essay, "A Modest Proposal for a Divorce Ceremony," Pierre Berton proposed that Canada institute a formal divorce ceremony, which would be like a formal wedding ceremony, but all the symbolism would be reversed.
10. The bride, for example, would wear black, and immediately after the ceremony, the newly divorced couple would go into the vestry and scratch their names off the marriage register.

UNIT SEVEN: Grammar

Chapter 32: Subject–Verb Agreement

EXERCISE 1

1. They sell used essays to other students.
2. He often spends the weekend on his sailboat.
3. The women maintain that their boss has been ogling them.
4. Their flights have been delayed because of the storm.
5. Those new computers affect the entire office procedure.
6. They like to work with children, so they are looking for jobs in a day-care centre.
7. All those who shop at Pimrock's receive free cans of tuna.

8. Those girls' fathers are looking for rich husbands for them.
9. Civil servants with indexed pensions stand to gain from future inflation.
10. Both of her sons are successful in their own ways.

EXERCISE 2

1. Atari games are Vince's first love in life.
2. Movies are what Marcia spends most of her time on.
3. The only junk food Tim eats is Hostess Twinkies.
4. The cause of his downfall was frequent nights of debauchery.
5. A good pitcher and outfielder are what the team needs now.
6. Clean living and Lois Lane are what keeps Superman strong.
7. Frequently, the cause of failure is absences from class and failed exams.
8. What I least like to eat is brown rice and tofu.
9. Accounting procedures were something that I didn't understand.
10. The reason for your success in the aluminum-siding business is your stunning good looks.

EXERCISE 3

1. know
2. is
3. is
4. are
5. repel

EXERCISE 4

1. is
2. has
3. inflicts
4. is
5. keeps

EXERCISE 5

1. is
2. loves
3. was
4. is
5. is

EXERCISE 6

1. is
2. involves
3. has
4. wants
5. believes

EXERCISE 7

1. is
2. prefers
3. leave
4. brawl
5. was

EXERCISE 8

1. was
2. seems
3. is
4. is
5. seems

EXERCISE 9

1. My sense of the schools is that none of them is . . .
2. Neither of them remembers . . .
3. Every one of the SUNshine Boys appeals . . .
4. My whole family, with the exception of Fido, dislikes . . .
5. Popular belief notwithstanding, quicksand does . . .
6. It is the suction created by the victims that is . . .
7. correct
8. Eight hundred dollars per term, all students agree, is . . .
9. The birth of quintuplets was . . .
10. Everything that we agreed to last night seems . . .

EXERCISE 10

Quebec City, along with Montreal, Toronto, and Vancouver, *is* among Canada's great gourmet centres. While Toronto is a relative latecomer to this list, neither Quebec City nor Montreal *is* a stranger to those who *seek* fine dining. Indeed, travel and food magazines have long affirmed that the inclusion of these two cities in a Quebec vacation *is* a "must." Montreal is perhaps more international in its offerings, but Quebec City provides exquisite proof that French Canadian cuisine and hospitality *are* second to none in the world. Amid the old-world charm of the lower city *are* to be found some of the quaintest and most enjoyable traditional restaurants; the newer sections of town *boast* equally fine dining in more contemporary surroundings. The combination of the wonderful food and the city's fascinating charms *is* sure to make any visitor return frequently. Either the summer, when the city blooms and outdoor cafes abound, or the winter, when Carnaval turns the streets into hundreds of connecting parties, *is* a wonderful time to visit one of Canada's oldest and most interesting cities.

EXERCISE 11

The interest in wrestlers and their managers, fans, and friends *is* fascinating proof that our society needs cheap thrills. The concept of good and evil fighting it out in epic battles *is* an enduring one. In simpler times, everyone who felt the need to witness such struggles *was* able to watch westerns on TV and see the Bad Guy (wearing the black hat) gunned down at high noon by the reluctant Good Guy (wearing the white hat). The complexity of our society, where good and evil *are* constantly redefined, *means* that we seldom get a clear decision in the battles we see each day on the news, let alone witness the triumph of good over evil. Into this frustrating world *come* Rowdy Roddy Piper, Hulk Hogan, The Junk Yard Dog, and King Kong Bundy. The variety of names, personalities, and "show biz" tricks *is* bewildering. Though the staging of the various moves and even the outcomes of the matches are obvious, the immense popularity of the matches, both on television and in the arenas, *is* undeniable. Like Rambo and Dirty Harry, the professional wrestler cuts through frustrating complexity and represents good or evil in its simplest, most dramatic form. To a great many people, wrestling—not to mention wrestlers—*is* irresistible.

Chapter 33: Pronoun–Antecedent Agreement

EXERCISE 1

1. Yesterday's lecture was given by the English teacher who has a large wart on her nose.
2. Curling's most durable player is a man named Howard "Pappy" Wood, who competed in sixty-five consecutive bonspiels between 1908 and 1972.

3. Is this the car that was stolen by the man who escaped last night?
4. We are often attracted to people who are completely opposite to us.
5. When I entered the locker room, I knew the team that had lost had been there before me.
6. Liona Boyd is the musician who is scheduled to perform tonight.
7. correct
8. Rudolf's grandmother always told him that people who couldn't fly as well as eagles should stay out of airplanes.
9. He remembered that sage advice the stormy night when the DC-9 in which he was flying went into a sickening tailspin over Great Slave Lake.
10. The math problem that we worked out last night would have stymied anyone who hadn't attended class regularly.

EXERCISE 2

1. his
2. herself
3. her
4. his
5. their
6. his
7. itself
8. her
9. their, they
10. himself, he, his

EXERCISE 3

1. Everyone who works in this car wash should pick up his cheque on Monday.
2. Women are treated as equals when they work in the fields.
3. A good manager must have an understanding of every employee and what makes her tick. (*or* . . . what makes him tick.)
4. Do you know whether anyone in this neighbourhood wants to have his windows washed?
5. correct
6. Virginia claims that every one of her male friends has a room of his own.
7. It is now time to listen to the voice of your conscience and what it has to say.
8. No one living in Canada today believes the country is thriving economically.
9. Anyone who has completed introductory sociology should know what a "peer group" is.
10. Most people know that Gordie Howe is the man who played 25 years in the NHL, but do they also know he collected 500 stitches on his face?

EXERCISE 4

1. The gorilla was mean and thirsty because he had finished all the water in the morning.
2. If your pet rat won't eat its food, feed the pellets to the kitty.
3. Hockey is his favourite game, and he badly needs new skates.
4. Tim told Rocco, "My teeth are falling out."
5. Whenever Dennis and Bob played poker, Bob stacked the deck.
6. Every time Rudolf sat on the frog, it croaked.
7. You know that smoking is very bad for your health, but you won't throw your cigarettes away.
8. Daphne dented her car by backing it into a garbage truck.
9. Lefty was suspicious of handgun control because he thought everyone should have a pistol for late-night subway rides.
10. If Pierre and Joe begin to argue, Pierre will tell him that he's never had any use for Joe and that Joe ought to keep his crazy ideas to himself.

Chapter 34: Tense Agreement

EXERCISE 1

1. Rolly goes home and <u>kicks</u> his cat.
2. Hank Aaron broke Babe Ruth's record of 714 home runs in a lifetime when he <u>hit</u> number 715 in 1974.
3. Children are quite perceptive and <u>know</u> when you are lying to them.
4. We had just finished painting the floor when the dog <u>ran</u> through.
5. When Knowlton Nash walked into the room, the ladies <u>went</u> crazy.
6. correct
7. Tim walked into the room, took one look at Lefty, and <u>smashed</u> him right through the wall.
8. First you will greet the guests; then you <u>will show</u> them to their rooms.
9. The largest cheese ever produced took 43 hours to make and <u>weighed</u> a whopping 15 723 kilograms.
10. He watches television all evening until he finally <u>goes</u> to sleep.

EXERCISE 2

1. correct
2. I tried to warn him about her evil ways, and what thanks <u>did</u> I get?
3. The embarrassed girl didn't say anything. She just <u>blushed</u> and <u>ran</u> from the room.

4. Before Roger noticed the snowstorm, he <u>was</u> already up and dressed.
5. They agreed to our living here after we <u>offered</u> them a substantial bribe.
6. In the interests of good community relations and to prevent them from blowing up our house, I vote that we <u>pay</u> what they asked for.
7. Drusilla looks like a sweet young thing; when she <u>speaks</u>, however, the toughest truck drivers blush.
8. Whenever I skip chemistry, it <u>seems</u> old Mr. Bunsen <u>is</u> lurking in the hall to catch me.
9. correct
10. We attempted to change Rudolf's mind all day, but we didn't know he <u>had</u> already voted.

EXERCISE 3

1. Are you going to see *The Blob?* It <u>is</u> a great movie!
2. *Prince of Space* and *The Blob* are the best movies I <u>have</u> ever seen.
3. The film begins with a clever sequence in which a girl <u>meets</u> a boy and his dog.
4. Little do we realize what kind of dreadful creature our young lovers will encounter, or that it <u>will</u> terrify the whole town.
5. The Blob originates in a test tube as a tiny bit of green ooze that then <u>grows</u> to enormous proportions.
6. The slimy, pulsating mass gathers both speed and size as it <u>moves</u> towards our young lovers necking in a pick-up truck.
7. They repel the fearsome Blob with the defrost button and <u>realize</u> the monster <u>can't</u> stand heat, so they <u>rush</u> off to save the town.
8. The Blob is devouring patrons at a local bowling alley, and its increasing girth <u>indicates</u> that it <u>enjoys</u> every morsel. What gruesome sights <u>does</u> this movie have in store for us next?
9. Much to our relief, our hero arrives and <u>builds</u> a huge bonfire out of five-pins; the Blob <u>withers</u> and <u>shrinks</u> away before our very eyes. The town <u>is</u> saved!
10. Is it any wonder that this movie <u>is</u> my favourite? I only wish I <u>could</u> see it with 3-D glasses.

EXERCISE 4

As a boy, Jeffrey had a remarkable knack for making predictions. At age 7, he *predicted* to anyone who would listen that he would be a millionaire by the time he *was* old enough to vote. When he *was* 11, he *predicted* that he *would star* in a major motion picture by the time he could legally drive. At 14, he *prophesied* that he *would be* elected mayor before his 23rd birthday. Incredibly, his predictions came to pass, one after the other. At 16, he *became* the youngest person ever to play James Bond in a movie; this role *led* to other pictures and a salary well into six figures. Careful investing *made* him a millionaire within two years. With all that money behind him, there *was* no stopping Jeffrey's campaign to become, at 22, the youngest mayor in Moose Factory's history. However, his amazing early successes *were* not repeated, and Jeffrey *became* a has-been by the time he *turned* 25.

Chapter 35: Person Agreement

EXERCISE 1

1. you
2. you, your
3. they, themselves
4. she
5. we

EXERCISE 2

1. After the unfortunate brawl, Tim learned that if a person stomps on policemen, he can expect to end up in jail.
2. People can expect to experience the horrors of nuclear war unless they raise their voices against nuclear proliferation.
3. If you leave garbage at your campsite, you may well have bears as midnight callers.
4. correct
5. One will always think about the opportunities he's missed, even if he's happy with what he has.
6. Canadians who worry about street violence should keep in mind that, in comparison to New York, they are safe in downtown Kapuskasing after dark.
7. You should always wear garlic around the neck if you fear vampires.
8. Any woman who wears garlic won't have to worry about men harassing her, either.
9. Can you really know another person if you have never been to his home?
10. A sure way to lose your friends is to eat all the Baskin-Robbins ice cream yourself.

EXERCISE 3

You can enjoy classical music if you are willing to give it a chance and really listen. If *you* listen closely, you will find relaxation and enjoyment quite different from that which *you* might experience when listening to "pop," rock, country and western, or any of the other varieties of music. Of course, not all classical music appeals to everyone, but then, everyone doesn't find all rock music *enjoyable* either. Nevertheless, there are some classical selections *you* are sure to enjoy. Go to the public library and borrow one or two of the following records and put them on your turntable. If *you* then *relax, put your* feet up, and really *listen,* you will be guaranteed an enjoyable experience. For your introduction to classical music, *you* might try Beethoven's Sixth Symphony (*Pastoral*), Grieg's *Peer Gynt Suite,* and Tchaikovsky's *Romeo and Juliet.* These pieces appeal to almost everyone and are ideal selections with which to begin *your* exploration of a new musical world.

EXERCISE 4

1. If you're ready to learn how to operate a motorcycle, you should involve yourself in lessons, especially if you are interested in safety.
2. We often go to wrestling matches at the Gardens, and we're always sure of having a stimulating evening as we watch the Sheik make mincemeat of the Masked Marvel.
3. I don't know whether I can complete the program on time because it always seems either I must wait for a terminal, or the machines are down.
4. Until last week Marcia had us all believing her unlikely story; then we realized that she was lying.
5. You know that Cindy Nicholas holds the record for completing a double crossing of the English Channel, but are you aware that she has swum it a total of six times?
6. You know Orville is a troublemaker when you see his sneaky little face.
7. When we considered the issue carefully, we thought better of the more expensive proposal. After all, quality workmanship was what we were looking for.
8. When summer arrives, our patio is where you find us, relaxing and enjoying our leisure hours.
9. Many women think that the only way they can succeed in the business world is by wearing conservative three-piece suits similar to those men wear.
10. Actually, while you should dress appropriately, you needn't spend undue amounts of time and money trying to ape "the executive

look." Competence and ability have always had more impact than appearance.

UNIT EIGHT: Punctuation

Chapter 36: Question and Exclamation Marks

EXERCISE 1

1. question mark
2. question mark ·
3. period
4. period
5. question mark
6. period
7. period
8. question mark
9. period
10. question mark

EXERCISE 2

1. exclamation mark
2. exclamation mark
3. exclamation mark
4. exclamation mark, exclamation mark
5. exclamation mark and period
6. two exclamation marks or exclamation mark and period
7. exclamation mark
8. exclamation mark
9. exclamation mark
10. exclamation mark, exclamation mark

EXERCISE 3

1. period
2. period
3. question mark
4. period
5. question mark
6. exclamation mark
7. question mark
8. exclamation mark
9. period
10. exclamation mark and period

EXERCISE 4

1. The question was whether we would spend the night in Cornwall or push on for Montreal.
2. "Help!" he screamed. "The piranha has my finger!"
3. Just think! We have two glorious weeks free of English class.

4. Tim thought he looked lovely in his new sharkskin suit.
5. If you think you're confused, just imagine how I must feel.
6. correct
7. Catherine asked Arthur if he would like to stay over.
8. Her Ph.D. didn't seem to impress her co-workers at the doughnut shop.
9. Despite the fact that he was busy with his weightlifting, jogging, swimming, tumbling, etc., Jacques always had time for a little drinking.
10. We studied the poems of Irving Layton, who was born in Rumania, I think.

Chapter 37: Quotation Marks

EXERCISE 1

1. "Pardon me, boys, is this the Transylvania Station?" asked the man in the black cape.
2. Every day Rudolf asked the same question: "When do you think E.T. will return?"
3. correct
4. "This film," exclaimed Granny, "is more explicit than *National Geographic*!"
5. As the *Globe and Mail* put it, "The Canadian dollar went on a roller coaster ride yesterday."
6. It was the philosopher Ludwig Feuerbach who first said, "Man is what he eats," and we here at Big Boy restaurants certainly agree with that.
7. correct
8. "Your every whim will be catered to," promised the Sybaritic Spas brochure.
9. correct
10. "If not," I asked my friend, "why should we spend $800 for a weekend in Collingwood?"

EXERCISE 2

1. The *Guinness Book of World Records* claims that the oldest living thing is the California bristlecone pine tree, which is almost 5,000 years old.
2. "Did you see the strange look on his face?" asked Roderick.
3. correct
4. "Of course," she answered, usually willing to oblige.

5. "Have you read my new essay, 'Dreaming Your Way to an Energized Future'?" Dr. Piffle asked his numbed audience. "It's in my next book entitled *Upscale Networking in a Self-Actualized Cosmos.*"
6. The fellow to my left hissed, "I'd sooner be horsewhipped; where do they find these guys?"
7. I forget whether it was John Paul Jones or George Chuvalo who said, "I have not yet begun to fight."
8. The vice-president had bad news for the staff: "Due to lack of funds and excessive vandalism at the parking gates, you're all terminated."
9. correct
10. "Wow!" I said. "That's amazing!"

Chapter 38: The Colon

EXERCISE 1

1. incorrect
2. incorrect
3. correct
4. incorrect
5. incorrect
6. correct
7. incorrect
8. correct
9. incorrect
10. correct

EXERCISE 2

1. correct
2. Unless you work consistently throughout the term and prepare thoroughly for your final exam, you will achieve only one result: failure.
3. There are several troublesome implications of biological engineering, but one in particular is frightening to most people: the cloning of human beings.
4. Their credit consultant asked them an important question after their bankruptcy: "Why don't you cut up your credit cards?"
5. Only one thing prevents me from pulverizing you: the Masked Marvel, who is standing behind you.
6. correct
7. The bulk of Canada's population is worn out and exhausted at the end of a long, hard winter, but most people console themselves with one thought: spring will arrive sometime in May or June.
8. There are a number of activities that will improve physical fitness: swimming, tennis, jogging, even brisk walking.
9. Melanie is trying very hard to accomplish two things: a significant weight loss and success as a restaurant critic.

10. Several of the animals on the endangered species list are native to Canada: the wood bison, the Northern kit fox, and the whooping crane.

EXERCISE 3

1. The three people having trouble with their nursing techniques course are Tanya, Eddy, and Rufus.
2. There are three people having trouble with their nursing techniques course: Tanya, Eddy, and Rufus.
3. correct
4. The only thing we lacked was money.
5. Our friends are certain to remain loyal if we treat them with courtesy, kindness, and honesty.
6. correct
7. Two places I wouldn't want to visit are Tuscaloosa and Moose Factory.
8. correct
9. Roderick's needs in life were sex, drugs, and rock 'n roll.
10. correct

Chapter 39: The Comma

EXERCISE 1

1. Be sure to pick up gin, tonic, limes(,) and ice.
2. correct
3. Labatt, Molson(,) and O'Keefe are major breweries and patrons of sport and culture.
4. correct
5. Tim stomped into the room, threw himself into a chair, drained a six-pack of Budweiser(,) and crushed the cans against his forehead.

EXERCISE 2

1. The cheetah is, of course, the fastest animal on earth.
2. correct
3. Malcolm Lowry, an alcoholic British expatriate, wrote *Under the Volcano*, perhaps the finest novel ever written in Canada.
4. Many children in this school, it seems, are coming in the morning without having had an adequate breakfast.
5. The lead singer, in a bid for notoriety, bit the head off a bat during the performance.

EXERCISE 3

1. I refuse to wear that turkey costume to the party, nor will I go as a horse's rear end.
2. Yesterday he broke up with her, but today he is begging for forgiveness.
3. correct
4. The boss told him to stop leering at the ladies, or she would fire him.
5. Waving a red flag in front of a bull is supposed to enrage him, yet experiments have shown that bulls are colour blind.

EXERCISE 4

1. Third, insert your finger into the electrical socket.
2. Overwhelmed by the generous offer, we spent the evening watching Paul's home movies.
3. If you work for an airline, company policy states you are entitled to one free trip a year.
4. In addition, your next of kin is entitled to reduced fares.
5. Unless you learn to use commas properly, your writing will lack sophistication and polish.

EXERCISE 5

1. Caffeine, which is present in coffee, tea(,) and cola, stimulates the heart and raises blood pressure.
2. If a thing is worth doing, it is worth doing badly. (G.K. Chesterton)
3. The agency interviewed, tested, investigated(,) and rejected thirty applicants.
4. That man is guilty, in my opinion, and should be convicted of murder.
5. Roger checked his parachute carefully before take-off, but he forgot to pull his rip cord after he jumped out of the plane.
6. Fortunately, he landed in a tree and, later that afternoon, was found dangling helplessly.
7. Unfortunately, he had some very nasty contusions and developed an entirely justifiable fear of flying.
8. correct
9. Having left my wallet at home, I am unable to buy lunch.
10. correct

EXERCISE 6

1. Fascinating, challenging, high-paying jobs are available to the people who transfer to our exciting Beirut branch office.

2. Oswald, your lawyers agreed to work with you, not against you, didn't they?
3. Our guard dog, a Doberman pinscher, caught an intruder and maimed him for life.
4. Unfortunately, my Uncle Ladislaw was the intruder, and he intends to sue us for every penny we have.
5. correct
6. All warm-blooded animals that give live birth and suckle their young are classified as mammals, but no one knows how to classify the warm-blooded, egg-laying, chick-nursing platypus.
7. We are pleased with your résumé, and we are offering you an interview this week.
8. correct
9. Although Tim begged, his girlfriend refused to wear a tattooed heart with his name in the middle.
10. Igor asked, "May I show you to your quarters, or would you prefer to spend the night in the dungeon?"

EXERCISE 7

I sometimes wonder what our ancestors, were they able to observe us now, would think of some of the activities we take for granted. I'm sure that breakdancing would seem peculiar to them, as would surfing, water-skiing(,) and hang-gliding. However, I suspect that our forebears would find even those strange activities understandable, perhaps even enjoyable, compared to jogging. The sight of otherwise perfectly reasonable people decked out in various types of colourful underwear, doggedly puffing and sweating along every pathway, road(,) and trail would, I am convinced, put The Fear into Great Grandad and send him scurrying back whence he had come.

All kinds of people jog: there are short joggers, tall joggers, fat joggers, thin joggers; serious joggers, light-hearted joggers, fashionable joggers(,) and practical joggers; joggers with outfits of every hue from black to white and every shade in between. In fact, there may be more people who jog than who don't!

I gave up jogging some years ago with the excuse that, although I adored distance running, an old basketball injury prevented me from measuring up to my own expectations. This pitiful story, together with a wistful sigh for lost youth, usually gets me off the hook. While my friends claim to be fit and keen, I take satisfaction in quoting Satchel Paige, the famous baseball player, who, at age 60, pitched three scoreless innings in the major leagues. In his "Six Rules for a Long Life," Satch warns, "On no account, run." This is sound advice, and I intend to live by this sensible and energy-efficient rule.

Chapter 40: The Semicolon

EXERCISE 1

1. incorrect	6. incorrect
2. correct	7. incorrect
3. incorrect	8. correct
4. incorrect	9. incorrect
5. incorrect	10. incorrect

EXERCISE 2

1. We've eaten all the goodies; it's time to go home.
2. correct
3. Your instructor would like to pass you; however, there may be a small fee involved.
4. Florence is going to Hollywood; she wants to appear on "Let's Make a Deal."
5. We knew that the party was a huge success: Uncle Morty tap-danced across the top of the piano, Aunt Madeline did her Big Bird imitation, and Tim wrestled two of his cousins.
6. Many people dislike hockey because some of the players act like goons rather than athletes.
7. Orville tried and tried, but he couldn't get the teacher's attention.
8. correct
9. First, we'll have a cool drink; then we'll see if we can find a way to start this car.
10. Dudley left his clothes by the pool, so it's no wonder people in the lounge are looking at him strangely.

EXERCISE 3

1. Mrs. Reagan had a message for the unemployed: "There is no hunger in America; let them eat Kraft Dinner."
2. Most computer languages have been developed for a specific purpose; for example, COBOL is used in business whereas FORTRAN is used for mathematics, science, and engineering.
3. Some sociobiologists believe that human beings have evolved socially because female humanoids learned to barter sex for food and protection; however, this theory is controversial in academic circles.
4. Louis Riel led a Métis rebellion in Manitoba in 1885, but he was defeated, tried, and executed the same year. His death caused a deep rift between English and French Canada.
5. correct

EXERCISE 4

1. The entire town is in an uproar; it seems Rudolf has been missing since yesterday.
2. Of course, everyone knows Rudolf is a bit wacky; he's been very strange since his close encounter of the fourth kind.
3. He claims that a hamburger-shaped, chrome-coloured, smoke-belching UFO pinned him under its wheels, and its inhabitants kept him prisoner for several hours.
4. The creatures spoke to him through little slits; however, Rudolf says he got a good look at them.
5. According to him, the aliens looked like a cross between Bonzo the Chimp and Sylvester Stallone.
6. The creatures told Rudolf many secrets; one thing they told him was that they had searched the universe for a perfect specimen like him.
7. correct
8. In fact, Rudolf later told us he is under the aliens' control; perhaps this explains why he talks like Donald Duck.
9. But now everyone is beginning to worry; there's an unexplained burned spot in Rudolf's yard, and he's been gone since yesterday.
10. correct

EXERCISE 5

1. I have grown fond of semicolons in recent years. The semicolon tells me that there is still some question about the preceding full sentence; something needs to be added.
2. It is almost always a greater pleasure to come across a semicolon than a period. The period tells you that that is that; if you didn't get all the meaning you wanted or expected, you got all the writer intended to parcel out and now you have to move along.
3. But with a semicolon there, you get a pleasant little feeling of expectancy; there is more to come; read on; it will get clearer.
4. Colons are a lot less attractive, for several reasons: firstly, they give you the feeling of being rather ordered around, or at least having your nose pointed in a direction you might not be inclined to take if left to yourself, and, secondly, you suspect you're in for one of those sentences that will be labeling the points to be made: firstly, secondly, and so forth, with the implication that you haven't enough sense to keep track of a sequence of notions without having them numbered.
5. correct

Chapter 41: Dashes and Parentheses

EXERCISE 1

1. The aboriginal tribes of England—I've forgotten their name—painted themselves blue.
2. My purpose in moving from Vancouver to Hope—like that of hundreds of people before me—was to find affordable housing.
3. We shall have to start without her—again!
4. Skiing and skating—if you like these sports, you'll love Quebec.
5. Tending to his garden, writing his memoirs, and dining with friends—these were the pleasures Arnold looked forward to in retirement.
6. What is missing in his life is obvious—rest and relaxation!
7. Zoe should do well—in fact, I'm sure she will—in the engineering program.
8. Rudolf was amazed—positively thunderstruck—when he learned Uncle Ladislaw had won a million dollars.
9. Historians, diarists, and chroniclers—these are the recorders of our past.
10. Dashes allow you to insert—with a kind of a shout—the occasional exclamation into your sentences.

EXERCISE 2

1. Five of the students (I was asked not to name them) have volunteered to be peer tutors.
2. The apostrophe is explained in the unit on spelling (pp. 347–86).
3. Jason complained that being a manager (he became one in March) was like being a cop.
4. I have enclosed a cheque for one hundred and fifty dollars ($150.00).
5. More Canadian servicemen died in World War I (1914–1918) than in any war before or since.
6. Although Mozart lived a relatively short time (he died when he was thirty-six), he composed hundreds of musical masterpieces.
7. As news of his "miracle cures" spread (patients began to come to him from all over the province), the country doctor had to move his clinic to a more central location.
8. The new contract provided improved working conditions, a raise in salary (5 percent), and a new dental plan.
9. After years of producing undrinkable wine, Ontario now boasts a few very good wineries (Inniskillin and Hillebrand are two that come to mind).

10. "One of the most important tools for making paper speak in your own voice is punctuation; it plays the role of body language; it helps readers hear you the way you want to be heard" (Baker, "How to Punctuate," 48–49).

EXERCISE 3

1. Lord Dunsany (1878–1957) wrote many fantastic tales.
2. A hoe, a rake, a spade, and a case of beer—these are the essential tools for the weekend gardener.
3. Now that *Dick Tracy* has been so successful at the box office, I wonder if we will be treated (heaven forbid) to *Dick Tracy II, III, IV, V*, and even more?
4. Three of our best athletes—Anne, Mei-ling, and Philomena—have been declared ineligible.
5. At the last department meeting—you should have been there!—Ruth threw a lemon at Margaret.
6. Carefully arranged on a lacquer tray were deviled eggs, sushi, and kim chee—all favourites of my wife and her lover.
7. These two famous satirical novels (*Animal Farm* and *Gulliver's Travels*) ought to be on every college student's reading list.
8. Do we—*can* we—graduate truly educated men and women after only three years of study?
9. The prisoner is supposed to have escaped (if one can believe the witness) by bending the bars of his cell.
10. The explanation is lengthy but easy to follow if you study the diagram (see p. 77).

UNIT NINE: Spelling

Chapter 42: Three Suggestions for Quick Improvement

EXERCISE 1

1. desperately
2. crackling
3. generator
4. atonement
5. mating
6. rarely
7. elevator
8. emerging
9. positively
10. apologizing

EXERCISE 2

1. excitement
2. interference
3. desirable
4. continuance
5. abridging
6. removable
7. dissolutely
8. acquiring
9. shakable
10. aerating

EXERCISE 3

1. apologizing
2. encouragement
3. noisy
4. issuable
5. famous
6. abridgement
7. movable
8. officiating
9. valuation
10. realizing

EXERCISE 4

1. blotting
2. spanning
3. submitted
4. failing
5. blurred
6. regrettable
7. admitting
8. batting
9. begging
10. entailed

EXERCISE 5

1. forgetting
2. conferred
3. referring
4. stripped
5. shooting
6. expelling
7. grabbed
8. jarring
9. knitting
10. hindered

EXERCISE 6

1. deferring
2. remittance
3. regretful
4. cuddled
5. acquittal
6. concurred
7. flagging
8. pinning
9. barred
10. referred

EXERCISE 7

1. occurrence
2. persistence
3. emergence
4. recurrence
5. perseverance

6. consistency
7. sufferance
8. resistance
9. concurrence
10. deterrence

EXERCISE 8

1. brief
2. friendly
3. fielding
4. achieve
5. relieve

6. retrieval
7. deceive
8. leisure
9. receipt
10. grieve

EXERCISE 9

1. pier
2. hygiene
3. hierarchy
4. deceit
5. fierce

6. pieced
7. foreign
8. weight
9. receive
10. species

EXERCISE 10

1. either, their, beliefs
2. deceived, perceive
3. conceivable, receive
4. relief, neither
5. neighbour, conceited, weird

EXERCISE 11

1. heroes
2. histories
3. criteria
4. ghettos
5. personnel

6. crises
7. data
8. phenomena
9. nuclei (or nucleuses)
10. appendices (or appendixes)

EXERCISE 12

1. loneliness
2. copied
3. craziness
4. easier
5. prettiest

6. replies
7. replying
8. thirtieth
9. unnecessarily
10. trafficking

EXERCISE 13

1. em—ploy—er
2. con—sists
3. suc—cess
4. man—age—ment
5. pro—cess
6. ship—ping

7. ac—count—ing
8. through (Words of one syllable cannot be divided.)
9. dis—tri—bu—tion
10. busi—ness

Chapter 43: Sound-Alikes, Look-Alikes, and Spoilers

EXERCISE 1

1. course, affect
2. Are, accept
3. then, dessert
4. you're, losing
5. quite, here

6. whose, conscience
7. assured, number
8. It's, its
9. choose, course, advice
10. dining, does

EXERCISE 2

1. principal's, principles
2. chose, fourth
3. continuously, site, sight
4. Your, conscious
5. incredible, credulous, councilors

6. Except, minor
7. Morals, too, loose
8. farther, disperse
9. imply, continually
10. woman, who's, does

EXERCISE 3

1. hear, here
2. To, stationary
3. Losing, it's
4. you're, minor
5. piece, later, complimented

6. weather, whether
7. coarse, effect
8. fewer, faze
9. Women, whose
10. chose, accept, principal's

EXERCISE 4

There must be a better way to cope with house renovations. If I were to describe my personal agony during the months it took for the construction workers and contractors to achieve their final effect, your heart would bleed. Plaster dust was the worst problem, because it gets into everything, making even dining an uncomfortable experience. As the walls were torn loose and the house was gradually reduced to its skeleton, plaster dust found its way into every crack and corner. The noise and confusion affected my morale, and I became inclined to use coarse language, particularly with those who insisted on giving me advice. Later, when my conscience got the better of me, my feeble attempts at apology were not accepted. In the end, the renovations cost me my peace of mind, my friends, and more money than I dreamed possible.

EXERCISE 5

By the time we discovered that there was too much cholesterol in fried foods, we were already addicted. French fries and chicken wings, battered fish and doughnuts were an accepted part of our diet. The effect that dining on such foods has on us is evident in our waistlines and in the nation's heart disease statistics. The desserts we tend to choose are the worst offenders, according to diet counselors, but our main course can be equally dangerous if its cholesterol count is high. Experts now advise us to be guided by the principle that "less is more." But this advice is more difficult to follow than one might expect in a society that has been conditioned to believe "bigger is better." The moral seems to be that we must choose between foods that taste good and foods that do good.

Chapter 44: Capital Letters

EXERCISE 1

1. Why on earth would you buy a Toyota?
2. We need to get rid of some of our high-school habits when we start college.
3. Have you read Dr. Ernie L. Piffle's new book, *I'm OK — You're Fat: A Self-Help Guide to Fitness Fascism?*
4. The Loyalists were considered patriots by inhabitants of Upper Canada but traitors by people in the United States.
5. I didn't do very well in my fluid power course; maybe I'd better switch to culinary arts.
6. Well, look who's here; it's Mr. Olympics.

7. Take a right at Yonge Street, a left at Lawrence Avenue, and a right at Avenue Road.
8. My English teacher also teaches French to Asian immigrants.
9. Marcia's father, being conservative in his tastes, disapproved of Ronald's leather jacket and Harley-Davidson 750.
10. Neither was he amused when Marcia ran off with Ron's rock group, The Stoned Angels.

EXERCISE 2

1. Several psychiatrists in California are developing computer programs to treat patients with mild forms of depression or neurosis.
2. They envision computer therapy programs within the next fifteen years that will diagnose the patient's problem (to be confirmed by a psychiatrist) and select a treatment program.
3. The computer would interact with the patient and switch to various subprograms to analyse his mental problems.
4. A TV camera could view the patient to see if he exhibits signs of stress, nervousness, or lying.
5. correct
6. Most psychiatrists are against such unorthodox treatment methods, but proponents of computer therapy argue that it has many advantages.
7. These advantages include low cost and convenience: the computer would function as a cheap psychiatrist, available on weekends and holidays, summer or winter.
8. Other advantages are the long-term total memory of the computer and its appearance of honesty and objectivity.
9. Personally, I am surprised that anyone in the medical profession takes such a proposal seriously; treatment of complex human problems by machine seems perverse to me.
10. Taking my own personal depressions, fears, and phobias to a VDT would be likely to trigger a massive anxiety attack.

Chapter 45: The Apostrophe

EXERCISE 1

1. he'll
2. you've
3. I'm
4. don't
5. who's

6. wouldn't
7. we're
8. who'll
9. you'll
10. didn't

EXERCISE 2

1. can't
2. you're
3. they're
4. shouldn't
5. who'll

6. don't
7. you'll
8. we're
9. they've
10. it'll

EXERCISE 3

1. Yes, it's a long way from Halifax to Vancouver, but we've been in training for three months.
2. We're taking the train to Antigonish and we're biking to Halifax; then we'll begin the big trip west.
3. There isn't a dry eye in the theatre when Spielberg's film reaches its climax.
4. Those two haven't made it through a meeting since the college adopted its No Smoking policy.
5. Wasn't it Mark Twain who said, "It's easy to stop smoking; I've done it dozens of times"?

EXERCISE 4

1. their
2. Chris's
3. her
4. gentlemen's
5. strawberries'

6. mystery's
7. one's
8. Burgess' *or* Burgess's
9. chairmen's
10. ladies'

EXERCISE 5

1. week's, his
2. day's, dogs'
3. church's, its, minister's
4. children's, his, their, mother's
5. Today's, producers', tomorrow's

EXERCISE 6

1. A floppy disc's quality is measured by its ability to store information without error.
2. Diplomatic ambassadors' wives or husbands are often as important to a mission's success as the ambassadors themselves.

3. Near Chicoutimi is one of the country's most beautiful parks, where the skills of canoeists, fishermen, and wildlife photographers can all be put to the test on a summer's day.
4. The Leafs' forward and the Oilers' defenceman were exchanged during the last day's trading at the NHL meetings.
5. Janis's career got its start when she sang fishermen's songs in the yacht club's dining lounge.

EXERCISE 7

1. It's, its, turtle's, turtle's
2. It's, they're
3. you're, your, your
4. Joan's, Society's, province's
5. Someone's, whose
6. There, Joneses', their, it's
7. Countries, their, they're, powers'
8. Brothers', today's
9. father's, uncle's, fox's, woods
10. people's, workers', sides', strike's

Chapter 46: The Hyphen

EXERCISE 1

1. Nell decided to sublet her fifth-floor apartment.
2. Anwar claims he is allergic to classical music but addicted to new-wave music.
3. Chretien won most of the ethnic vote, which gave him a two-thirds majority in a hard-fought contest.
4. Hand-knitted sweaters are usually more expensive than factory-produced ones.
5. In 1950, at the age of forty-seven, George Orwell died of tuberculosis.
6. For months after Nicolae Ceaucescu was overthrown, the world was shocked by revelations of the repression suffered by the Rumanian people.
7. Would you relay this message to Mr. Chan: the masons would like to re-lay the bricks this evening?
8. Our next door neighbour teaches in a high school but does not like to be known as a high-school teacher.
9. A face-to-face meeting with an anti-intellectual always gets my adrenalin going.

10. Because Angela was an attorney-at-law and had once been an all-Canadian athlete, her forty-five-year-old former coach was not surprised when she became Minister of Recreation.

UNIT TEN: The Finishing Touches

Chapter 48: Wordiness

EXERCISE 1

1. Even then, corpses were treated with respect, just as they now are by civilized nations.
2. I think as you do about the value of Bargain Barry's sale items.
3. Despite his being small and being surrounded by children he didn't know, the brave seven-year-old took on the class bully.
4. Again the sergeant said to the new recruits, "I'll call you at 5:30 in the morning. Circle the barracks on the double until 5:45. At 6 o'clock, report to the barracks mess for breakfast."
5. The new recruits called a secret meeting after the 7 o'clock breakfast to discuss their revenge on a sergeant who woke them up one hour early.
6. Believing the sergeant would play his dirty trick every day, they planned an appropriate response.
7. Their plan was to get the sergeant very drunk in the evening and put him to bed at about 4:30 A.M. in the bunkhouse next to the officers' quarters.
8. I thought it was a great idea.
9. They had made sure the sergeant would believe, in the morning, that he was in his own bunkhouse; they bribed their friends who lived in that bunkhouse to leave it empty and arrange it like the sergeant's.
10. At 5:30 A.M., true to his promise that nothing would prevent his wake-up call, the sergeant staggered into the bunkhouse next to his and blasted with bugle and voice. He never did a 5:30 reveille again.

Chapter 49: Abusages

EXERCISE 1

1. Nell should have gone with us to the beach; now she can't go anywhere.

2. Many of us thought he might be prejudiced, but actually he turned out to be a really nice man.
3. I'm supposed to see whether the reason for the delay is that it's raining.
4. They are supposed to get the ball themselves, regardless of where it is when they come off the field.
5. Because I won't lend her my homework, she thinks I'm showing prejudice, but she is supposed to do her own homework.
6. If you don't do anything about boarding the windows, you'll have pieces of glass everywhere in the house.
7. It's very sad to see signs of prejudice in young children, who must have been influenced by their parents.
8. It is irrelevant whether she fell or was pushed off her bicycle; she is disqualified anyway.
9. They should have finished the race even though they were behind, since every entrant is supposed to finish unless disqualified or injured.
10. I didn't talk to anyone about seeing him cheat, since the judges don't consider a spectator's remarks to be relevant.

EXERCISE 2

1. No one except you and me would go camping in this rain.
2. He and I can't push this car any farther than you and she could.
3. She and I did a really stupid thing.
4. He is a better cook than she, and she plays baseball better than he.
5. You and I can use the Caravan passports all week, and you and she can use them on the weekend when I'm not here.
6. As we walked along Bloor Street, we saw Marie and him going into Toby's restaurant.
7. The police stopped him and me at the door of our apartment building.
8. correct
9. We are not very good friends anymore.
10. No one is happier than I that you got the job.

EXERCISE 3

1. Leila was late because it was she who drove the boys home.
2. She is one of the accountants who made the error in my income tax.
3. She who laughs last, laughs best.
4. The hedge at the back of the garden is slightly shorter than I.
5. Geoff wasn't as hungry as I, so he gave his lunch to Brian and me to share.

6. She and I wanted to see the circus, especially the horse that sings.
7. We four girls have been friends since before you were born.
8. I think it was she who had the nightmare.
9. The woman who won the lottery bought more tickets than you or I.
10. When asked to give the motto of the Dominion of Canada, either Jonah or he responded, "It's mainly because of the meat."

Index

To the owner of this book:

We are interested in your reaction to *Essay Essentials* by Sarah Norton and Brian Green.

1. What was your reason for using this book?

    _____ college course   _____ continuing education course
    _____ university course   _____ personal interest
                                     _____ other (specify)

2. In which school are you enrolled? _____

3. Approximately how much of the book did you use?

    _____ ¼   _____ ½   _____ ¾   _____ all

4. What is the best aspect of the book?

5. Have you any suggestions for improvement?

6. Is there anything that should be added?

7. What could be deleted?

Fold here
- -

(fold here and tape shut)

0116870399-M8Z4X6-BR01

Heather McWhinney
Publisher, College Division
HARCOURT BRACE & COMPANY, CANADA
55 HORNER AVENUE
TORONTO, ONTARIO
M8Z 9Z9